GODS AND RITUALS

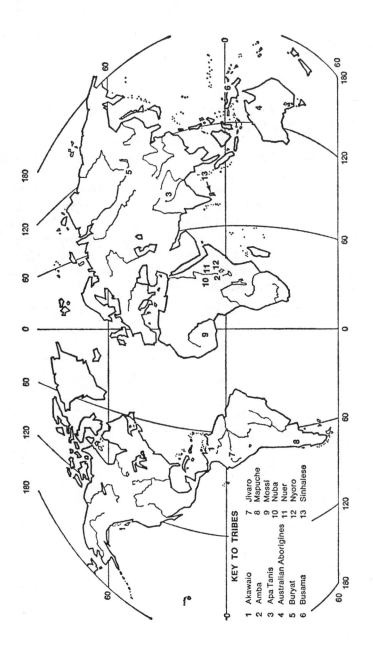

KEY TO TRIBES

1	Akawaio	7	Jivaro
2	Amba	8	Mapuche
3	Apa Tanis	9	Mossi
4	Australian Aborigines	10	Nuba
5	Buryat	11	Nuer
6	Busama	12	Nyoro
		13	Sinhalese

John Middleton
received his D.Phil. from Oxford in 1953. He has taught
anthropology at Capetown, Northwestern, and New York uni-
versities, and at present he is professor of African anthropology
at the School of Anthropology and African Studies, University
of London.
   He has done field research in Uganda, Zanzibar, and Nigeria.
He is the author of *Black Africa* and *Lugbara of Uganda*, and,
with David Tait, he edited *Tribes without Rulers*. Dr. Middleton
also edited four other volumes of the Texas Press Sourcebooks
in Anthropology series: *Comparative Political Systems*, with
Ronald Cohen; *Myth and Cosmos*; *Magic, Witchcraft, and
Curing*; and *From Child to Adult*.

Texas Press Sourcebooks in Anthropology
were originally published by the Natural History Press, a division of Doubleday and Company, Inc. Responsibility for the series now resides with the University of Texas Press, Box 7819, Austin, Texas 78712. Whereas the series has been a joint effort between the American Museum of Natural History and the Natural History Press, future volumes in the series will be selected through the auspices of the editorial offices of the University of Texas Press.

The purpose of the series will remain unchanged in its effort to make available inexpensive, up-to-date, and authoritative volumes for the student and the general reader in the field of anthropology.

Gods
and
Rituals

Readings in Religious Beliefs and Practices

Edited by John Middleton

University of Texas Press

Austin and London

Library of Congress Cataloging in Publication Data

Middleton, John, 1921–   comp.
   Gods and rituals.

   (Texas Press sourcebooks in anthropology; 6)
   Reprint of the ed. published for the American Museum of
Natural History by the Natural History Press, Garden City, N.Y.,
in series: American Museum sourcebooks in anthropology.
Bibliography: p.
Includes index.
1. Religion, Primitive—Addresses, essays, lectures. I. Title. II.
Series. III. Series: American Museum sourcebooks in anthropology.
[GN470.M48 1976]   291'.042   75-44032
ISBN 0-292-72708-9

Published by arrangement with Doubleday & Company, Inc.
Previously published by the Natural History Press in cooperation
with Doubleday & Company, Inc.

CONTENTS

INTRODUCTION

THE ANTHROPOLOGICAL study of religious beliefs and practices has a long history, from the psychologically oriented studies of the evolution of religious beliefs by Tylor, Frazer, Müller and their followers, and the more sociologically oriented work of Durkheim, Robertson Smith, Mauss, Levy-Bruhl and others. The early phase of anthropological interest in the religions of pre-literate peoples may be said to have ended with the field research of Radcliffe-Brown among the Andamanese and of Malinowski among the Trobriand Islanders. Since then the study of the religions of non-literate peoples has, with some monumental exceptions, met with a curious lack of interest by ethnographers. For this there have been three main reasons.

One was the cessation of attempts to produce evolutionary schemas of the development of religious beliefs (as distinct from those of technologies or social organizations), although these attempts have persisted to some extent among folklorists and historians of religion; also lay opinions on these matters are still largely determined by the continual reprinting of anthropologically out-of-date works from the height of the evolutionary period. A second reason has been the ever-increasing interest in functional studies of the social organizations of those non-Western people affected by colonial impact; in times of rapid and radical social change, ethnographers have tended to become more aware of the need to analyse kinship, political and legal systems than to devote themselves to religion. A third reason has been that in the anthropological tradition most writers on religion have tended to be agnostic, and have not felt at home with the concepts and aims of theology; they have felt both a superiority to those who have studied religions theologically and also an inferiority toward them on account of their apparent wider scholarship.

In the past few years the situation has changed. Instead of armchair theories there have appeared a number of analyses of religions based upon actual field observation by anthropologists who have set their studies within a strongly sociological framework; some of them are presented in this volume.

This book consists of readings in the beliefs and rituals of people who see themselves in a particular kind of relationship to gods or other "supernatural" powers. The distinction between the subject matter of this book and that of its companion volumes (on myth and cosmology, and on magic, witchcraft and curing) is not, of course, all that clearly marked, and may be considered as convenient rather than as reflecting any inherent distinctions. I have not attempted to give examples of the "classical" writings of theoretical importance, but to present detailed ethnographic accounts of actual religious systems as they have been observed by modern field workers. It has been possible to cover the main problems of the anthropological analysis of religion—beliefs in the supernatural, rituals of several kinds, the spread of new religions and the religious reaction to rapid social change. It has not proved possible to provide a really adequate geographical coverage: most recent work has been in Africa rather than in America and Australia, formerly the areas of main interest in this field. But it seems of greater use and importance to have concise accounts written by contemporary anthropologists who are trying to answer the contemporary problems of anthropology, rather than merely to cover every corner of the ethnographic world.

JOHN MIDDLETON

GODS AND RITUALS

1 MORALITY AND THE SOCIAL ORDER AMONG THE APA TANIS

Christoph von Fürer-Haimendorf

WHILE THE Apa Tanis' economy and political system are without parallel among the tribal populations of the North-East Frontier Agency, their religious practices and ideas conform in general to an overall pattern common to such tribes as Abors, Miris and Daflas. This similarity between the world-view of as stable a community as the Apa Tani tribe and the insecure and turbulent society of the Daflas must appear as a challenge to the theory that religion is basically a reflection of social situations and suggests the possibility that an ideology rooted in a specific cultural background can persist with little modification in societies of very different structure and character. Yet, before the theoretical implication of this situation can profitably be elaborated, both Apa Tani and Dafla religion needs to be investigated much more intensively than it has so far been done. My own inquiries among the Apa Tanis, often overshadowed by political and administrative preoccupations, were least intensive in the sphere of religion, a sphere in which mere observation yields few results, and nothing can replace the insight gained by long and undisturbed work with selected informants. Such work was seldom possible, and the following observations are offered as a preliminary sketch of an apparently very complex system of ideas and ritual practices.

Reprinted from Chapter VIII ("Religion and the moral order") of *The Apa Tanis and their neighbours: a primitive civilization of the Eastern Himalayas,* London, 1962, by permission of the author and Routledge and Kegan Paul, Ltd.

THE NATURE OF DEITIES AND SPIRITS

The Apa Tani feels himself surrounded by invisible beings capable
of affecting his welfare and health, beings who are accessible to
the approaches of men. He thinks of these beings as similar to humans in some of their reactions to requests, offerings, promises
and threats, but as different in substance and infinitely superior
to all men in the power to influence natural events. The number of
these beings is believed to be very large and though Apa Tanis
attach to some of them special attributes, it is doubtful whether the
tribesmen think of deities and spirits as divided into definite categories. If for want of a better term we refer to such beings as 'gods'
or 'spirits' we must do so without implying that the Apa Tanis
necessarily look upon such 'gods' with feelings of reverence or
piety. The word *ui* which precedes the name of some of such superhuman beings indicates their divine character, but the same syllable
ui is used in connection with natural features such as rivers and
regions to signify that they are not of the world of the Apa Tanis'
experience but belong to a sphere of divine and mythical beings.

While I have little concrete information as to how ordinary Apa
Tanis imagine the majority of deities and whether they associate
indeed any visual pictures with the beings whom they invoke in
prayers and invocation, there is some evidence that seers and
priests have in their own minds a fairly clear and entirely anthropomorphic picture of certain deities. All the priests of my ac-
quaintance asserted that they could see these deities in their
dreams, and they described them as male and female resembling
human beings.

The Apa Tani gods are not arranged in the order of an accepted hierarchy, and a society lacking any agreed system of precedence except the basic division into *mite* and *mura* provides indeed no model for a pantheon presided over by any particular
deity. Various deities are described as 'the greatest' in different
contexts, and it would seem that in doing so priests think of their
importance for the world of men, rather than of any absolute pre-
eminence.

Two deities known as Kilo and Kiru were described to me as
the most powerful, and the fact that the greatest annual festival,
the Mloko, is devoted to their worship bears out the importance

which Apa Tanis attribute to this divine couple. Kilo and Kiru are husband and wife, and Apa Tanis envisage indeed most deities and spirits as pairs and never invoke them singly. The dual character of supernatural beings is so firmly established that I doubt whether Apa Tanis pronouncing the two linked names are always conscious of appealing to a duality of deities, or whether it is taken for granted that every supernatural being has a female counterpart.

Kilo and Kiru live now in the earth and have been there from its beginning. They had no part in the creation of the earth, but when Chandun, a male god, made the earth, Kilo and Kiru had already been in existence. It is not very clear in what manner the power of Kilo and Kiru manifests itself, for though living in the earth they do not seem specifically associated with the fertility of the soil; they are believed, however, to influence the general welfare of men.

The male god, Chandun, to whom the creation of the earth is ascribed, has a female counterpart known as Didun, and this goddess is believed to have made the sky. This reversal of the far more usual association of a male god with the sky and a female deity with the earth remains for the time without satisfactory explanation, particularly since it does not seem to occur among other tribes of the region, most of whom associate the sky with a male deity (see von Fürer-Haimendorf 1954: 593).

Another creation myth current among the Apa Tanis does not mention Chandun and Didun but tells how at the beginning of time there was only water. Next a rock and finally the soft earth appeared, and this was created by three female deities known as Ui-Tango, Ui-Ngurre and Nguntre, and three male deities known as Ei Karte, Rup Karte and Ain Karte. These six deities created all trees, plants, animals and birds, and even the sun, the moon and the stars. The priests now recite on certain occasions long lists of heavenly bodies created in the sky, objects and plants created on earth, and animals of all kinds created to live on the earth.

The origin of man, however, is associated with a deity of another category known as Hilo. In one myth the term Hilo is applied to a specific deity credited with the making of the first ancestor of the Apa Tanis, Abo Tani,[1] whereas usually Hilo is a generic

[1] According to another myth Abo Tani was not 'made' by a Hilo deity, but was the son of Rika and Ritu. This couple existed from the very beginning of the earth, in which they dwelt. They were not gods but the ancestors

term referring to a number of separate gods. A short list of some of these Hilo deities may serve as an illustration of the variety of supernatural beings peopling the world of the Apa Tanis:

Ploti Hilo—a couple living in the forests and hills; concerned with the welfare of men, cattle and crops; worshipped once a year—but not at a fixed time—with offerings of cattle, pigs or fowls, which are sacrificed close to the homestead of the worshipper.

Niro Hilo—a couple living in the vicinity of villages; appealed to with requests to make people wise and restrained; every house gives a monthly offering to Niro Hilo, and the day is observed as a day of abstention from work. Cattle, pigs, dogs and fowls are acceptable offerings.

Dadu Hilo—a couple living close to the village; bringers of disease and worshipped only in case of illness.

Lel Hilo—similar in nature and function to Dadu Hilo.

Yadu Hilo—a couple living under the earth; bringers of illness and propitiated only in case of sickness.

Nili Hilo—similar in nature and function to Dadu Hilo.

Dani Hilo—a couple living in the sky; bringers of eye-ache, head-ache, chest-ache; propitiated in case of such sickness.

Rosa Buyu Hilo—couple living near the sun; cause vomiting and headache; propitiated in case of such afflictions.

Mloro Hilo—couple living in the forest; cause headache, dizziness and fever; propitiated in case of such sickness.

From this list, only part of which is here produced, it appears that Apa Tanis imagine the world peopled with Hilo deities, and that according to the nature of a disease or affliction the one or other Hilo deity is thought responsible and duly propitiated.

Different from these gods are the deities specifically associated with certain natural phenomena. Prominent among these are three deities collectively known as Korlang, and worshipped annually at a rite performed by a priest representing his village or in some cases two allied villages. Niri Korlang is a deity who resides in the sky and provides protection against hailstorms. Tagung Korlang, who also dwells in the sky, is propitiated to ward off thunderstorms and excessive rain, and Anguro Korlang, who dwells in the plains of Assam, is believed to protect Apa Tanis visiting the plains against disease. A rite known as Korlang-ui is performed before the work of transplanting the rice begins, i.e. at the end of

---

of all mankind. Rika and Ritu came out onto the surface and lived there. They neither cultivated nor did they need to eat. They had one son Abo Tani, and ultimately they died.

March. Each village maintains a place for such rites on one of the communal grounds outside the settlement, and there a priest sacrifices a chicken and calls upon the spirits of lightning, water and earth, and certain local deities to ward off dangers from the young crop. This, as many other rites, is followed by a two days' period of abstention from work outside the village.

In 1944 the Korlang-ui rite for the villages of Haja and Duta was performed by a priest of Duta. This performance covered both villages and the inhabitants of both abstained from work for two days. Not all Apa Tani villages perform the rite on the same day, nor do the priests of Duta and Haja undertake the task of worshipping the Korlang deities strictly in turn. One priest who claimed the ability to see these gods in his dreams told me that they looked not like Apa Tanis but like Daflas.

Within a few days of the Korlang-ui a rite in honour of Mokum, a female deity dwelling in the earth, is performed by one of the priests of each Apa Tani village, and it seems that this rite must be done separately for each village, a joint performance being not considered adequate even in the case of such closely allied villages as Haja and Duta.

Apart from the deities associated with the forces of nature there are others who stand in a special relation to certain human activities. Thus the gods Ui-Kasang and Nia-Kasang are associated with war, and before going on a raid Apa Tanis pray to these deities to give them strength and courage, and afford them protection in the fighting. On that occasion a dog, pig or mithan may be sacrificed at the *lapang* of the raiders, and a further offering is promised in case the raid is successful. The animal sacrificed at the *ropi*-rite which follows a successful raid is intended for Ui-Kasang and Nia-Kasang. The former is believed to live inside the earth, and the latter above the earth. A seer, who claimed to have seen them in his dreams, told me that Ui-Kasang looked alternatively like a Dafla and like a man from the plains,[2] while Nia-Kasang, though a female deity, looked like an Apa Tani man.

Also connected with the vicissitudes of war are two other deities known as Pila and Yachu. They are believed to live under the earth, and to assist captured persons to escape from the bonds of their enemies. When a family learns of the capture of one of its

[2] The seer had never been to the plains, but had seen Gurkha soldiers.

members, a fowl is sacrificed inside the house and a priest, or any other man knowing the appropriate prayers, addresses himself to Pila and Yachu, begging them to help the captive in finding a way to escape. And again when go-betweens are sent out to negotiate the prisoner's ransom, the same two deities are begged to make the captors listen to the negotiators' words. Further offerings are promised in the event of the captive's escape or release, and when he returns he himself offers the promised sacrificial fowls. Even if a mithan is stolen, the same deities are asked to enable the animal to break its ropes and return to its owner's grazing grounds.

Besides the gods known by specific names or associated with special activities or needs, there is according to Apa Tani belief a host of spirits inhabiting the surface of the earth, and most of them are worshipped only in connection with activities taking place in the locality where they are supposed to dwell. Thus at the construction of a new sitting-platform (*lapang*) the spirit of the site is invoked and fowls and dogs are sacrificed to gain the spirit's favour for all those who will use the *lapang*.

Outstanding natural features, such as unusual outcrops of rocks, are often thought to be seats of particularly important spirits, and the people of the village on whose land they are situated offer sacrifices to such spirits at the time of the Mokum or other seasonal rites.

Multitudes of spirits (*ui*) inhabit Neli, the Land of the Dead, and it is not unusual for such spirits to entice the straying soul (*yalo*) of a sick person to their houses. We shall see that priests journeying in their dreams to Neli may bargain with the spirits for the *yalo's* release, and whatever animals they promise as ransom must be sacrificed by the patient's family. This idea that the Land of the Dead is peopled not only by the departed but also by a large number of spirits is shared by many of the hill-tribes of Assam and also by such middle Indian tribes as the Saoras of Orissa (see Elwin 1955). The assumption is that whereas on this earth the gods and spirits, even when dwelling close to the habitations of men, remain invisible to all except those endowed with the gift of visionary dreams, in the Land of the Dead spirits and departed humans meet face to face without any bar to full communication.

The deities and spirits of the Apa Tanis appear thus as invested with human qualities and a likeness to men which make a meeting on common ground possible. The very belief that the supernatural beings known as *ui* covet the same things which men consider desirable is the basis of all sacrificial rites, and all the efforts of priests and seers.

SEASONAL RITES

There passes no day in the Apa Tani valley without one or another priest (*niubu*) approaching gods and spirits on behalf of individuals who seek their help in a personal crisis. Indeed it is common to find priests in ceremonial dress reciting incantations on a public *lapang* or to hear their monotonous chants resounding in the interior of a dwelling-house. The occasions, however, when all the inhabitants of a whole village, or even of one of the three groups of villages, combine for the worship of gods are confined to certain times of year, and it is only then that sacrificial rites are accompanied by public festivities.

The two main public festivals are the Morom and the Mloko, and both seem to be associated with the beginning of the agricultural season. The celebration of the Morom is begun by the villages of Bela, Hari and Hang, where the rites start at the end of Kume (December/January), but the villages of the Haja-Duta group do not commence the rites until the first day of the month of Kuye (February/March). The principal public functions at this festival are processions of young men and boys dressed up in their best clothes which, headed by a priest in ceremonial dress, move in single file from village to village. The priest waves a fan of feathers and scatters husked rice-grains as he walks across the fields, and the boys and young men brandish swords and beat brass plates in the manner of gongs. As they lift the flashing blades of their Tibetan swords, they utter rhythmic shouts, but the priest keeps on chanting prayers until the procession reaches a village. An older man accompanies the procession carrying a basket of rice-flour, small quantities of which he distributes in the villages visited by the procession.

Each procession spends a whole day visiting all the villages of the valley. In each village the young men and boys are entertained with rice-beer, which they drink while standing in line, and here and there they are also offered small snacks of food. In the open squares of the visited villages, they dance and chant, but seldom leave the formation of their file.

The Morom's character as a fertility rite can be deduced not only from the scattering of rice-grains on the fields to be soon taken under cultivation but also from phallic dances performed by young boys now and then leaving the procession and prancing about with huge bamboo phalli.[3]

Apart from the procession jointly undertaken by all the young men and boys of a village, there are at the time of the Morom also individual ritual performances held by wealthy men, intent on increasing their prestige. These performances, which fall into the general category of feasts of merit so highly developed among Nagas and other tribes of the Assam-Burma border area, culminate in the slaughter of mithan, the meat of which is widely distributed. There are two rites of this type. The greater and more expensive one is known as *un-pedo,* and this necessitates the slaughter of at least five to six mithan. In this case the meat must be distributed throughout the Apa Tani valley. When such a rite has been performed representatives of all villages and *khel* in the valley come to the house of the donor of the feast and tell the exact number of households in their village or *khel.* The next day men of the donor's clan carry the shares of meat to all the villages. They are accompanied by the messengers, who indicate the number of households and help in the distribution of the meat. No favouritism is supposed to influence this distribution; important men and men of lower status receive similar shares, and it is only large households with many mouths to feed that get extra shares.

Men who cannot afford the performance of an *un-pedo* rite may give a feast known as *padu-latu,* and for this only two to three mithan are required. Their meat is distributed only among the inhabitants of one or two villages belonging to the donor's own group.

The performance of these feasts lends the donor social prestige, but does not invest him with any tangible privileges or the right to specific ornaments or other prestige symbols. Neither selection to the office of *buliang* nor recognition as priest is in any way dependent on the conspicuous expenditure of wealth connected with the rites of *un-pedo* and *padu-latu.* But as these are regarded as a regular feature of the Morom celebrations, there must be considerable speculation every year as to who would devote a portion

[3] For a more detailed description of the procession and dance see von Fürer-Haimendorf 1955: 167.

of his cattle wealth to the common good, and wealthy men who have never performed either rite may well be subjected to some pressure of public opinion. Particularly a wealthy clan-head could hardly maintain his status without devoting some of his resources to such a feast of merit. The subsequent distribution of shares of meat serves no doubt to reaffirm the sense of corporateness pervading the whole Apa Tani tribe.

It is significant that the Daflas, who rely for their security much more on individual alliances than on a general tribal solidarity, have no ritual performances which involve a comparable wide and even distribution of material resources. Among them prestige is gained by the ceremonial exchange of valuables, but the meat, rice and beer given away in connection with the many visits entailed in such an exchange benefit only the two families concerned, and there is no conscious attempt to spread benefits as widely as in the course of the Apa Tanis' feasts of merit at the time of the Morom.

While the Morom is performed every year by all Apa Tani villages, the second great public festival, the Mloko, is held by each village only once in three years. But a system of rotation assures that in the Mloko month, which corresponds to March/April, there is a celebration every year of the Mloko festival in the valley. According to this system Hang performs the Mloko one year, Bela and Hari the following year, and the group consisting of the villages of Haja, Duta, Mudang-Tage and Michi-Bamin in the third year, after which Hang begins a new cycle. Preparations for the festivities extend over many weeks and include the purchase of sacrificial animals, the collection and storing-up of firewood, and above all the erection of tall poles, which at the time of the Mloko are used for a game of acrobatics performed on strong cane ropes attached to these poles. By pulling on one of the ropes and causing the poles to swing, people get themselves propelled high up into the air and the sport is popular among the young people of both sexes, though even older men and women sometimes show their skill. The poles for this sport, known as *bobo,* are dragged to the village by the common effort of the men of the individual wards, and are then erected close to the *lapang.*

The religious side of the Mloko consists mainly of sacrificial rites celebrated separately by the different clans, but intended for the general welfare of the people. The priest representing his clan or sub-clan performs these rites at a clan-sanctuary in a garden inside the village; pigs, chickens and a dog are sacrificed. The deities invoked are the divine pair, Kilo and Kiru, as well as Kiriliyari, a deity associated with the earth. The timing of the Mloko at the beginning of the cultivating season, the performance of the sacrificial rites in a village garden, and the worship of an earth-deity are obvious pointers to its character as a spring festival aimed at the enhancement of the fertility of the land. My informants, however, did not specifically emphasize the fertility aspect of the Mloko, and until the texts of the prayers recited at the sacrificial rites become available, little more can be said about the deeper religious meaning of the celebrations.

The social implications of the Mloko, however, are more easily observed. As only one group of villages performs the Mloko every year, the celebration is an occasion for inter-village visiting and the entertainment of guests from other villages. There is, moreover, a regular exchange of gifts. Shares of the sacrificial animals killed during the Mloko are given to the *buliang* of villages or village-quarters linked by traditional ties to the village of those performing the rite. The system regulating this exchange is complicated, and provides for a number of contacts across the limits of the three groups of allied villages. Every ward of a village has certain ceremonial ties with corresponding wards of villages outside its own group, and the exchange of Mloko gifts occurs between such wards. Thus in a year when the Mloko is performed by the two villages of Bela and Hari, the distribution of shares is roughly as follows: The shares of meat of half of the Reru *khel* and half of the Tajang *khel* of Bela go to the *buliang* of Haja, and the shares of meat from the other halves of these two *khel* as well as some of those of Kalung *khel* go to the *buliang* of Duta. Some shares of meat of Hari village go to the *buliang* of Mudang-Tage and Michi-Bamin, while certain wards of Bela as well as of Hari send shares of meat to the *buliang* of Hang. These gifts of meat are fairly substantial. A *buliang* of Hang, for instance, told me that he received seven pieces of pork from a man of Haja when the latter village celebrated the Mloko, and when it was the turn of Bela and Hari, he received seven pieces of pork from a man of Tajang *khel* of Bela.

This system of mutual obligations does not extend equally over all villages, however, and when Hang celebrates the Mloko no shares of meat are given to the *buliang* of Duta.

It would seem that the ceremonial links of the *buliang* of one village with specific wards of another village serve as channels for inter-village contacts, and that negotiations for the settlement of disputes, for instance, run often along the lines of these permanent channels. The comparative peace and orderliness in the Apa Tani valley, which contrasts so significantly with the turbulence among Daflas, may well be partly due to the strength and durability of these ceremonial inter-village contacts which would seem to make up for the lack of any institutionalized tribal authority.

At the Mloko the unity of the tribe is being given ritual expression, and the way in which men and women of all villages join as visitors and guests in the celebrations of one village-group serves to cement friendly relations across village boundaries and to counteract tensions and jealousies between the inhabitants of different villages.

There are no other seasonal rites comparable in complexity and social impact to either the Morom or the Mloko, but in certain months prescribed rituals are performed by priests acting on behalf of individual villages. Thus, in the month of Pume (June/ July) a small pig, a dog and some chickens are sacrificed in the name of Potor, Met and Tamu, three deities believed to dwell in the earth, and in Puje (July/August) a chicken and eggs are offered to Yapun, the god of thunder, Mloru-Sü, Punglo and Korlang, in order to protect the crops against hail. For ten days after this rite no villager may go outside the cultivated area or even visit other villages in the valley and it is feared that any breach of this injunction would lead to the crops being damaged by hail.

The harvest of the rice is neither preceded nor followed by any public celebrations, but when people first eat of the variety of rice known as *emo*, individual families sacrifice pigs in their houses.

In a society so passionately devoted to the cultivation of the soil and the growing of crops, one might well expect a great number of communal rites specifically associated with such agricultural operations as sowing, transplanting, or harvesting, but among the Apa Tanis only a few of these activities are occasions for significant ritual intervention. In this respect the Apa Tanis differ greatly from such tribes as the Nagas, who accompany every phase in their agricultural work with elaborate ritual, and have even such religious village dignitaries as a First Sower and a First Reaper (cf. von Fürer-Haimendorf and Mills 1936).

THE RITUAL DISPOSAL OF THE SLAIN

Though the Apa Tani valley is an oasis of peace in the war-torn world of Daflas and Miris, the Apa Tanis do not always live in peace with their neighbours of different ethnic stock, and we have seen that feuds with tribesmen of settlements beyond the confines of their own country are by no means unusual. The ritual preparations of a raid have already been described, and here I am concerned only with the rites that follow the killing of an enemy in battle or in ambush, or even the execution of a prisoner of war or criminal.

The rite accompanying the disposal of human trophies, such as an enemy's hand, eyes or tongue, is known as *ropi,* and I have elsewhere (1955: 46–48), described a *ropi* ceremony performed in my presence in Bela village. Unlike Nagas, the Apa Tanis do not make ritual use of the heads of slain enemies. If possible, they sever a hand from the victim's body, and secure the eyes and tongue for burial in their village. All these trophies are kept in a *nago* shrine until the performance of the *ropi*-rite, when the hand is burnt, and eyes and tongue are buried close to the slayer's *nago.* The idea underlying this practice is the belief that the burial of these vital organs will prevent the dead man from seeing his slayer and pursuing him with his wrath. The incantation, of which I recorded the basic text, reflects this idea, and may here be quoted in a free translation:

'Go to your own place; we are sending you under the earth; go there, we are closing the gate of the earth. It was your fate to be killed by swords and arrows; the rain from the sky has washed you. For ten generations to come you shall be powerless to harm our descendants. Do not be angry with us; do not turn on us in wrath; you have been buried in the earth, and we have sent you off; do not come to us, but move on to other places.'

After the burial of eyes and tongue in the section of a bamboo, the slayer takes rice-beer in his mouth and spits it on to the stone covering the interred trophies. What remains of the hand after its ritual cremation is disposed of in the same way as eyes and tongue, and similar words are spoken over the burial place.

The *ropi*-rite is performed not only in the case of slain enemies, but also in conclusion of the execution of a criminal member of the Apa Tani tribe. Thus when Chigi Duyu, a patrician of Duta, was executed at a *lapang* in Hang, his body was burnt in front of one of the Hang *nago* shrines, and the spears and shields of the executioners piled up on the *lapang* where he had been killed and left there for nine days until the *ropi*-rite could be performed. A mithan, the price of which was raised by public subscription, was sacrificed during the *ropi*, and the men of Hang danced and chanted as if they were celebrating the victory over an enemy slain in battle.

The similarities between the Apa Tanis' *ropi*-rite and the head-hunting ceremonies of the Nagas are unmistakable, but there are also significant differences in the respective attitudes to slain enemies. Whereas the *ropi*-rite seems to aim mainly at warding off the wrath of the victims, the Nagas preserve their enemies' heads in order to gain for their community the magical powers inherent in the skull. Their rites and the annual libations offered to the skulls are intended to integrate these forces into the accumulated store of their captors' magical virtue.

The Apa Tanis, on the other hand, do not expect benefits from attaching the soul-power of slain enemies to their villages, nor are they particularly concerned with any influence which the souls of their own departed might have on the fortunes of the living.

ESCHATOLOGICAL BELIEFS

In general outline the Apa Tanis' beliefs in the life after death co-incide with the eschatological concepts of other Tibeto-Burman speaking hill-tribes on the borders of Assam. Nagas, Lusheis, Garos, Abors, Daflas and Apa Tanis appear to have basically similar ideas about the fate of the departed in the Land of the Dead (von Fürer-Haimendorf 1936) and their beliefs are clearly set off from the ideas current among the Hindu populations of the plains. The most characteristic feature of the eschatological beliefs of most of these tribes is a very detailed picture of the Land of the Dead, including the often tortuous path by which it is reached and the figure of a guardian of the underworld. This picture is provided by shamans or seers who visit the world beyond, either in their dreams or while in a state of trance.

The Apa Tanis believe that the souls (*yalo*) of all those who died a natural death go to Neli, the region of the dead, which looks exactly like an Apa Tani village with long rows of houses. At the entrance to Neli, they are met by Nelkiri, the guardian spirit, who questions all newcomers about their exploits in the life on this earth. He inquires how many enemies and wild animals a man has slain, how many slaves he has bought, and how much land he owned. As an Apa Tani lived on earth so will he live in Neli: a rich man will be rich and a slave will serve his old master; in Neli a man finds the cattle he has sacrificed during his lifetime, but those animals which have passed to his heirs are forever lost to him. Every woman returns to her first husband, but those who died unmarried may marry in Neli, and beget children. Life in Neli is similar to life on this earth; people cultivate and work, and ultimately they die once more and go to another Land of the Dead.[4]

When a man is ill and loses consciousness his soul or *yalo* may leave his body and stray to Neli. A shaman priest (*niubu*), called to minister to the sick man, may succeed in tracing the soul to the dwelling of one of the many spirits (*ui*) who together with the *yalo* inhabit Neli, and who are ever avid to draw straying souls into their sphere. Once the shaman has located the *yalo* and identified the spirit that detains it, he offers to ransom the *yalo* with the sacrifice of an animal. If the spirit accepts the ransom, the *yalo* is set free and returns to its earthly body, and as soon as this happens the patient regains consciousness.

Neli is believed to be under the earth. It is a real underworld, but without any gloomy associations. Another Land of the Dead is situated somewhere in the sky, and to this abode, known as Talimoko, repair all those who died an unnatural or inauspicious death. Men who were killed by enemies and women who died in childbirth go to this Land in the Sky, and they are referred to not as *yalo* but as *igi*. There is no suggestion that the fate of *igi* is one of suffering or unhappiness, but it would seem that life in Talimoko is not considered to the same extent a continuation of life on earth as is the existence of the departed in Neli. Both those in Neli and in Talimoko are believed to return at times to the dwellings of the living but their visitations are not welcome and the Apa

---

[4] In my Frazer Lecture, I have suggested that the idea of an interminable series of 'Lands of the Dead', and the inevitable death of a person after a span of life in any such 'Land of the Dead' may have contributed to the development of the Hindu concept which was foreign to Rig-Vedic Aryans. Cf. von Fürer-Haimendorf 1953: 45.

Tanis do not think they could result in any benefits to the surviving kinsmen.

MORAL CONCEPTS

The Apa Tani idea of life in the Land of the Dead as a more or less automatic repetition of life on this earth does not provide any motivation for conduct aiming at anything except gratification in terms of immediate self-interest. The belief that the rich are going to be rich again and the powerful have the prospect of enjoying the services of their slaves' dependants in the world beyond places a premium on worldly success, and the idea of a transcendental reward for morally positive acts has no place in Apa Tani thinking. I can recall no other allusion to morality in connection with their beliefs in the after-life than a priest's brief statement that in the Land of the Dead good people will be good again and bad people bad.

This does not mean that Apa Tanis lack any sense of moral values. They do not admire the strong and ruthless man to the same extent as the Daflas, but value industry and business sense, skill in negotiations and the power of leadership in influencing the deliberations of a council of *buliang* or clansmen. To attain one's aims by peaceful means is considered preferable and more laudable than to resort to violence, and we have seen that in situations when a dispute between equals has defied a negotiated solution, the adversaries may try to shame each other into submission by a competition of *potlatch* type, rather than use physical force. The very fact that such moral pressure is thought effective is indicative of a sensitivity to public opinion, and it is the support of public opinion in the moral judgment on criminals which enables the *buliang* to take punitive action against habitual offenders. In this respect the Apa Tanis have gone far beyond the Daflas' attitude to inter-personal relations. Among Daflas there is no provision for preventing or even limiting the encroachment of the powerful on the rights of weaker fellow tribesmen, either by legal sanctions or by the pressure of public opinion. As long as a man can get away with violence and the disregard of the interests of others, he retains his position in society and there is even admiration for the strong man and successful organizer of raids. The Apa Tanis, on the other hand, have developed a collective sense of right and wrong, which finds expression in the enforcement of customary law through the chosen representatives of public opinion. Their ideas on the desired and socially approved conduct in inter-personal relations are not embodied in set rules or commandments, but there is nevertheless broad agreement on the moral evaluation of behaviour. Unprovoked infliction of an injury to a fellow tribesman, murder, theft, cheating in trade deals, adultery, clan-incest and the failure to repay a debt are all considered morally wrong, though the general reaction to any of these offences depends largely on the nuisance or harm it causes to the community as a whole. An isolated case of theft, for instance, arouses little comment, whereas a habitual thief may be executed. A couple guilty of clan-incest are expelled from their village, but no objection to their union is raised by the inhabitants of any other village where they may find shelter. There is no idea that clan-incest may produce supernatural sanctions or place the guilty couple into a state of pollution dangerous to those with whom they consort. Sexual relations between persons not tied by the bonds of marriage are regarded as morally neutral, and this toleration of premarital sexual attachments includes even relations between girls of patrician status and men of slave class. Otherwise a distinction is made between the actions of a free man and that of a slave. Whereas a free man can be subjected to serious punishment only with the agreement of a majority of the village dignitaries, a slave whose criminal habits have made him an embarrassment to his owner may be put to death without much ado on the latter's initiative. In this case conduct is determined not only by the status of the actors, but also by that of the person who is the object of the action.

The Apa Tanis are sensitive to social approval and disapproval, and the fear of being 'shamed' is a powerful incentive to conformity. There is, however, no sense of 'sin' and no corresponding desire to acquire 'merit' in a system of supernatural rewards. The approval of fellow tribesmen and a favourable place within the social and economic system of this world is the ultimate aim of Apa Tani conduct, and there is—unlike in more sophisticated societies—no distinction between actions which are meritorious within a system of supernatural values, and actions approved because they are in conformity with tribal custom. All relations with members of other societies stand outside the sphere of morally prescribed action. The Apa Tani cannot conceive of right or wrong conduct other than as a response to the requirements of his own society and relations with outsiders are hence considered as morally neutral. The idea that an individual is responsible for his actions not only to his immediate social environment but primarily to a universal moral order has no place in Apa Tani thinking. Hence there is a complete lack of any sense of 'guilt' or 'sin', such as might be felt by those acting contrary to the values of such a higher order. In their moral thinking and sentiments Apa Tanis remain always close to the earth, and if they think of the fate that awaits them after death, they think of it as a reflection of life on this earth. A happy fate in the world beyond is not gained by austerities and acts of charity or self-sacrifice, but by success and prosperity in this life—achievements which perpetuate themselves automatically in the Land of the Dead. Immediate gratification and the gratification hoped for in another life are thus not antithetical, and any thought of making sacrifices for the sake of living up to moral ideals is foreign to Apa Tanis. In short, the aim of all conduct is purely 'this-worldly' and tribal morality lacks the 'other-worldly' incentives of the ideologies associated with such religions as Hinduism and Buddhism.

In conclusion we may consider a problem which eludes any satisfactory solution. Throughout this book we have encountered basic differences in the economy, pattern of settlement, social structure and general way of life of the Apa Tanis and their Dafla and Miri neighbours. While Apa Tani economy is characterized by stability and wealth, mainly derived from the ownership of land, which is handed from generation to generation, a general instability is typical of the Dafla social order. Settlements are frequently shifted, there is no private property in land, and a man's wealth in cattle and ornaments is subject to many perils. Whereas an Apa Tani has security of life and property as a member of a closely knit society, the Dafla depends entirely on his own strength and his ability to support it by forging a net of alliances. Similarly there is a high degree of rigidity in the Apa Tani class structure; a patrician can never sink to the position of a slave, and no device can raise a person of slave class to patrician status. Compared to this, Dafla society is of extreme flexibility. A rich man of high status may lose all his wealth and his freedom as a result of a raid, and a man born as a slave may rise to affluence and a respected position in society. There is thus a high degree of social mobility which stands in sharp contrast to the static nature of Apa Tani society. Equally great is the contrast between the elaborately organized system of village dignitaries (*buliang*) among the Apa Tanis and the absence of any institutionalized authority in Dafla society.

Even a brief enumeration of some of the characteristic features of the two societies reveals that each conforms to a way of life which is consistent within itself, and we have seen above that the different social reactions to certain aspects of human conduct are in accordance with these contrasting trends of Apa Tani and Dafla society. How can it then be explained that both tribes hold virtually identical views on man's fate in the world beyond, that they do not differ in the moral evaluation of the deeds which will determine this fate, and that their approach to the deities and spirits capable of influencing human fortunes is basically the same? While it is consistent with Dafla ideals that the guardian of the Land of the Dead approves of deeds of valour, and honours not the meek and peaceful, but the strong man who has killed many enemies, married many wives, and acquired many slaves, one might well expect that the Apa Tani, whose social and economic system depends for its smooth functioning on peaceful co-operation, would consider acts of charity and social responsibility earning a reward in the world beyond. In fact there is, however, no discernible difference between the ideologies of the two tribes. Both among Daflas and Apa Tanis we find a moral system which is basically utilitarian and prudential, directed towards 'this-worldly' goals, and devoid of both supernatural sanctions and any link between moral and eschatological concepts.

Must we then assume that an ideology can exist more or less independently of a social order, in the same way perhaps as such culturally conditioned phenomena as a language or an art style are not directly linked with a particular social or political system? The data here assembled hardly permit so broad a generalization, but they suggest to my mind the hypothesis that while an economic development such as that which enabled the Apa Tanis to progress materially far beyond the level of all neighbouring tribes will of necessity be accompanied by changes in the social system, change in the sphere of ideology and ritual may be so slow that an ideology congruous with an earlier social order may persist in the face of dramatic economic and social changes. Thus the ideology and world-view of the Apa Tanis may have remained basically unchanged since the days of the migrations which brought them to their present habitat, a time when their economy and general style of living were presumably similar to that of Daflas and Miris. The growth of population and economic development which followed upon their settlement in the uniquely favourable environment of the Apa Tani valley, produced far-reaching changes in the social structure, without as yet engendering a comparable development in moral concepts and world-view. These remain in line with the ideology of all the other tribes of the Subansiri region, and hence they are to some extent inconsistent with the complex and stable community life the growth of which has given birth to the Apa Tani civilization as we know it today.

2   AMBA RELIGION

Edward H. Winter

THE WORLD OF the Amba is not confined to human beings but includes a host of supernatural spirits. In fact, the latter outnumber the living people for all of the ancestors belong to the supernatural world. For present purposes the supernatural world may be seen as divided into two categories; first, the ancestors and second, all other supernatural entities who may be referred to as gods. The Amba themselves do not draw this or, in fact, any distinction within the supernatural world for all such entities are referred to by one word—*Balimu*.

It is difficult to systematise the beliefs of the Amba concerning this other world and the ritual means with which they deal with it. The whole system is characterised by a lack of rigidity. For instance, no definite list of gods may be given since, although there are well known ones, particularly those personifying natural phenomena such as the sun, the moon, the rainbow, fire and storms, there are countless other spirits and new ones seem to be constantly invented. Again, although many rituals adhere to a basic pattern, there is great variation in detail between various ceremonies. Great scope is allowed for improvisation. People have a general idea of the basic procedure to be followed and within this framework they are allowed great freedom. Thus, when songs are being sung, there is no set order in which the songs must be sung or, in fact, any prescribed list of them. People may introduce completely new songs they have composed on the spur of the moment.

Reprinted from Chapter V ("The supernatural") of *Bwamba: a structural-functional analysis of a patrilineal society,* Cambridge, 1956, by permission of the author and the East African Institute of Social Research.

Some people specialise in supernatural affairs. Most prominent among these are the doctors,[1] male ritual specialists who are, more or less, jacks of all trades as far as the supernatural world is concerned. Again, there are some women who spend a great deal of their time carrying out the activities of priestesses. Many other people, although they do not specialise in such activities, nevertheless play active rôles in various rites. Great numbers of women become priestesses for various gods and adult men often carry out sacrifices for their ancestors.

Adults in this society are "caught" by gods. This may happen to men or women and there are certain gods which "catch" only men, while others confine their attentions to women. In practice, however, the majority of people who are caught by gods are women, with two exceptions, doctors and the men who are in charge of a few of the lineage shrines. Gods characteristically catch women when the latter are outside their homesteads gathering firewood or collecting water from a stream. The gods are thought to dwell in trees or in the water, where they lie in wait for women whom they wish to seize. When a woman comes into contact with a god she usually becomes ill. The major symptoms of this illness are fainting or feelings of dizziness. In some cases, visions and trance states occur. In other cases the woman undergoes no such experience, but the god manifests itself by causing the illness of one of the woman's children or perhaps her husband. Gods are said to seize people in order to enter homes where they will receive sacrifices. The disturbances which they create are merely the means by which they announce their desire. But, should no action be taken, they may make the person seriously ill and may even cause her death. A doctor is consulted as to whether particular events do indeed denote the presence of a god, and if so, which god or group of gods is responsible. He resorts to divination to find out. After this the woman's husband, or her father, since she is occasionally seized while living at her parental home, visits a priestess and asks her to conduct the necessary ceremony. The priestess is asked to "heal the patient" by "putting the god on her head" and by "bringing it into the home." Soon

[1] It is significant that the same words, *Nboka* in Kwamba and *Omufumu* in Lubwezi, which are used to designate these native ritual experts, are also applied to European medical men and the dispensers in the Government dispensaries.

after this, the priestess, with her retinue, which always includes at least two other junior priestesses and usually also a man, go to the house where the patient lives and begin the ceremony.

The ceremony may be broken down into two parts, or it may be carried out in its entirety at one time. In the former case there is a preliminary ceremony which usually lasts for four days, followed some months or even years later, by a longer rite, a week in length. The ceremony, which is usually carried out on one occasion, chiefly consists of a series of three or four hour sessions held at night within the house. The patient takes an increasingly active part as she becomes "stronger." On the next to last day the ceremony is carried on through the night until dawn. On the final night the rites are again continued throughout the night, ending at seven or eight in the morning. After this the participants rest for a few hours and, in the afternoon, the final activity occurs. On this occasion, for the first time, the participants dance outside the house, usually before a large group of spectators. The god is shown the location of the house and the entrance to the courtyard and it is also introduced to the spectators.

Commonly the gods involved in these ceremonies have no connection with the lineage, either of the woman or her husband. Such gods are not passed from the woman to her daughter or to her daughter-in-law after her death. When the woman dies the gods leave her home and return to their wild haunts. The gods are primarily the responsibility of the woman, but they may cause illness among other members of the nuclear family if they do not receive sacrifices often enough. They do not affect people beyond this immediate group.

Priestesses are very loosely organised and do not form a secret society. Most women who have undergone the ritual described above do little more than make occasional sacrifices to their gods. However, some women decide to specialise in this type of work. They make a point of going to a number of ceremonies and usually they become attached to some priestess who is often called upon to conduct ceremonies. Usually the priestess to whom a woman attaches herself is a consanguineal relative, although in some cases she may be an affinal relative. Later such women may begin to conduct ceremonies themselves. The women who act as ritual leaders are almost always beyond the menopause. Priestesses are paid for their work and their fees are very high; fifty shillings for a

week-long ceremony being typical.[2] Widowed or unmarried
women are able to retain these fees, but the sums paid to married women are collected by their husbands.

The rôle of a priestess who conducts a ceremony is almost
the only one which accords a woman status and power outside the
bounds of her immediate family. While they are engaged in their
work, they are in complete charge and the husband of the patient
and other men of his group must be very careful to avoid annoy-
ing them.

Very few men undergo ceremonies of the above type; although
many have hunting gods. Almost every man who takes hunting
seriously has such a spirit. No elaborate ceremony is involved.
The man merely builds a small model house on the edge of the
courtyard where he sacrifices before and after every successful
hunting expedition. Usually these gods are not inherited by the
man's sons, although this happens in some cases.

All men have ancestors and most of a man's ritual activities
are concerned with the ancestors. Since individuals achieve the
status of ancestors by their death, consideration will first be given
to the ritual and attitudes which surround death.

DEATH AND BURIAL

As soon as death occurs those who are on the scene give themselves over to intense expressions of grief. However, after an hour
or two the men cease wailing, although the women continue in a
highly stylised manner until the burial has taken place. The funeral almost always occurs on the same day unless death has occurred in the late afternoon, when it may be deferred until the
following morning. The burial party is generally confined to the
members of the village.

The men who are present busy themselves with the preparation
of the grave, an occupation which requires several hours, since the
grave is usually dug to a depth of some six feet and the only tool
used is a hoe. The men who are most closely related to the dead
person, the brothers and sons of a man for instance, are not usually
required to aid in this work. The grave-digging party is not a
particularly solemn affair and occasional jokes are not out of order.

[2] A man working as an unskilled worker receives less than half this amount
for a month's work.

All people are not buried in the same location. A man, his wives and older children are buried in the courtyard. Infants and young children are buried in the courtyard, although not in a central position but rather in the cleared area between the walls of two houses. Adult female members of the lineage, that is women who have not yet married or who have been married but have left their husbands, are buried behind the house and not in the courtyard at all. The differential placing of these graves may be seen as symbolising the social position of these categories of people. The man, his wife and older children are all full members of the local group. Thus they are buried in the courtyard which is the focal point of interaction in the group. The infant, since he is a member of the lineage, is buried in the courtyard. However, his short life did not allow him to become a full social personality; therefore he is not buried in the centre of the courtyard. An adult lineage woman should, in the normal course of events, be living with her husband at the time of her death and should be buried at his home. Thus when she dies at her parental home she is buried, not in the courtyard, but in the uncleared ground behind the houses which represents the outside world. When a woman of the lineage who has not given birth to a child is buried, a piece of plantain stem is laid across her chest and she is told "Here is your child! Do not come back and trouble our children."

Other people who are considered to be abnormal or dangerous in some way are also buried outside of the courtyard when they die. Madmen are always buried in the forest and told not to return and afflict people with their madness. Twins are buried under a special tree in the forest. People who died with greatly distended bellies are also buried away from the dwelling unit. A woman who dies in childbirth is buried behind the house. When she is laid in the grave a man who has performed circumcision rites should cut open her abdomen and remove the unborn child, which is then wrapped separately and laid beside the mother, the point of greatest interest being the sex of the child. At the present time most people, through fear of the Toro chiefs who disapprove of this procedure, do not carry out the autopsy but content themselves with placing a symbolic plantain stem in the grave with the woman.

The graves of those who are buried outside the courtyard are left unmarked, as are the graves of children within the courtyard. The graves of the adult men and their wives are always marked.

The degree to which these markings are elaborated differ greatly. The simplest merely consists of four upright poles supporting a small platform composed of a few logs upon which some thatch is laid. Others are model houses some three to four feet high with mud and wattle walls; while in a few cases very large tombs, as large as the average house, are constructed. These last are built only over the graves of leaders of large residential groups.

A period of mourning, which commences at the moment of death, lasts until the death ceremony which takes place on the fourth day following the burial. During this period, no work except that which is absolutely essential is done by members of the residential group. In the past, and still to a certain extent today, when the deceased is a circumcised man, this is the time of the buffalo. The adult men of the village construct a temporary grass hut near the grave, which they use as their headquarters, and as the house of the buffalo. On the first evening the men go to the nearest bit of forest in order to get the buffalo, which is then taken to the hut. The buffalo is in reality a drum, the head of which has been moistened. A stick is placed upon it in an upright position. When a man slowly draws his hands up and down the stick, a sound is produced which is not unlike that of an automobile engine. The fact that there is in reality no buffalo, but only a drum, is a great secret of the men, and no women are supposed to realise the truth of the matter. In the evening, men take their buffalo about to various houses in surrounding villages and beg for food, salt, chickens, etc., to "feed their animal." All of the gifts are taken back to the hut and consumed there. While they are visiting the various residential groups, and while they are in the hut, they sing songs. These are for the most part of a lewd nature and insulting to women. They also make loud noises and shake the branches of trees which they say strikes terror into the hearts of the women. There is nothing gloomy about this part of the death ceremony and it is greatly relished by the men, who consider it a great joke. I have been told that in the past, the buffalo was kept in the house for three months, or until the second death ceremony, but at the present time it is never kept for more than four nights, after which it is returned to the forest.

The first ceremony after the death is the most important mortuary rite. At dawn on the morning of the fourth day all the men and women of the residential group, plus the men who are in the house of the buffalo, take a bath at the place at which water is normally obtained for the residential group. After bathing these people shave their heads. This is also the occasion upon which widows don their mourning garb, which should consist of dried plantain leaves, bound around the waist. They should also smear the entire body with castor oil. Today, however, most women limit themselves to the plantain leaf and omit to cover their bodies with oil.

After this the courtyard is carefully cleaned and plantain leaves are set out on the ground to serve as temporary seats. In addition a temporary sun-shelter is sometimes erected. All this is in anticipation of the number of people who are expected to arrive. The ceremony itself usually starts at about ten-thirty or eleven in the morning, but people begin to arrive as early as nine o'clock. These events are attended by some of the largest crowds to be found in Bwamba, with the exception of the markets, for groups of five hundred or more people are by no means uncommon. All people in any way connected with the dead person are expected to attend and a great number of others, particularly men, attend purely out of curiosity.

The ceremony is conducted by the lineage of the village in most cases: that is to say, it is conducted by the dead man's own lineage or, in the case of a woman, of that of her husband. If the deceased man was an immigrant in the village of another lineage some confusion occurs. His own lineage should conduct the ceremony, but in some cases, only a few members of his lineage may attend, and in a situation in which he has effectively cut himself off from his lineage, none of its members may attend. In such cases the ceremony is conducted by the members of the lineage with which he has been living.

Although in a normal case the ceremony is conducted by the man's own lineage, or, in the case of a woman, by her husband's lineage, the most important people are, in the case of a man, his mother's brothers' lineage and, in the case of a woman, her own lineage. These people are the ones primarily responsible for deciding the question of guilt in the subsequent inquest. Their appearance is eagerly awaited and they usually arrive in a solid body, unlike other people, who arrive singly or in little groups of two or three. They always make a point of carrying their spears and they appear extremely angry. Usually they enter silently and stalk to a suitable place where they seat themselves in a group.

Sometimes, though, a man may start to bewail the loss of the dead one and cry out against the witches. When they appear, a dead silence falls upon those present, a silence which is maintained until they are seated. When they have taken their position they are welcomed to the village by one of the men of the resident lineage. The most striking feature is the dominance which is accorded to the lineage of the mother's brothers or to the woman's own lineage upon this occasion. The visitors act in a very belligerent manner while the local lineage is quiet and subdued and attempts to placate them. When the newcomers have been greeted they should be given a goat, known as the burial goat. This goat must be given to them before the ceremony continues. Sometimes an argument develops at this point, when the visitors demand a larger goat than the one which is offered to them. I have seen ceremonies end at this point amidst great confusion as the mother's brothers or the woman's male relatives leave, furious at not having been offered a large goat. It was interesting to note how carefully the goats of the residential group were kept out of the reach of the visitors, for fear that they might later seize one of them.

Once the matter of the burial goat has been satisfactorily settled, the members of the resident lineage hold a short conference at which the case to be presented is discussed for the last time. Following its conclusion the "speaker of the case" stands up and, grasping his spear, walks to the centre of the courtyard where he begins to deliver his oration. This speech may take as long as three hours to deliver. Almost always the life of the deceased person is sketched and the events leading up to the death are described in great detail. It is at this point that the names of the people suspected of having killed the dead person by witchcraft are introduced. In some cases only one person may be suspected but, in other cases, more than one name is introduced into the discussion. The reasons for suspecting them are set out. At the conclusion of this the "speaker of the case" resumes his seat. Then the suspects are given opportunity to refute the charges made against them. They are allowed to make whatever statements they wish and to shift the blame to others should they desire to do so. They may ask people questions and they may be questioned in their turn by anyone present. When all have been heard, people shout out their decisions and usually there is almost complete unanimity. Very often, at this point, the ceremony which, although it has had its tumultuous moments, has been on the whole very orderly may disintegrate into confusion, people shaking their spears and fists and uttering threats against the person whom they believe to have been guilty of witchcraft.

A second ceremony is held some three months after the first one. This is a much smaller ceremony and is usually attended only by the members of the local lineage and the mother's brothers or the woman's lineage. There is a ceremonial meal followed by a beer party. It is at this time that a successor is appointed and the man's property divided among his sons. However, this is not always adhered to. In some cases the successor may be appointed and seated upon the stool at the first ceremony and the property may also be divided on that occasion. The second ceremony offers a forum in which any new suspicions concerning the death may be brought forward. Also upon this occasion the house in which the deceased lived is destroyed. This is only done in the case of an adult. A house is not destroyed after the death of a child. There is some variation after a man's death. In some cases only one house is destroyed, while in others all of the dead man's houses are pulled down. A man's widows move into a special house which is built for them after the death of their husband. They remain there until the period of mourning is completed. There is considerable variation since some women end their period of mourning on the occasion of the second ceremony three months after the death, while others remain in mourning for six or even nine months. When the period ends they are given a hen by the son who has succeeded his father, after which they are free to go home to their own lineage, to remain under the care of the successor, to stay with their adult sons in the group, or to become the wives of other men in the same lineage under the provisions of widow inheritance.

The attitude towards the dead is ambivalent, for, in addition to the grief which is demonstrated by the survivors, particularly in the period immediately following the death, fear is also shown. The fact that people leave houses in which adults have died and the fact that these houses are destroyed testifies to this. Men and women fear the return of their spouses from beyond the grave. This fear seems more marked in the case of women for they take more elaborate precautions than do men. They fear in particular that the dead spouse will return and attempt to have sexual intercourse with them. All women formerly covered themselves with

oil and some still do so. Even the most modern woman is careful
not to bathe during this period. It is thought that if women keep
themselves in such a state their husbands will not be tempted to
have intercourse with them. Again, should a husband visit his wife
and find her in this condition, he would immediately realise that
his wife had been faithful to him for no other man would be interested in her under such circumstances.

The grief for the loss and the fear of the dead person gradually
decline so that after a few months these attitudes have been largely
replaced by calmer ones. It is at this time that the dead man may
be said to have assumed the full status of an ancestor.

ANCESTORS AND THE UNDERWORLD

When people are buried they are wrapped in barkcloth. A slit is
cut in the bottom of these grave clothes in order to allow the spirit
to leave the body and proceed to the underworld. In the cosmog-
ony of the Amba there is another world under this one and our
earth is the sky of this other world. Rain, for instance, soaks
through our earth and rains once more in the world below. The
Amba know very little about this underworld for, characteristically, they have no myths concerning it. In general, it is believed
to be very much like this world, and Bwamba in particular. People
live there in lineage villages and they cultivate the same range of
crops and raise goats, sheep and fowls. The underworld is not
considered to be either desirable or undesirable. People neither
fear nor desire to go there.

Although most people go to the underworld from their graves
by individual routes, all of the members of some lineages go by a
common avenue. These exceptions occur in the few instances in
which a village has a pond within its boundaries. The hot springs
are also thought to be used by the members of one lineage. These
ponds, therefore, become closely associated with the ancestors and
sacrifices are made at them which, in most other cases, can only
be made at real or supposed sites of graves.

The Amba are not absolutely certain that all people, without exception, go to the underworld. It is thought that people who are
buried outside the courtyard such as twins, or women who have
died in childbirth, may wander about in the forest instead.

When a person becomes an ancestor he does not lose his connection with the lineage, but many individuals disappear from the memory of the lineage members of subsequent generations. An ancestor may retain a closer connection with his lineage by having a child named after him. It will be recalled that infants, when they cry in the initial period of their lives are thought to be troubled by ancestors who wish to have the children named after them. The relationship of the person and the ancestor after whom he is named is not altogether clear. The person is not said to be a reincarnation of the ancestor. On the other hand, certain traits, such as a quick temper or generosity, when noticed in the namesake are attributed to the ancestor. Again, in certain situations, the person is treated as if he were the ancestor. Thus at a beer party, a young man, who bears the name of a father of one of the elders, may demand to be served before the latter. Again, a widow of a man may treat the child named after him in certain ways as though he represented him.

In most cases illnesses which afflict the child after its earliest years are not attributed to the influence of the ancestor. I have often been told that such an ancestor never interferes in the affairs of the person named after him when the latter is an adult. I have, however, come across one case in which an illness of an adult was attributed to the ancestor after whom he was named. Another man also sacrificed to his ancestor because he was not achieving the success in life he expected, a state of affairs which he thought might be due to the displeasure of his ancestor.

A man's father, after death, becomes for him the most important figure in the underworld. The father is seen as the one who links the individual to the rest of the lineage ancestors. Individuals usually sacrifice to their own fathers. Nevertheless, all the lineage members of past generations who are in the underworld are ancestors of the individual and he is linked to all of them. Thus an individual may participate in a sacrifice to an ancestor of whom he is not a direct lineal descendant.

Ancestors reveal themselves in various unpleasant ways. They may cause a member of the lineage to become ill, they may cause him to suffer economic loss or they may cause him to have difficulty with his wives. Of these, sickness is by far the most common manifestation of the ancestors. When the spirits of the dead act in this manner they always act as individuals, never as a group. There is never any indication that the ancestors, as a total group, are angry with their descendants, either individually or collectively. It is always a particular ancestor who is held responsible.

Ancestors also appear to people in their dreams and, in this way influence people's actual behaviour. The Amba say that an ancestor may appear to any member of the lineage or to any woman who is married to a member of the lineage. But the only cases which have come to my attention have been those in which fathers and mothers have appeared to their sons, daughters and daughters-in-law. As an example of a dream in which a parent appears, the following may be given. The dreamer was a woman. She said, "My father appeared to me in my dream last night and he said, 'Why do you stay here and not visit my home? Now do you understand what I told you? Have you seen that you have not given birth to another child? You did not obey my instructions, which were that you should marry another man in the home of your first husband.' I replied, 'Father, I was not interested in anyone in the home of my first husband.' Then my father told me, 'If you refuse to go back to the home of your first husband, then get a hen and sacrifice it to me and then you will have a child.'" The woman concluded by saying that she wanted her husband to give her a hen which she would have sacrificed to the father. The woman had been married to a man who subsequently died. After his death she left his lineage and since she had been exchanged, it meant that her father's group had to return the women whom they had received. At the present time she is married to another man and although she is reaching the age at which she could hardly expect to have another child, yet she would still like to have just one more. The whole dream may be seen as a very clear exposition of her anxieties and of an easy solution to them. We see her guilt at having disobeyed her father, the fear that she will not have another child, her desire to do so, and the sacrifice to the father as a solution. Other dreams are often similar to this in that the ancestor upbraids the person for some misdemeanour or offers advice towards the solution of a problem, or both.

Sacrifices are continually being made to the ancestors as a matter of course. When a man brews a pot of beer, a small amount is always set aside for the ancestors. Lineage members, and people who stand in the kinship category of sister's sons, are the only ones who are allowed to drink this beer, which they do after it has been offered to the ancestors. When beer is proffered to the ancestors the man speaks to them in terms such as the following, "Here, my father, is your beer. Come and invite the people with whom you used to drink beer to share it with you." Again, whenever hunters kill an animal, or when domestic animals are slaughtered, a token offering must be made to the ancestors.

In addition to these routine offerings, sacrifices are made to the ancestors when it is believed that they have brought about some misfortune, such as sickness. The ancestors are seen as individuals who must be continually pacified in order to keep them in good humour. When misfortune befalls an individual it may mean that an ancestor has become annoyed. Thus, in addition to a feeling of filial piety, all sacrifices are made in order to prevent the ancestors from causing trouble or if they have already done so, in order that they may cease their attacks. People very rarely sacrifice to them in order to solicit their aid. Except for the dreams, which have been mentioned above, the ancestors are, at best, a neutral force in people's lives and, at worst, an actively harmful force. By regular sacrifices a man hopes to ensure that at least one area of potential trouble will be eliminated from his life and thus he will be able to devote his attention to other obstacles on the path leading to his goal. Unfortunately there is no absolute certainty in the efficacy of regular sacrifices because at times ancestors cause misfortunes completely arbitrarily.

The ancestors include not only the male members of previous generations of the lineage but also the female members. In addition, the women who gave birth to children while married to men of the lineage are included. The male ancestors, however, are far more important. Female ancestors are primarily of significance as a source for names to be given to girls born into the lineage. The majority of sacrifices are made to the male ancestors, although men occasionally make sacrifices to their own mothers.

Sacrifices are made almost entirely by men. Occasionally a woman may sacrifice to her own parents, but, in most cases, such sacrifices are carried out by the woman's brother or husband should they prove necessary. A woman may suffer as a result of the neglect of either her paternal ancestors or of those of the ancestors of her husband. However, the responsibility for placating these ancestors falls upon her brothers and her husband respectively and a woman should not have to make sacrifices upon her own account. When a man's father is still alive the latter is primarily responsible for carrying out the ancestral rites. Thus, should an adult son brew some beer, his father normally makes the sacrifice to the ancestors which is required upon such occasions. For the son to carry out the rite in the father's presence is considered to be a usurpation of the parent's rôle, which is tantamount to a death wish against the father. However, the son is not forbidden to sacrifice to the ancestor under other circumstances. For instance, should the son brew beer in the absence of his father, he may carry out the rite. Again, if the son is living in another village he normally makes his own sacrifices to the ancestors as a matter of course.

Normally, a man sacrifices to his own ancestors; that is, to the ancestors of his own lineage. However, there are certain exceptions to this. As noted above a man may carry out sacrifices for his wife's parents, but this is extremely rare. Again, a man may attend the sacrifices of lineages which are linked to his own by exogamous ties. Of great importance is the rôle of the man in rites at the home of his mother's brothers. A man may always attend such cere- monies and may, for instance, drink the beer which is set aside for the ancestors. He is permitted to do so because the ancestors of his mother's lineage are also his own forbears. On the occasion of major rites, at which shrines are built, it is imperative that at least one sister's son be present. Although a sister's son may thus par- ticipate in rites conducted by his mother's brothers, he does not sacrifice to his maternal ancestors himself at his own home.

ANCESTORS, LINEAGE SHRINES AND GROUP STRUCTURE

Most sacrifices to the ancestors are carried out at the home of the individual making the sacrifice and not at some spot sacred to the ancestor in question. Thus, a man who moves to another village may sacrifice to his own ancestors at his new home. He need not return to his own lineage village in order to carry out such rites. Thus, to a large extent, the ancestors are not tied to any locality and a group does not lose contact with them should it cease to live in the land inhabited by the ancestors. There are, nevertheless, certain sites which are sacred to particular ancestors and at which rites are carried out. Quite often such sacred places are the sites of graves and very often they are found within a grove of fig trees which were planted at the time of the burial. Sometimes a stone upon which the ancestor is said to have sat during his lifetime to catch the warming rays of the early morning sun, or a stone which he used to sharpen his knives and spears may be used as the ritual site.

Sacrifices carried out at such places are rather elaborate. They include a march to the spot by the members of the maximal lineage, during which horns are blown and at least one drum is beaten by a sister's son. At the spot the land is cleared of all underbrush and a small thatched hut some two to four feet high is built. Two chickens, or perhaps a goat, are slaughtered. The blood is scattered about the spot. The meat is then cooked together with some bananas and mushrooms. The food, together with some beer, is then offered to the ancestor at the doorway of the shrine. Then those present eat the meal and drink the beer. All of this is accompanied by much singing and dancing and a general air of festivity reigns. The participants are the male members of the lineage and at least one sister's son. No women are present.

These shrines do not reflect, with any degree of exactitude, the internal structure of the maximal lineage. A situation can readily be imagined in which every lineage of a certain generational order would have its own shrine, a shrine dedicated to its own founding ancestor. Ceremonies at this shrine would express the integration of this group as a distinct unit. Then, at the next level of integration, there would be another shrine dedicated to the founding ancestors of the larger group, which would serve as a focal point for the expression of the integration of the sub-units in this larger collectivity. But this is not the case. What appears to happen is that the leading men of a generation, those who have held the position of leader of a large residential unit, or those who have had a large number of sons, are chosen for special emphasis. Whereas the ordinary man, after his death, is only sacrificed to by his sons in their own houses, these men received sacrifices at sacred places in addition to those made at the homes of their descendants. It is true that these men are the ones about whom lineage relationships are reorganised and, therefore, they become significant ancestors in contrast to other men who lose their significance. However, these shrines are usually limited to ancestors on the first or second generational level above the people who carry out the sacrifice. Shrines associated with the founders of sub-lineages are very uncommon and I know of only one case of a shrine dedicated to the founding ancestor of a maximal lineage, although, *a priori,* one would suspect that shrines dedicated to the founding ancestors of maximal lineages would be the rule. One other anomaly is that although but few men of any given generation ever have shrines built for them, occasionally more than one shrine will be built for a single individual and I know of one case in which rites have been carried out for one ancestor at three different places.

Ritual activity at these sacred spots is intermittent and is not based upon a calendrical system. Also, no attention is given to them during the period between ceremonies. The underbrush is allowed to grow and the shrine is not repaired but is allowed to fall apart. Individuals do not have recourse to them once the ceremony has been completed. As a rule, it would seem that two or three years are allowed to elapse between ceremonies. What seems to occur is that after a certain time has elapsed, someone suggests that the various difficulties which the group has been experiencing may be attributed to the fact that no ceremony has been carried out recently at the sacred spot. This view quickly gains adherents and finally it is decided that a doctor should be consulted in order to find out whether this is indeed true. His divinations almost invariably support their suspicions, with the result that plans are made and the rite is carried out.

When such a sacrifice is planned, in the case of the deceased father of a group of brothers for example, these would be the men who would take the most active interest in the affair. However, other members of the maximal lineage are supposed to participate, for attendance is not confined to the direct descendants of the particular ancestor. Thus, we see again the double significance of a particular ancestor. An ancestor is the reference point for the group directly descended from him and thus he is primarily of significance to the men of this group, since it is by virtue of him that they do form a group. On the other hand, a member of the lineage who has gone to the underworld belongs to all the surviving members of the maximal lineage. This is seen in the fact that a child of any sub-group in the lineage may be named after him; the child need not be his direct descendant. In the ancestor cult this is seen in the greater interest of a man's direct descendants coupled, at the same time, with the participation of the entire lineage in rites directed to him. The fact that each individual ancestor is viewed in this double light as being relevant, in one sense, to a particular sub-group, but in another sense relevant to the maximal lineage as a whole, is probably a factor which prevents a higher degree of pattern conformity between the ancestor cult and the structure of the lineage.

Lineages have, in addition to ancestral shrines, others which are associated with gods of non-human origin. These gods are considered to be similar to the gods which "catch" women but they have "caught" an entire lineage at some time in the past, rather than a single individual. Every maximal lineage has one of these gods associated with it and in some cases, sub-lineages also have them. The ceremonial activity associated with them is exactly the same as that carried out in connection with the ancestral shrines.

The ponds through which the dead of certain maximal lineages are thought to descend to the underworld are also sacred spots at which shrines are built, but they occupy an intermediate status. Sacrifices made at these places are thought to be directed to all the ancestors of the maximal lineage. However, the sacrifices are addressed not to the ancestors, but to a particular spirit with an individual name. One man explained the situation to me as follows: "It is like this tent in which we are now sitting. All of us are sitting together and the tent covers us all. If we were ancestors, we could all be called Tent."

In a few cases, there are shrines which are associated with more than one maximal lineage. Almost always these shrines are associated with maximal lineages belonging to the same exogamous group, but I know of one case in which a god is shared by two maximal lineages between whom marriage is permitted. It is said that the god at one time was associated with one maximal lineage but, at some time in the past, it moved to the other, although still retaining some contact with the original lineage.

Of these lineage gods whose influence extends over more than one maximal lineage, there are four in Amba which differ from all others. Shrines are built for these gods which are as large, or larger, than the average house. Each of them is in the care of a priest who is said to have been caught by the god as an individual. The normal type of lineage god has no one who is individually responsible for his care, rites being carried out by the lineage as a group under the direction of the elders. These four gods also are renowned for their death-dealing powers. Regular lineage gods are sometimes thought to have such powers, but this is the exception rather than the rule, and people do not seem to have great con-

fidence in their power. Anyone wishing to kill someone takes a
piece of clothing belonging to the intended victim and gives it
to the priest, who then shows it to the god whom he asks to carry
out the execution. Fees are charged for this service and become
the property of the priest. Sometimes it is feared by a maximal
lineage that one of its members has gone to one of these powerful
gods and requested the death of all the members of the group. This
danger may only be averted by the payment of seven goats to the
priest, who then asks the god to cease his programme of destruction. Anyone may make use of the services of these gods. It is not
required that the individual belong to one of the maximal lineages
with which the god is associated. One of these deities also insures
the good harvests for the members of the associated lineages.
This is unique, since otherwise the Amba gods have no association
with agriculture.

NYAKALA

Of all the supernatural spirits which affect women, there is one
in a distinct category of its own. This is the goddess known as
Nyakala. Unlike the others, this goddess has significance for the
entire maximal lineage. Further, the obligation to care for her is
inherited. Amba tell me that in the past only one priestess of
Nyakala was to be found in each maximal lineage. Now, however,
it seems to be more common for one to be found in each sub-
lineage and sometimes more than one are to be found even within
it.

When a priestess of Nyakala dies, she is buried in a special
manner. Certain rules have to be observed by the mourners and
the corpse itself is painted with red and white clay. A deep grave
is dug on one side of which a chamber is hollowed out. A stool is
placed in the chamber and the priestess is seated upon it with the
earthenware pot which she used in her sacrifices to the goddess
placed over her head. A reed partition is then erected sealing off
the chamber from the rest of the grave. Then the grave is filled
in the usual manner.

It is said that a woman who becomes a priestess of Nyakala is
forever wedded to her husband. The reason given for this is that
if such a woman leaves her husband, the latter merely has to take
a piece of her clothing or a bit of her fingernail, or hair, and, plac-

ing it in the section of the house sacred to Nyakala, he asks her to force the woman to return home. When appealed to in this manner, Nyakala causes the woman to become ill. If the woman should refuse to return she would die. In spite of this I have known of several priestesses of Nyakala who left their husbands.

Nyakala herself is seen by the Amba as being the most powerful and dangerous individual in the entire supernatural host, and great precautions have to be taken with her. All domestic animals and fowls which are kept in the house in which her priestess lives, may not be sold or slaughtered without first requesting her permission. Again no one with the exception of the priestess and her husband may have sexual intercourse in the house without endangering both themselves and the priestess, the penalty for the infringement of this being an attack of intestinal worms.

Nyakala has certain powers which are at the disposal of the lineage as a whole and which may be utilised through the medium of the priestess. By sacrificing to her, barren women may be able to conceive and give birth to children. Also she may be asked to kill an enemy of any member of the lineage. It is said that in time of war it was forbidden to burn her house, and anyone taking refuge there was safe from his pursuers, who could only capture or harm him at the risk of incurring the enmity of Nyakala.

THE ANCESTORS AND THE MORAL ORDER

An important negative point is that the ancestors are not very closely concerned with the institutionalised patterns outside of the specific context of the ancestor cult. It has been noted that parents sometimes appear to their children in dreams and point out to the latter that they have committed a misdemeanour. They may also advise their children to do the right thing. Thus, a man may be asked to give his brother a goat or two in order to help the latter arrange a marriage. The man may feel disinclined to do so but his father may speak to him in a dream and tell him that he should help his brother. This, however, is better seen as the operation of the individual's conscience in terms of internalised norms than as a contribution to the system of sanctions by the ancestor cult.

Ancestors do not normally punish individuals for infringement of the patterns of the society. Thus, if a man does not aid his brother to gather the necessary bride-wealth, he does not have to fear any automatic punishment by the ancestors. Should he subsequently fall ill, he does not suspect that he has angered the ancestors and that he is now being punished for his meanness. The only thing which the ancestors do punish is the failure of their descendants to sacrifice to them often enough.

Misdeeds, which are punished automatically, are not tied to the ancestor cult, even though it might be thought that they would be closely connected with it. Incest is a case in point. If a man and a woman belonging to the same maximal lineage have sexual relations with one another they have committed a very serious misdeed and they have endangered not only themselves but the entire lineage. It is thought that people may be attacked by intestinal worms, and that they may get leprosy while the couple themselves may even die as a result. However, this is an automatic consequence and the punishment of the misdeed is not visited upon the guilty pair and the lineage as a whole by the ancestors. The ceremony which must be held to avert the feared calamity is therefore not an appeal to the ancestors for forgiveness but a purely magical rite.

The Olympian detachment of the ancestors from the moral order can only be seen, I believe, as a serious weakness in a system with a set of sanctions which is not too strong at best. The ancestor cult is probably of indirect significance, however, in that it increases the sense of group identification and group solidarity among members of the lineage. This acquires increased importance, due to the fact that the system places so much emphasis upon subjective feelings of solidarity in order to achieve group harmony. However, it should be noted that the ancestor cult is only of significance for members of the lineage and thus it is not tied directly to the local community. Thus immigrants, unless they are sister's sons, are not affected by it. This means that should the present lineage villages develop into villages composed of *ad hoc* groups of relatives, the ancestor cult would have no significance whatsoever for the community.

3 PAGAN RELIGION
IN A NEW GUINEA VILLAGE

H. Ian Hogbin

THE AIM of this paper is to give the picture which the present-day natives of Busama paint of the religion of their forefathers. The village is situated in an area which has been subjected to the influence of a mission for over forty years, the west coast of the Huon Gulf between Lae and Salamaua, and only three or four of the oldest of the six hundred odd inhabitants have ever seen any of the ancient rites performed (see Hogbin 1948). Even the magic has disappeared, leaving not so much as a mangled spell. For the immediate purpose this is not a disadvantage, however, as my concern here is less with what the past actually was than with what it is believed to have been. This latter is of greater importance for an understanding of the present.[1]

The golden age, as in probably all primitive religions, lay not in the future but in the past, and great stress was accordingly placed on tradition. Goodness, in the final analysis, consisted

Reprinted from *Oceania* 18, 1947–48: 120–45, by permission of the author and of the editor, *Oceania*.

[1] At the same time, it may be well to point out at once that there can be little doubt about the accuracy of the general outlines, so closely do these follow the pattern for the rest of New Guinea. The beings which I have referred to respectively as the land spirits and the monsters of the male cult are so general, indeed, that there are terms for them in pidgin English, the "masalai" and the "tambaran."

Those who are interested in a faithful reconstruction of Busama religion should consult the literature dealing with the Bukawa' people of the north coast of the Huon Gulf, where the culture was identical. Much of this is unfortunately not readily accessible, but the following titles may be mentioned: R. Neuhauss (1911: 397–485); S. Lehner (1930, 1935).

The religions of other New Guinea peoples are discussed in M. Mead (1934, 1935); G. Bateson (1936); H. I. Hogbin (1935); P. M. Kaberry (1941); and the various publications of F. E. Williams.

in following ancient customs as faithfully as possible, and it was thought that if everyone could be persuaded to do this the world would necessarily return to its former state of bliss.

Such a belief is readily understandable in a community where conditions can have changed only slightly if at all in the course of centuries. There is no evidence of any contact with the outside world prior to 1900, and the natives must long before that date have come to terms, within the limits of the technology available, with the physical environment. Their houses are still the most suitable for the climate, there is nothing which we can teach them about hunting or fishing—they are not permitted to use firearms—and until new crops or artificial manures are introduced there will be little for them to learn about agriculture. Modifications of the political structure may have occurred from time to time, but, as every New Guinea village has always insisted on maintaining complete independence, it is difficult to see how a great deal can have been accomplished. In the circumstances there were no unfamiliar problems to solve, and harking back to precedents was the only practical wisdom.[2]

The other feature of Busama religion which is so immediately striking is the way in which it reflects, and also validates, the social organization. As the latter is somewhat unusual a short preliminary account will be desirable.

SOCIAL ORGANIZATION

The world of the ancestors was a small place, being confined to the waters of the Huon Gulf and the land on each side of it. In shape it was supposed to be like a plate turned upside down,

[2] It was probably no accident that the first peoples to place the golden age in the future, the Jews, occupied the natural corridor between East and West. Enormous changes occurred in this area with each passing generation, and following tradition too literally would have been an illusion.

A number of anthropologists have recently been insisting that native societies in pre-European times were not as static as I have suggested. Professor Malinowski, for example, has criticized those who, when setting out to examine culture-contact, presume what he calls a zero point, the moment when changes began with the arrival of the first Europeans. I cannot speak for Africa, where migrations are known to have taken place, but there seems to me to be no reason for adopting any other approach in the southwest Pacific (cf. the slight effect of casual Malay contacts on the cultures of northern Australia: W. L. Warner [1932]). *Vide* B. Malinowski (1938, 1945).

with the edges curving downwards. Right in the centre was Busama, and around the rim lay the Waria River to the south, the mountains of the Kai and Kaiwa peoples to the south-west, the mountains of the Buang peoples (Kaidemoe) to the west, the Markham plains of the warlike Laewamba (known locally as the Lahiwapa) to the north-west, the mountains behind the Bukawa' coast to the north, the Tami and Siassi Islands to the north-east, and the sea to the east and south-east. A journey beyond these limits, it was thought, would have involved the voyager in a climb up the blue vault of the sky, which was supposed to be solid, "just like thatch."

The Busama and some of their near neighbours to the south have the same speech as the Bukawa' peoples across the Gulf, but the region is otherwise the usual New Guinea babel, about a dozen different languages being spoken. Yet the settlements have always been linked together in a trading circle not unlike the *kula* ring of eastern Papua. From the south and the middle Markham valley came pots; from the Busama-Salamaua area hard stone suitable for adze blades, surplus taro, sago, and pigs; from the western mountains dogs' teeth and bird-of-paradise plumes; from the mouth of the Markham woven baskets; from the Bukawa' coast pandanus-leaf mats and string bags; from the Tami Islands carved wooden bowls; and from Siassi the obsidian (volcanic glass), imported from New Britain, from which knives were made.[3]

Within the village one of the main kinship units was, and still is, the matrilineal joint family, the group tracing descent through females from a common great- or great-great-grandfather. These persons held their land and much of their magic together. To explain how this came about a short digression into history will be necessary.

The earlier home of the natives was at Lutu on the Salamaua peninsula. The ground here is poor, and with the growth of population three separate migrations to the mainland opposite became necessary in turn, the first to Asini' in the south in the year 1800, as near as I can judge, the second to Busama in the north be-

---

[3] *Vide* map in H. I. Hogbin 1947d: 120. An account of the exchanges appears in H. I. Hogbin 1947b.

tween 1840 and 1850, and the third to Buakap in the centre in 1910.[4]

Each of the Busama settlers chose the areas of land which took his fancy, eighteen to thirty in all—small strips along the beach for planting coconuts, sections of swamp for stands of sago palms, large plots in the river valleys and on the hillsides nearby for cultivating taro, and remote tracts of forest for timber for houses and canoes. This selection established permanent rights which have been handed down through the generations to certain of the man's descendants. Local custom provides for real estate passing exclusively to men but in the female line; so to-day each set of areas is the property of a matrilineal joint family consisting of the sons of the women who trace their descent through females from the original owner. The average membership is six men, all related to one another either as brothers, real or classificatory, or as mother's brothers and sisters' sons.

The inheritance law for magic was the same as for land, and the joint family also owned the various spells of its founder.

Another unit of some significance was that associated with a ceremonial house (*lum*), of which there were in all some fifteen to eighteen. This group collaborated in undertakings which required the efforts of perhaps twenty or thirty persons. The marriage of one of their number was of interest to all, for example, and each paid a contribution to his bride-price and helped him with pigs and other food when the wedding feast took place.

Membership of the ceremonial-house group was not quite as strictly defined as in the case of the joint family. In theory everyone belonged to two, that of his father and that of his mother's brother, but in practice he nearly always made a choice, sometimes of the one, sometimes of the other. At the present time fifty-five per cent. of the community join the group of the maternal uncle and nearly thirty per cent. that of the father. (The remainder go with more distant kinsmen.)

The reason why so many men go with the father is that almost the same stress is laid on his relatives as on those of the mother. Further, though land and magic are inherited from her brother,

---

[4] The Busama were joined some thirty years later by remnants from the bush village of Awasa, which had been the object of a number of attacks from the peoples of the surrounding hills.

other kinds of property descend in the male line. Thus a man's house and chattels, his valuables, his pigs, and any trees which he has himself planted go not to his nephews but to his sons.

The senior men of the different ceremonial houses had considerable influence over their respective followers, but the person with most authority was the headman. He presided over the council of elders which was entrusted with the management of village affairs, and in all the deliberations his voice carried the greatest weight. The position depended not upon birth but upon wealth, and to achieve it the man had to have larger gardens and bigger herds of pigs than anyone else. To become socially distinguished it was therefore necessary to be industrious and have organizing ability and the personal qualities likely to attract helpers. Possessions had to be used, however, for the benefit of everybody, and the headman was under the constant obligation of entertaining his fellow villagers with elaborate feasts.[5]

Other village leaders included the fishing experts, the directors of overseas voyages, and the principal warriors. These men had to be highly skilled and the possessors of special knowledge acquired only through long training, and it was perhaps on this account that, unlike the headman, they held their titles by hereditary right.

As there was a male cult, it will be advisable also to speak about the relative status of men and women. Social differentiation has always been apparent, and looked at from a purely legal point of view the women are at a certain disadvantage. They have no overt authority, for example, either in the home or in the village and, apart from household goods, own little property. Land belongs to the men, and it is the men, too, who decide how the family valuables and pigs shall be disposed of. Again, no woman may sue for compensation, any demand for damages having to be made by the male guardian, either the father, brother, husband, or son.

Yet it must not be concluded that in practice women are of no consequence. Many of them exert great influence indirectly, and in a number of families the husband is only nominally in con-

[5] The duties of the council and of the headman are discussed in H. I. Hogbin 1947a.

trol.[6] Further, although they have never owned land, they have the right to demand that gardens shall be cleared for their use; and, when handicapped by being unable to sue, they can take comfort from the knowledge that they cannot themselves be sued.

The division of labour is fair and reasonable, the heavier tasks and those involving long absences from home being performed by the men. It is they who accept the responsibility for clearing new gardens, for bringing heavy logs from the forest for housebuilding and canoe making, and for providing the family with fish and game. Women's work is by contrast fairly easy; and for the most part it radiates from the hearth. They weed the crops, carry the daily supplies of vegetables, firewood, and water, take care of the house and everyday cooking, and mind the young children.

The women of to-day, however—and one may presume that this was true also of their grandmothers—rather resent the fact that their jobs are never finished. A man may take a day's holiday after clearing an area of jungle or if he has a mild attack of malaria, they point out, but water bottles are always having to be filled, fires are always needing attention, and children are always hungry. Women are never called upon for the great bursts of energy, it is agreed, but they have little opportunity for taking a rest.

Female vanity furnishes consolation, and all women take great pride in their fortitude and indifference to pain and fatigue. They parade their importance as they hurry to and fro when a child is born and openly snigger that if the men suffered from labour pains the village would long ago have ceased to exist.

This attitude is reflected by the men, who refer to themselves in self-pity as a tidal creek (*buka saung*), in comparison with the women, who are like a broad river (*buka atu*). Women are so constructed that weariness and disease flow away from them with the same speed as a flooded stream empties itself of driftwood. (This is not a reference to menstruation.)

[6] For information concerning the strong-mindedness of some of the women see Hogbin 1947d: 229–33.

SKY SPIRITS

The words *ngalau* and *balum* are used almost indiscriminately for supernatural beings, but several different types were distinguished, and it will be convenient here to give them separate names—the sky spirits, the spirits of the land, the spirits of the dead, the lonely female spirits, the spooks, and the monsters of the male cult.

The beings which dwelt in the sky were supposed to look like humans but to carry torches always. The two largest of these, representing the sun and the moon, were borne by the headmen, the rest being content with stars.

These spirits, particularly the sun and the moon, were looked upon as culture heroes or high gods, and to them were attributed all the characteristics of the various societies around the Gulf. They were believed to be responsible for everything—the annual rhythm of work resulting from the seasonal cycle, the distribution of resources, the technical skills, the languages, the social organization, even the marriage rules.

A myth related that in the remote past mankind lived in chaos. Each person had his own private speech and dwelt alone, and there were no households, no villages, no groups speaking a common tongue. But by and by the sun and the moon sent some of their followers down as instructors in the proper way to behave. These men gave the people their languages, showed them how to build houses, told them about marriage, the family, and group life, and taught them how to cultivate the soil and catch fish. It was at this time, too, that the natural resources were allocated and trade began. One area received pottery clay, another stone for manufacturing implements, a third grasses for weaving baskets, and so forth. In the end the culture of the earth duplicated the culture of the sky.

The sun, the moon, and their followers, having completed their task, seem like culture heroes and high gods in other parts of the world to have forgotten all about their handiwork, or at least to have displayed no further interest in it. Their presence was felt only in the wet season, the rain being ascribed to the displeasure of certain of the spirit men at the goings on of the spirit women, and when the ground was shaken by earthquakes as a result of their wars. The natives considered that a debt was owed, however, and as an acknowledgement always set aside baskets of food at ceremonial distributions. Such offerings, like the sacrifices made to the spirits who were more directly concerned with human welfare, were left for some hours in a special place in the ceremonial houses to allow the essence of the food to be consumed, after which the elders ate its corporal substance.

SPIRITS OF THE LAND

Every set of areas owned by a joint family somewhere includes a spot which is noteworthy because of its gloom, chill atmosphere, or danger—a cave with a fern-covered entrance perhaps, a waterfall drenched with cold spray, a lonely pool where a stray crocodile may be lurking, or a slippery precipice. Each of these places was formerly considered to be set apart as the abode of a colony of the beings to which I have given the name spirits of the land.

Normally invisible, land spirits occasionally took the form of an eel, snake, or lizard but were then easily recognizable by their bright and varied colouring. Their breath was of the same radiant hues and was to be seen in the sky from time to time forming the rainbow. Tempests, thunderstorms, and heavy downpours were attributed to them, especially when out of season, and they were thought to have the power also to cause a variety of diseases and even madness. They particularly disliked women and were apt to inflict them with difficulties during labour, sometimes involving the death of the infant.

Dangerous as these spirits were believed to be, however, it was thought that the group dwelling at each sacred place had made a promise to the first claimant of the surrounding area to leave him and his heirs unmolested. The members of the joint family accordingly felled the timber growing close by without anxiety, convinced that they would enjoy protection. The only exception occurred when one of them had recently been indulging in sexual intercourse. These spirits hated women so intensely that even the faintest smell of menstrual blood was a source of grievance. Men who had been sleeping with their wives took the precaution therefore of keeping at a distance, and young husbands always made their gardens as far away as possible. (This taboo is not to be confused with that prohibiting cultivation for some days after sexual indulgence: a breach of the latter was followed by the failure of the crop only, not by illness.)

Persons who had no claim to ownership, on the other hand, imagined that any unauthorized approach to a sacred place would be fraught with danger. Not being members of the joint family, they were ignored in the contract and could expect no favours. Remnants of this fear linger to this day, especially amongst the women, who usually prefer when walking about in the bush to take the safer routes even if heavily laden. The village idiot, who lost his wits after a severe illness six or seven years ago, is presumed by many to owe his condition to having cut bamboo for a fishing rod from the vicinity of a forest pool.

The proper course when a person suspected that the wrath of the spirits might have been aroused was to make a sacrifice. Sometimes he did this immediately, but in general he postponed the analysis of his past actions until the next time he was ill. If he remembered trespass on land where there was an abode of hostile spirits, he caused a message to be sent to the owners. Begging pardon for the offence, he entrusted a small collection of valuables to them, perhaps a couple of boars' tusks or a short string of dogs' teeth, with a request that these might be offered to the spirits as a means of appeasing their anger. The leader of the group carried the valuables to the sacred place, where they remained hanging from a tree for a couple of days. By this time the spirits were thought to have taken their essence, and the outer form was returned.[7] Forgiveness was now assured, and lack of improvement in the man's health was accepted as proof that other forces were at work and that a new course of action must be followed.

Gase', now an old man, told me that during his childhood he was once afflicted with acute inflammation of the throat. At first nobody took any notice of the complaint, but eventually, after he had lost his voice, his father enquired where he had been playing during the previous few days. The boy thought for some minutes and then recalled that when passing through the neighbouring

---

[7] The handing back of the sacrifice is in line with what happened to the other sacrifices. The Wogeo natives, living on an island near Wewak, in circumstances of this kind, however, make offerings of fruit peelings and coconut husks, the argument being that land spirits are so stupid that it is unnecessary to take the trouble to give them valuables even temporarily.

settlement of Gwado he had thrown a stone at a bird and missed. From where he was standing at the time, he said, there was some chance that the stone might have gone beyond the limits of the village into the pool at the base of the waterfall on the Bula River. This must be the explanation, the father decided, and within an hour he had arranged for one of the men from Gwado to hang some of his dogs' teeth on a bush alongside the waterfall. "From that moment," Gase' concluded, "my throat started to improve."

The sky dwellers were believed to be responsible for the bad weather which was always to be expected during the height of the trade-wind season, in July and August, but for prolonged storms at any other time the land spirits were blamed. If heavy seas day after day made fishing impossible therefore, or if flood rains threatened the crops, it often happened that an elder who was partial to sea food, or one whose gardens were in the greatest peril, or even one who wished to create a favourable impression amongst his fellows, would try the effect of a gift of pork on the beings who dwelt in the sacred place on his land. After the pig had been ceremonially carved a plateful was carried to them, but the villagers ate the rest of the meat. These occasional storms seldom last longer than a week, and there was little chance of the sacrifice failing to achieve its object.

Land spirits were also venerated as the source of much of the magic. To cement the agreement to give the different ancestors protection, it was supposed that they handed over a number of their spells. These formed a valuable part of the man's fortune and were transmitted to his heirs along with his land rights.

As a mark of appreciation for the gift, the joint family adopted the name of one of the spirits as its battle cry and ceremonial greeting. There was no idea apparently that the call would bring supernatural aid in time of peril, but it was felt that the word had a peculiar appropriateness for rallying purposes. A man surrounded by the spears of his enemies was fortified by a reminder of the spirits of his land and of what they had done for his ancestors.

SPIRITS OF THE DEAD

The relatives were summoned as soon as anyone became gravely ill, and it was unusual for them to be absent at the time of death. The great lamentation which went up informed the other villagers of what had happened, and from then till after the body was buried all work had to cease.

The members of the dead person's family gashed themselves with knives in the agony of their grief and sometimes tore the lobes of their ears, making the wearing of ornaments afterwards impossible. Often, too, they destroyed some of their property, perhaps chopping down two or three coconut palms and driving an axe through the hull of one of their canoes.

Meantime some of the women shaved the corpse, bathed it, and arrayed it in new garments for the lying in state, which was arranged to take place in one of the larger houses. The body rested in the centre surrounded by the weeping family, but the remainder of the floor space was cleared to make room for the various members of the community, who now paid short visits to express respect and sympathy. All the adults, youths, and girls attended, but the children were excluded for fear that the chill of death might seize them and carry them off. As a sign of grief the visitors beat their breasts and pounded their ears with coconut shells till their cheeks and necks were lacerated and swollen.

The family continued to weep without rest during the whole of the night, alternately embracing the corpse and flinging themselves on the floor. For several hours, too, the villagers sang dirges. As many as could be accommodated packed into the house, the rest seating themselves on the verandah or under the eaves.

Burial took place the following morning. The job of preparing the grave, which was usually dug in front of the residence, fell to the distant relatives, who so far had had no very prominent part to play. The hole was only about three feet deep, but the body was always wrapped up tightly in a thick covering of mats to prevent the smell of decomposition becoming apparent in the village. A small basket of taro was set at the side before the earth was replaced to furnish nourishment for the soul on the journey to its new home. A hut was then built on top, and to this the members of the family retired to continue their mourning. Kinsmen

gave them food, most of which had to be eaten raw, and also
fuel sufficient to keep a fire burning constantly in order that the
body might be kept warm. They were absolutely forbidden to
wash, and the men were also not allowed to shave.

At length, after an interval of from one to three months, depending on the dead person's status, a feast brought the period
of seclusion to a close. The heirs furnished the pigs and taro,
squandering much of what they would otherwise have inherited.
Funeral feasts were distinguished from all others by the fact that
the food was roasted on an open fire instead of being boiled or
steamed, as is usual.

The soul, which had so far been hovering around the village,
was now thought to have taken its last farewell. The natives had
no belief, however, in a single afterworld where all the departed
were assembled: the doctrine was that each one went to dwell
with the particular land spirits which had previously granted
him their protection. The tie with these beings was thus presumed to last for ever—the persons whom they allowed to approach them in life took up residence with them after death. I
was unable to discover for certain what happened to the souls of
the women but gathered that if they were single they joined the
land spirits of their brothers and if married they went to those of
the husband.

It follows that the joint family had reason to regard its sacred
place as doubly hallowed. Here not only were its land spirits
congregated but also the souls of its ancestors, the men who
in times past had belonged to the group, owning the same ground
and carrying out the same magical rites.

Yet although the two sets of spirits lived side by side, they
were always clearly distinguished. Their supernatural power was
equally extensive, certainly, but was exercised in an entirely different way. Ancestral spirits never became incarnate as eels or
reptiles, for instance, and, far from inconveniencing mortals with
bad weather, they preferred to help them with large hauls of fish
and increased herds of pigs.

As a return for their kindness, a basket of fish was presented
to them every time a big catch was secured and a plate of pork
whenever a pig not consecrated to another spirit was killed.

The ancestral spirits sometimes inflicted the living with disease,
it is true, but here again there was a difference. They were con-

cerned on such occasions with punishing not trespass on their dwelling place, which left them unmoved, but such breaches of custom as neglect of kinship obligations and wilful setting aside of marriage rules; moreover, they ignored strangers and struck only at their descendants, the very persons who were normally immune from the wrath of the land spirits. The whole group was considered to be at fault for allowing the offence to take place, and all had in consequence to pay the price. Responsibility was thus attributed to the ancestors only when two or three members of the extended family fell ill simultaneously. The sacrifice of a pig was considered to be sufficient to assuage their anger and secure a renewal of goodwill.

LONELY FEMALE SPIRITS

Deaths of adults, unless they were killed in battle, were generally thought to be the result of sorcery, and, as we shall see later, the survivors not infrequently sought out the man alleged to be responsible and put him to death. The Busama infant-mortality rate, as in other parts of New Guinea, was, however, so high that such a doctrine might have had serious disruptive effects had it been extended to young children.[8] There was accordingly an alternative belief in childless spirits which were supposed to make a practice of kidnapping the souls of babies.

Continual precautions had to be taken. Thus when leaving her baby at the edge of the garden the mother always made a loud noise by banging two sticks together to frighten away any of them which might have been in hiding close by, and when sitting on the beach she was careful to see that no tiny footprint was left in the sand to attract unwelcome attention. She refrained from venturing on the sea, too, till the child was at least a year old. In the depths of the ocean one of the spirits was supposed to lurk in the form of a giant octopus whose long arms could clutch infants no matter how tenderly they might be nursed.

If the baby was fretful or irritable the mother at once thought that one of the female spirits was either frightening it by making faces or already attempting to take away its soul. She retired to

[8] The reason for differing beliefs concerning the deaths of infants and adults is discussed by M. Mead (1934) and R. F. Fortune (1932).

the family dwelling and had one of the older children periodically
scatter hot ashes round about. At night, too, blazing fires were
kept burning just outside the doors to prevent the spirits from
going inside. If there was still no improvement the services of a
magician were sought to recover the stolen soul. He took his
spear to a rocky promontory and murmured a spell to conjure the
spirit to appear. As soon as it was visible to him he flung the
weapon, thus causing it to drop the bundle containing the soul.
Making his way as speedily as possible to the village, he returned
this to the owner with the aid of incantations and magical herbs.

SPOOKS

Such beings were of little significance beyond serving as the explanation for the profound dread which the natives had—and
still have—for the dark. They were not considered to have any
power to harm humans but were supposed to take delight in
frightening them. To this end they banged doors in empty houses,
rustled the leaves on calm days, rolled stones down hillsides,
and jumped from behind patches of shadow at night. Such
manifestations, besides being alarming in themselves, were regarded as the forerunners of misfortune. If at the time someone
in the village was seriously ill, it was taken for granted that he
would probably die.

THE MALE CULT

The foundation of the cult was the belief that the sexes were in
substance entirely different. Men, it was claimed, were akin to the
spirits and could at certain times acquire the same sanctity, a
state indicated by the expression *dabung,* a close equivalent of
the Polynesian *tapu.* Women, on the contrary, were outside the
spirits' pale—they were essentially profane and could never
attain sacredness. Contact between the two was accordingly held
to be ritually dangerous, though only to the men, and likely to
lead to loss of virility. The cult had as its object the overcoming
of this disability and bringing about the restoration of ritual
purity.

The most vital of the ceremonies was concerned with blood
letting, the means adopted for removing the women's contami-

nating influence. The penis, the organ which actually penetrated the female body when contact was at a maximum, was the obvious choice for the cut.

Incising the penis, apart from the pain and inconvenience involved—the gash had to be of some depth—was not to be undertaken lightly. Maleness was now renewed to the full, and, as a result, the affinity with the spirits was at its height. Because of the supernatural forces present, a period of preparation was necessary beforehand and some days of seclusion afterwards. During these times even the most superficial contact with women was prohibited, and the man retired to a ceremonial house. All sorts of diet taboos were imposed, too, and various other restrictions had to be observed. Fluids were barred, for instance, thirst having to be quenched by sucking a piece of sugar cane, and many varieties of fish. Further, if the food could not be eaten raw—and this was considered to be preferable—it had to be roasted on an open fire: in no circumstances could it be prepared in the normal manner by steaming or boiling.[9]

The operation was supposed to be performed at more or less regular intervals, but many men, probably the majority, were apt to delay until jolted into remembering their growing impurity by an attack of illness.[10] They then retired to the ceremonial house to take the preliminary precautions. These were considered to be complete after two days, and at dawn on the third the men proceeded to a lonely spot on the beach armed with a sliver of obsidian. The blood was allowed to drip into the sea, and they afterwards bound the wound up with leaves.

Most important undertakings also involved a preparatory incision for those taking part, thereby ensuring that defilement would not bring about disaster from weakness or any other cause. Warriors purified themselves before a raid, weavers before the manufacture of a large fishing net, builders before the erection

[9] Women were on two occasions subject to the same diet restrictions, (i) when they were in mourning, and (ii) when set apart after their first menstruation. The loss of a near kinsman was supposed to have the effect of pulling them to the brink of the spirit world (though they did not become *dabung*); and the ceremonial associated with first menstruation was obviously based on that carried out at the initiation of youths (see below).

[10] The attitude to confession is to-day similar. *Vide* H. I. Hogbin 1948: 26–28.

of a new ceremonial house, and gardeners before engaging in collective cultivation to furnish supplies for a feast.

Other ceremonies of the cult involved the impersonation of supernatural monsters. The women and children were told that these were like enormous crocodiles but were never allowed to approach near enough to see. Instead, on hearing the monsters' "voices," they had to run into hiding, reputedly on pain of death. The noise was in fact the sound made by bullroarers.

The myth giving the origin of bullroarers relates that their special properties were discovered accidentally in a village on Mount Yambi, near the mouth of the Waria River, to the south. One of the women when chopping firewood struck off a chip which flew into the air with a whirring noise. Picking it up, she discovered that it had a slight twist, which she rightly concluded was responsible. She thereupon bored a hole through one end, attached a piece of string, and returned home twirling it round her head. The husband, interested, borrowed it to show his friends in the ceremonial house, first warning her to make no mention as yet of what had happened. The men agreed that here was an object which could well be incorporated into their cult, from which hitherto they had had difficulty in keeping the members of the other sex. They would say that it was the voice of a spirit, they decided, which women were forbidden to look upon. The difficulty was that one woman had already seen it and would no doubt laugh at them as humbugs. It was accordingly declared that she must be killed. The husband was at first reluctant but at length gave his consent when promised a substitute. He sent a message to her to bring his supper, and as soon as she stepped on the ladder of the house the men despatched her with their spears. The body was buried in secret, the rest of the women being told that she had been eaten by a fearsome spirit monster which had come into the area. From that time onwards the men alone possessed the bullroarers.

The story may perhaps give the impression that the hoaxing of the women was uppermost in the men's minds when carrying out their ritual. From my experience in other New Guinea communities where pagan rites are still being carried out I am convinced that, although this aspect of the matter cannot be ignored, it would be a mistake to pay too much attention to it.

Every ceremonial house had two bullroarers, both named, a

"male" about thirty inches in length, and a "female" somewhat shorter, often only a foot. The surfaces of both were engraved with designs of mythological significance. When not in use they were preserved in a carved bowl of the most exquisite workmanship on a special shelf, and when removed for a ceremony they were reverently painted and decorated with feathers.

One of the chief occasions for the impersonation of the monsters was when a headman wished to put a taboo on certain kinds of food as a prelude to a feast. A rite to summon them from their lairs underground was carried out some time beforehand, and from then on till the date of the feast the consumption of coconuts or bananas and the killing of pigs were forbidden. They appeared, too, if a new ceremonial house was to be erected or if a leading man of a neighbouring community was ill or had died, when it was said that they had come to mourn because his kinsmen had not taken better care of him.

The bullroarers themselves were also put to special uses. A headman wishing to communicate with another village usually entrusted one to the messenger as an indication that he was on official business. The holy object gave him complete immunity from attack, for to kill or wound him would have been sacrilege. When an alliance or a truce had been concluded between two settlements, too, several bullroarers were exchanged to cement the relationship. It was said that if treachery occurred afterwards the guilty parties were liable to be the victims of supernatural vengeance.

INITIATION

Youths were excluded from the cult until physically mature, when they were put through a series of tests first and then formally initiated. So much food had to be provided for the accompanying feasts, however, that the appropriate ceremonies—there was a whole cycle, known as *sam*—could seldom take place oftener than at intervals of ten years. The younger lads involved were therefore only about fifteen, whereas the eldest were more than twenty-four. The headman gave the word as he had to supply the major part of the food.

The first procedure was the announcement of what was contemplated to the surrounding countryside. Messengers went out to invite two men from each settlement to visit the village on a certain date, and when all had assembled the headman gave notice of his intentions and presented them with bullroarers. This marked the beginning of a taboo period, during which no minor feasts could be held. Quarrelling and fighting were also outlawed, and it is said that from this time till the ceremony was over anyone found guilty of murder, adultery, or other major offences had to be killed by his own kinsfolk. The visitors later returned to their own homes, where similar taboos now operated.

The villagers next selected two old men to undertake the arduous duties of guardians (*songoboi*) during the tests. Once these had been chosen a large building (*po'labu* = cave) was erected in the bush to house the boys. This had to be fairly substantial as they remained there for five or six months. A meeting then decided which lads exactly were ready. Each had to be sponsored by a man who had himself been initiated only at the last ceremonies, so that he was not a great deal older than his ward. The pair subsequently became bond-friends and were at all times mutually considerate and helpful. This institution has now disappeared, but the two were "like the dugout and outrigger float of a canoe, always together and lost if separated." The word for bond-friend was *nengga'*, which is also the kinship term used by men married to a pair of sisters.

On the day fixed for the beginning of the ordeals the various sponsors sought out their wards and told them of what was about to take place. The youths had to climb on the men's backs, and the party left the village for the house in the bush in procession. Meantime the older men had lined up along the track, taking with them firebrands, sticks tipped with obsidian fragments, and bundles of nettles. These were used to administer a sound thrashing to the boys as each passed by. The sponsors did not escape unscathed, and by the time the house was reached everyone was covered in blood.

The initiands, at this stage known as *saga,* were received by the guardians, who told them that during the next few months they would be tested to see whether they were fit to be presented to the monsters as a sacrificial meal. If they proved worthy there would be no cause for fear, as they would pass through whole and be evacuated. But anyone who failed to measure up to the requirements would remain fast in the monster's belly and never be heard of again. The tests prescribed included further beatings, being kept awake for several days on end, and partial suffocation. Huge fires were lit inside the house and piles of green boughs put on top. The doors were then kept tightly closed until everyone was practically insensible.

During the whole of this period, which lasted for upwards of three months, the boys were only allowed to eat minute portions of the coarsest types of food either raw or roasted. All liquids were forbidden, though if they were thirsty permission was occasionally granted for them to chew a piece of sugar cane provided by the sponsors. The mothers and sisters handed over plates of delicious stews daily, but these were taken by the elders. There was also a ban on leaving the house at any time except just before dawn, when each youth had to bury his fæces in a deep hole. A watch was then kept to see that he did not wash himself afterwards.

At length the day arrived for the summoning of the monsters. Word had been sent out to the villages which had proclaimed the taboo, and a vast concourse of people was by this time in attendance. They remained till the last rite ended, causing severe strain on their hosts' resources.

The pretence was that the monsters lived underground, and a hole was accordingly dug from which they could emerge. At first only a faint humming was heard, and the women murmured amongst themselves that the tree roots must be scraping their flanks. Soon afterwards a man covered with earth went along to the village to announce how deep down the monsters had been but that they had at last appeared. The humming now became louder, till in the end the whole countryside rang with the booming of dozens of bullroarers.

The boys had to listen for a few days and were then brought out and shown by their guardians, with much impressive ritual, how the noise was made. A poisonous fish was later flourished in front of their mouths, and they were warned that if a word of what had been disclosed crossed their lips they would perish as assuredly as if they had swallowed a deadly toxin.

This revelation was followed by the incision rite. This time the boys were cut by one or other of the guardians, but on all subsequent occasions each person operated on himself. A long low shed had been built to represent one of the monsters, and inside

the two men waited with their obsidian knives. The lads were
taken in turn, each one being carried on the back of his sponsor,
who also served as a support while the gash was being made.
The blood, as the first which they had shed, was especially sacred,
and the sponsors gathered it in leaves for use later as face paint.

The men spoke of the wound as the mark of the monster's
teeth as the boy was swallowed. Informants stated that at times
some of the candidates bled to death or died as a result of the
cut becoming septic and that occasionally those who had
offended the guardians by their weakness or disobedience were
deliberately put to death. The bodies were buried in the bush,
the mothers being informed that unfortunately the monsters had
failed to digest their sons.

The hosts now made ready a great feast, supposedly for the
entertainment of the monsters but in fact for the guests. The
youths, however, were hurried back to the shelter, where they
were subject to the same taboos as before. They remained shut
up until the wounds were quite healed, generally a couple of
months. Different men took turns swinging the bullroarers day
and night, and it is claimed that the lads had barely any sleep on
account of the noise. At the same time, no further tests were
held, and instead the guardians delivered long moral homilies.
Respect must always be paid to the elders, they said, and it was
necessary for everyone to bear in mind that he now had a bind-
ing obligation to help his various kinsfolk, those on the mother's
side as well as those on the father's side. They made a great
point also of the rule that sexual intercourse outside wedlock
was forbidden and urged the lads to avoid entanglements by
concentrating on their work and refraining from sitting for long
gossips in the houses of others.

Before the boys could emerge the monsters had to be sent
back underground, a rite accompanied by another feast for which
sometimes hundreds of pigs were slain. The villagers liked to
boast that so much food was provided that a large quantity became rotten before it could be eaten.

Now called *gwale,* the youths next day went to a stream and
were given a ceremonial bath by their sponsors. Richly painted
and decorated, they were then led one by one into the village,
where the women welcomed them with tears of joy. A secular
feast, which all could share, had in the meantime been prepared

and a platform erected outside one of the ceremonial houses. On this the boys sat while their relatives and friends danced and sang songs in their honour.

This concluded the celebrations, and the guests made their farewells and departed. One duty alone remained, a purely private matter for the boys' families. Most of them liked to show their appreciation of the sponsors by showering them with gifts.

The taboo period was also over, and fighting was no longer regarded as sinful. The ancestors used to insist that the effect of the restrictions continued, and that peace could confidently be expected for a year or two. This the natives to-day dismiss as a pious hope. Outbreaks of violence often began, they say, before a month had elapsed.

SOCIAL CONSEQUENCES OF INITIATION

The rites made a drama of the lads' change of status. Their childhood came to an abrupt close, and, after a period when they were under close observation, their manhood had an even more violent beginning. The obvious intention was to impress upon them that irresponsibility must now give way to earnest fulfilment of obligations to kinsfolk and the community as a whole.

Informants who are themselves of middle age, while admitting all this, insist that the ceremonies also had the effect of ensuring that at all times due respect would be paid to the elders. So forceful a demonstration of knowledge and power, they urge, humbled the initiates and left them with a meekness which they never afterwards threw off.

When giving me detailed accounts of what used to take place these older men always dwelt longest on the belabouring of the boys during their ride on the sponsors' backs to the place of seclusion. The ostensible function was said to be the encourage-ment of growth by magical means, but they invariably added that the beating was of extra importance as a demonstration that authority rested in the hands of the senior generations. Whether or not the blows were administered with sadistic abandon it is now impossible to say, but everyone insisted that this was so.

The alleged laziness and moral laxity of the youths to-day, in my opinion somewhat exaggerated, are attributed to the abandon-

ment of the custom, and many elders expressed a desire for
its revival in some form by the mission. "I'd make the youngsters
heed me," one man exclaimed. "I'd hit them till the blood flowed
like rain. Then we'd see whether they'd sit talking all day instead
of helping us in the gardens. They'd bring some of their money
home from work, too, and not gamble it away as fast as they
earn it."

It is unnecessary to point out that any changes in the young
people's behaviour cannot be accounted for so simply and that
many other factors must be at work.

WOMEN'S CEREMONIES

Just as men reached the highest levels of sanctity when renewing
their masculinity by incising the penis, so women gravitated
towards the lowest depths of the profane when their femininity
was at a maximum during childbirth and menstruation. Yet
though at such times the two sexes travelled in different directions
and ended up poles apart, they had one thing in common: both
were wrenched out of the ordinary world of every day. The
women no less than the men therefore were subject to restrictions
—they had to avoid all contact with males and were forbidden
to eat certain foods. A ceremonial house into which they could
retire was lacking, but the difficulty was overcome by preventing
the menfolk from visiting the family dwelling.

As the time for the wife's delivery approached the husband
pulled the floorboards aside and dug a hole underneath to receive
the placenta and the blood. These preparations concluded, he
withdrew to wait on the beach or at some other convenient spot.
The woman was attended by certain of her female relatives, who
brought firewood, water, and clean mats. Progress was announced from time to time, and as soon as the child was born a
message was sent to the father telling him of its sex. He was not
permitted to see it, however, or even to go near the house for
several days.

The mother remained indoors for about a week devoting all her
attention to the care of the infant. The only food permitted, in
contrast with the raw or roasted vegetables eaten by men under
a taboo, was hot soup, preferably made from the shoots of
young sago palms, which her husband and brothers were expected

to provide, one every alternate day. At length, if she was considered to have regained her strength fully, her kinswomen went out with their nets to catch a dish of freshwater fish. After these had been eaten her seclusion ended. She was allowed to come out of the house into the village, and the husband could now examine his offspring and perhaps nurse it for a few minutes.

The girl's entry into womanhood at her first menstruation was something of an event, the accompanying ceremonies being not unlike those carried out at initiation. At the same time, they were not nearly so elaborate, and, as only one girl passed through at a time, there was no general disturbance of village life.

On the first appearance of the blood the girl was ordered to go to bed. She was considered to be ritually cold and had thus to be heated, a process achieved with the aid of massage with warmed oil in which ginger roots had been steeped. The rubbings continued for several days, during which she did not sit up.

This was the beginning of a period of seclusion lasting for six or seven months. Permission to go outside was only granted when it became necessary to answer the calls of nature, and at such times a shroud of mats was worn as a cover not only for the head but for the whole body. If the father or brothers wished to remain in the dwelling a small compartment was made for the girl in one corner, but the men usually preferred to stay outside and eat their meals in the ceremonial house.

Unlike the youths, the girl was not called upon to undergo any ordeals, but washing and drinking were forbidden, and her diet was also confined to raw or roasted foods. Three or four girls of approximately her own age attended to her wants, companions to whom the word *nengga'* was applied, the term used by the boys and their sponsors.

When at last the father considered that he had sufficient food for a small feast he announced to his relatives that the time for emergence had come. The next morning the companions took the girl to the stream for a ritual bathe. An old woman always went with the party, and on the completion of the toilet it was her duty to give a certain amount of elementary instruction in sex. Using a gourd or a green banana, she told of the male organs of generation and showed the girl how the penis would be inserted in her vagina, rupturing the hymen as she did so.

A member of the train carried the girl back to the village. Many

persons, men as well as women, stood in readiness, and as the
two appeared they were beaten with stalks of the ginger plant.
They were afterwards expected to become bond-friends, *sangung*
being used for the girl herself and *ise'* for the companion. (These
are not kinship terms: women married to two brothers call one
another *dawatang*.)

The feast took place on the following day, the girl, now known
as an *aku'wi*, being painted and decorated with all the family
ornaments for the occasion. The food was displayed in front of
the house with a mat on the ground in front. To this she was led
by her brothers, who protected her from observation with a screen
of mats until she was seated and arranged to the best advantage.

When menstruating later, women were not confined quite so
strictly to the house, though they rarely came outside. The beach
was absolutely barred, however, on the ground that the fish
might afterwards smell the contamination on the canoes drawn
up above high-water mark and keep their distance. Gardening
and the preparation of the family meals were also forbidden, and,
to tide the husband and children over, the neighbours sent along
provisions. The women cooked for themselves but had to limit
their meals to hot broth.

SORCERY

Three types of black magic were recognized—*mwi'sinang*, resulting in illness only; *katon*, leading to the annihilation of whole
populations; and *balu*, bringing about the death of particular
individuals.

Mwi'sinang

Each minor ailment with which the people were commonly afflicted was associated with one or more systems of magic. Thus
there were systems with rites to cause tropical ulcers and cure
them afterwards; systems to cause and cure diarrhœa; systems
to cause and cure conjunctivitis; and so forth. Nearly everyone
in the community had a knowledge of at least one system, a fact
which he did not as a rule attempt to conceal. The details of the
rites, however, especially the spells which had to be chanted, were
carefully guarded from all but the legal heirs, who learnt them as
part of their heritage.

The chief use of such magic was to prevent theft from palm groves and orchards. The trees were often planted at a considerable distance from the village where no watch could be kept, and to protect them the owners carried out the first of their rites. They then hung a warning sign on a bush close by or else twisted it around one of the trunks to inform the potential thief that from thenceforth he meddled at his own risk. If he was undeterred and stole any of the nuts or fruit it was thought that he would inevitably be taken ill.

Spells to cause the disease were also used as a means of taking vengeance when an offence was committed by a fellow villager—failure to pay a debt perhaps, destruction of property, or borrowing tools without first asking permission. The whole community was linked together by such a never-ending chain of reciprocal obligations that an open breach would usually have been inexpedient, and persons who considered themselves to be injured preferred to punish the offender in secret through their magic. The necessary rites were carried out in the depths of the forest over a leaf or some other convenient substance, which was then buried in his garden or thrown on to his bed. He himself was unaware of what had occurred, but the magician was satisfied because convinced that sickness would follow.

It is possible that persons with a guilty conscience may occasionally have imagined themselves into illness. But New Guinea is not a healthy country, and as few drugs are obtainable the average villager even to-day spends at least a fortnight or three weeks in each year confined to his bed. Subsequent events must accordingly have confirmed the magicians in their belief—sooner or later the culprit always suffered. The disease with which he was afflicted was sometimes different from the one intended, but this was not regarded as of much consequence. The magic had perhaps worked itself out in a new way, or else another person who had been wronged had used more powerful spells.

The fact that the rites could be performed by stealth meant that they were sometimes resorted to also for the satisfaction of private grudges. The victim, that is to say, was sometimes innocent of all offence and ought not to have been expected to pay any penalty. His ignorance was on such occasions his protection. Being unconscious of the enmity which his conduct had aroused, he had

no suspicion that magical forces might have been directed against
him.

The normal treatment for minor illnesses was to have the
remedial rites performed. Patients who were aware of having
trespassed on a sacred area or who felt that an incision of the
penis might be due had recourse first to the appropriate religious
ceremony, but in ordinary circumstances no further action was
taken than to request the assistance of a man with a knowledge
of the correct magic. Any one of them served the purpose, and it
was not regarded as necessary to locate the person actually responsible for the onset of the complaint. Natural resistance was
generally in itself sufficient to ensure recovery, and once again
the current belief received apparent corroboration.

Katon

This was the most lethal sorcery of all, being thought to be capable of wiping out everyone in a village. It was only employed with
the consent of all the elders, and then solely against a neighbouring settlement which had given serious offence.

Each village in the locality had one or two *katon* sorcerers,
men who had inherited their spells from a brother of their mother.
So deadly was this form of magic that during their apprenticeship
they were compelled to withdraw from the rest of society to a
cave in the forest, where they lived for upwards of a year, con-
fining their diet solely to uncooked food.

The essential ingredient of *katon* sorcery, apart from the spells,
was a length of a species of creeper which when left in the sun
gradually disintegrates into powder. If the elders agreed that the
sorcery was to be carried out the magician collected his creeper
and that night journeyed to the outskirts of the offending settlement. Having lit a fire, he murmured his incantations over the
stalks and then cut them into short lengths. These he held over
the flames one by one till they were ignited, afterwards hurling
them in the direction of the houses. If by chance while the ceremony was in progress he heard the mournful cry of a night bird
he was doubly certain that his mission would be crowned with
success.

It is said that within a couple of days one of the women began
to sicken, to be followed later by everyone whom she had touched,
then by everyone with whom they had been in contact, till in the

end not a single healthy person remained. If steps were not taken to have the magic undone, death carried them all off within a few weeks. Anxious to prevent such a catastrophe, the offenders sent compensation for their misdeed to the group which they had injured, with a message also to the headman to have mercy upon them. A meeting was called to decide whether the gifts were acceptable, and if it was agreed that this was so the sorcerer was ordered to undo his work. He bespelled a length of sugar cane and chopped it into four pieces, one for himself and one each for a man, a woman, and a child from amongst the wrongdoers.

Bula

This is the familiar sorcery of food remains, common throughout the primitive world. The magician collected a few crumbs which had fallen to the ground while his victim was eating a meal and later, in the privacy of his house, recited spells over them. The man began to feel pains soon afterwards, but it was believed that death could not take place until the food had been burnt. The only hope of a cure was to find the sorcerer as soon as possible and persuade him to neutralize the magic by putting the crumbs in cold water.

The headman and one or two other persons of importance were supposed to have *bula* spells, the net weavers and the stone workers alone being always excluded—black magic would have been incompatible with the white magic which they were called upon to perform. If a man wished to become a sorcerer and had not inherited the necessary knowledge he could buy it for a large fee from someone more fortunately placed who was willing to sell.

As with *katon,* the main purpose of *bula* was to score off the inhabitants of other places. To aim it at a fellow villager would normally have been the height of folly—the sorcerer would have been depriving himself of a helper and his group of a warrior. It was one of the duties of the headman to rid the community of troublemakers and habitual criminals, however; and leaders were occasionally suspected also of bewitching possible rivals who were beginning to be as wealthy as themselves.

People fell back on the *bula* explanation only after simple home treatment by sacrifices, the incision of the penis, and remedial magic had failed to effect any improvement. The patient then began to cast about in his mind to discover whether anyone in a neighbouring community might have a grievance against him. If he came to the conclusion that this was so, he persuaded one of his kinsmen who was friendly with the man in question to make a few discreet enquiries. Confirmation of the suspicion was followed by a plea that the crumbs might now be placed in cold water, a request which was seldom, if ever, refused. The questioner was often met with a blank denial, nevertheless, making further search necessary. In cases where this was still unsuccessful, and the patient began to recover, it was taken for granted that the sorcerer must have relented of his own accord. If, on the other hand, death took place, the only possible conclusion for the relatives was that the food had been burnt.

Here then was an explanation which could be put forward on practically every occasion when anyone save a young child had died. For infants another reason was given; as has been mentioned, they were thought to have attracted the attention of lonely spirits. There is some probability, too, that *katon* was held responsible for serious epidemics. The villagers even supposed that *bula* was at work when a man died as a result of some misadventure, such as a fall from a tree, the bite of a snake, the wreck of a canoe, or goring by a wild boar. Had he not been bewitched his hand would have kept a firm hold, the snake would have wriggled away, the canoe would have outsailed the storm, and the boar would have been less fierce.

It is important to note that there was never at any time a suggestion that the dead man might himself be to blame either for ignoring the sacrifice due to an offended land spirit or for delaying the incision of his penis. These remedies were within the same easy reach as our aspirins and castor oil and were tried out, like them, during the early stages of the illness while there was still hope of a speedy recovery.

One may be reasonably certain that *bula* magic was actually performed, but there is considerable doubt about whether it was as common as was generally believed. For the natives, however, death was in itself proof that the rites had been carried out—had they not been the person would have been still alive. The kinsmen were accordingly filled with rage against the sorcerer believed to have been responsible, their desire being to make him pay in full for what was, to their way of thinking, unjustifiable homicide.

The first requirement was the man's identification, a job for which a diviner had to be called in. He had several methods at his disposal, but all involved the conjuring of the spirit of the dead into some object. A series of questions was then put to it, each one phrased in such a way that the answer was a simple yes or no—"Did the man who killed you come from the west?" "Does he live in Gwado?" and so forth. The commonest object was probably a stunned eel, a convulsion at the appropriate moment being accepted as an affirmative. A trochus shell was also used. It was poised on the base of an upturned pot shaped like a cone, and when it fell off the answer was "yes." Again, some men employed a length of bamboo containing one of the dead man's ornaments: this remained still for "no" but rolled about on their hand to indicate "yes." It seems that gossip had usually fixed upon the name beforehand, and that all the diviner did was to give confirmation. This was easy as every method was susceptible of manipulation.

The elders decided what was to be done. They sometimes organized a raid to put the alleged sorcerer to death immediately —the last time this took place was in 1900—but more usually, for fear of causing a war, they asked the headman to arrange for him to be bewitched in his turn.

MAGIC AND LEADERSHIP

Many different methods of fishing were practised, but seining was always one of the most popular and probably on a yearly average supplied more than half the total catch. Five nets were available, never more and, except when a new one was in process of being made, never less. Each was technically the property of a single individual, though there was, of course, no possibility of him rounding up a shoal without a large team of helpers to man the canoes and pull the ropes.

The significant fact was that ownership, and in consequence leadership, were based on a knowledge of the magic carried out while the netting was being manufactured—the man who performed the rites automatically claimed the finished seine, and persons who were ignorant, no matter how wealthy they might be, could never hope to do so. The spells were inherited in the normal way and before death were always taught to one of the sisters' sons, who thereby in due course became the owner-leader.

I have observed in other communities that the abandonment of magic as a result of mission influence has led to the disappearance of seine fishing even before the weaving skills have been forgotten. The Busama can no longer make nets but are lucky in that a few natives have always had enough money to purchase them at the stores.

The owner of the seine had to organize and direct its repair and renewal as one of his main duties. He carried out regular inspections and gave the word for holes to be mended, for sections to be replaced, and, if required, for a whole new net to be woven. It was his job also to decide when it was to be taken out, which areas were to be fished, how the members of the team were to arrange themselves, and what proportion of the haul each was to receive. Of necessity he became thoroughly acquainted with the winds and the tides and the feeding habits of the different kinds of fish and an expert at predicting changes of weather.

The value of a director for an undertaking of this sort requiring communal effort cannot be over-emphasized. The chances of the equipment becoming damaged or worn through neglect or carelessness were reduced by its being made the responsibility of one man—his property and his reputation were now at stake. The background of skill and knowledge was also an obvious advantage, and the fact that the right to give orders was recognized meant that everyone was kept informed of exactly what he had to do.

These points were brought home to me when in 1945 I had the good fortune to secure a seine as a partial replacement for those which had been destroyed when the village was obliterated by bombing two years before. (There were at this time no stores where the natives could obtain nets for themselves.) I had intended to make a gift to the community at large but was dissuaded by a number of my friends. "Give the net to your brother Nga'gili'," one of them urged. "He can't use it by himself, and we'll all share the catch. But if it's his he'll take care of it; if it belongs to the village no one will bother. Besides there'd be trouble then if two groups both wanted to have it on the same day." The example of a communally owned canoe, a present from a District Officer, was cited in support. As it had been nobody's particular job to renew the lashings and patch the hull, the craft had become unseaworthy after only a few weeks and was lying derelict on the beach (Hogbin 1947c).

Membership of the team depended partly on kinship with the owner, partly on descent from persons who had belonged to the group in the past. The team not only fished with the seine but was under the obligation of providing either labour when a new one was made or supplies for the feast with which its completion was celebrated.

The making of a new net was a highly ceremonial business, for, apart from the specialist ritual of the owner, the workers, about thirty in all, were under the strictest of taboos from the time when the materials were first gathered till the final feast. They lived apart in a special house on the beach eating only roasted vegetables and drinking no water, and, after the task was completed, an incision of the penis was insisted upon.

Warfare was another communal enterprise in which leadership was bound up with the hereditary possession of special magical knowledge. There were half a dozen war generals in the village, each of whom had inherited a spirit familiar from his ancestors. This was represented by a carved stone figure about a foot high over which spells were recited when an expedition was contemplated. The incantations translated the spirit to the enemy settlement, where it clubbed all the menfolk, making them "heavy with sleep like blocks of stone" so that they could be taken by surprise. The only risk was that if a watch had been set the heavy tread of the spirit sometimes gave warning of its intentions.

The choice of a general for a particular campaign rested with the headman and the elders. They took various factors into consideration, such as knowledge of the geographical features in the vicinity of the enemy village—what sort of cover was available and where hazards and defences might have been placed—familiarity with the habits of the people, natural sagacity, and proven ability to inspire followers. Once the man had been named he was in complete authority and was implicitly obeyed.

On the evening of the day fixed for the attack the general had the duty of divining the probable result and, if success was assured, of endowing the weapons of his band with the magical ability to find the target. A pot was filled with a mixture of water, a small piece of his excrement, bespelled ginger, and other herbs, and round it the spears were planted firmly in the ground. The

warriors then lined up in the background while the general lit the
fire under the pot and kept watch on the liquid. If it boiled first
on the side where the warriors stood success was a foregone
conclusion, and the spears were dipped in one by one. But if
instead the bubbles appeared on the other side the party returned
home. The ceremony was then repeated on the next day and, if
necessary, on the day after. Not until defeat had been prophesied
three times was the project abandoned.

The general was also skilled in reading omens, and as the band
proceeded by stealth through the jungle he had to watch for the
signs given by certain birds and reptiles.

Other leaders whose position depended on magic were the men
in charge of the overseas trading voyages and of the quarrying of
stone to be ground into adzes.

The explanation of the absence of a special gardening magician
to discharge the functions of agricultural leader probably is that
the cultivation of the staple crop, taro, is carried on throughout
the year, new areas being cleared by each householder as soon as
the old ones become exhausted. Gardening magicians are to be
found in New Guinea only in places like the Trobriands, where
there is an annual rhythm of agricultural work, with a regular
season for planting and another for harvesting. Most of the
Busama possessed individual systems of gardening magic, however, with spells to make the plants grow, spells to repel the wild
pigs, and spells to keep insect pests and plant diseases in abey-
ance.

VILLAGE MAGIC

The systems of magic which were individually owned, apart from
those concerned with gardening, related to fishing with lines and
hooks, to hunting, and to beauty, the last being carried out before a dance. Love magic may appear to be a striking omission,
but its absence will be readily understood in the light of the Puritan sexual code and the privilege claimed by the elders to arrange
all the marriages.

Mention must also be made of a number of magical taboos,
especially those associated with the care of young children, so
many of whom died in their first year. No one was permitted to
kindle a fire or light a cigarette with embers taken from a house

in which there was a baby, for example, for fear that it might contract a fever. The excrement of infants had to be burnt most carefully, too, lest by being trodden about it should cause a rash to appear. Finally, the parents had to avoid eating certain kinds of fish—those with large scales which might result in skin diseases, those with prominent eyes which might lead to the child developing a cast, and so on. Similar taboos related to gardening, fishing, and hunting—the men refrained from going out in a canoe for a few days after eating pork, and if hoping to spear a pig they always pretended that a rat was the quarry.

CONCLUSION

The link between social organization and religion, adumbrated in the introduction, will have been apparent on almost every page of the account. The principal economic and religious groupings, for example, have proved to be identical: the men who owned and worked the same areas of land were united also by a common bond with certain ancestral and other spirits, and those who joined together for some of the bigger enterprises belonged to a single ceremonial house and had a similar ritual relationship with the mythical monsters. Co-operation for daily tasks was thus not merely a social matter: behind lay the full force of the world of the supernatural.

The various leaders played a dual rôle, too, taking charge of both secular and spiritual matters. The headman, as well as presiding over the village council, acted as the chief sorcerer and had the final say in calling up the monsters from the underworld for initiation and other ceremonies; and the director of the fishing team and the war general were alike expert magicians. Even the differentiation of male and female was given religious backing, the one being held to be sacred and the other profane.

This curious attitude to sex calls for further comment. The basis for it, I believe, was the women's high social status. They were so prominent in community life that the men fell back on a cult as a means of self-assertion.

A comparison with Wogeo Island, where there is a similar culture except that the women are of still greater importance than they were in Busama, is in this connection instructive. The theory here is that contact between the sexes is equally perilous for both, and the women in consequence have a separate cult to themselves founded on menstruation, the natural function which, they say, obviates the necessity for a cleansing operation. The incision of the penis is actually regarded as an imitation of their monthly periods and is commonly spoken of by the same term. The men ignore most of the ceremonies of this rival cult with great ostentation but, in the end exasperated, bring the biggest of them to a close by falling upon those taking part and driving them home with sticks and stones. The leading women retaliate, though only when by themselves, by saying that they know all about the initiation monsters but have no objection to their husbands deluding themselves with the belief that the whole thing is a close secret.

The myth relating how everything originated with the sky dwellers served as a means of elevating and consecrating the accepted standards of behaviour. These, it was insisted, had been ordained not by men such as we are but by superhuman creatures who were above and beyond criticism. Custom, that is to say, acquired a mystical value which made the slightest murmur of complaint an act of the grossest blasphemy. The man who followed established traditions must have felt that he was playing his allotted part in the divine purpose of the universe.

Some of the customs had features which are to our way of thinking barbarous, but in those concerned with the relations of fellow villagers the keynote was always loyalty. Persons who lived only a few miles away may have been treated as enemies and killed for sorcery or for no reason at all as opportunity offered, but near neighbours were trusted kinsmen and friends to be supported if necessary at the cost of ease and convenience. Within certain narrow limits, then, it may be asserted that the sky spirits gave a charter for conduct which we would ourselves accept as moral.

Additional moral sanctions were provided by some of the other beliefs. Property rights were preserved, for instance, by the doctrine that the land spirits were concerned to punish trespass and by the faith in black magic as a means of bringing thieves to book. Again, the ancestral spirits were supposed to harry their descendants when marriage rules had been disregarded or kinship obligations remained unfulfilled. On the other hand, there was no invocation of supernatural penalties against either the murder of a relative or adultery. Perhaps these offences were adequately condemned in being treated as evil customs specifically forbidden by the sky spirits; though adulterers, in any case, had little chance of escaping the avenging spears of the wronged husband and his kinsfolk.

Much has already been written about the general effect of magical and religious rites, and it will suffice to say here that in Busama as elsewhere these gave the natives confidence that, in spite of all the unforeseen difficulties against which no practical measures could be taken, their desires would in the end be achieved. The recitation of spells and the elimination of what were supposed to be contaminating influences by means of an incision assured the success of many of the enterprises, sacrifices to the land spirits brought about the return of good weather, offerings to the ancestors secured fine hauls of fish and abundance of pigs, and more magic guaranteed recovery from illness. Further, if the unexpected happened and the patient perished, the survivors were able to take comfort from the funeral ceremonies, which not only allowed due outlet for their grief but also reaffirmed their hopes for immortality by insisting that death was but the beginning of a new life on another plane.

4 TWO NUBA RELIGIONS: AN ESSAY IN COMPARISON

S. F. Nadel

I PROBLEM AND METHOD

THIS STUDY is, methodologically, a sequel to a previous "Essay in Comparison," exemplifying the same approach and a very similar *Problemstellung* (Nadel 1952). It is concerned with two groups in the Nuba Mountains, the *Heiban* and *Otoro,* whose cultures coincide over a wide range while exhibiting certain limited though marked divergences: these will be regarded as constituting a series of "concomitant variations" significantly interrelated and hence permitting the construction of certain explanatory hypotheses.

Since the general ethnography of the two groups has been presented in the writer's monograph on the Nuba tribes a few introductory remarks will be sufficient to provide the context for the present inquiry.

The Heiban and Otoro are racially identical and live in the same environment, being in fact close neighbors with villages and homesteads of very similar design. They speak almost identical languages (as various vernacular terms will show) and have identical economies based on the same types of resources and technology. They intermarry, though not very frequently. With few exceptions their clan and kinship systems are closely alike: their kinship terminologies, for example, show no differences. The same close similarity also characterizes the legal conceptions of the two groups, their simple, nonrealistic art, and their dances and other

Reprinted from *The American Anthropologist* 57 (4), 1955: 661–79, by permission of Mrs. B. Nadel and the American Anthropological Association.

forms of recreation. As will be seen, numerous common elements also link their religions.

It is in the field of religion that the crucial "variations" occur, accompanied by others in the field of social and political organization; further differences, not so easily summarized, will be introduced later. Our explanatory hypotheses will bear primarily on the types of religious beliefs and practices characterizing the two groups. In describing these the present study fills a gap in ethnographic knowledge, since the Nuba monograph contained no account of Heiban and Otoro religion.

II   CONCEPTION OF THE UNIVERSE

The Deity

The pivotal concept in either group is that of a supreme being. It is pivotal in the sense that all the other beliefs about the nature of the world presuppose, however vaguely, its creation and arrangement by the deity. Equally, the concept of a supreme being is a "final" concept, entirely self-satisfying and inviting no further speculation. God is called *kalo,* which is also the common word for "earth." But he is understood to be in the sky as well, being, in fact, ubiquitous, invisible and unknowable, with neither sex nor any other human likeness ascribed to him. Though God has created everything, the act of creation is tacitly accepted rather than explicitly asserted or specified. Much the same is true of his guardianship over the universe and his concern with human fate. Thus the conception of the deity has only weak moral implications: though certain forms of supernatural punishment of evildoers come ultimately from God, since he created and still governs the agencies executing the punishment (lightning, certain diseases), their intervention must be solicited or engineered by human action. The deity is, essentially, morally neutral, and the existence of evil in the divinely created universe is not seen as a problem.

It is in keeping with this conception that neither group conceives of a beyond where goodness is rewarded and evil punished. The Heiban formulate this conception more sharply by insisting that punishment, such as it is, takes place in this life; in the next life good persons and evil fare equally.

In the conception of the beyond the two groups differ a little. Both picture it as an exact copy of this life, where men live in houses, keep livestock, farm the land, marry, and so forth. Logically, both groups provide the dead with food for the journey and make other, similarly realistic, preparations. The Heiban are somewhat more realistic in this respect, for example, in burying two sheep with any man of adult age so that he might have brideprice for remarriage in the other world, and in providing him with fire to light his pipe. Also, their beliefs are more detailed and concrete. Thus they have a special name for the beyond—*kwereny,* "in the back"—though they are not sure where it is located, on the earth or in the sky. The Otoro have no such special name, describing the beyond as being somewhere, probably in the sky, "where one can see God." The Heiban maintain that the soul of the dead bores a tiny hole through the earth covering the grave, through which it escapes shortly after the burial. Kinsmen will visit the grave to discover the hole and so obtain proof of the soul's escape, for a soul which remains imprisoned in the grave may harm the living. In the Otoro view the soul simply leaves the dead body and the grave, which event is neither visualized in detail nor thought to involve any risks or dangers. Both groups believe that the souls of dead people may visit the living, sometimes bringing illness to a person or ill luck to a house. But in Otoro this belief rarely crystallizes in concrete fears. Furthermore, only the Heiban have developed it further, into a belief in ancestral powers. For them, the dead show continued concern in the fate of their progeny, which leads to interventions both helpful and (more often) threatening. Thus, in the event of domestic quarrels which require some solemn reconciliation, the Otoro invoke and sacrifice to God, while the Heiban address themselves to (unnamed) ancestors. Equally, the Heiban are always ready to detect the anger of ancestors over, say, a funeral feast negligently or niggardly performed, in various forms of illness or disaster.

The beliefs of the two groups differ even more sharply as regards the intervention of the deity in human life. The Otoro accept the given form of their rituals as an adequate means of communicating with and influencing the deity. The feelings that should go with the rituals are humility and trust: the priest will address the deity as "God of mine" in the same way, it is ex-

plained, as a "child would call his father." In Heiban it is positively stated that the mere observance of the ritual rules is not
enough and that God must be stirred out of his apathy by other
means as well—through loud and violent pleas, complaints, and
even accusations. Thus the typical Otoro ritual is quiet and subdued; when, in extraordinary crises, a more agitated mood breaks
through, this is specially commented on and considered an exception. Few Heiban rituals present a similarly quiet aspect, an
excited and violent mood being the rule. Indeed, at certain sacrifices, private or public, individuals may loudly abuse God, accus-
ing him of unconcern and weakness. The explanation is readily
and uniformly given: "God does not listen to you if you just
pray; you must make him angry first, then he will do what you
ask, just to show you his power." This attitude the Otoro consider
absurd and unintelligible.

The Heiban notion, that mere appeals and offerings to the deity
are insufficient, reveals itself also in another aspect of their rituals.
In the "great" cultivation ritual, for example, one beats cornstalks
violently against the rocks until the stalks are broken, which
means that the rains will similarly be "broken"; in another ritual
empty gourds, formerly containing beer, are shaken three times
in the direction prescribed by ritual, so that they may be filled
again after a prosperous harvest; branches placed across the path
to the place of sacrifice after the latter is concluded are meant to
"bar the way" to storms which might harm the crops; and at all
rituals concerned with cultivation the congregation executes certain elaborate gestures which realistically symbolize the precise
effects expected of the particular rite—the height to which the
plants should grow, the sprouting of the leaves, the filling out of
the ears of grain, and so forth. Though the violent mood mentioned before reappears only in the first of these ritual acts, they
are all alike in that they add to the sacrifice and invocation
manipulations meant to compel and force nature and hence the
deity behind it.

Similar symbolic-compulsive acts are not unknown in Otoro.
But they occur only in one or two rituals and do not approach
either the elaboration or the precise significance of the Heiban
observances.

Spirit Beings

Neither group admits the existence of other deities. There are, however, anthropomorphous beings, local genii or spirits called *nyibor,* which live in rocks, trees, or streams. They are invisible to ordinary humans, though I was once told (in Otoro) about a child who had seen the spirits and for a time lived with them. Medicine experts, on the other hand, combine with their other gifts that of being able to see and discover spirits. The spirits can be of either sex and both good and evil. The good spirits do not do anything in particular; the evil ones haunt certain localities, strike people who go there with sickness or sudden death, and occasionally attack human beings without provocation.

The Heiban conception of these spirits is both more bizarre and more sinister than that of the Otoro. The Otoro believe that the spirits look like ordinary human beings though they are much stronger; the Heiban picture them as being white of skin, with red hair, and one-legged. They also believe that the female spirits entice certain male humans (who are born with "a second head") to join them in the spirit world; and when the humans are tempted—as they often are—to take advantage of this visit by stealing some of the spirit wealth, grain or livestock, the spirits punish them with illness or death.

In addition to the spirits and the souls of the dead, the world contains certain other invisible creatures—the "people from below" (i.e., living inside the earth), who are "good" people, for example, anxious to insure rain for the humans. The Otoro also speak of "people from above," once more good and helpful, though nothing more precise can be said about them.

Body and Soul

The rest of creation consists of inanimate and animate beings, the former including plants and trees, the latter animals and men. There are no theories or speculations about sun, moon, or stars. The difference between animate and inanimate beings lies in the possession or nonpossession of a "shadow soul"—*dgrim*—which is the word for the shadow of men or animals, the shade thrown by objects, trees or plants being differently named. The shadow soul is already present in the embryo in the womb; on death, it is separated from the body and embarks on a new existence in the beyond, the body turning to dust. Illness always attacks the shadow soul, causing it to "grow weak." Though it would seem more logical to attribute the effects of illness to a loosening of the bond between soul and body, neither group has seized upon this idea or finds the assumption of a "weakening" soul (which yet survives the body) self-contradictory. Nor are there decided views on the nature of dreams, which may show the sleeper the shape of other persons, live or dead. It is thought possible that the persons appearing in dreams may be souls seen by a soul, but here speculation rests. It is, however, positively asserted that the *dgrim* both of living and of dead people can be seen, if only by medicine experts in virtue of their uncommon gifts.

The Otoro conceptions of soul and body are somewhat richer and philosophically more ambitious than those of the Heiban. The Otoro define three constituents of the living being: shadow (or "soul"), breath (or "life principle"), and blood (epitomizing the organism as such). For "breath" one also says "heart," using a special word with a metaphoric meaning, not the name for the physical organ. The shadow is of two kinds, "white" and "black." The living person throws both kinds of shadow (as informants were anxious to demonstrate), the dead body only the "white" one, while the "black" shadow, being the soul that survives death, becomes invisible once life goes. The "breath" ceases at death, while the "blood" disappears gradually with the disintegration of the body. Logically, since the Otoro assume that the soul leaves the body immediately upon death, the dead body is at once called a corpse (*kumdi*). The Heiban, less logically, distinguish between the dead body before interment (called simply "dead person") and after interment (when it becomes a "corpse," *karu*), even though they believe in a period of transition when the soul still clings to the body in the grave.

The Otoro, incidentally, present their ideas about soul and body in the form of a rudimentary genesis, thus: "When creating man God first made blood; then he added breath; finally he gave man his shadow soul." There are two other attempts, as crude and bare, to account for origins—for the origin of rain making and of certain female food taboos. There is no need to quote the stories, which are not very widely known and which, apart from being flimsy, also refer in a highly inaccurate manner to the observances they are meant to explain. These three accounts contain all there is of Otoro cosmology or mythology, and, if the Otoro are poor "myth builders," the Heiban are none at all.

Miraculous Gifts

The beliefs of Heiban and Otoro lack, as we have seen, any conception of abstract, mystic "forces" which exist autonomously in the world and might become subject to human control. Both groups, however, conceive of certain mysterious enhancements of human capacities, both for good and for evil, which are as fortuitous as they are nonnormal (or "supernatural"). They are referred to simply as "possessions" or "things owned," sometimes by owners initially unaware of the gift, and are best described as "miraculous gifts." These may make a man a rival of spirits (though one doomed in the end), or at least an intermediary between spirits and humans, and between the visible and invisible world.

Such is the medicine expert (called *kumaŋ* in Heiban and *miyaŋ* in Otoro), who can diagnose and cure spirit-caused ailments and see the souls of the dead. Though the calling tends to run in kinship lines (paternal or maternal), it is held to be unpredictable, depending neither on heredity nor on acquired skills but only on a "gift" miraculously bestowed, both on men and on women. In Otoro, meaningful dreams announce its possession; in Heiban, it is even more mysterious, the expert-to-be simply "knowing" that he (or she) has the gift. The expert may well be deceived, as would be shown by the failure of his ministrations. But there is no other test of his capabilities, which, as will be seen later, have in fact no empirical foundation.

The Heiban liken the powers of the medicine expert to those of another mysterious and miraculously gifted individual—the "person with two heads." This is the free translation of the vernacular term *kugi kweti lra,* "man of the head," or *lra* ("head") for short, which is usually explained by saying that such persons have "four eyes" or "another pair of eyes in the back of their head." The "second head" is, of course, invisible, and ordinary people do not recognize a *lra,* though one would suspect one in newborn children who cry all the time and beat their bodies with their fists. In this event a medicine expert may be called in, and if the latter confirms the suspicion he will advise that the infant be killed at once, by crushing its skull and hence destroying the mystic, and unlucky, "double head." But often the *lra* grows up unsuspected and unsuspecting, for his magic power lies not in his visible body but in his shadow soul, which would roam about at night, harming other shadow souls or plundering the wealth of spirits, as already mentioned. Any person suddenly and unexpectedly grown rich is suspected of being a *lra*. Of this, too, the human owner of the gift may be unaware, thinking only that he was exceptionally lucky, until the spirits punish him—with sudden death, with death by lightning, or with a form of paralysis affecting only the left side of his body. But the suspected owner of a *lra* is in no way ill-treated or ostracized by his fellow men; rather, one appreciates the fact that he is the unwilling vessel of an evil power.

The Otoro have a somewhat similar belief in exceptionally gifted individuals, though it is conceived both more vaguely and on the whole less pessimistically. Thus a person may suddenly discover that when he curses someone or wishes him good luck, e.g., on a hunting expedition, his curses and wishes come true. Other men are said to possess a gift called ŋraba, which word again has no other meaning and cannot be illustrated by any would-be concrete analogy such as the Heiban "double head." The owner of ŋraba is credited, primarily, with an entirely beneficial gift, that of easing difficult confinements by spitting on and massaging the mother's womb. The gift is thought to be hereditary in the same sex, but children brought into the world with the help of ŋraba will possess the same powers. Ordinarily friendly, the gift may turn into a threat: if its owner is angered by the parents of a child to-be-born, he may cause it to be born deformed, but once his anger is pacified he would be able to remedy the effects by a simple treatment (once more, by spitting on the afflicted part of the body and massaging it with water and red clay). Also, there exist evil ŋraba which attack newborn infants without provocation and without the "owner's" desire or knowledge; in this evil version the powers of ŋraba may turn even against the owner's own flesh and blood.

We note the close connection between the "miraculous gifts" and afflictions of the body. The discussion of healing practices will bring further evidence to bear on this "ownership" both of ailments and of their cure.

III   RITUAL

General

Like other primitive societies the Heiban and Otoro lack any conception of worship in the abstract, of a self-satisfying and exalting communion with the deity. Rather, all acts of worship are severely pragmatic, revolving upon needs to be satisfied, risks to be reduced, problems to be resolved. Equally, all acts of worship are ritualized, the appeals for supernatural aid being bound to more or less standardized procedures, to appropriate times and places, and to the manipulation of objects. Sometimes, especially in Heiban, the procedures and manipulations become all-important and are credited with autonomous efficacy (as in the "compelling" gestures mentioned before). But ritualization goes together with conscious expressions of appeal. This is evidenced, in both groups, in the loosely phrased prayers addressed to God (more rarely, to ancestors) which accompany all rituals and never approximate to precise verbal manipulations (i.e., to magic spells). Taking the belief in the efficacy of manipulations (of words, gestures, objects) to indicate a more "magical" orientation, and the belief in the power of spontaneous prayers or appeals one that is more "religious," we may regard the rituals of the two groups as embracing both, if in different degree.

For the sake of brevity we shall here concentrate upon the major and "public" rituals, meaning by this phrase not so much their scale of celebration as the import ascribed to them, i.e., their concern with the needs or problems affecting the community at large rather than the lives of individuals or kin groups.[1] Of the "private" rituals we need only say that they are linked with birth, death, and marriage, with domestic calamities or fortunes, with the conclusion of pacts of friendship or the settling of quarrels, and with similar personal or family matters.[2]

It is difficult to describe a "typical" ritual, since its features vary

[1] The scale of celebration has of course an importance in its own right in that it indicates both the degree to which the religious activities tax the economic resources of the group and the manner in which rituals implicate (and reinforce) social structure. Both these viewpoints will here be disregarded.

[2] Several of these "private" rites have been outlined in my Nuba monograph (1947).

widely with the occasion. But the following brief account of a
cultivation rite in Heiban presents all the important features.

Priest and congregation assemble in the morning at the place of
sacrifice, which is marked by a stone cairn serving as altar. First,
some newly cut grain is placed on the cairn, being weighed down
with a stone. The priest, assisted by the congregation, lifts the
sacrificial animal over the cairn, puts it down again, and kills it
with a spear. Everybody touches the blood on the spear blade,
and then all clasp hands across the cairn. These acts are accompanied by brief prayers spoken by the priest and congregation in
chorus, thus:

> God, give us things today,
> Cause the sacrifice to be good today.
> God, give us grain, give us beer, give us children,
> Give us all things good.

After being skinned the animal is cut up, and the meat is boiled
with some grain and heaped on a platter. The people sit down in a
circle facing the food and, extending their folded hands toward it,
repeat the prayer. Then everyone helps himself to the food. After
the meal one leaves the bones, the stripped grain stalks, and
morsels of the food on the cairn as a final offering to the deity,
whereupon the gathering breaks up without further ceremony.

Let me note a few variants. At minor ceremonials there may be
no cairn "altar," a simple flat stone serving the same purpose.
Animals already killed, other crops, or prepared food and beer
may be added to or replace the sacrificial offerings just described.
In rituals involving the idea of consecration (of first-fruits, of a
newly filled granary) one also burns certain animal fats, incense
fashion, over the things to be consecrated.

Normally there is no music or singing. Women and young people are admitted only at minor ceremonials, but the ritual procedure is by no means secret, everybody knowing what takes
place. It is on the whole uncomplicated and loosely formalized, and
involves the handling of only a few objects—plain vessels for food
and drink, the spear with which to kill the animal, the crude altar,
a splinter of wood on which to place the "incense." Rarely is the
choice of the sacrificial animal subject to special rules or mystically significant; often it is determined by practical considerations
alone. The animal is invariably a common species, domestic or

wild, and the conceptions underlying this as all other offerings are once more unsophisticated, the offering being simply regarded as a gift to the deity (or to spirits and the souls of the dead). In calling the sacrificial food a "gift" the people further underline the character of the ritual as an "appeal." The problem involved in this offering of material substances to nonmaterial beings disturbs no one; if the people speculate at all on this question, they answer it simply by saying that it is the "shadow souls" of the sacrificial items and not the items as physical substances which are offered to and accepted by the transcendental beings. As regards the meal with which the congregation concludes the sacrifice, it has in no way the significance of a "communion."

The simplicity and informality of ritual admit of certain exceptions. Various ceremonials in both groups entail rigid prescriptions as to the direction in which one must face during the ritual acts, the number of items to be sacrificed, and the kind of incense to be used. These rules, however, signify nothing that bears on the aim or success of the ritual but only certain social implications of its performance, namely, the clan membership of priest and congregation (Nadel 1947: 96–97). Another exception is more significant since it distinguishes sharply the religious attitudes of the two groups. We have mentioned the symbolic gestures which, in Heiban, complicate the ritual (and render it more "magical"). The Heiban similarly surround one of the common ritual objects, the sacrificial spear, with more elaborate ritualization. It is treated as a sacred instrument, hidden away on normal occasions and requiring to be consecrated before it is first used. Also there is only one such spear in each kin group (a feature especially important in private rites), where it usually belongs to the oldest male member. If the sacrifices thus performed appear to be unlucky, the spear will change hands, passing to another man who, one hopes, will handle it more auspiciously. In Otoro, the sacrificial spear is neither as sacred nor as rare, and new ones are often taken in use without consecration, e.g., when a kin group grows and scatters. Ordinary spears, even knives, may equally be employed without courting disaster. Let me stress that the Heiban beliefs indicate more than merely a greater preoccupation with ritual detail: they introduce into ritual not only an additional mystic manipulation but also an additional risk—the possible ill luck of the spear's owner.

Cultivation Rites

The public rituals have one of two professed aims—to secure rain or to prosper the crops. Only the latter kind of ritual is also public in the sense that it is performed on a communal scale. But though the rain ceremonial is executed in the privacy of the priest's house and by him and his kin alone, the whole community takes cognizance of it and may even have to take steps to insure an adequate performance. Both kinds of ritual, too, exhibit their public character in that they constitute specific offices, held by publicly acknowledged experts—the local "grain priest" or "rain maker."

The Heiban grain priest is in charge of five annual rites (called *lobo*), which accentuate various phases of cultivation. The first rite precedes planting and involves, apart from the usual sacrifice, also the burning of incense over the seed grain. The second rite takes place when the crops are about foot-high (and must be "made to grow"). The third rite coincides roughly with the last weeding (when backward plants must be "helped on"), and the fourth, with the first reaping. The last ceremonial once more involves the incense rite, now performed over the newly threshed and stored harvest. The first three rites take place on or near cultivated land; the fourth, on a group of rocks overlooking the farmlands of the community; the last, in the priest's own house. The first and fourth rituals also serve as signals for the respective agricultural activities, the priest being the first member of the community to undertake them, on his land. The premature planting or harvesting by others is believed to destroy the fertility of the land, and such acts call for special purificatory sacrifices as well as for the imposition of fines on the culprits.

The fifth ritual, called "great" *lobo*, is on a much larger scale than the rest. It concludes with a big feast in the priest's house, attended by everybody and celebrated with singing, dancing, and much drinking of beer. It also marks the end of an important, severe taboo: this is imposed, after the third *lobo*, on all singing, dancing, and on certain boisterous games played by the young. All these forms of enjoyment, and even mere whistling or shouting in the standing grain, are thought to endanger the crops, perhaps (there is no agreement on this) because they might provoke the jealousy of the spirits.

Here another magic threat to the fertility of the land may be mentioned. It lies in any crime (such as rape, homicide, or assault) committed on cultivated land; even a scuffle or exchange of blows which leads to blood dripping on the ground would threaten fertility. The crime and breaches of the peace are thereby aggravated, and the disastrous consequences to the land must be warded off by special sacrifices of purification. One does not think in this connection of spirits and their quasi-human idiosyncrasies; rather, the underlying conception is a firm linkage between the moral universe (which is disturbed by such crimes) and the natural universe (sensitive to all kinds of disturbances).

The priesthood of the *lobo* is hereditary in certain lineages, though the succession is far from rigid. Thus, where there are several sons, any one may be chosen, not for reasons of seniority or other obvious qualities such as cleverness or virility (one grain priest I knew was a eunuch), but in virtue of some mysterious, not readily discoverable gift. This gift might be suspected or guessed by fathers or relatives, but would ultimately prove itself in the success of the rituals; nor are "false starts" unheard of or unexpected. The grain priest lives the life of an ordinary peasant save for one special taboo: he must not eat in the presence of strangers anything that "grows on the ground"; when his wife carries food to him on the farm, she carefully covers it up so that no one should even see the food.

To turn to the Otoro cultivation rites: there are only two of a public character; the others either are missing or are reduced to "private" ceremonials. Only one of the two public rites is called *lobo,* and corresponds to the "great" *lobo* of Heiban in its combined ritual and festive character. It falls, however, in the middle of the rainy season, not coinciding with any of the Heiban dates, and lacks the significance of a "signal" rite. In some Otoro communities both the local and seasonal significance of the rite have disappeared; here the sacrifice has been joined to the triennial age-grade ceremonial ŋ*ajo,* which is celebrated on a tribal scale and has the strong connotation of a festivity demonstrating political solidarity (Nadel 1947: 145–46). The second Otoro ceremonial precedes the first planting and also ceremonially opens the new hunting season. It consists of a sacrifice of the newly killed or trapped game and of the incense-burning rite, being also known by that name (*kurregyo*).

Unlike the *lobo,* which is entrusted to the local grain priest, the

second ritual is the responsibility of the rain maker. If this combination of religious duties suggests that Otoro priestship is less
highly specialized than priestship in Heiban, this is evidenced also
by another fact. In order to ascertain the precise date of the first-
planting rite, the Heiban grain priest must rely on the knowledge
of special calendar experts—old men experienced in observing the
rising and setting of the sun but holding no office proper. In Otoro
there are no such specialists; rather, the rain maker is himself a
calendar expert.

Very little need be said about the Otoro grain priest. He assumes
his office exactly as in Heiban, though he stands under no taboos
indicating his unusual position or mystic powers. Nor do the Otoro
practice any of the seasonal taboos which, in Heiban, are a constant reminder of possible disasters. Nor yet do the Otoro believe
in the supernatural threats to fertility entailed in crimes committed on cultivated land. Again they see in the performance of
rituals and in the simple appeal of prayers a sufficient guarantee
of divine protection.

Rain Ritual

The appointment or election of the rain maker closely resembles
that of the grain priest and follows the same rules in both groups.
But the character of the office differs sharply. In Otoro the rain
maker's special powers come into play only when the seasonal
rains fail. In this event he is expected to perform the appropriate
rite without waiting for any request on the part of the people. The
rite takes place at night and in secrecy. The priest kills a "red"
sheep and, invoking the deity, fills two gourds with water, which
he throws high up in the air: as the water drops down to the ground
so rain will fall on the earth. Yet it is thought possible that the
priest might, from personal resentment against someone in the
community, refuse to perform the ritual. The morality of such a
step is not questioned as such; all one would try to do is to remedy
the situation. If the person who is the cause of the rain maker's
anger is known, the people will try to persuade him to make
amends; failing in this, they would climb to the top of the mountain
or assemble in front of the rain maker's house, wailing and crying
"as in a funeral" and begging God for rain (as I have witnessed),
whereupon the rain maker would always relent and perform the
ritual.

Here it is important to emphasize that, for the Otoro, the rain maker is only an intermediary between the people and God. God himself causes the rain in response to sacrifice and prayer. Thus, if the rain maker were to persist in his refusal, it is thought likely (though no one could visualize such a situation) that the direct approach to God by the crying and wailing congregation would even then secure the rain.

The rain maker and his sons (i.e., his potential successors) observe certain food taboos and special rules of personal cleanliness. The rain maker also officiates at the death of people killed by lightning, when a sacrifice is needed to neutralize the supernatural contagion ascribed to this kind of death. This duty the Otoro rain maker shares with his Heiban counterpart.

The Heiban, unlike the Otoro, expect the rain maker to perform the secret, rain-causing ritual every year, and not only when the rains appear to fail. The beginning of the rainy season in fact depends, in their view, on the regular performance of the rite. Again, they are much more ready to suspect the rain maker of omitting the rite because of some private grievance, and any delay in the rains is at once interpreted in this sense. Though the rain maker is firmly expected to deny any such motive, rumors of this kind will at once spread and gain credence. The countermove now lies not in persuasion but in coercion, in forcing the rain maker, by threats and even bodily attacks, to perform his duty. There is some concrete evidence of rain makers' having left their villages, emigrating to other parts, when the rains were late and these threats likely to materialize. As in Otoro, the rain maker is still an intermediary between humanity and deity, but he is an intermediary who is both more indispensable and more unreliable.

This pessimistic and anxious outlook is further accentuated by the duplication of rain experts in Heiban. In addition to the expert responsible for making rain, there is one responsible for stopping or "holding" the rain. He is expected to do so, normally, when the rainy season draws to an end. But once more it is thought possible that resentment or anger might cause the expert to "hold" the rain out of season, so that the person responsible for his mood must be discovered. But now no threats are used against the expert, even if no culprit can be found. Rather, if this is the case, one assumes that the drought must be "natural" and can be broken by the offices of the rain maker proper.

In this view the rain "maker" is a more sinister figure than the rain "holder," for the former cannot plead "natural" causes, and his denial or apparent lack of motives for revenge is inevitably disbelieved. It is interesting to note that in an adjacent community, culturally identical with Heiban, the roles are reversed, the rain "holder" being regarded as dangerous and on occasion evil, while the rain "maker," though not immune from the human weakness of wishing to vent his anger on others, is on the whole considered a friendly and helpful agent. Thus there is some attempt at balancing good and evil, the friendly and the hostile forces of the universe. In Otoro, where the hostile attitude of the rain maker, apart from being thought less likely, can be neutralized by the direct appeal to the deity, this balance seems unnecessary. Nor is the danger of the season failing traced to two different sources and hence doubled, the notion of a special rain "holder" being simply ridiculed.

IV HEALING PRACTICES

The logical transition from "ritual" to "healing practices" may be seen in a variety of the latter which employs the typical procedures of ritual and represents, with the other observances provoked by domestic calamities, an instance of "private rites." In a sense the healing rites are the least private of all the "private" rites. For while in all others the ritual procedure is in the hands of ordinary individuals (a family head, a father or husband), the treatment of illness usually involves the services of publicly acknowledged experts. Also, certain illnesses carry a far from private import, being understood to represent supernatural sanctions for offenses against tribal or kin group morality.

In Nuba eyes hardly any form of illness is "natural." Various diseases and ailments are in fact traced to specific mystical causes; others, though they cannot be thus identified, are yet "unnatural" in that they are believed to come from the unexplained presence in the organism of some foreign body such as a stone or splinter of wood. Only in the case of minor complaints, which may not call for treatment at all, or of injuries due to obvious accidents is there no search for a hidden cause. Female sterility and male impotence are classed with the mystically caused disabilities.

When there are doubts as to the type of illness afflicting a person, the medicine expert must diagnose it before applying the appropriate treatment. The diagnosis involves nothing in the way of an examination based on acquired skills or experience but is entirely intuitive. The intuition in turn is taken to be part of the "miraculous gift" which makes the medicine man. Nor does the treatment rest even on crude empirical knowledge, say of medicinal herbs or of some simple form of surgery. The mystically induced diseases are treated by ritual entirely; in the others the treatment is ostensibly technical, aiming at the "extraction" of the foreign body, which usually lodges in the chest or abdomen. This is done by massaging the afflicted part with oil, spittle, or animal blood until the intrusive element remains in the hands of the medicine expert and can be triumphantly displayed. Though this spurious surgery simulates a strictly mundane skill, the miraculous and supernatural source of that skill is never forgotten.

As will be seen, the list of mystically induced ailments is much fuller in Heiban than in Otoro. This does not mean, of course, that the respective complaints are unknown in the latter tribe. But it does mean that the Otoro are aware of fewer causes of disease and hence reckon with fewer risks and mystic dangers. Conversely, the more extensive and precise anticipation in Heiban of these risks and dangers also entails much greater overt anxiety.

The mystic causes of illness may lie in the direct action of God, in the machination of spirits, in the anger or malevolence of the dead, in sorcery, and in the efficacy of magic "roots." The different treatments corresponding to these different causes are often tried out one after the other or even combined.

The forms of illness caused by God directly are the same in both groups—lunacy and leprosy. Both are incurable; while nothing further is known about the first, leprosy is invariably considered a supernatural punishment for grave kinship offenses, such as incest or neglect of blood revenge. This threat is more sweeping in Heiban than in Otoro, for, while the Otoro think only of true incestuous relations (between siblings or parents and children), in Heiban any illicit sexual relationship between kin is believed to invite this penalty.

Spirit-caused diseases, which are of various kinds, or those caused by the souls of the dead require some conciliatory gift or sacrifice or some rite of exorcism. In the latter, the medicine expert sprinkles animal blood over the patient, his kin, and his dwelling, or drags the branch of a thorny shrub of magic qualities through the house and out to some wasteland or river bed, where it is weighted down with a stone. As has been mentioned, only the Heiban believe in revengeful ancestors, who may inflict illness, impotence, or female sterility.

Sorcery, called *kudigrinna* in both groups (lit., "seizing the soul"), is essentially punitive magic, which any man or woman can work against a person by whom he or she has been harmed. Unless the subject of the sorcery is in fact guilty, the magic act has no effect. If effective, it causes swellings on the body and eventual death, unless the culprit repents and remedies the wrong he did. The techniques involved are simple: anything belonging to the person to be bewitched will serve (a piece of clothing, food, grass from the roof, also earth scratched from the footprints), if it is taken, hidden, and finally thrown in the fire. As the victim's possession burns to ashes so his "soul" will disintegrate and vanish. In Heiban one may also take the leaves of a certain tree, dip them in the blood of an animal, and sprinkle the blood in the air; at the same time one calls upon God to "send evil to the person (unnamed) who wrought evil."

If Heiban sorcery is simpler and more widely applicable (since it is unnecessary to possess oneself of the victim's property or even to know his identity), it is also thought more destructive, for everybody is believed to be capable of it, though certain clans are credited with particularly effective powers of this kind. In Otoro these powers are thought to belong to certain individuals only, who need not be aware of it until some chance trial convinces them of their gift.

The only remedy open to the victim is to conciliate the sorcerer and, if there is still time, to make him or her lift the curse. There is no protection against *kudigrinna* save one's innocence; nor do kinship bonds, of any degree, offer immunity. In a case I witnessed in Otoro a husband thought himself bewitched by his wife; in a case in Heiban, a son by his father. Yet *kudigrinna* is talked about quite openly without any attempts at secrecy or, for that matter, show of fear. The Otoro even state explicitly that it is senseless to be afraid of something that cannot be helped and is, in any event, worked in secrecy, unbeknown to the victim. Though the Heiban in similar discussions admit to being afraid, there are no overt indications of anything like an ever-present obsession with this particular anxiety. But the act of sorcery itself is viewed differently in the two groups. The Otoro call this magic self-help unequivocally "evil," and informants would admit only that they might resort to it "very rarely." The Heiban regard it as perfectly normal and even as capable of being improved and made easier. They are now also utilizing the services of itinerant shamans from a neighboring tribe, paying them a goat for each "bewitching" of a victim, known or anonymous. The Otoro, then, import moral inhibitions into their belief in punitive magic; the Heiban turn the magic revenge almost into a business proposition.

The belief in magic "roots" (*towa*) is once more limited to Heiban, where it serves to explain a variety of ailments—sores and boils on the legs, inflammation of the eyes and of the throat, and severe rheumatic pains. In spite of the concrete name, which refers to "real roots in the earth," these are invisible to the layman's eye and entirely mystical in nature. They work automatically, without the intervention of the deity, and in largely unexplained fashion. Only the roots responsible for boils and sores are associated with a tangible entity and observable causes, the roots being those of a special, "evil" kind of grain which causes the affliction when, by chance, the grain (or any of its products, such as beer) touches the human skin. At the same time, the evil quality of the grain is said to come not from the plant as such but from its planter or "owner," who is called the "owner" of the disease as well. The other magic roots are similarly "owned" by certain individuals. The "ownership" is hereditary, both in the paternal and maternal line, though nothing can be said about its origins or beginnings. The owner of the disease is frequently capable of curing it, and a number of these "experts" are widely known. But while the harmful gift is hereditary, the cure must be specially learned. Not everybody is sufficiently "clever" to master the skill, which involves extremely complicated manipulations such as repeated sacrifices of unusual animals, accompanied by elaborate and symbolic passes and gestures. Let us note that the highly "magical" character of these cures also renders them precarious, since the slightest error or lapse of memory would invalidate the whole procedure.

A similar mystic "ownership," though much deadlier in its effects, is attributed to one Heiban clan (*Lgoko*). Without any action on the part of the owners, this magic brings sudden death upon any person attempting to steal from a *Lgoko* man. Now this type of automatic "punitive magic" does not fit into the framework of Heiban beliefs. Indirect evidence in fact suggests that the *Lgoko* represent an immigrant group (though long since absorbed in the Heiban community) from one of the neighboring tribes which possess precisely such a system of clan-bound magic. A similar anomaly, to be similarly explained, also occurs in Otoro, where two clans are credited with corporately "owning" certain magic powers. But these are entirely beneficial, consisting in the cure of intestinal complaints, rheumatic pains, and of a wasting disease (probably sleeping sickness) by a simple ritual manipulation or by the "laying of hands." In the tribes from which the two Otoro clans appear to have come the gift of curing a particular disease is usually combined with that of inflicting it, much as in the "root" diseases of Heiban. It is possible, therefore, that the Otoro, in incorporating the alien clans, have adopted only their beneficial powers, and the Heiban only the malevolent ones. But even if this assumption were incorrect, the fact remains that Otoro culture permits the persistence of an anomaly which adds to the benevolent aspects of the universe, and Heiban culture the persistence of one that adds to its threats.

V   SUMMARY AND FIRST HYPOTHESIS

It is now possible to summarize the character of the two religions and to contrast the basic attitudes or tendencies visible in them.

In Heiban, the acts of worship are more highly ritualized and lean more heavily on "magical" manipulations and symbolic, or symbolic-compulsive, meanings. The greater concern with details of ritual also means a greater awareness of chances of failure —from technical errors, lapses of memory, and the like. Let me here add that this awareness is often visible in the anxiety with which the congregation watches the ministrations of a young or in-experienced "expert." The Heiban tend to multiply and particular-ize not only the features of ritual but also the supernatural entities (think of their conception of spirits, of "men with two heads," or of revengeful souls of the dead), but they do so only to increase and specify the mystic threats in the world. Altogether, the Heiban world view is more sinister than that of the Otoro and gives greater play to aggression, real or fancied (for example, in their attitude toward the rain maker). For the Otoro, the universe is fairly ordered by a dispassionate deity, so that relatively few, unexcited observances insure the desired normality of life and nature. In Heiban, one feels the need for repeated ritual interventions (think of the more numerous cultivation rites), for excited protestations, and for the coercion of the deity. Only the Otoro have attempted to rationalize their beliefs in a rudimentary cosmology and mythology.

Attempting a more concise (if oversimplified) summary, we may call the Heiban more magically oriented, more aggressive, emotionally tense, coercive and pessimistic, and the Otoro more "religious," calm, dispassionate, submissive, and optimistic. There is no need to point out that the traits in each group hang together in something like a coherent "syndrome." What is important is that the same cognitive and emotional traits reappear both in other provinces of religion (i.e., in the "private" rites) and in the attitudes or biases visible in mundane life. In other words, they add up to two consistent, contrasted "mentalities" (or "orientations," forms of "ethos," "personalities"—whichever description one may choose) (Nadel 1947: 171–74).

To accept this consistent "mentality" is not, however, to dispose of the problem of explanation. To some extent the syndromes themselves contain explanatory clues, for within each, certain traits appear to be causally interconnected so that the presence of one would explain that of the other. Thus the bias of the Heiban toward "magical" manipulations and compulsive symbolism might well be a consequence of their more sinister world view; and the latter is more likely to be accepted (and perpetuated) by children brought up in an atmosphere of violence and aggression.[3] But we will for the moment disregard these internal, short-range, and essentially circular linkages. We will assume that it is possible to go beyond them and to establish more significant, because more far-reaching, causal relations, connecting religion with social facts of an altogether different order, that is, with conditions which are

[3] It is further possible that an existing cosmology or mythology, as it attempts to explain and rationalize the universe, also reduces mystic fears and felt uncertainties, while its absence (as in Heiban) would foster a neurotic, pessimistic outlook (see Nadel 1952: 27). But the difference in this respect between the two groups seems too slight to warrant any definite inference.

functionally autonomous and hence represent "independent" variables (upon which the facts to be explained are "dependent"). I
am referring here to the social or cultural divergences which, as
explained in the beginning, appear together with the divergences
in religion. They concern (A) the size and political integration of
the two groups; (B) the regulation of adolescence; (C) the jural
status of wives; and (D) sexual morality.

The preliminary hypothesis, then, is that one or more of these
factors will prove capable of explaining, in causal terms, the difference in the religious orientation (or "mentality") of the two
groups.

Verification

A   While the Heiban form a small group, occupying a small,
compact territory, the Otoro, more than ten times their size, are
spread over a large hill massif. Though the Otoro are still in many
ways split up into separate communities, each roughly corresponding to the type of group exemplified by Heiban, an embracing
tribal unity has also emerged, helped by the centralized chieftainship now several generations old. Neither development took place
in Heiban. But the resulting differences in social organization
offer no evidence in support of our hypothesis, rather the contrary.
It can be shown that both the wider tribal unity and the centralized
chieftainship have created new problems and moral dilemmas,
such as conflicts of loyalty and uncertainties about the duty of
blood revenge (Nadel 1947: 154). Their emergence thus fostered
tensions and anxieties rather than lessened them.

B   Only the Otoro have evolved a system of age-grades providing a step-by-step framework for adolescence, both male and female. Offering as it does planned occasions for competition in
aggressive sports and games, the age-grade system may be assumed to release as well as canalize violent tendencies and implant
the values of self-restraint. It does so, further, by its rules of eti-
quette and team co-operation, and by its hierarchy of authority.
Equally, it lessens adolescent sexual tensions through associating
the two sexes in acknowledged and balanced relationships. More
generally, the Otoro age-grades habituate the adolescent to a well-
ordered, predictable scheme of roles and relationships in which
uncertainties of expectation and anxieties over right and wrong
conduct are reduced to a minimum. In Heiban, adolescence is

without such marked steps and set relationships, being essentially unregulated. Here, then, the observed covariations demonstrate an intelligible, meaningful, causal nexus, in the sense of our hypothesis.

c All societies operating with unilinear descent groups must resolve the problem of the ambiguous position of wives, for the wife comes as a stranger to her conjugal kin group yet remains in it not only as a domestic partner but also as the progenitress of the continuing descent line. Otoro and Heiban have in this respect worked out opposite solutions. In Otoro, the wife is completely adopted into her husband's lineage, being jurally and symbolically severed from her natal kin group. In Heiban, the adoption and severance are alike incomplete, wives and mothers belonging to their conjugal kin groups only for life and for the explicit purpose of giving sexual satisfaction to the husband and offspring to his lineage. Detailed evidence to support this interpretation has been given elsewhere (Nadel 1947: 107–8, 120, 122, 124). Here I would argue that the "incomplete" adoption of wives entails serious conflicts of loyalty, anxieties over the success of the marriage, and jural ambiguities which must engender tensions both within and between kin groups. Their reality is borne out by the many family quarrels in Heiban, and by the marked concern of the men over the fecundity of the women no less than the sexual satisfaction they provide. These data, too, may be said to support our hypothesis.

d The Otoro are markedly reserved when discussing sexual matters, and never do so in large company. Only in privacy, between two friends, is there any bragging about sexual adventures. Marital experiences are never discussed, nor are sexual topics normally touched upon in the presence of the other sex. At the same time, the Otoro show no traces of embarrassment, shame, or guilt in this connection. Sexual dreams are considered meaningless, and young men do not feel ashamed to talk about them, even to their girl friends. In Heiban, sexual bragging and joking among the men is strongly pronounced and one's sexual adventures are openly discussed, in provocative fashion, even in the presence of the other sex; also husbands generally complain about the frigidity of their wives and the fact that they "tire easily." Yet a feeling of guilt is equally noticeable, for it is considered shameful to talk about sexual dreams, which are found puzzling and disturbing.

In both groups, finally, male homosexuality occurs. But while in Heiban the homosexuals have no special niche in cultural life, being simply regarded as "abnormal," in Otoro they are allocated a special role, allowed to dress like females and to live in most respects a woman's life.

In certain respects the attitude to sex is accounted for by facts previously discussed—the habitual association of the sexes in the Otoro age-grades, and the "incomplete" adoption of wives in Heiban. But the Otoro "reserve" in sexual matters, and the Heiban "freedom," could as convincingly be related to "mentalities" which are the exact opposite of those actually observed, on the assumption that "reserve" might connote repression (and hence anxiety and tension), and license, the absence of inhibitions and their psychological consequences. The possibility of constitutional differences in sexuality being unverifiable, we can presume no further causal linkage, only the extension of the two contrasted syndromes now to the sphere of sex morality. The different treatment of sexual deviants, more "orderly" in Otoro and unregulated in Heiban, would similarly fit into the picture.

VI   CONCLUSIONS

It will be noted that the two causal interrelations which proved verifiable have a closely similar import: both refer essentially to the presence or absence of social norms which would increase the set patterns of roles and relationships and decrease ambiguities or uncertainties of conduct. Differently expressed, the causal efficacies here suggested derive from aspects of the social system which reduce or enhance anomy. The more specific, observed interrelations, then, between the character of religion on one side, and regulation of adolescence and jural status of wives on the other, can be generalized in this sense, now predicating the dependence of the religious orientation on the varying pressure of anomy (or its opposite, normativeness). Expressed schematically, and as a balance of opposed tendencies: anomy $\geqq$ normativeness $\therefore$ religious pessimism (etc.) $\geqq$ optimism. However imprecise and preliminary this formulation, it indicates (or foreshadows) a general social regularity or "law."

But even our observed specific correlations can only be stated in a form in some measure imprecise and preliminary. For example, we cannot, on the facts at our disposal, decide whether the two particular instances of anomy, unregulated adolescence and ambiguous position of wives, exercise their presumed effects singly or only in combination and to an equal or unequal degree. Nor can we estimate the relevance for this efficacy of all the other features of the two cultures, that is, the features which happen to be identical, satisfying the crucial condition of *ceteris paribus*.

Furthermore, the "far-reaching" causality we postulated is not only incomplete but also as nonsequential.[4] No precise genesis can be suggested whereby the institution (for whatever reason) of age-grades or of the rule of complete adoption precedes in any definable historical sense the appropriate religious development. All that can be assumed is that the social norms provide a continuous causation for the emergence of particular religious conceptions. Nor does the causal nexus account for every characteristic of the two religions; and those not so accounted for (e.g., the concern or unconcern with compulsive symbols) must be taken to be the effects of some secondary causality, implied in the internal, "short-range" linkages mentioned before. Equally, the emergence of the religious conceptions must be understood to entail additional circular linkages at all stages (such as that between upbringing and the readiness to embrace a particular world view).

Finally, on the grounds of general psychological knowledge, we must admit that the scope of our "law" is likely to be limited. The nexus here assumed presupposes psychological mechanisms whereby tensions and anxieties arising from the normlessness of social life are *projected* into an analogous, "pessimistic" religion. There are, however, two other possibilities. (1) Anxieties and tensions might be engendered not only by the lack of normativeness but by its over-rigidity, which would be felt as frustrating; and (2) the anxieties and tensions might, instead of being projected, be *compensated* by a contrasted, "optimistic," religious orientation. Some such limitations are true of most or all scientific "laws"; in our case it must be left to further investigations to specify the relevant conditions.

Though these qualifications detract not a little from the preci-

[4] It is, however, a true causality, i.e., nonreversible, for it would make no sense to assume, say, that freedom from anxiety can account for the complete adoption of wives, or a pessimistic world view for adolescence left unregulated.

sion of the causal nexus, they do not affect its validity. When we previously spoke of the causes to be discovered as "independent" variables, possessing "functional autonomy," we were merely stating the logical requirement of any assumption of valid explanatory relations (Nadel 1951: 243–44). The social norms here adduced satisfy this condition in that they can be thought of apart from the facts they are meant to explain. More precisely, they are intelligible in their own right, as solutions of given, ubiquitous problems of social existence. But here the causal nexus must end. It is perhaps not meaningless to try to carry it further by asking why the problems of what to do with adolescents and how to fit marriage into a unilinear descent system have been resolved in this contrasted fashion by the two groups. But it is, in the narrow context of this inquiry, unprofitable to do so.

5 BURYAT RELIGION AND SOCIETY

Lawrence Krader

THE BURYATS are the northernmost Mongol-speaking people, occupying the steppes and river-sides to the east, south, and west of Lake Baikal. They have been subject to acculturative processes since early in the 17th century when Russian explorers and colonialists first came into contact with them, the contact having extended uninterruptedly since then down to the present day. The Buryats are by tradition a pastoral nomadic people with a considerable investment in hunting. They are the northernmost of the complex pastoralists as well; their herds consist of cattle, sheep, goats, horses, and even a scattering of camels; in the same latitudes, but to the west and east are simple herdsmen, whose sole domesticated animal is the reindeer, on the slopes of the Sayan and Altai mountain chains and in the Amur region. The bulk of reindeer breeding, however, is to the north of the Buryat forest-steppe, while the *locus classicus* of complex herding in eastern and northern Asia lies in the steppe to the south, in Mongolia. Buryat mythology assigns a central place to bull-ancestors, horses whose wisdom is superhuman, and sheep endowed with magical properties. During the course of the 19th century, however, they developed sedentary agriculture through Russian contact, while dependence on the hunt for livelihood shrank almost to nothing, at the same time that pastoralism appreciably diminished. The Buryats are approaching the number of 300,000 for the second time in their history; the central tendency in their population density is 2–5 per km sq, which is a typical figure for complex pastoralists.

Reprinted from *The Southwestern Journal of Anthropology* 10 (3), 1954: 322–51, by permission of the author and the editor, *The Southwestern Journal of Anthropology.*

Buryat social organization is centered around the joint principle of patrilineal descent and agnatic relationship, which they have applied with a consistency matched by few other societies in the world. All Buryats trace descent from a single common ancestor, a mythical figure who may differ from group to group within Buryat society. Thus, a Buryat of Cis-Baikalia (to the west of Baikal) will impute descent from his primary ancestor to all Buryats, while a Trans-Baikal Buryat (to the east and south of Baikal), who traces descent from a different founding ancestor, will do the same. All Buryats are theoretically related by ties of agnatic consanguinity. Moreover, there is a relationship between neighborhood and kinship; the closer the kinship relation between two Buryats, the closer their proximity to each other in residence. A man's closest kin are residents of the same nomadic kin-village, *ulas.*[1] The lineage, *urag,* comprising a group of related kin-villages, forms the next largest social grouping, and a number of lineages form a clan, *xolbōn* or *obag.* There are instances of still larger Buryat groupings, among them clan federations, but in these structures the ties of consanguinity are necessarily distant and loose, hence they are organs of political power rather than kinship relationship; but since the manipulation of political power in a state structure is but poorly conceptualized by the Buryats, these confederations and principalities are ephemeral phenomena.

The eastern and southern Buryats have had more stable political organizations than the western, which may be attributed to the greater proximity and closer relationships of the former, the Trans-Baikal Buryats, to the Khalkha Mongols, i.e., the Mongols of Outer Mongolia, who are their neighbors to the south. To this must be added the greater Russian impact on the western than on the eastern Buryats. The closer relationships of the Selenga River and Khori Buryats (the Trans-Baikal Buryats in question) with the Khalkha Mongols may be shown in the religious sphere as well, for these Buryats assign a greater role to Lamaism than do the western and northern Buryats. However, all the Buryats are fundamentally shamanist, despite an overlay of Lamaism; Lama-

[1] Where possible, the transcription of Buryat names and terms has followed Cheremisov's Dictionary (1951). I should like to voice my thanks to Cora DuBois and David Aberle for their criticisms and comments on this paper.

ism has had a lesser but yet perceptible influence on the Cis-Baikal Buryats as well.[2]

We may regard the Buryat clan, lineage, kin-village, and other formations already described as diachronic or vertical organizations of the society, vertical or ascending and descending in time, because they depend for definition on relationship to a given paternal ancestor. Relationship by agnation and hence group membership is therefore determined by establishing a common ancestor and tracing the genealogical line to and from him. In addition to the vertical organization of society, in which time as reckoned in the generation count is the paramount criterion, there is the composition of society by its contemporary members. In the Buryat tradition, all members of the society are distributed in three social classes or strata—the aristocratic, the commoner, and the slave —which may be viewed as the synchronic or horizontal organization of the society.

Through further analysis of the dynamics of Buryat patrilineality, both those modes of social organization, the diachronic and the synchronic, may be derived from a single set of principles. In order to establish these principles we must first set on one side the question of the slave stratum, which is formed by capture, and is not a product of the relationships among *consanguinei*. The aristocrats and the commoners between them form the synchronically interrelating members in a group of common descent. (In archaic times, the slaves as a third stratum were subordinated to the first two.) Time as an analytic device is not necessary to establish the required relationship of superiority-subordination, prestige-respect, authority-obedience which exists between the aristocrats and subjects. The relationship is established through personal recognition, through the identification of external marks or signs, sumptuary clothing or the lack of it, and so forth. Nevertheless, both aristocrat and commoner are the descendants of one and the same ancestor, and it is upon the anvil of the common descent group that the pattern of diachronic organization of the society is hammered out. In the diachronic organization, time is an analytic device in the establishment of relationship in con-

---

[2] Pallas (1771), vol. 3, pt. 1, p. 177 on the political organization of the Khorin Buryats in the 18th century; Georgi 1776–1880: 420–22; for the 19th century, *Khori-Buriaty*, 1899: 61–63. Comparative materials in Khangalov 1894: 102–4, 113, 127–28, 132 and Okladnikov 1937, *passim*.

sanguinity. The genealogical principle in reckoning kinship is the opposite of the technique of social differentiation, for in establishing kinship it establishes community and group membership. Consanguineal differentiation is established by preferment of the eldest son and the eldest son's line in primogenitary succession. Thus, within the Buryat world, descent lines are ranked according to the seniority of the founder, i.e., the rank-order of birth in relation to founders of other descent lines in the same generation. The senior descent line or lines are the aristocracy, the junior descent lines are the commoners.

As to the two different modes of social organization—by social strata and by lines of descent—even though they may be related through a common set of principles, nevertheless they must be kept separate because with each one a different type of religious phenomenon is associated. Both modes are conceptualized and explicitly set forth in Buryat intellectual life, mythology, and religion.

In addition to these two modes, there is a limited amount of craft specialization, notably the shamans and the smiths, *both* of whom have a religious function. Finally there are traces of a dual organization of society—very weak traces—and these will be alluded to only in passing. On the contrary, the dual organization of the spirit world is of paramount importance.

Far older than Lamaism, far more widely distributed among the Buryats, is the somewhat amorphous body of doctrines, beliefs, rites, myths which constitutes the form of shamanism particular to themselves. Buryat religion has been described in several of its aspects in the western anthropological literature: there is an excellent summary article by Demetrius Klements (1924) on shamanism and the spiritual hierarchy and ritual; by Garma Sandžeyev (1927–28) on the world-view of the Buryat shamanists; and latterly by Pater Schmidt (1951), which presented the Buryat religion in the aspect of its cult of the supreme being.

There is one problem in the study of Buryat religion which has not been treated hitherto, but which constitutes a classical question in ethnology—the relationship between the social organization and the organization of the religious conceptions of a given people. Durkheim has carried farther than any other ethnologist the study of the relationship between the specific structuring of the world of the sacred and of the profane. His conclusions took on a dialectic form, through the interpenetration of religious phenomena in society and of social phenomena in the religious world. "If religion has engendered all that is essential in society, the idea of society is the soul of religion" (Durkheim 1912: 599). As a further expression of this dialectic he postulated that the individual does not innately conceive of the collective ideal of religion, but rather that it is in the school of the collective life of society that the individual learns to realize the religious ideal (Durkheim 1912: 604). The materials toward these formulations were the close parallels between the social structure and the cosmology of given peoples, among them the Zuñi and the Arunta. More recently, a similar correlation was made by Evans-Pritchard when he submitted his monograph on *Witchcraft, Oracles and Magic among the Azande* to re-thinking in the course of a lecture given in 1950. The monograph had first been prepared in the 1930s and its author then started from the premise of the lack of inner coördination of Zande magic, the lack of system or nexus in the magical rites (Evans-Pritchard 1937: 540). In later examination of his own researches, Evans-Pritchard developed a more architectonic view of Zande magic religion, and concluded that the entire political hierarchy of Zande society as well as its fabric of kinship is closely reflected in the pattern of magical rites (Evans-Pritchard 1951: 101–2).

In the following pages, no integral picture of Buryat religion will be offered; neither the religious doctrines nor the social organization of the Buryats form a single, coherent, internally consistent whole. Nevertheless, a few formative principles upon which both society and religion rest may be established, and a number of correlations between the two as well. The very number of these correlations is a matter of considerable moment. Moreover, the correlated phenomena lie at the core of their respective spheres. From these considerations it follows that the essences of the Buryat worlds of the sacred and profane are twin and coördinate with each other. *In part these coördinations of the two worlds must be derived from that which is implicit in the ethnographic material, but to the greater extent they have been formulated* expressis verbis *by the Buryats themselves,* and are therefore primary data.

The major corpus of these materials covers the period from the 1870s to the mid-1920s, and is the contribution of a number of Russian-educated Buryats, Agapitov, Khangalov, Džamtsarano, Mikhail Bogdanov, and Garma Sandžeyev, working either alone or in collaboration with Russian scholars of the period, the chief of whom were Krol', Klements, and N. Poppe. The work of another fine Buryat thinker, Dordži Banzarov, belongs to an earlier era and another body of literature. The sum of the contributions of these Buryats constitutes a veritable awakening of Buryat intellectual culture of the era. Their written record is extensive, varied, and rich in information, in the form of autobiographic recollections, scientific investigations, and scholarly text-redactions. Their themes are the cosmology, religion, world-view, social life, and folklore of their people. As a group they have accomplished a victory of the human spirit through the simultaneous pursuit of a double path: they were at once the spokesmen for and the recorders of their culture. Within the institutional and linguistic framework of another culture they were able to set down what they observed and learned as Buryats, viewing the same data likewise from the standpoint of the objective disciplines which they later mastered. They lived in two worlds, their native and that of the western academic culture, moving outward from their own culture in the opposite sense to that of the ethnographer.

THE ORGANIZATION OF THE COSMOS BY THREES

The primary element in the coördination of the two worlds is the triple division of the social world, the triple division of the spirit world and the three souls of men (Klements and Khangalov 1910: 132–33). The spirits are the most important features of Buryat religion; they include the deities at the highest level; they are prayed to, sacrificed to, invoked for blessing, and for the exorcism of evil and of sickness, both human and zoötic. The spirits are divided into the higher spirits, the middle, and the lower. The higher spirits, called *tengeri* (plural *tengeriner*) live in heaven, direct and control everything, take care of mankind. These *tengeriner* are in their turn divided into three; the two lower ranks within the superior category functioning as intercessors between man and the highest beings. The spirits of the middle rank, *bōxoldoy,* are considered the spirits of the commoner Buryats (the term is rendered *bōxoldey* by Castrén [1857: 169] with the meaning "spirit in the service of the shamans"). Finally, in the presentation of Klements and Khangalov, there are the spirits of the lowest rank, the spirits of the slaves. Both the middle and lower order of spirits were fully subordinate to the higher order.

The religious doctrine of the triple division in the Buryat cosmology is paralleled by the triple division in the Buryat doctrine of man. Man is conceived as being composed of three parts: the body, *beye,* i.e., the physical organism of man; *amin,* the breath and life-principle resident in the living organism; and *hünehen,* the soul of man (Podgorbunskiy 1891: 18).

The soul in turn is submitted in Buryat pneumatology to a triple division, again hierarchized in an upper, a middle, and a lower order. There are two basic descriptions of the Buryat doctrine of the soul, that found in Klements and Khangalov (1910: 132–33) and that of Sandžeyev (1927: 578–85): both are in agreement on the fundamental traits. Sandžeyev prefaces his remarks on the soul with the note that in one group, the Alar-Buryats, there are numerous souls, but that these are grouped in three chief categories. The first of these is the soul which is housed in man, more precisely, in the skeleton of man, and in the skeleton as a whole, not in any one part. This soul is an invisible copy of the skeleton, and if the skeleton is injured, e.g., if a bone is broken, this soul is harmed. Animals also are in possession of such a soul, and at a sacrifice, a deep concern is to protect the bones of the sacrificial animal. For if the bones of the offering are broken, the soul would be injured and the sacrifice would be rejected by the deity to whom it was offered (Sandžeyev 1927: 578–79). This soul corresponds to the lowest soul in the presentation of Klements and Khangalov; one of its attributes is its existence among animals as well as among men.

The second soul of man has the capacity to leave the body and dwell in the world; it can transform itself into a flying thing, such as a wasp or a bee, and can undertake activities of which its possessor is unconscious. In its non-transformed state it is anthropomorphic, however, and its seat is in the organs of the trunk of man: the heart, the liver, the lungs, also the larynx, possibly the blood as well. This soul is readily alarmed and is disposed to flee from danger, e.g., the barking of a dog, and must then be tempted back, especially in the case of the second soul of a child (Sandžeyev 1927: 579–81). It is this soul which is invoked, projected and manipulated in shamanistic ceremonies, e.g., in the ceremony for the curing of illness. It corresponds to the middle soul, *dünda hünehen,* of Klements and Khangalov, who add that this soul corresponds not only to the appearance of man, but to the physical condition of its resident body. If the man owns a horse, the second soul rides the same horse; it wears the same clothes; and most important, continues in this condition after death (Klements and Khangalov 1910: 133).

The third soul of Sandžeyev is the highest soul of Klements and Khangalov. It is this soul which is called on death by the chief *tengeri,* who is, according to the Kuda River Buryats, Esege Malān Tengeri (Agapitov and Khangalov 1883: 4), and its passing marks the end of the mortal span of the man to whom the soul was attached. Aside from this feature, it is little distinguishable from the second soul, for both reflect the physical and social condition of the possessor in health and wealth in this life and during the life beyond (also Khangalov 1888: 15).

Petri's data on the Buryat conception of the soul agrees in the main with the foregoing accounts by Klements and Khangalov and by Sandžeyev, adding at the same time certain other attributes (Petri 1925: 34–35). The Buryat has three souls. As to the first, after death this soul (the chief soul) goes upward to the afterworld; there it lives for a term as it had on earth, and then is born again. The second remains on earth as a wandering being after the death of the man; this soul resembles the defunct. At night it amuses itself by frightening people, but in general it is harmless, although sometimes it may attach itself to sick or drunken men and cause much harm. The third soul is called *mū* (literally bad, evil) by both Khangalov and Klements and Petri (Klements and Khangalov 1910: 133; Petri 1925: 34–35). This soul remains with the body, and when the corpse disappears, the body vanishes. The chief soul may have a good or bad character, according to the character of the man in whom it dwelled. If this soul was that of a good man, it is asked by the kinsmen to intercede on their behalf before the *tengeri.* If the deceased had an evil character, then this soul too is evil and dangerous; it is the cause of suffering to children, and of female illnesses among women. It must be placated by propitiatory offerings of sheep.

Petri's observations were drawn from the Kuda River Buryats, a branch of the western Buryats, i.e., among those farthest from the influences of Buddhism and Lamaism. It is therefore interesting to note the spread of the doctrine of rebirth and transmigration as a trait diffused from the Buddhist world. Thoroughly indigenous traits of the triple division and hierarchization of the souls among these Buryats are substantiated by Petri. His data add another dimension still, the relation between soul worship (propitiatory sacrifices, prayers for intercession) by close kin. M. E. Opler and A. I. Hallowell have reported on the close relations between in-group sentiments and the attitudes of the living toward the dead in Jicarilla and Saulteaux communities. It has been noted that the suppression of the resentments, hatreds, or fears toward living kin takes expression as the projection of these sentiments into the animal embodiments of the spirits of the dead. Among the Buryats an opposite inversion takes place: negative sentiments toward men of ill character continue after their death, for the principal soul has the same attributes as the dead man. But on death the soul acquires greater power; evil souls must therefore be propitiated and not attacked as an evil person would be. In the terms made available by this comparison, the Buryat relationship with the world of life and death is pragmatic, manipulative, and optimistic, for in the struggle to master his fate, there are control-bearing techniques at man's disposal.

It will be recalled that a system of three social estates or classes was found among the Buryats, not during the period of Russian domination but in the immediately preceding era, and this social structure is still preserved in the mythology and cosmology of the Buryats. Not only has this formation been noted by outside observers, it also has been verbalized—this is the crucial consideration—by Buryats themselves. The triple division is arranged in hierarchical form—always highest-middle-lowest. This triple division and hierarchization is then repeated within one of the divisions, for instance, in the three grades of the highest spirits, or in the case of the three souls which together form one of the composite parts of the human being (on hierarchization, cf. Schmidt 1951: 446–48).

The number three and its multiples (9, 90, 99) are constantly recurrent in Buryat mythology and ceremonial. The number of major communal sacrifices, *tailgan,* during the year is three (Potanin 1881–83, vol. 4: 80). The bride at the wedding ceremonial feeds the hearth in the husband's tent three times with bits of fat, then sprinkles the garments of the husband's father three more times with fat (Potanin 1881–83, vol. 4: 34). The shaman can cure a sick Buryat but has the power to prolong the man's life only for three or nine years—and seven as well (Potanin 1881–83, vol. 4: 87). The heavenly spirits, *tengeriner,* are 99 in number; 3 and 9 occur as the combination, division, and order upon which the entire organization of the spirit world is based, as we have already seen, and to which we will return. The number 7 is an intrusive variant on the basic 3-9 system. Only 3 and 9, and not 7, are mentioned in another version of the account of the number of years a man's life can be prolonged (Batarov 1890: 13).

BURYAT SHAMANISM

The shaman is an ecstatic, a soul-projector, a spirit-master; he has special powers over and special relations to the extra-mundane sphere. These powers he obtains through a special gift, having undergone a specific kind of experience of self-abnegation and vision-quest. Accompanying the shaman-cult are a number of rites and myths relating to the worship of rocks, high places and peculiar features of the landscape; of fire and the hearth. The shaman is often a transvestite who may be of either sex, a highly nervous person, one subject to nervous disorders; his powers, when they are not disposed to harm mankind, are sought in the cure of (psychosomatic) illness. These are general traits of shamanism in its distribution from the Caspian Sea to the Bering Strait. I leave open the question of shamanism in South Asia and in the Western Hemisphere.

In regard to the peoples of the north, Ohlmarks has distinguished two types of shamanism, the "great" shamanism of the peoples of the Arctic littoral and tundra, and the "little" shamanism of the peoples of the taiga and to the south of the taiga. The Arctic shaman is a true aberrant, subject to unmistakable psychically-meditated seizures. To restate Ohlmarks' position, the status of the Arctic shaman is a highly personalized one, for he is outside his society; the means whereby he has achieved his status is likewise highly personalized, for he has established his relationship to the spirit world through his own quest. The sub-Arctic shaman in this view is only a quasi-shaman; characteristically, he is not self-led into his trance but is narcotized, stimulated, or depressed into the shaman's state. He achieves his status through training, indoctrination, the trappings of institutionaliza-

trén has characterized the *bōxoldoy* as that spirit which is
service of the shaman. Batarov calls it the spirit of a dead
n (Castrén 1857: 169; Batarov 1890: 10). These spirits
ls (for now they are one) are again ambivalent beings, for
ork both good and harm. There are two sources of sickness
eath; one, by decision of Erlen Khan (Erlin Khan, Erlen-
-khan), the other, by inadvertency. The former source, by
n of the highest order of being, is regular, in the nature of
a stabilized matter—although it too can be temporarily
d by a shamanistic intervention. The source of disease and
by inadvertency is attributed to the actions of the *bōxoldoy;*
e malignant activities of these beings may be bought off
rifices. These *bōxoldoy* have different degrees of power,
ing on the power of the shaman during his life. Thus,
is a continuation of the attributes of being from this world
next among shamans as among ordinary people. More
his, Batarov makes use of the Buryat word *utxa/udxa* in
ing how the varying degrees of power of the *bōxoldoy*
on the power of the shaman during his life. The term *udxa*
primarily essence, significance, but it also means descent,
tion (Cheremisov, s. v.); it is rendered as ancestral spirit
džeyev (1928: 977). After death, these shamans remember
in and help them in sickness and death. The ideas of in-
ss, immanence, and of inheritance and descent are joined
Buryat world-view. The shaman's power is not his own, but
f his descent line's, just as the individual in the Buryat
is not a fully articulated being, but is the momentary
ent of the earthly existence of his lineage. The demonstra-
f the last statement rests on analysis of the Buryat pattern
ship and lineage and the practices of inheritance, and must
to another occasion.

shaman has been regarded thus far as a single, undifferen-
kind of being, albeit one with a dual relation to the spirit
that of seizing and that of being seized, of controlling and
ig controlled; and his power has been regarded as single,
nbivalent only in the sense that it is powerful, easily out of
and dangerous to manipulate. This, of course, requires
st careful estimation of his capacities by the shaman; for
ndertakes a task beyond his powers, he may be crushed by
rit whose control he has lost, and his client crushed as well.

tion, as opposed to the charisma of the Arctic shaman (Ohlmarks 1939, *passim*).

One significance of this contribution is that it views shamanism
neither as a single, unanalyzable entity, nor as a phenomenon too
complex for generalization, and varying from people to people.
Furthermore, it distinguishes that which is constant, such as the
trance or fit or seizure, and that which is variable, the method of
inducement of the shaman's spell, of which there are roughly two.
On the other hand, it oversimplifies the relationship between the
shaman and the spirit world, the relationship between the shaman
and society, and the relationship between the shaman and his
calling. These may be shown to vary according to the complexity
of organization of the society, and the societies of Siberia are
simplest in their organization in the extreme north, and become
more complex the farther south they dwell. The Chukchi, the
Eskimo, the Koryak of the Arctic coast and tundra have the
simplest organization and the most personalized role and quest
of the shaman. The Yakut, the various Tungusic peoples, and
indigenes of the Altai (Turks and Turkicized Samoyeds) have a
more complex social organization and the beginnings of institutionalization of shamanism, in terms of a quasi-hereditary transmission of the calling and a professional relationship of master
shaman to disciple.[8]

The Buryats are the most complexly organized of the peoples
under discussion, are closest to the great civilizations, and are
endowed with the most favorable environmental conditions of
them all. They continue that form of shamanism which existed
among the Mongols during the era of Chingis Khan (13th century). Under Chingis Khan, in the early days of his rule, the head
of one descent line, the Ba'arin, in which the specialization of
shamanism was hereditary, supplied him with his Arch-priest
(*Secret History:* para. 216; Barthold 1928: 391 ff.; Vladimirtsov
1948: 57–60). The nephew of Chingis Khan was named Yesünge,
forming another point of contact between the modern Buryat
shamanism and the medieval Mongols. Among the Buryats, the
shaman-candidate at the time of his initiation has nine assistants

[8] Mikhailovskiy-Wardrop 1892: 85 ff.; Shirokogorov 1935: 74–75; Dyrenkova 1930: 267–68. Harva (1938: 485–96) has contrasted the relative
simplicity of the Yakut, Tungus, and Goldi rites of initiation of the shaman
with those of the Buryat.

called *yihüngüt,* literally the nine (*yesün/yihün*—nine) (personal communication from N. Poppe).

It is necessary to distinguish between the receipt of the shamanist power or gift which descends upon the subject after the death of the shaman-kinsman, and the shamanist status into which the subject is born. The former is quasi-hereditary, and is found chiefly among the people of the taiga; the latter is fully hereditary, and is found chiefly among the medieval Mongols, whose steppe lay to the south of the Buryat, in what is today Outer Mongolia. In addition to this form of shamanism, the fully hereditary, the Buryats also have the quasi-hereditary. In the quasi-hereditary shamanism, the power is not inherent in a descent line, for the kinsman from whom it was transmitted to the shaman in question may have received the gift personally, from no one else in his kin group (Agapitov and Khangalov 1883: 44; Sandžeyev 1928: 977–78).

Where the shaman is a member of a shamanist descent line, i.e., where members may become shamans by right of birth, this right is a hereditary specialization of function in society. And this very specialization of function contributes to the greater complexity of organization of the society. The nascent development of a hereditary priesthood was noted at the turn of the century "which keeps up not only the education of the people, but also the memory of the achievements of their ancestors" (Klements 1924: 15). This is not to say that personally, as opposed to institutionally and hereditarily endowed shamans, do not exist among the Buryats, but they are of an inferior status, possess an inferior spiritual power, and cannot compete with the hereditary shaman. Sandžeyev has made the categorical statement (1928: 977) that the shaman's office is open only to those who have shamans among their ancestors; the ordinary person cannot become a shaman. It may be that Sandžeyev's report, valid for the 1920s, marks the end of the line, the final outcome of the tradition.

Klements, who worked with Khangalov's materials gathered two or three generations earlier, in the last third of the 19th century, qualifies this view: the Buryat shamans (which ones are not specified) believe in their origin from the eagle, son of a *tengeri,* and maintain long genealogies. Although any Buryat can become a shaman if the call descends on him, yet he would find

himself unable to compete with other sham[a] line from shamans and a series of shaman cestral shamans mediate for their client and tary shamans are helped in another way, f[o] their business from infancy on (Klements 192

These shamans, far from being solely the voyagers in the spirit world as they are in [ ] a veritable political force among the Burya 18th century, after about one hundred and contact and rule in the area, the shamans sought to seize the political power for t learned the lesson of political combination. [ ] learn it too well, for the Russians suppress[e] tablished the office of hereditary prince (*tayš* Buryats, and thus a lay ruler over all wester[ ] for the first time (Khangalov 1894: 113).

The Buryat shaman is as bold in relation was in political matters; often he is overbol[d] possessed unlimited power, according to an mighty shaman bit the cheek of Erlen Khan dead) in a struggle, and their power has since of this defiance. Khangalov recounts a grea shaman and an emissary of Esege Malān Te[n]́ spirits) with much trickery involved and t[ ] human to animal form. It is difficult to say wh the shaman must die eventually and live amo ing them and interceding with them on behal scendants, nevertheless he has succeeded in

The shaman's relation with the spirit world seized by spirits for his future calling; but he derived to seize the spirits (souls of the dea[d] the high gods) to his own ends. The power dangerous power; it is ambivalent: the same nant to one person and beneficent to another 933). Sacrifices and shamanistic rites can effec the activities of the spirits, and eventually th[ ] back on the power of the shaman who acts [ ] hopefulness, but not always with success.

[4] Khangalov, 1890: 19–23. The legend becomes the west Baikal Buryats, the Bulagat and Ekirit.

However, there are two types of shamans, two sets of relations to the spirit world, and two kinds of shamanist power. The shamans and their spiritual powers and relationships are divided as good and evil, white and black; the good shamans, together with the good powers and the good heavenly spirits not only have a color opposition with the evil, white versus black, they have also an opposing compass direction. The location of the good is in the west, the evil and black in the east (Agapitov and Khangalov 1883: 46 ff.; Sandžeyev 1927: 933; Khangalov 1890: 1 ff.). There is a brief intimation in one report (Agapitov and Khangalov 1883: 46 ff.) that the black shamans are less the masters of and more in the service of the evil spirits. The implication is that man is by his nature more prone to good; that if the shaman were not seized by evil, his control of the spirits would work for the weal of man.

Thus, in addition to the dual relationship of the shaman to the spiritual powers, and the dual source of shamanism (by heredity and by charisma), there is the dual nature of the shamans (white and black), and two kinds of shamanist consecrations as well (Agapitov and Khangalov 1883: 44–45). There are distinctive terms for both male shamans and female (Agapitov and Khangalov 1883: 41; Sandžeyev 1928: 778). The white shamans preside at births, adoptions, weddings, illnesses, and deaths; the black shamans are invoked against illness primarily (Khangalov 1890: 85). Only the good shamans are remembered; the bad are gradually forgotten by their people. Every dead shaman—white, i.e.—as far as he possibly can, continues to aid and protect his kinsmen and descendants, and the good shaman is a powerful source of support in the struggle against disease and death. These spirits of past shamans intercede on the part of their kin before the mighty powers of heaven—that is, before the good, white, western spirits and *tengeriner*. Therefore, every locality, every clan, every *ulas* has its separate spirits, the souls of dead shamans and shamanesses who act for their kinsmen-neighbors (Khangalov 1890: 83–84). On death they usually go to dwell on a neighboring mountain or wood, and are therefore called *xada ūlan öbögöd*, forest-mountain-ancestors or elders. Each individual kin-village has its own mountain elders to whom offerings and sacrifices are made at communal rites—and individual rites as well. These spirits have significance only for their own people and are not honored by others (Khangalov 1890: 84). The relationship between communal rites and the kinship structure will be examined below. So much for the white shamans.

The black shamans on the other hand are not honored after death; instead they are forgotten. They are not honored during their lifetimes either; they are feared. However, they are brought in during times of crises to intercede before the evil spirits, the eastern *tengeri* and their minions. The Buryat family or kin-group faced with a threat or disaster will usually bring in an outside black shaman to shamanize on its behalf. He then returns to his own people after effecting a cure; should one of his own group then die, the black shaman is suspect, for he is thought to have borrowed a soul of one of his own kin to cure that of another. Evil influences are central to the Buryat theory of psychosomatic disease—they distinguish these from such matters as breaking a leg, etc.—and soul-borrowing is central to the theory of curing.[5] There is also a mode of substituting an animal for a human being in the case of illness and death (Sandžeyev 1927: 938).

One of the most famous black shaman lineages was that of Tarsay. A Buryat of the Tarsay *ulas* came to live in the Kulunkun *ulas* of the Kuda River Buryats, and there married a daughter of a black shaman. From their union were born two sons who likewise became black shamans; from the younger son descended the line of black shamans notorious for their power at the end of the 19th century. In this notice a number of traits are evident. The status of the black shaman is hereditary just as the white is, and is inherent in a descent line. The residence pattern is inverted, for the marriage is matrilocal: the husband is the foreigner, not the wife. The black shamanist power descends in the maternal line to the grandsons, and specifically to the younger son rather than the elder, although the elder too was a black shaman. All the relevant patterns of Buryat life have been inverted in this genealogy and the powers it sustains (and which sustain it): descent, marriage, residence, and succession. The power in this line is double black because the founding ancestor was a stranger and his wife the daughter of a black shaman. A similar account of the foreign origin of a black shaman is found in the genealogy of a then-famous line, the Öbösin on the north shore of Lake

[5] Khangalov 1890: 85; for comparative Yakut material cf. Mikhailovskiy-Wardrop 1892: 92.

Baikal (Khangalov 1890: 86–87). That the shamanist calling can be inherited in the female line is also attested by Sandžeyev (1928: 978), who gives the genealogy of his shaman-informant Batta. This shaman's ancestor in the ninth generation was a foreigner who came to the Buryat country from Mongolia. In this case, the shaman was a white and not a black practitioner.

In both the white and black practice of the shaman's art, the normal patterns and values of Buryat life are inverted, possibly more so in the black than in the white, but that difference is minor. The important consideration is that both dare to call up powers which are dangerous both to the shaman, to his kin, and to his client—kin or not. While the shaman's call is hereditary, that is, is innate in a given descent line, it is arbitrary rather than regular: not everyone in the lineage is called, but only those who are psychologically predisposed. The shaman, because of his nervous and psychic aberrancies, is a difficult person in social life; the Buryats regard the shaman as the worst kind of man (Sandžeyev 1928: 983). They are so regarded for several reasons. First of all, they are individualists, odd, abnormal, queer, in a society noted for its communal living; second, because they live in a hectic, excited manner, and in a dangerous world which is not the world of everyday life. Because of their life in the mid-world they perform services special to themselves, and are respected, honored, feared for these services.

The Buryat shaman is an anomalous person, even as a shaman, for while he is a psychologically unstable individual, nevertheless his social position has been stabilized as an occupational group and as a descent line. The shaman's social position has led one observer, Petri, to believe that there is actually a schooling to which the shaman is submitted (Petri 1923: 18–19). It is clear that their training and their social status are both more formalized than are the training and status of shamans in the less complex societies of northern Siberia. The shamans among the Buryats have their disciples, and form, not a set of isolated individuals, but a social group apart from the rest of Buryatdom. Sandžeyev has written of the social costs in the training of the shaman, which are defrayed by the entire kin-group (Sandžeyev 1928: 982; see also Schmidt 1951: 432–36). In the accounting of his social role, one must reckon in the fear and dysnomia which are embodied in his powers. These powers have their spiritual origin.

The shaman repays the social cost with his religious and psychiatric services.

Because the shamans among the Buryats are a group of specialized occupation, and not a group of pure individualists, they have their own ideology of religion, and their own doctrines. Petri (1923: 18) depicts their religious thought in terms of doctrinary disputation, religious reform, etc. This statement contains a measure of truth because there is ample testimony to the high degree of religious culture of the Buryats which could only have been produced by a specialized group with sufficient leisure to engage in such speculations. The existence of the Buryat shamans as a specialized social and occupational group is a mark of the complex society and economy of the Buryats.

THE SMITHS, BLACK AND WHITE

Another special occupational group besides the shaman, one also formed in lineages, and in whose line of descent a mystical power inheres is the smith. There is a special group of heavenly spirits called the smiths (*darxad*), and the practitioners of the craft on earth are descended from one of them—although which varies according to the group supplying the information. There are also two kinds of smiths—good and evil—white and black (Khangalov 1890: 38–39). The good smith-spirits protect men from the eastern spirits generally, not only the eastern smith-spirits. The chief of the good smith-spirits is Božintoy, who had nine sons and one daughter: this western smith-spirit taught men the art of ironworking by the Tunkinsk mountains, and settled there. The smiths of this Buryat group (the Tunkin Buryats) are called *saganī darxad* (*sagan,* white) by virtue of this origin myth (Khangalov 1890: 39). A close variant of this myth is given by Sandžeyev (1928: 539 ff.). The white smiths (human) of the Balagan Buryats—both they and the Tunkin are western Buryats —have their own family and lineage spirits, and thus form a group or groups of common descent apart from the rest of the Balagan Buryats. These spirits of the Balagan white smiths have their own *ongon* or spirit represented in the form of a doll. Black smiths are not reported in this group (Khangalov 1890: 73).

The craftsmanship of the Buryats in the working of metals, both iron and silver was admired by the 18th century voyagers among them (Gmelin 1751–52, vol. I: 707 ff.; Georgi 1776–1880: 425; cf. also Sandžeyev 1928: 541–44). Their knowledge of the arts has a much higher antiquity, and have fallen into disuse of late with the increase in Russian trade articles among them. Whether there is any relationship between the high development of this art among the Buryats and the spiritual power of the smith has not been established. As Sandžeyev points out, the smith has always had an honored position in Mongol (including Buryat-Mongol) society, appearing as a hero or free warrior in many epics (1928: 538). Again in many steppe-nomad groups of Asia, the smith has enjoyed a tax-free status from the period of Chingis Khan and earlier, down to the present. The Africanist may find here the inverse of his picture of the social position of the smith among the Buryats. The genesis of the relationship of craft specialization to the spirit world aside, there is a similar hereditary structure of the smiths as in the case of the shamans. They not only have their own *ongons* and genealogies, they also have their own protective (western) spirits from whom they trace their descent (Sandžeyev 1928: 538). Iron and metal work generally are an important part of shamanism, in the paraphernalia of the shaman (metal disks, etc.).

DUAL ORGANIZATION OF THE SPIRIT WORLD
AND A POSSIBLE DUAL SOCIAL ORGANIZATION

The division of the spirit world into forces of good and evil forms the basis for division of shamans, of smiths, and of the entire heavenly hierarchy. The highest beings are the *tengeri,* who are 99 in number, divided into 54 western white and good heavenly spirits and 44 eastern, black, and evil; and in addition, there is one, *segēn sedbek* (*segēn*—blue, *sedbek*—?), who is the border-marker, *obo,* between the two, although he is actually a western *tengeri.* The highest *tengeri* is also the oldest, for the principle of seniority applies equally to the sacred and the profane worlds. Although this senior *tengeri,* Khan Tyurmas Tengeri, leads the struggle of the western spirits against the eastern on behalf of man, this figure is not primary in the concern of the Buryat religionists. The principal object of their concern is the second *tengeri* in order of rank, Esege Malān Tengeri ("Father Bald Tengeri") who is invoked by the shaman in calling up a lesser

spirit, the *zayan*. Each of these highest *tengeri* has three sons
(Khangalov 1890: 1–2; Agapitov and Khangalov 1883: 1–2).
What is an evident instance of the projection of social values into
the religious world is the constant reference to the many sons of
the higher beings, in ritual numbers of 3, 9, and so forth; for this
is the chief desire of the Buryat and the chief source of happiness.
The sons of the highest beings form a secondary rank of higher
being; for the highest deities are the most sacred and rarely reveal
their activity; while their children, or more truly, their further
descendants are in closer contact with man, being intercessors
between earthly inhabitants and the inaccessibly distant deities
(Agapitov and Khangalov 1883: 2). Parallel hierarchization of
the heavenly beings exists in the case of the eastern spirits.

In the origin myth of the Kuda River Buryats, a descendant of
the second supreme being, Esege Malān (his son in one version)
is Buxa-Noyon ("Bull Prince"): from Buxa-Noyon all Buryats
are descended (Agapitov and Khangalov 1883: 3–4). However,
certain descent lines of the western Buryats trace their ancestry
to yet another supreme being, Šara Xasar Tengeri ("Yellow-
Cheek-Tengeri"). This being acts as protector for his descendants, who form the Sarat and Xangin clans (Khangalov 1890:
3–4). In general, all Buryat groups have their own supreme deities, either special to themselves or shared with the rest of the
Buryat world; with these deities they stand in a relationship of
direct descent and they invoke the deities in time of need. The
supreme ancestor of a given group may be one to whom that
group attributes the descent of all Buryats.

One such genealogy has been transmitted by Mikhail Bogdanov
(1926: 92–93), himself a Bulagat Buryat (west of Baikal). It
is a genealogy set down in the year 1847 by Bogdanov's grandfather, and at that point, in the second ascending generation,
breaks with Western tradition, and gives a true Buryat account
of the descent line. It originates in the divine ancestor of all
Buryats, the being who is part bull, part man, Buxa-Noyon, and
his wife a shamaness. It then enumerates eighteen generations to
the recorder, Bogdan, the paternal grandfather of M. Bogdanov.
It accounts for the ancestor and relative seniority of at least a
dozen clans and descent lines, comprising most of the Buryats
living west of Lake Baikal.

A more circumstantial account of the same origin myth was

recorded in an earlier generation by another man of Buryat origin, Khangalov (1890: 23–24). Two shamanesses found a baby in an iron cradle beside Lake Baikal; the younger shamaness recognized it as the son of Buxa-Noyon, and they raised him as their own, naming him Bulagat, or more fully, *buxa dorhō oldohon Bulagat,* Bulagat-found-under-the-bull. Bulagat played with a boy who rose out of Lake Baikal, and a meal was prepared for that boy by the shamanesses which put him to sleep (so that he would not disappear into the lake again). They then retained the boy and raised him together with Bulagat, naming him Ekirit; each of the shamanesses took one boy for her own, the senior shamaness taking Bulagat, the junior, Ekirit. The descendants of these two boys form the two Buryat peoples of Cis-Baikalia, and each of the descent groups has its own ancestor (and ancestress) and protectors.

In Bogdanov's account of the interrelation of the various segments of Buryat social organization, he divides his people first into Cis- and Trans-Baikal Buryats, which correspond to the western (or northern) and the eastern divisions; the latter he groups collectively as the Khori Buryat. The eastern Buryat are then divided into the Bulagat and Ikhirit (Ekirit), and the latter are placed on the lower course of the Angara River. The Ekirit Buryats are then further divided as the east or left bank and the west or right bank Ekirit (Bogdanov 1926: 39). Now plainly this is not exhaustive of the social divisions of the Buryats; on the other hand, the communal hunt of the ancient Buryats was conducted on the basis of a formation in two great wings or divisions. Whether this is an indigenous Buryat trait or one borrowed from the higher military organization of the Mongols to the south cannot be discussed here (Vambotsyrenov 1890: 32; Khangalov 1888: 6). Traces of a system of dual organization may be found in many sectors of the Altaic world; e.g., the ancient Mongols were divided in their socio-military organization into two wings, the right *barūn* and the left, *dzün.* The latter survives to this day as a place name in Inner Asia: Dzungaria, the country of the left (west) hand or left flank. Traces of dual organization may be found also among the Kalmuks, the Turks of Turkestan and of the Altai.

The concept of dual organization of the spirit world as being coördinate with the dual organization of the social world is of-

fered with considerably greater reservation than that of the triple
division of the two worlds as mutual reflexes of each other. The
triple division of both worlds is a conceptualization of the Buryats
themselves, that of the dual organization is not; three is a magic
number, two is not; the triple has been more fully explored and
conceptualized by the Buryat philosopher.

THE SACRIFICIAL RITES OF THE KIN-COMMUNITIES

The communal sacrifices of the Buryats, *tailgan,* are rites undertaken by kinship groups of varying size, from the *ulas* or village
community to the lineage and the clan as a whole, depending on
the importance of the rite and its occasion. These sacrifices are
distinguished from private rites or those performed by a family,
rites which are called *kirik* (Klements 1924: 14–15). The *tailgan*
may be conducted for any one of a number of reasons: as a
propitiatory offering to influential spirits which the *ulas* regards
as its own; as popular festivals on the occasion of seasonal clan
gatherings; in the face of calamity, such as an epidemic or an
epizoötic (Agapitov and Khangalov 1883: 36 ff.; Klements 1924:
14–15; Petri 1925: 5–6).

The cost of these sacrifices is borne by the participating households; the paraphernalia in addition to the animals to be offered
(horses, sheep, cattle) are milk-brandy (*tarasun*), wine, fire for
purification of the participants, and the shaman's implements.
Having purified themselves by going by or through a fire, the
members then proceed to the traditional place of sacrifice, on a
hillside near the *ulas-* or the clan-center. Thus far we have two
of the more significant accompanying traits of shamanism—the
fire-ceremonial and the role of high places.

The Buryat *ulas* has spirits which it does not share with other
ulases, even though these others may be all related as members
of a common lineage and of a common clan. The *spiritus loci* of
a given *ulas* are beseeched for protection and support; these
spirits are called *bümal burxan,* descended or manifest Burkhan.
On the other hand, there are certain manifest Burkhans who are
worshipped by great numbers, and have lost their significance as
local spirits (Agapitov and Khangalov 1883: 38; Shashkov 1864:
24). Certain manifest Burkhans reside in mineral springs and
have great powers of healing attributed to them (Shashkov 1864:

27). The term Burkhan occurs throughout the Mongol world as a designation for the Buddha; however, it has become generalized to mean deity, god, spirit. At minor *tailgans* the shamans play no role, at least among the Alar Buryats (Potanin 1881–83, vol. 4: 80). Another set of spirits which is particular to a given community and shared by no others is comprised by the souls of dead good shamans to whom their kin and descendants look for guidance and protection (Khangalov 1890: 83–84).

The great ceremonial or *tailgan* of the Balagan Buryats is that performed to the western Khans (deities just below the Tengeris in rank). It is conducted in the spring, and the entire clan gathers on a mountainside, facing south in a row with the senior and most respected clan-members in the west, the lesser members in the east. (Married women, widows, and girls who have passed menarche are not permitted to participate.)[6] In the course of the ritual, when the sacrifice itself has been completed, the shaman becomes Buxa Noyon, the Bull-god, and butts at the participants and at the altars and birch-trees set up by the place of sacrifice. After butting, he goes off in the southwestern (the holiest) direction, and cries nine times on the way. Thus the participants know that he is leaving the ceremonial entirely, and that it is over (Khangalov 1890: 116–17). Other, lesser ceremonials are built around the driving away of evil spirits from a household by a shaman, and the fire purification ceremony here is central (Khangalov 1890: 112).

Again, in the organization of the *tailgan,* the entire clan is divided into groups of more closely related kin, so that the distribution at the sacrifice is the same as that in the profane world. Each sub-group within the clan or lineage has its own camp, its own fire and sacrificial altar, carries on its own rites, and makes its own animal-offerings.[7] In the genealogy recounted by Bogdanov (1926: 92–93), he describes the formation of four lineages, *urag,* founded by four brothers, in the seventh ascending generation from himself. Each of the lineages was in existence in the first decades of this century. The great-grandfather of Bogdanov, Marxay, together with his brother Bayanxi, were the

---

[6] Cf. Petri 1925: 15–18. On the other hand, Petri points out that pregnant women can join in one specific *tailgan.*

[7] Bogdanov 1926: 94. A description of a *tailgan* bearing much the same import is to be found in Curtin 1909: 44–45.

founders of two *ulases,* for each had three sons and a rich progeny. However, the two *ulases* were formed only recently, around
the turn of the century, and until that time the descendants of
Maldžigi had lived in one *ulas* for approximately a century, and

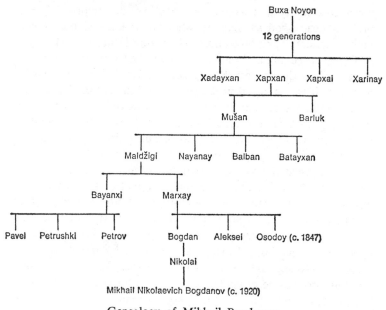

Genealogy of Mikhail Bogdanov.

lived as a unit, joining in making arrangements for marriage, in
communal hospitality and in the *tailgan.* Of late, i.e., since the
turn of the century, they rarely came together in the *tailgan* as a
group. On the other hand, grandsons of the three brothers, Bogdan, Aleksei, and Osodoy, joined in the *tailgan* (Bogdanov 1926:
92–94). (We have, by the way, an excellent criterion for degree
of acculturation in the adoption of Russian names by the
Buryats which increases with each generation.) We have thus a
detailed account of the close correlation between the organization
of the communal sacrifice and the organization of the Buryat
kinship system.

There are a number of taboos to which women are submitted.
It is clear from the nature of these taboos that women are never
fully adopted into their husbands' clans on marriage, unlike the

Manchus. They cannot participate in the husband's clan sacrifices, and are barred from the *tailgan* of the natal kin as well from menarche on. Menstruation is regarded by Petri (1925: 10–11), as a mark of ritual uncleanliness. Women are also subject to another taboo. On the birth of a son, a rope of horse-hair is stretched across the family tent, and only closely related women can come under the rope to enter the tent, such as the wife's mother, and then only after purification. Women from the farther end of the *ulas* cannot enter; nor can the husband's sister, for she has married out of the kin-group. Petri comments on the Buryat concept of their co-religionists: Tungus women come under the same interdiction as Buryat women—"the shamanistic faith is the same." But Russian women are not subject to this taboo because they fall under a different religious system. The Buryats regard their religion and that of the Tungus as the same, for they have the same gods in common. Unfortunately, this comment by Petri has not been corroborated elsewhere.

The role of women in the religious practices and concepts of their husbands and fathers may be viewed in a different manner from that of the ritual impurity of menstruation, although the two views complement each other, relative to the lower ritual and social status of Buryat woman. The Buryat kin-community, whether the village, the lineage, or the clan, has spirits which it does share with broader kin groupings. The girl until her marriage, which is a time approximately coincident with menarche, is a member of her natal kin-group, and may participate in its ceremonies. From another point of view, she may participate or not, for her presence does not count—she has no social, religious, or legal personality as yet. When she comes of age, she achieves a certain measure of social personality, but it is ambivalent, for she never fully leaves her father's group, she never fully joins her husband's. She is, therefore, never fully divested of the spiritual influences of her father's line, even though she undergoes the rite of fire-purification as part of the wedding ceremony, a rite which is designed to keep out the antipathetic, foreign spirits. For while these spirits are not per se malignant, they would not combine peacefully with the local spirits. The pregnant woman can attend the *tailgan* of her husband's community, because the spirit of her husband's line is within her, in the child she will bear. Finally there is the one great *tailgan* in which all

Buryats, both men and women, join; it is not specific to any one line of descent, or to any particular body of spirits.

Each Buryat descent line has a spirit or spirits particular to itself, inherent within itself. The smallest group, the *ulas* or village-kin-community, has a spirit of its own in addition to that which it shares with other villages as joint members of a lineage; each lineage has its own spiritual relations and powers specific to itself, and others still which it shares with other lineages as joint members of a clan; each clan has its own set of spirits and spiritual relations which it holds, and which in their turn hold the clan apart from all other Buryat clans. Finally there is the entire pantheon of Buryat spirits which govern all things, and which the Buryat shaman seeks to manipulate in the interests of his group and of himself.

In this way we establish the broadest and at the same time the most intricate correlations between the worlds of the sacred and the profane, between the religious order and the order of society. The inner hierarchy of the spirit world parallels the composition and articulation of the Buryat descent lines; and these descent lines are the all-embracing units of Buryat social organization, for they comprise within themselves the class strata and the specialized occupational groups.

THE EXTENDED FAMILY, THE HEARTH-SPIRIT, AND THE WEDDING

The Buryat kin-village is composed of extended families, and these extended families are the microcosms of Buryat society, with all the characteristic features of that society. The extended family too has its own spirits in the form of hearth-spirits and *ongons* which it shares with no other family, while at the same time joining with the other neighboring families in the invocation, exhortation, or propitiation of spirits venerated in common. The hearth-spirit is the house-deity, the defender of the tent of the family, and each tent or yurt has one (Agapitov and Khangalov 1883: 4). This spirit looks like a man, but during his stay in the fire he is small. . . . One must not poke the fire with a knife or anything else that is sharp, for one can thus poke out the eye of the fire spirit accidentally. The householder will then suffer mischance. The fire spirit when he is blind cannot protect the family of the host very well against evil spirits, since he keeps sharp watch that they do not come into the yurt. Moreover, the descendants of the household can become blind in such cases; like fire spirit, so householder (Account by a Buryat woman to Sandžeyev [1928: 967]).

The son or brother who leaves the family when a family divides, takes with him the fire from the common family hearth, which he lights in the new yurt; here a new fire spirit appears. To the question whence he comes, the Buryat answers: "As many children as you have, just that many does the fire spirit of your hearth have." It is clear that we have in the given case the same principle of the mutual dependence between the condition of the spirit of the fire and that of the householder. Hence the saying exists among the Buryats in regard to a family that has died out, "Their hearth fire has died out." (Sandžeyev 1928: 968).

The fire is the symbol of fertility of the family, and as part of the wedding ceremony, the bride must feed the fire with bits of fat, which she does three times, symbolizing by the enrichment of the fire the enrichment of her own marriage and of her husband's descent line through the birth of many children. The fire in the new yurt has been brought there from the husband's father's yurt by the husband's mother, symbolizing likewise the continuity of the line from father to son.[8] On the birth of a son, the wife bows to the fire again in the Balagan Buryat ritual (Khangalov 1898: 74).

One final relationship between kinship and the religious ritual remains to be described, that of the avunculate. Unlike many other societies which are organized on an agnatic principle, the Buryats do not assign a great role to the relationship between the mother's brother and the sister's son. There is, however, one formalized relationship between the two whereby the sister's son is forbidden entry into the house of the mother's brother if he does not wear a taboo belt. The tradition exists that in olden times there was practiced the strangulation of old men and women. This strangulation was performed by the sister's son (or the daughter's son: the term *zē* has both meanings) by means

[8] Khangalov 1898: 57; Potanin 1881–83, vol. 4, p. 34. These reports hold for the Cis-Baikal Buryats. Cf. Krol' 1894: 72 for similar data on the Trans-Baikal Buryats of the Selenga River valley. Here the bride in the wedding ceremony bows three times to the fire and three times feeds it with fat.

of a special belt. Before the strangulation, the *zē* offered to his mother's brother a gift of fat. It is this belt which is no longer worn for fear of committing a great sin as well as insult to the mother's brother. At the wedding ceremony, the sister's son continued to offer at the time of the report a gift of fat to the mother's brother (Khangalov 1898: 63–64).

CONCLUSION

In the foregoing pages the principal features of the Buryat religion in its relationship to the social organization have been set forth. The formative principles upon which Buryat society is based may be reduced to the following: descent in the paternal line from a single common ancestor, and hence the agnatic relationship among all the descendants; the concentric organization of these agnatic kin into extended families grouped into kin-villages, kin-villages grouped into lineages (these are the units of exogamy); lineages grouped into clans, and clans into clan confederations and principalities. The descent groups are collaterally ranked by the principle of primogeniture, which forms the basis of social differentiation into the aristocratic (primogenitary) and the commoner social strata; to this dichotomy, a stratum of slaves was subordinated, forming a triple class-division of society. There exist also descent lines of shamans and smiths, forming groups of specialized occupation.

The joint concepts of division and hierarchization by ranking is the basis for social inequality in a society where all men trace descent generation by generation from a common ancestor. These joint concepts are operative in the two worlds, the sacred and the profane, in application to the triple division of the spirits, of the human soul, of the entire being of man, and of society itself. Each group, from the extended family to the clan, takes its place in the hierarchy of Buryat society, and this hierarchy is extended to include the specialized groups: to each unit of social organization, such as an extended family, kin-village, etc., and to each level of social organization, such as the commoner stratum, there corresponds a unit or level of the spiritual hierarchy. The relations of the group to its own spirits are necessarily more intimate than those of any other group, and this despite the fact that the two groups may have spirits in common by being members of a larger inclusive group, such as villages or lineages in a clan. Therefore, a member of one lineage entering another (such as a woman in a lineage-exogamic marriage) must be purified of the spiritual influences of her natal group-spirits, even though both lineages may have joint spirits, joint sacrifices and myths as members of the same clan. The spirits which are not shared, and therefore those of whose influence the new member must be purified by fire, are not per se maleficent; but they are mutually antipathetic. All of earthly Buryatdom is so organized in the conception of each Buryat as to reflect in point-for-point detail the spiritual organization of the cosmos, and the spiritual organization in its turn the social, in mutual interaction.

The organization of society into a series of concentric circles, to which the threefold organization of society and of the cosmos was traced is but one mode. The Buryats in a *tour-de-force* have been able to conceptualize the coördination of a complex social order and an equally complex spiritual order. There is, however, another mode or order, the dual organization of the spirit world into good and evil, black and white, west and east respectively. Moreover, certain types of human beings, the shamans and smiths are likewise so divided (for the sake of simplicity I shall speak only of shamans). The dual classification does not have a real analogue in the social organization; despite certain traces of dual organization of society, no analogy can be drawn because of the overwhelming difference in emphasis between the dual in society and the dual in religion and morality.

If the measure of the cosmic trichotomy was found in the society and its three strata, the measure of the dual cleavage must be sought in the Buryat shaman. The shaman is the repository of these double relations, to the good and to evil; for, regardless of whether the shaman is white or black, he has relations to both sectors of the spirit world. And these very relations to the spirit are reciprocal ones, that of possessing and that of being possessed. The relationships beyond these are also ambivalent: the good spirits protect men from the bad, yet the good spirits decree, execute, and report man's death; and evil spirits in conjunction with the force of the black shaman are invoked to prolong a man's life and stave off imminent death. The shaman's power is not intrinsically evil, any more than the spiritual influence to be purified by fire is malignant; the shaman's power in the one case, and the spiritual influence in the other, are dangerous and hence ambivalent. If they are properly channelized and controlled they are benevolent forces; the shamanist-spiritual power may on the other hand out-reach the shaman and do vast harm. The shaman maintains the most delicate balance between maximalizing and over-reaching, between curing and killing.

The Buryat non-shaman is spiritually neutral, possibly with a slight balance in favor of the good; Buryat society as a whole is similarly appreciated from the viewpoint of morality. The fundamental cleavage of the social plane is that between the aberrant who is the shaman and the forces of conformity embodied in the organization of the society—indeed the hyper-organization of society may be inferred from the proliferation of modes of social organization of the Buryats. The shaman is the breaking away from the bounds of organization; the shaman is the transcendence by the individual of the social norm. The struggle between good and evil within the shaman as spiritual representative dramatizes the conflict between norm and ab-norm in the shaman as a man. In this attitude toward both the natural and the supernatural environments, the Buryat is daring, forceful, cunning and optimistic. The Buryat shaman and the Buryat layman both know that the parallel journey through life and through the spirit world is fearsome and beset with dangers; all Buryats know the risks and how to overcome them.

The interpretation of the religious and social conceptions of the Buryats as coördinate is not without parallel in world ethnography; but it is rare, especially at the given degree of complexity of the two conceptual spheres. That these spheres have been coördinated at various levels by the Buryats is the achievement of their cosmology and their social thought. They have the means to pursue and support objectification and abstraction in all spheres except that of the shaman himself.

6 SOME FEATURES OF NUER RELIGION

E. E. Evans-Pritchard

I SHALL GIVE you in this address a brief account of some features of the Nuer concept of God, *Kwoth a nhial*.[1] The word
kwoth[2] is used by Nuer to refer to divers spirits which, though
they are of different kinds and of varying significance, are identical
in essence. Nuer place them in two categories: *kuth nhial*, the
spirits of the sky or of the above, and *kuth piny*, the spirits
of the earth or of the below, which are principally totemic spirits.
I am not concerned here with the tellurian spirits, and I shall
only speak a few words about the superior category of spirits in
general, leaving a fuller discussion of them for some future occasion. They present a difficult problem of interpretation, which
is further complicated by the historical evidence which has to be
taken into consideration. The spirits of the above are *Kwoth nhial*
or *Kwoth a nhial*, the spirit of the sky or the spirit (who is) in
the sky, who can, for reasons which will I believe appear adequate, be appropriately spoken of as God; the *kuth dwanga* or

Reprinted from *The Journal of the Royal Anthropological Institute* 81,
1951: 1–13, by permission of the author and of the Council of the Royal
Anthropological Institute.

[1] Other aspects of Nuer religion have been treated in the following articles: Evans-Pritchard (1949a, b, c, d, e, and 1951).

[2] The word has been variously spelt by those who have written about
the Nuer or compiled vocabularies of their language. Professor Westermann gives *koth* (1912a: 86); Mr. Jackson (1923: 156) gives *kosz* or *kott;*
Captain Stigand gives *kuth* (1923: 16); Miss Huffman gives *kwoth* (pl. *kuth*)
(1929: 27); Father Crazzolara gives *koth* (pl. *kuuth*) (1933: 6 and 40);
and Father Kiggen gives *kuodh* (pl. *kuth*) and also *kuoth* (pl. *kuuth*) (1948:
162, 164). The variations are probably due to dialectical differences as well
as to the different ways Europeans hear and write this exceedingly difficult language. I shall throughout use *kwoth* (pl. *kuth*) neglecting the geni-
tive and locative forms.

gaat Kwoth, the spirits of the air (or of the breezes) or the sons
(or children) of God; and the *col wic* spirits, which are the souls
of persons killed by lightning and taken by God to dwell with
him in the above. The spirits of the air and the *col wic* spirits
may be regarded, for reasons which I do not enter into here, as
divers manifestations or hypostases of God. Consequently the
Nuer concept of God cannot be fully treated without taking them
into account; but it seems to me desirable to pay attention first
to the distinctive features of their concept of God and then to see
later how this concept is related to, and influenced by, other
aspects of their religion, and also by their culture and social
order. It is possible, if difficult, to proceed in this manner, and it
is the logical order of procedure because the other spiritual
beings cannot be understood except in relation to God.

There are two important characteristics of Nuer religion
which have great importance for our present discussion. Firstly,
it is throughout concerned with spirits. Indeed, if we want to sum
up its most general and characteristic features in one word, it
would best be described as "spiritual." Secondly, these spirits
are classed into two categories, those of the above and those
of the below, the superior and the inferior, the free and the earth-
bound. In a study of Nuer religion it is necessary, as we will
see, to give special attention to this symbolic dichotomy between
heaven and earth.

I have translated the word *kwoth* by "spirit" and I have said
that Nuer religion can best be described as "spiritual" because
the Latin *spiritus,* like the Greek *pneuma* and the English deriva-
tives of both words, suggests, as does the Nuer word, both the
intangible quality of air and the breathing or blowing out of air;
though it does not perhaps cover the sense of *kwoth* so well as
does the Hebrew *RWH,* which like *kwoth* is an onomatope and
denotes violent breathing out of air in contrast to ordinary breathing (the Hebrew *neshamah,* the Nuer *yiegh* or *yie*) (Snaith 1944:
Chap. VII). *Kwoth,* in its verbal form, is used to describe such
actions as blowing on the embers of a fire; blowing into the
uterus of a cow, while a tulchan is propped up before it, to make
it give milk; to snort, the blowing out of air by the *bulyak* or puff
fish; and the hooting by steam pressure of a river steamer. The
word is also found, and has the same sense, in some of the other
Nilotic languages; in Dinka *koth,* to blow on a fire, to blow the

nose, etc.; in Shilluk *kodho,* to blow on a fire or to play on a wind instrument; and in Lango, *kuto,* and in Acholi, *koto,* with the same and related meanings. Professor Westermann says that it is the same word as the word for "rain," *koth* or *kot,* in the Shilluk-Luo group of languages (Nebel 1936: 16, 87; Westermann 1912a: 86; 1912b: 263; Driberg 1923: 389; Crazzolara 1938: 261). I feel very doubtful whether this is so, but it is not a matter about which I am competent to judge.

In the Nuer conception of him, God is *kwoth,* a being of pure spirit, and he may simply be so called. He is further, and is often specified as, *Kwoth nhial,* or *Kwoth a nhial,* the spirit of the heavens or the spirit (who is) in the heavens, the copula *a* in the second designation being the verb "to be." *Nhial* is the sky and combined with certain verbs the word may also refer to natural processes associated with the sky, as raining and thundering; but it may also have merely the sense of "on high" or "above." We may certainly say that the Nuer do not regard the sky or any celestial phenomenon as God and this is clearly shown in the distinction made between God and the sky in the expressions "spirit of the sky" and "spirit (who is) in the sky." Moreover, it would even be a mistake to interpret "of the sky" and "in the sky" too literally. They are to some extent to be regarded as metaphors, just as are similar expressions throughout the Old and New Testaments where heaven is represented figuratively as the habitation of God.

It would equally be a mistake to regard the association of God with the sky as pure metaphor. It is more than a religious symbolism, even if we regard the symbol as both standing for something and, through this special association, partaking of the thing itself, though without being identified with it. For though the sky is not God, and though God is everywhere, he is thought of as being particularly in the sky, and Nuer generally think of God in a special sense as being on high. Hence anything connected with the firmament has associations with him. Nuer sometimes speak of him as falling in the rain and of being in lightning and thunder. Mgr. Mlakic (in *The Messenger* 1943–44) says that the rainbow is called the necklace of God. I have never heard a spontaneous reference to the sun as a divine manifestation, but if one asks Nuer about it they say that it too belongs to God. They also say that if a man sees the sun at night this is a divine manifestation, and one which is most dangerous for him; but I think that the light they say is occasionally seen is not regarded as an appearance of the physical sun but some peculiar luminous vision. When Nuer see the new moon they rub ashes on their foreheads —the Nuer act of dedication—and they throw ashes, and perhaps also a grain of millet, towards it, saying some short prayer, as "Grandfather, let us be at peace" or "Ah moon, nyadeang (daughter of the air-spirit Deng) we invoke that you appear with goodness. May the people see you every day. Let us be (akolapko)." Mgr. Mlakic (1943–44) says that they mark their foreheads with ashes in the form of a cross and that it is called ngei Kwoth, God's sign. I must add that the language is here figurative, even playful. They may address the moon, but it is God to whom they speak through it, for the moon is not regarded, as such, as a spirit or as a person.

It would be quite contrary to Nuer thought, as I have remarked, and it would even seem absurd to them, to say that sky, moon, rain, and so forth are in themselves, singly or collectively, God. God is a spirit who like wind and air is invisible and ubiquitous. But though God is not these things he is in them in the sense that he reveals himself through them. In this sense he is in the sky, falls in the rain, shines in the sun and moon, and blows in the wind. These divine manifestations are to be understood as modes of God and not as his essence, which is spirit.

God being above, everything above is associated with him. This is why the heavenly bodies and the movements and actions connected with them are associated with him. This is why also the spirits of the air are regarded as gaat Kwoth, children of God, in a way other spirits are not, for they, unlike other spirits, dwell in the air and are also thought of as being in the clouds, which are nearest to the sky. This is why also the col wic spirits are so closely associated with God, for he touched them with his fire from heaven and took them to himself. Some birds also are spoken about by Nuer as gaat Kwoth, especially those which fly high and seem, to us as well as to Nuer, to belong to heaven rather than to earth and therefore to be children of light and symbols of the divine. The feeling that they are in a measure detached from the earth is enhanced in the case of migratory birds by their disappearances and reappearances. I have heard the idea expressed that in their absence from Nuerland they have gone to visit God's country. This is probably no more than poetic fancy, but we can say that the disappearance of these birds strengthens the allegory of God's children which arises from their ability to do what man cannot do, fly towards heaven and God. Twins also, in a very special sense, are *gaat Kwoth,* for Nuer say that twins are birds, a dogma which is emphasized by many observances concerning them. When a twin dies Nuer never say that he has died, but that he has flown away. The Jikul clan and the Gaanwar clan, whose ancestors fell from heaven, are also *ji Kwoth,* God's people, for that reason and are thought to have special powers.

Thus anything associated with the sky has virtue which is lacking in things earthly. Nuer pathetically compare man to heavenly things. Man is *ran piny,* an earthly creature and, according to the general Nuer view, his soul is also earth-bound: *"joah e ran piny,"* "a ghost is a person of the earth," that is, he is not a *ran nhial,* a person of the sky. Between God and man, between heaven and earth, there is a great gulf, and we shall find that an appreciation of the symbolism of the polarity of heaven and earth aids us in our attempt to understand Nuer religious thought and feeling and also sheds light on certain social features of their religion, for example, the greater importance of prophets than of priests, the prophets being inspired by heavenly beings while the leopard-skin priests, although they have received their powers from God, are in themselves wholly of the earth.

Before discussing further the separation of God from man I will mention some of the chief attributes of God. God is in the sky, but his being in the sky does not mean that he is not at the same time elsewhere, and on earth. Indeed, as will be seen, Nuer religious thought cannot be understood unless God's closeness to man is taken together with his separation from man, for its meaning lies precisely in this paradox.

Nuer say that God is everywhere, that he is "like the wind" and "like the air." According to Father Crazzolara (cited by Schmidt 1949: 10, 23), God may be spoken of by the epithets *jiom,* wind, and *ghau,* universe, but these words only stand for God in poems or in an allegorical sense and are an illustration of the liking the Nilotic peoples show in their poetry for metonymy and synecdoche. God is not *jiom,* the wind, but *cere jiom,* like the wind; and he is not *ghau,* the universe, but *cak ghaua,* the creator

of the universe. Another poetic epithet by which he may be referred to is *tutgar*. This is an ox-name, taken from an ox of the
kind Nuer call *wer*, which has wide-spreading horns and is the
most majestic of their beasts. The name is a combination of two
words: *tut*, which has the sense of "strength" or "greatness" and
gar, which has the sense of "omnipresent," as in another of God's
titles, *"Kwoth me gargar,"* "the omnipresent God."

The commonest Nuer way of trying to express their idea of the
nature of God is to say that he is like the wind or the air, a
metaphor which seems appropriate to us because it is found
throughout the hierological literature of the world and we are
particularly familiar with it in the Old Testament, where the *RWH*
of the Hebrew and the *pneuma* of the Septuagint are variously
translated, according to the context, "spirit," "wind," and
"breath," in the English version (Snaith 1944: Chap. VII, and
179 *seq.;* Trench 1871: 260–62). Among the Nuer the metaphor
is consistent not only with the absence of any fixed abode of
God but also of any special places where he is thought particularly
to dwell, for air and wind are everywhere. Unlike the other spirits
God has no prophets or sanctuaries or earthly forms, I do not
discuss this point further here, but it will be appreciated that the
somewhat amorphous, though monotheistic, character of Nuer
religion is in harmony with the absence of a developed and politically important priesthood.

God, the spirit in the heavens who is like wind and air, is the
creator and mover of all things. The American Presbyterian missionaries at Nasir have written in an unpublished manuscript that
he is especially the creator, the giver, and the sustainer of life.
This accords with my own conclusions and with those of the
Catholic missionaries at Yoahnyang. Mgr. Mlakic (1943–44)
has written that the Nuer "believe in one supreme God, creator
of the world, of human beings, and eventually of the spirits."
Father Crazzolara has said that he is "the creator, the almighty,
he who rules the destiny of man; he is especially the lord of life
and death" (Schmidt 1949: 29).

Since God made the world he is addressed in prayers as *Kwoth
ghaua*, spirit of the universe, with the sense of creator of the
universe. The word *cak*, used as a noun, can mean the creation,
that is, all created things; it can be used in a very special sense to
refer to an abnormality, for example, *cak Kwoth*, a freak; and,

though I think rarely, it is used as a title of God, the creator. As a verb, to create, it signifies creation *ex nihilo* and when speaking of things can therefore only be used of God. As a phrase quoted by Father Kiggen has it: *"cagh e dung Kuodh ke rode,"* "to create is proper to God alone." However, the word can be used, as implied by another example of its use by Father Kiggen (1948: 502), *"caghe diid,"* "composer of songs," for imaginative constructions in the same figurative sense as when we say that an actor creates a part. In quoting these phrases from Father Kiggen's dictionary I am vouching for their genuine ring of Nuer thought and expression, a ring lacking in some of his examples of the use of Nuer words which have a religious significance.

Professor Westermann wrote at the dictation of a Nuer an account of how God created the world and made all things in it. It begins *"Me chak koth nath, chwo ran thath,"* which Professor Westermann (1912a: 115) has translated "When God created the people he created man." Here again I must say that the phrase is genuine Nuer thought and expression, because Professor Westermann's sources might be held to be suspect, having been, in part at any rate, soldiers, and therefore possibly Muslim slaves, and certainly influenced by Islam (Westermann 1912a: 87). It will be observed that he has translated two different words, *cak* and *tath*, by "create"; but they have not quite the same sense, for whereas *cak* means creation *ex nihilo*, *tath* means to make something out of something else, as when a child moulds clay into the shape of an ox or a smith beats a spear out of iron. The sentence would therefore be better translated "When God created people then he made (or fashioned) man." The distinction is similar to that between "created" and "made" in the first chapter of Genesis, "created" there being a translation of the Hebrew *BR'*, which can only be used for divine activity.

The complementary distinction made in Genesis between "The heaven and the earth" is made, by implication at least, in a slightly different way by the Nuer. A parallelism often heard in their prayers in *"e pinydu, e ghaudu,"* "it is thy earth, it is thy universe." *Piny* is the down below, the earth in the sense of the terrestrial world as the Nuer know it. *Ghau* has many meanings—world, sky, earth, atmosphere, time, and weather (Kiggen 1948: 121)—which taken together, as they should be in a context of prayer, mean the universe. Another common, and related, strophe in prayers is "*e ghaudu, e rwacdu,*" "it is thy universe, it is thy word." *Rwac* in ordinary contexts means speech, talk, or words, but when used in prayers and invocations in the phrase "*e rwacdu,*" "it is thy word," it means the will of God; and when used in reference to creation it has almost the meaning of the creative word: "He created the world, it is his word."

The Nuer can hardly be said to have a creation myth, though our authorities (Jackson 1923: 70–71; Fergusson 1921: 148–49; Schmidt 1949: 15) record some fragmentary accounts of the creation of men, parts of which I have myself heard. These state that men were created in the Jagei country of western Nuerland at a certain tamarind tree, at the foot of which offerings, and according to Mr. Jackson sacrifices, were sometimes made till it was destroyed by fire in 1918. Many details in the versions given by Mr. Jackson and Captain Fergusson are clearly foreign, either Dinka or, in Mr. Jackson's account, Shilluk, and in Captain Fergusson's account, possibly even Atwot or Mandari,[3] and I regard Father Crazzolara's version as the closest to Nuer tradition. In this version the tamarind tree (Father Crazzolara gives the correct Nuer word *koat,* but incorrectly translates it "fig-tree" instead of "tamarind"), called Lic, was itself the mother of men who, according to one account, emerged from a hole at its foot or, according to another account, dropped off its branches like ripe fruits.

Whether they are speaking about events which happened *me walka,* in the beginning or long ago, or about happenings of yesterday and today, God the creative spirit is the final Nuer explanation of everything. When asked how things began or how

[3] This is clear on internal evidence, and Mr. Jackson himself says that he has combined Nuer, Dinka and Shilluk stories to make a more coherent account. I will not here enter into a discussion of the difficulties involved in an attempt to determine whether a story found among both Dinka and Nuer has been borrowed by the one people from the other, but I must point out that it is always possible, as in the case under consideration, that an authority has taken down a Dinka story, and not a Nuer story, from a Dinka informant in Nuerland. Mr. Jackson's account of the Nuer was written entirely from information supplied by a single informant who was a Dinka who had settled among the Nuer and later resided in Malakal under a Muslim name. Captain Fergusson's immediate entourage was mainly, if not solely, Dinka or Atwot. Even in the case of Father Crazzolara it must be taken into consideration that not only is the area in which his mission was situated saturated with Dinka influences but also that Dinka as well as Nuer attended the mission.

they came to be what they are they answer that God made them or that it was his will that they have come to be what they are. The heavens and the earth and the waters on the earth, and the beasts and birds and reptiles and fish were made by him, and he is the author of custom and tradition. The Nuer herd cattle and cultivate millet and spear fish because God gave them these things for their sustenance. He instituted their marriage prohibitions. He gave ritual powers to some men and not to others. He decreed that the Nuer should raid the Dinka and that Europeans should conquer the Nuer. God has made one man black and another white (according to one Nuer account our white skins are a punishment by God for incest committed by our ancestor with his mother), one man fleet and another slow, one strong and another weak. Everything in nature, in culture, in society and in men is as it is because God made it so. Above all else God is thought of as the giver and sustainer of life. He also brings death. Nuer say that since it is his world he can take away what he has given. It is true that Nuer seldom attribute death—in such cases as death by lightning or following the breach of a taboo—to the direct intervention of God, but rather to natural circumstances or to the action of a lesser spirit, but they nevertheless regard the natural circumstances or the spirit as agents of God; for it is he who causes a man to die and the final appeal in sickness is made to him. Nuer have often told me that it is God who takes the life, whether a man dies from spear, wild beast, or sickness for all these are *"nyin Kwoth,"* "instruments of God."

In the Nuer conception of God he is thus creative spirit. He is also a person. I have never heard Nuer suggest that he has human form, but though he is himself ubiquitous and invisible he sees and hears all that happens and he can be angry and can love (the Nuer word is *nhok,* and if we here translate it "to love" it must be understood in the preferential sense of *agapao* or *diligo:* when Nuer say that God loves something they mean that he is partial to it). As a person he is the father of men.

A very common mode of address to the Deity is *"gwandong,"* a word which means "grandfather" or "ancestor," and literally "old father," but in a religious context "father" or "our father" would convey the Nuer sense better; and *"gwara"* or *"gwandan,"* "our father," are also often used in prayers. God is the father of men in two respects. He is their creator and he is their protector.

He is addressed in prayers as *"Kwoth me cak gwadong,"* "God who created my ancestor." Figuratively, and in conformity with Nuer lineage idiom, he is sometimes given a genealogical position in relation to man: a man of the Jinaca clan, for example, after tracing his pedigree back to Denac, the founder of his clan, may explain that Denac was a son of Gee, who was a son of *Ran,* man, who was a son of *Ghau,* the universe, who was a son of *Kwoth,* God. When Nuer thus speak of God as their remote ancestor and address him as "father" or "grandfather," and likewise when in praying to him they speak of themselves, as they commonly do, as *"gaatku,"* "thy children," their manner of speech is no more to be taken literally than are those frequent passages in the Old Testament in which Israel is spoken of as the spouse or son of Jehovah. Also, when Nuer speak of spirits, birds and twins as *"gaat Kwoth,"* "children of God," they speak in an allegorical sense. Similarly, when children are named after God or one of the spirits of the air, for example, Gatkwoth, son of God, or Gatdeang, son of (the air-spirit) *deng,* all we are to understand from these theophorous proper names is that the child was conceived in answer to prayer or sacrifice. Even in Nuer family and kinship usages the word *gat,* son, does not necessarily, or even usually, signify a natural son but a son in one or other of several social senses. That the language is here allegorical is shown by the use of the word *cak* in the expression *"Kwoth me cak gwadong,"* "God who created my ancestor," for *cak* means to create and not to beget. It is also shown by the fact that the word *dieth,* to beget, is not only not used in this expression but is never used in reference to God. It is true that Father Crazzolara records the sentence *"Gwandan ce nadh dieth ke diedh nadhe,"* which, as he rightly says, means "God did not beget men with the begetting with which men are begotten," but he adds that the word *"dieth"* (which he has translated *"zeugen"*) was only used by his informant because the question he himself had asked required its use (Schmidt 1949: 15). Nuer do not think of God as the begetter of man but as his creator.

God is also the father of men in that he is their protector and friend. He is *"Kwoth me jale ka ji,"* "God who walks with you," that is, who is present with you. He is the friend of men who helps them in their troubles, and Nuer sometimes address him as *"madh,"* "friend," a word which has for them the sense of intimate friendship. The frequent use in prayers of the word *rom* in reference to the lives, or souls, of men indicates the same feeling about God, for it has the sense of the care and protection parents give to a child and especially the carrying of a helpless infant. The Nuer habit of making short supplications to God outside formal and ritual occasions also suggests an awareness of a protective presence, as does the affirmation one hears every day among the Nuer, *"Kwoth a thin,"* "God is present." Nuer say this, doubtless often as a merely verbal response, when they are faced with some difficulty to be overcome or some problem to be solved. The phrase does not mean "there is a God." That would be for Nuer a pointless remark. God's existence is taken for granted by everybody. Consequently when we say, as we can do, that all Nuer have faith in God the word "faith" must be understood in the Old Testament sense of "trust" (the Nuer *ngath*) and not in that modern sense of "belief" which the concept came to have under Greek and Latin influences. There is in any case, I think, no word in the Nuer language which could stand for "I believe."

Kwoth a thin means that God is present in the sense of being in a place or enterprise, the *a* being here again the verb "to be." When Nuer use the phrase they are saying that they do not know what to do, but God is here with them and will help them. He is with them because he is spirit and being like wind or air is everywhere, and, being everywhere, is here now.

But though God is sometimes felt to be present here and now, he is also felt to be far away in the sky. However, heaven and earth, that is, God and man, for we are justified here in treating the dichotomy anagogically, are not entirely separated. There are comings and goings. God takes the souls of those he destroys by lightning to dwell with him and in him they protect their kinsmen; he participates in the affairs of men through divers spirits which haunt the atmosphere between heaven and earth and may be regarded as hypostasizations of his modes; and he is also everywhere present in a way which can only be symbolized, as his ubiquitous presence is symbolized by the Nuer, by the metaphor of wind and air. Also God can be communicated with through prayer and sacrifice, and a certain kind of contact with him is maintained through the moral order of society which he is said to have instituted and of which he is the guardian, a matter I discuss briefly later. But in spite of these communications and contacts the distance between heaven and earth is too great to be bridged. In a sense, therefore, but not, I think, in the sense in which some writers have used the word—of being functionless and of serving no purpose—but in his separateness and uniqueness, his "holiness" in the Old Testament sense of the word, *Kwoth a nhial* is otiose.

God's separation and remoteness from man are accounted for in a myth recorded by Father Crazzolara which relates that there was not always a complete separation of heaven and earth and that there might never have been but for an almost fortuitous event. I did not myself hear this myth, and I judge it to be of Dinka origin, partly because it occurs among the Dinka but more because I think it is very probably only current among Nuer to the west of the Nile, which would indicate recent introduction into Nuerland from Dinka sources; but, whether it is Dinka or not, it accords well with Nuer religious conceptions in general. The myth relates that there was once a rope from heaven to earth and how anyone who became old climbed up by it to God in heaven and after being rejuvenated there returned to earth. One day a hyaena—an appropriate figure in a myth relating to the origin of death—and what is known in the Sudan as a durra-bird, most likely a finch, entered heaven by this means. God gave instructions that the two guests were to be well watched and not allowed to return to earth, where they would certainly cause trouble. One night they escaped and climbed down the rope, and when they were near the earth the hyaena cut the rope and the part above the cut was drawn upwards towards heaven. So the connection between heaven and earth was cut and those who grow old must now die, for what had happened could not be made not to have happened (*"Aber was geschehen war, konnte nicht mehr ungeschehen gemacht werden"*). A variant of this myth has been recorded by Captain Fergusson (Schmidt 1949: 17–18; Fergusson 1921: 148–49).

It is in the light of their feeling that man is dependent on God and helpless without his aid and that God, though a friend and present, is yet also remote that we are to interpret a word the Nuer frequently use about themselves when speaking to or about God: *doar*. The meanings of this word given in Nuer-English dictionaries (Stigand 1923: 7; Huffman 1929: 13; Kiggen 1948: 78), "idiot," "stupid," "fool" and "weak-minded," do not adequately convey the sense of the word, especially when it is used to refer to man's relationship to God. Then it means rather "simple" or "foolish" or "ignorant"—"idiot" in the sense the word used to have in the English language and which the word from which it is derived had in Greek. Nuer say that they are just ignorant people who do not understand the mysteries of life and death, and of God and the spirits and why things happen as they do.

A favourite Nuer expression is *yie wicda,* "my head goes round" or "I am bewildered." They are at a loss because they are just foolish people who do not understand the why and the wherefore. In saying that they are simple or foolish or ignorant Nuer are not being modest in respect to other peoples, though I have often had the impression that they regard themselves as guileless compared with other peoples, especially compared with the Dinka, whom they regard as cleverer and more cunning than themselves, a difference dramatised in one of their myths. The story, which reminds us of that of Esau and Jacob, is cited by Nuer to explain why they have always raided the Dinka. Nuer and Dinka—the peoples are personified in the myth—were both sons of God, who had promised to give an old cow to Dinka and its young calf to Nuer. Dinka came by night to God's byre and deceived him by imitating Nuer's voice and God gave him the calf. When God found that he had been deceived he charged Nuer to raid the herds of Dinka to the end of time. In other words, the Nuer may be robbers but the Dinka are thieves. Another story relates that God offered men the choice between cattle and guns. Nuer and Dinka chose cattle and Arabs and Europeans chose guns. Here both Nuer and Dinka are figured as simple compared with Arabs and Europeans. Nuer regard themselves as having manly virtues exceeding those of other peoples, but compared with them they are artless. However, when they use the word *doar* in a religious context they are speaking of themselves being foolish in comparison with God and in his eyes. I think that the same idea is expressed in speaking of themselves as *cok,* small black ants, in their hymns to spirits of the air, that is, they are God's ants, or in other words what a tiny ant is to man so man is to God. This is a conscious and explicit analogy. Thus

Father Kiggen (1948: 60) quotes the phrase *"Kondial labne cuugh, ke min kueine ke Kuooth,"* which I would translate "We, all of us, have the nature of ants in that we are very tiny in respect to God," and *"Kondial gaad cuughni ke Kuooth,"* which I would translate "All of us are like little ants in the sight of God." The same metaphor has been recorded for the Dinka by Archdeacon Shaw (1915).

In speaking about themselves as being like ants and as being simple people the Nuer show a humbleness in respect to God which contrasts with their proud, almost provocative, and towards strangers even insulting, bearing to men; and indeed humbleness, a consciousness of creatureliness, is a further element of meaning in the word *doar,* as is also humility, not contending against God but suffering without complaint. Humbleness and humility are very evident on all occasions of religious expression among the Nuer; in the manner and content of prayer, in the purpose and meaning of sacrifices, which are generally made to avoid, stay, or restrict misfortunes, and, perhaps most evidently, in their sufferings. Here I want only to say that when misfortunes happen Nuer accept them with resignation. Whatever the occasion of death and other misfortunes may be, whether they be what the Nuer call *"dung cak,"* "the lot of created things," or whether they be the result of what they call *"dueri,"* "faults," they come to one and all alike, and Nuer say that they must be accepted as the will of God. The best that can be hoped for is that God will hear the prayers and accept the sacrifices of those who suffer and spare them any extra burden. Nuer do not complain when misfortunes befall them. They say that it is God's will (*rwac Kwoth*), that it is his world (*e ghaude*), and—I have often heard Nuer say this in their sufferings—that he is *goagh,* good. When a child dies women lament, but only for a little while, and men are silent. They say that God has taken his own and they must not complain; perhaps he will give them another child. This is a common refrain with the Nuer, especially in their invocations at mortuary ceremonies. They say of the dead man that God has taken him and that he was in the right in the matter, for it was his man; he has taken only what was his own. Also, when a byre is destroyed by lightning Nuer tell him that they do not complain. The grass of the thatch is his, and he has a right to take what belongs to him. Likewise if a cow or an ox of your herd dies Nuer say that you must not complain if God takes his own beast. The cattle of your herd are his and not yours. If you grieve overmuch God will be angry that you resent his taking what is his. Better be content therefore that God should do what he wishes, seeing not that he has taken one of your cows but that he has spared the others. If you forget the cow God will see that you are poor and will spare you and your children and your other beasts. I cannot convey the Nuer attitude better than by quoting part of the verse in the Book of Job: "The Lord gave, and the Lord has taken away; blessed be the name of the Lord."[4]

Father Crazzolara records much the same of the Nuer in this respect as I have done. He says, for example, that if God kills a man or destroys property by lightning, Nuer say: *"Grossvater, was du genommen hast, war dein Eigentum. Du hast recht gehabt"* (Schmidt 1949: 40). God is always in the right, always, as the Nuer say, has *cuong*, a word I discuss later. Nuer also say, when some calamity has happened to them, *"thile me lele,"* which means that there is nothing which can be done about it and that therefore it does not matter. It does not matter, not because it is unimportant for the person concerned, but because it is the will of God and therefore determined and beyond man's control.

People comfort a man who has lost cattle by telling him these things, but they find it hard to comfort a youth who has lost his *dil thak,* his favourite ox, for he is young and the ox was perhaps his only ox and has been his companion. He has cared for it and played with it and danced and sung to it. He now sits by himself and pines and his friends try to cheer him up and they tell him that he must not be tearful or God will be angry: "God is good, he might have taken you, but he has taken your ox instead." Here we have a further and very common reflection in adversity. God has been gracious and he has taken something belonging to a man and has spared the man himself. What appears to be misfortune is therefore really fortune. Nuer here use the word

---

[4] This quotation is also given by Professor and Mrs. Seligman (1932: 230). It was, however, like the rest of their account of the Nuer, except where they have stated to the contrary, taken from my notebooks. I mention this fact because I have found that Professor and Mrs. Seligman are often quoted, for example, by P. W. Schmidt in his *Der Ursprung der Gottesidee,* as independent authorities. This is no fault of Professor and Mrs. Seligman, but it makes nevertheless for confusion.

gang, to shield or protect, saying that the thing has shielded the man.

I was told that in spite of these encouragements a youth who has lost his favourite ox has to be pressed to partake of its cooked flesh, his friends saying to him, "What? Are they not all the cattle of God? And if he has taken one of them you must not refuse its flesh. Why do you sit moping?" I have also heard it said that if the owner refuses its flesh and puts his spear away in the rafters of his byre, the spear may cut his hand or leg some later day because it was put away as though useless. In any case, in the end no Nuer can resist meat. A Nuer once told me wistfully that a man's eye and heart are mournful at the death of his beast but his teeth and stomach are glad. Nuer say that the stomach prays to God independently of the heart.

In taking things God, as we have noted, takes only what is his, but he is compassionate and, as we have also noted, spares a man if he sees that he is poor and miserable (*can*). In talking about these matters with Nuer, I received the impression that, while of course they like to be rich, they think it safer for a man not to have too much good fortune. Pride in the number of his children or cattle may cause God to take them away. For this reason Nuer show great uneasiness if their good fortune is so much as mentioned. It is proper to praise a man's moral qualities, to say that he is brave, generous, or kind, but it is more than rude to remark on his physical well-being, the size of his family, or the number and quality of his beasts and other possessions, for evil consequences may follow. It is what the Nuer generally call *yop.* Thus to say to a man, "Well, you are fat," may make him thin; and it is the ambition of every Nuer to be fat, though I have never seen one who achieved it. It is also very bad to praise a cow, especially to remark on its exceptional milk yield, because it will then cease to give milk. I was told that "only when her husband has married a wife with a cow will a woman praise it," that is, after it has ceased to be her cow. It is also most dangerous to tell a lad who has recently been initiated that the cuts on his forehead are healing well, or indeed to make any allusion to them, because a favourable comment may result in an unhealed spot festering anew. I was often in trouble with Nuer on counts of this kind. I was always reprimanded if I counted children, saying, for instance, "Let me see, so-and-so has four children, has he not? So-and-so, so-and-so, so-and-so, and so-and-so." On one occasion I was eating porridge with Nuer and complimented my host on the size of the meal. Everyone was most embarrassed and I was later taken aside by a Nuer friend and told that I must never make such comments. On another occasion I got into trouble for asking a man in jest, and, I admit, in rather bad taste, whether it was food or beer inside him, for his belly was as tight as a drum. I was told that my question might well make the man sick, and one of those present said that once a man had remarked to him "Well, you are full," and shortly afterwards he was violently sick. The worst offence is to praise a baby. In referring to it one should use some such expression as *"giekeme,"* "this bad thing." When blessing children by spitting on them, which is the Nuer manner of showing favour to a child, kinsmen, and especially kinswomen, utter some opprobrious remarks, sometimes a string of obscenities, over them.

The idea here is not that of the evil eye (*peth*), though the two ideas may in some ways resemble one another and also overlap.[5] In Nuer opinion the evil eye is an act of covetousness or envy, whereas here, I think, the emphasis is on the danger of rejoicing in unusual good fortune lest it should be taken away. There is a feeling that God evens things out, so that if he helps the needy he may take away from those with superfluity. As I understood their view it expresses a certain uneasiness at attention being drawn to possessions lest pride should bring about retribution. That this is their view is further suggested by a number of their stories which relate how God punished hubris. I mention only one in this place, a short myth which reminds us of the story of Elijah and the priests of Baal, and which is obviously either taken over from some foreign people or is a fairly recent creation of Nuer imaginative thought, because it is about the *"Turuk,"* "Turks," a word which among the Nuer, as among the black peoples of the Southern Sudan in general, includes all lighter-skinned northerners with whom they have had dealings, that is, Turks, Egyptians, Arabs and Nubians of the Northern Sudan, and ourselves and other Europeans. The "Turks" compared their guns to God's thunder, and there was a trial of

[5] *Yop* is presumably the same word as the Shilluk *ywop* which Wilhelm Hofmayr (1925: 221) translates by *"böse Blick."*

strength between them and God. God made a huge mud image
of an elephant and told the "Turks" to shoot at it, which they
did to no effect. God then brought clouds and darkness and
thunder and lightning and smashed the image to dust and killed
many of the "Turks" as well because they had compared the gun
he had given them to his power. The point of this story is not
merely that God was stronger than the "Turks" but that he was in
the right and the "Turks" were at fault.

This brings me to an extremely important Nuer concept, an
understanding of which is very necessary to a correct appreciation of their religious thought and practice. This is the concept of
cuong. This word can mean "upright" in the sense of standing,
as, for example, in reference to the supports of byres. It is also
used figuratively for "firmly established," as in the phrase *"be
golle cuong,"* "may his hearth stand," which has the sense of *stet
fortuna domus.* It is most commonly employed, however, with
the meaning of "in the right" in both a forensic and a moral
sense, and when used in a religious context is perhaps best translated "righteousness" in the Old Testament sense of the word.[6]
The discussion in what we would call legal cases is for the purpose of determining who has the *cuong,* the right, in the case, or
who has the most right; and in any argument about conduct
the issue is always whether a person has conformed to the accepted norms of social life, for, if he has, then he has *cuong,* he
has right on his side. We are concerned with the concept here
both because it relates directly to man's behaviour towards God
and other spiritual beings and the ghosts and because it relates
to God in a more indirect way, in that he is regarded as the
founder and guardian of morality. Up to this point I have been
describing Nuer ideas about the nature of God. I shall now describe their ideas about what God requires of them.

I do not want to suggest that God is thought to be an immediate sanction of all right- and wrong-doing, but I must em-
phasise that the Nuer are of one voice in saying that sooner or
later and in one way or another good will follow right conduct and
ill will follow wrong conduct. People may not reap their rewards
for good acts and punishments for bad acts for a long time, but the

---

[6] Where it is a rendering of the Hebrew *SDQ. Vide* W. Robertson
Smith (1902 ed.: 71–72 and 1927: Stanley A. Cook's notes: 675 *seq.*),
also Snaith (1948: Chap. III and 165–67).

consequences of both follow behind (*gwor*) them and in the end catch up on those responsible for them. You give milk to a man when he has no lactating cows, or meat and fish to him when he is hungry, or you befriend him in other ways, though he is no close kinsman of yours. He blesses you, saying that your age-mates will die while your children grow old with you. God will see your charity and give you long life. Those who have lived among the Nuer must have heard, and received, their blessings. My lamented friend, Miss Soule, of the American Presbyterian Mission at Nasir, once related to me how a Nuer woman had told her that her husband wished to throw her monorchid child into a river and how she dissuaded him by saying to him, "May be if we take care of this baby God will do great things for us." Miss Soule was herself often blessed by Nuer, being told that she would have a long life because she cared for orphans and babies whose mothers were unable to suckle them. I have myself had similar experiences during my illnesses in Nuerland. Nuer, who appeared to be unsympathetic at other times, would visit me then and say gently "You will drink Nile water," that is, "You will return to your home"; or "Well, pray to God and tell him that you have come on a journey to the country of the Nuer and that you have not hit anyone or stolen anything or done any bad thing there, and then he will leave you alone"; or "It is nothing. You will not die. This is our earth and you shall not die on it. Why should you die? You have not wronged us, and you are friend to all our children. It (the sickness) is nothing. If you call on God it will finish. Let it blow there, and there, and there (pointing in different directions), let it go to the ends of the earth." As these admonitions imply, if a man does wrong God will sooner or later punish him.

The Nuer have the idea that if a man keeps in the right—does not break taboos, does not wrong others, and fulfils his obligations to spiritual beings and the ghosts and to his kith and kin —he will avoid, not all misfortune, for some misfortunes come to one and all alike, being *"dung cak,"* "the lot of created things," but those extra and special misfortunes which come from *"dueri,"* "faults," and are to be regarded as castigations or corrections. The word *duer* means "a fault" and the verbal form *dwir* means "to be at fault." Like the Hebrew *hātā* and the Greek *hamartia* (Smith 1902: 102–3; Trench 1871: 226–35) and similar words

in other languages, *dwir* has both the sense of missing a mark
aimed at—in throwing a spear, and today also in firing a rifle—and
also of a dereliction, a fault which brings retribution. Nuer class
as faults not only breaches of taboos, most commonly of the
incest taboo, but also wrong conduct towards persons. Any failure to conform to the accepted norms of behaviour towards a
member of one's family, kin, age-set, a guest, and so forth, is
duer, the commission of a fault. A failure to respect them brings
about evil consequences through either an expressed curse or a
silent curse contained in anger and resentment, but the misfortunes which follow are regarded by Nuer as coming ultimately
from God, who supports the cause of the man who has the *cuong,*
the right in the matter, and punishes the person who is at fault
(*dwir*), for it is God alone who makes a curse operative. Nuer
are quite explicit on this point. What then Nuer ideas on the
matter amount to is, in our way of putting it, that if a man wishes
to be in the right with God he must be in the right with men, that
is, he must subordinate his interests as an individual to the moral
order of society. A man must honour his father and his father's
age-mates, a wife must obey her husband, a man must respect his
wife's kin, and so on. If an individual fails to observe the rules
he is, Nuer say, *yong,* crazy, because he not only loses the support of kith and kin but also the favour of God, so that retribution in some form or another and sooner or later is bound to
follow. Therefore Nuer, who are unruly and quarrelsome people,
avoid, in so far as they can restrain themselves, giving gratuitous
offence. Therefore, also, a Nuer who is at fault goes to the person
he has offended, admits the fault, saying to him *"ca dwir,"* "I was
at fault," and he may also offer a gift to wipe out the offence. The
wronged man then blesses him by spitting or blowing water on
him and says that it is nothing and may the man be at peace. He
thereby removes the curse and any resentment he may have in
his heart. Nuer say that God sees these acts and frees the man
from the consequences of his fault. Similarly, the consequences
of faults which are more directly of a religious order like the
breach of a ritual prohibition or the neglect of some spirit, may
be avoided by a timely sacrifice, though Nuer say that sacrifice
without contrition will not avail. But—and this is the point I want
to bring out here—the fact that the consequences of a fault,
whether it be a wrong done to another or a transgression in the

eyes of God or of some spirit, can be stayed by contrition and reparation shows that the consequences of wrong-doing are not what we would call mechanical cause and effect.

That this is so, and there is a moral, and therefore uncertain, element involved is further shown by another fact. In estimating the likelihood, or degree, of misfortune that may be expected to follow from an act, Nuer take deliberation into the reckoning. They distinguish between *duer* and *gwac*. The word *duer,* as we have seen, means a fault, and it normally implies that the fault was deliberate, though, as will be seen later, this is not always or entirely so. *Gwac* means a mistake, an unintentional error and generally one of no great consequence, one in which a serious breach of religious or moral precepts is not involved, such as an unintentional lapse in manners or a slip of the tongue. It implies that the action was incorrect but inadvertent; and the man asks to be excused. In a certain sense, however, in the sense that the act was not deliberate, a more serious fault may be regarded as a mistake, even though it is at the same time a fault, and the fact that it was not a deliberate fault is held to some extent to alter the circumstances. This is very evident in affairs in which damage and compensation are involved, as, for example, in homicide. When a man kills another, how the damage is treated, both with regard to manner and to the amount of compensation demanded, much depends on whether the slaying was premeditated or was the unfortunate outcome of a sudden quarrel or an accident. God also takes deliberation into account in breaches of moral law. Thus it is not thought that children will fall sick if they have incestuous relations in their play "because the children are ignorant of having done wrong." They know no better. Likewise, if two kinsmen have relations with the same girl, which Nuer regard as incest, without knowing that the other was making love to her, "it is not incest because each was unaware that the other was making love to her." Again, it is not thought that a man who commits incest with a kinswoman, not knowing her to be a kinswoman, will suffer any serious, or even any, consequences: "This is not incest because he was unaware of the relationship between them." If a man who respects hearts or lungs of animals eats them not knowing the nature of the meat he eats "this is an accident and his spirit (the spirit of hearts or lungs) knows that it was not done deliberately." He may get a slight illness, but not a serious one. When I was living on the Sobat River news came to our village that some persons in an upstream village had found some meat and had cooked and eaten it, thinking that it was the flesh of some animal crocodiles had mutilated, and that they had later discovered it to be the flesh of a man whom crocodiles had killed and torn to pieces. I was told that these persons would at once have taken *wal nuera,* medicine to cleanse them from pollution, and that while the happening was very disgusting it was unlikely that it would cause death because the flesh was eaten in ignorance of its nature. Nuer say that God may overlook what was done in error. Similarly, they say that he will not allow a curse to harm a man who has done no deliberate wrong.

One can make too rigid distinctions between the meanings of words, and while an error or accident is clearly regarded by Nuer as different from a deliberate and premeditated act, the concepts of *gwac* and *duer* shade into each other. There is perhaps always an element of the unintentional in the worst fault, and a Nuer who has committed a bad fault is inclined to excuse himself, as we would do, by calling it a mistake; but it is also true that, except in matters of no moment, and although the consequences may not be so severe, a wrong act is always a fault, whether it was deliberate or was due merely to forgetfulness or even involuntary, and may involve liability. Thus the children who commit incest in play, the men who in ignorance have relations with the same girl, the man who unknowingly has relations with a kinswoman, and the man who by mistake eats the flesh of his totem have all committed *dueri,* faults, and they cannot be certain that evil consequences will not follow. Likewise a man who inadvertently eats from a dish from which a man with whom his kin have a blood feud has eaten, and a man who appears naked before a kinswoman of his wife (Nuer men normally have no covering), not having noticed her presence, have committed faults. It may well happen that a man does not know he has done wrong till he suffers the consequences of the wrong. For example, a man takes a woman for concubine not knowing that she is distantly related to him, and his children by her die. He then makes enquiries and discovers the relationship. He sinned, like Oedipus, in ignorance, but that did not alter what he had done and, like Oedipus, he paid the penalty of his fault. Even the innocent may suffer, as the example I have just given shows. Indeed the whole human race suffers death on account of what was no more than a trivial oversight. If man had prevented the hyaena and the durra-bird from escaping from heaven there would have been no death. This is the lesson of another story recounted by Father Crazzolara[7] about the origin of death. Like many similar stories it makes death follow from what appears to have been either a mere blunder or, at the worst, a trifling act of malice. When man was created God took a piece of a gourd vessel and threw it into water to indicate that man would live for ever just as the rind would float for ever on the water. He then sent a barren, or divorced, woman to men to tell them that they would live for ever, but, in explaining this to them, she threw, instead of a piece of gourd, a potsherd into the water, and it sank. She then told men that they would all die just as the sherd sank in the water and did not rise to the surface again. In what Father Crazzolara says is a rare variant of this myth, a dragon-fly takes the place of the woman and a piece of ambatch wood and a stone the places of the piece of gourd and the potsherd. Almost fortuitous though these happenings were, what had happened, as we have noted before, could not be made not to have happened. Men have to accept the consequences of their actions whether they are deliberate or not.

Hence when Nuer suffer a misfortune they ponder how it may have come about, for it follows from what has just been said, and from the fact we noted earlier that God is always in the

---

[7] (Schmidt 1949: 16–17). Father Crazzolara says that this myth *"allgemein bekannt ist,"* but I have never myself heard it, and I think that, for the reasons I have given earlier when speaking of the myth about the rope from heaven to earth, it is probably Dinka or of Dinka origin. Miss Huffman (1931: 90) records a different story accounting for the origin of death, though it attributes death to an equally fortuitous cause. The story she tells has probably been taken over by the Nuer in the vicinity of the American Mission at Nasir from the Anuak community who live there. The point of the story does not come out in Miss Huffman's version but is clear in the Anuak version I recorded in Anuakland (Evans-Pritchard and Beaton 1940: 56–57). In the Anuak version God threw a stone into a river so that men would die. Dog, realising the consequences of God's act, tried to persuade the people to get the stone out of the water and, when they refused to do so, himself dived after it. He was not able to lift the stone unaided, and the people, being simple, merely laughed at him; so he had to be content with biting off a bit of the stone and bringing it to them. So man, thanks to dog, lives a long life, even if he dies in the end. Before this happened men used to die for a little while and then came to life again.

right, that if a misfortune comes to a man it is most likely on
account of some fault. This is why on such occasions one hears
so often in Nuer prayers and invocations the plaint "What have
we done?" or "What evil have we done?" So we find that in
invocations at mortuary ceremonies they ask God whether the
man's death was just the lot of all created things or was some
special suffering he had sent them. This is also the reason why
Nuer sacrifices are so often propitiations, expiations, atonements,
and purifications. It is therefore probable that suffering usually
entails a measure of guilt. Nuer search their consciences to discover what fault might have brought it on them, though this is
more evident when a misfortune is only pending and may yet be
stayed or though it has fallen may yet be mitigated, for if the
fault can be determined they will know better what action to
take. When the misfortune is complete and their condition can
in no way be alleviated they are less interested in its cause and
accept its accomplishment with sorrow and resignation.

When Nuer suffer they sometimes at once know what is the
cause of their suffering because they are well aware of some
particular fault. They sometimes, as we would say, tempt God
by doing what they know to be wrong, hoping that it will not
matter very much, such as having relations with a woman which
are incestuous but not very incestuous. If trouble comes they
know that this is the cause, for they have said that whether the
relationship was too close for congress would be decided by any
consequences of it. They now discover that it was more serious
than they thought. Very often Nuer neglect their duties to their
various spirits. They omit or forget to sacrifice to them or they fail
to dedicate cows to them or they use their sacred cows for marriage and find that they cannot replace them or do not trouble
to do so. If a misfortune falls on them they then know that it is
due to the anger of a spirit. Often, however, they are in doubt
about the cause and confused and bewildered. It may be that the
suffering is just something, like death in old age, which had to
happen. It may be due to a fetish or the evil eye. It may arise
from bad intentions or evil dispositions. I will not discuss here
all the possible causes of suffering nor their moral significance for
Nuer. I wish only to stress that Nuer generally feel that suffering
is due to some fault of theirs, and it is probable that there is
always an element of this feeling in every situation of misfortune,

whatever its immediate cause may be thought to be; and also that they trust that God will intervene on their behalf if they pray to him for help.

It is in the light of the cardinal concepts of what we may call Nuer mystical and moral theology of which I have given some account in this address that their prayers and sacrifices are to be interpreted.

A. P. Elkin

To UNDERSTAND the nature of Australian totemism, it is necessary to study the significance and function of the various
forms of it that are found in Australia. By the form is meant the
manner in which totems performing the same function are distributed amongst the individuals or groups of the tribe; thus, there is
sex totemism, clan totemism, moiety totemism, and so on. By the
significance is meant the meaning which the form of totemism
bears to the individual concerned; it may be his assistant, his
guardian, his mate, or the symbol of his social or cult group.
Finally, the function refers to the part played by the particular
form of totemism in the general system of social integration; thus,
it may control the marriage relationships between clans, preserve
moral and social sanctions, or provide a psychological adjustment
to the problems of nature and life. It will therefore be obvious
that though we may systematize our study under the heading of
"forms," we must keep all three aspects of the problem continually before us.

INDIVIDUAL TOTEMISM

In several areas of Australia, more particularly in the eastern
States, medicine-men and those who work magic stand each
in a special relationship to one species of nature, usually some
animal or reptile. This species acts as the performer's assistant,
going forth either to work his will for good or ill on the patient
or the victim, as the case may be, or to gather information from

Reprinted from *Oceania* 4 (2), 1933: 114–31 by permission of the author
and of the editor, *Oceania*.

a distance. Thus, amongst the Kamilaroi and most tribes of New South Wales, any person who wishes to acquire skill in magic must acquire a special relation to some species of animal. Amongst the Kurnai, too, such a person had his "familiar" animal, or reptile. This was both in him as a spirit or second self, and also externalized in the species, perhaps especially present in a tamed member of the species. The taming and keeping of one of the medicine-man's personal or individual totemic species certainly impressed other persons, who readily believed that this very creature worked the will of its "owner," especially in the dark of the night (Howitt 1904: 147, 387–88; Radcliffe-Brown 1930; Elkin 1932a).

This is akin to the belief that the medicine-men of Central, North and North-Western Australia, like those of Eastern Australia, have in their "insides" spirit-snakes associated with or derived from the mythical rainbow-serpent. These spirit-snakes do the same work for their possessors as do the personal totems referred to, but they are not members of a natural species, and so cannot be seen under natural conditions.[1]

The personal totem in South-East Australia is usually given by medicine-men, and though it is usually only given to persons who are destined, or who desire, to work magic, yet the somewhat unsatisfactory evidence suggests that other persons may also receive one.[2]

Further, a dying medicine-man may leave his totem to someone else. Thus, there is a "property" aspect to the individual totem, but that is not all, for there is a living bond between the totem and the totemite. Amongst the Yualayi, an injury to the former

[1] Spencer and Gillen 1899: 481, 484–86; Spencer 1914: 297–99, 326; Elkin 1931a: 349–52; Howitt 1904: 405–8, 523. One of my informants in Dampier Land, North-West Australia, put a medicine-man to the test by asking to be shown the spirit-snakes and spirit-dogs which the practitioner claimed to possess. The latter responded by producing something, if only illusion, in the shadow of a tree made by the uncertain light of the moon. He also proved to my informant's satisfaction that he could send his "spirit-dogs" out and gather information of what was happening at a distance.

[2] It is given in the Wiradjeri tribe during initiation, by way of hypnotic suggestion so Howitt thought; amongst the Yualayi a medicine-man may give an individual totem which is a sort of "alter ego," not only to a person as a means of magical power, but also to a sick person as a means of recovery; the strength of the animal goes into the patient, making him strong again.

hurts the latter. Moreover, in South-East Australia the totemite does not eat his personal totem, while the totem on its part assists and guards the totemite. Now, this is as it should be, for the totem is "himself," being both within and without him; the totem-species symbolizes and is the sacramental form of, his own self or soul, likewise he is the sacrament of the "soul" of the species; thus personal totemism is akin to social totemism.

SEX TOTEMISM

In most of the tribes of South-Eastern Australia, from Lake Eyre east and south-east to the coasts of New South Wales and Victoria, each sex has its own totem; two specimens of small bush, Dieri tribe; bat and night owl, Kamilaroi, *etc.*, and Wotjobaluk; bat and wood-pecker, Worimi; emu-wren and superb warbler, Kurnai; bat and emu-wren, Yuin. The sex-totem represents the sex-dichotomy of the tribe, and symbolizes the solidarity of each sex. It is an emblem. If the men hurt the women's totem, it is regarded as an injury or an insult to the women, or, at least, it is a method of teasing them; such action is resented and quarrelling and fighting follow. The same happens if the women hurt the men's totem. But it is apparently more than an emblem, or the rallying point of the sentiments associated with the sex concerned. The Wotjobaluk say that "the life of a bat is the life of a man" (Howitt 1904: 148–51; Elkin 1932a and unpublished field notes). In other words, sex totemism enshrines a belief in a common life shared by man and natural species, though only symbolized by two representatives of the latter. Threlkeld gathered that the Awabakal based this belief on a transformation of a man and a woman respectively into the bat and the wood-pecker. R. H. Mathews interpreted the sex-totem as the friend of the sex concerned; in north-eastern South Australia the sex-totem is the mate, and amongst the Kurnai it is referred to as the brother or sister, as the case may be (Threlkeld: 92; Mathews n.d.: 137; Elkin, unpublished field notes; Howitt 1904: 273). Indeed, Howitt thought that the sex-totems Yeerung (emu-wren) and Djeetgun (superb warbler) were eponymous ancestors, one of either sex, who were commemorated in the initiation ceremonies; the great central idea of Kurnai society is community of descent. "Every descendant of Yeerung is a brother, every descendant of

Djeetgun is a sister; all else are Brajerak, savage men, aliens to their blood" (Fison and Howitt 1880: 232–33). The belief that all the women of a community have a different ancestral source from the men may seem strange to us, but the associated aboriginal belief in pre-existence of spirits makes it logical enough to the native mind. And, at least, it does emphasize the solidarity of each of the sexes.

Until quite recently this form of totemism had only been found in South-East Australia, and in most of this region it is associated with matrilineal moieties and with matrilineal social totemic clans. Thus, in a region where the matrilineal principle receives greater emphasis in social organization than elsewhere in Australia, with the possible exception of a small area in the south-western corner of the Continent (Radcliffe-Brown 1930: 216–19), we find this special emphasis on the difference between the solidarity of the sexes; it is as though the women said, "not only must descent of the moiety and clan be reckoned through us, but also we as a sex are to be marked off from the men as a sex, by the possession of a distinct symbol and by a certain type of standardized behaviour associated with it, namely, a ritual combat." This suggestion is supported by a Kurnai custom: If there were marriageable young girls and the marriageable young men did not propose marriage, the elder women took the initiative and caused a ritual combat, in the manner described; the men then killed the women's totem and so caused another fight. These sex-totem combats had the moral effect of inducing the young men to talk of marriage and arrange elopements with the young women (Howitt 1904: 149, 273–74).

This, however, cannot be regarded as a generalization, for the tribes of the coast of New South Wales and of Gippsland (Victoria) do not possess moieties, while their totemic clans are localized and apparently patrilineal, and, further, one small group of tribes with sex-totems on the immediate west of Gippsland had patrilineal moieties and possibly also patrilineal totemic clans.

Finally, sex totemism has recently been reported from the north-western part of the Aranda tribe on the Finke River, Central Australia, and the Matuntara, a neighbouring Aluridja tribe. Each sex is symbolized, as in the Lake Eyre group of tribes to the south-east, by a bush or plant.[3] The Aranda have patrilineal moieties which function in ceremonial life, while their cult totemism is local and conceptional. But though the latter tends to be patrilineal, as a result of patrilocal marriage, yet the actual determination of the child's totem depends on the mother, who announces the totemic locality in which she realizes conception, that is, the entry of the spirit-child into her womb, either in a dream or in waking life. The Aluridja tribes, which join the Aranda on the west and south-west, do not possess any moieties, but their method of determining the child's totem is the same as in the Aranda tribe. Incidentally, in the latter, a person always respects his mother's totem. The women, too, take part in a dance, the *Wuljankura,* which not only marks and strengthens their solidarity as a sex, but also initiates love intrigues, and, at times, fights between men over women (Roheim 1933: 211, 226, 241–48; Spencer and Gillen 1927, I: 76–78, 117; Fry 1933: 251–53). This is comparable to the initiative taken by the Kurnai women in elopement and marriage.

Thus, in this region sex totemism is associated with an emphasis on the rôle of motherhood in the determination of the totem, with a respect for the mother's totem, and with a definite ceremonial solidarity of women. But in spite of this, it is not yet possible to establish any absolute connection between sex totemism and a special prominence of the principle of motherhood in the descent or determination of totems. Sufficient evidence may be produced in the future to establish such a generalization, and a fuller knowledge of the social and totemic organization of the south-east coast might also have supported it, instead of appearing to invalidate it. But, of course, future field work may show that such theorizing is futile. At present we must be satisfied to say that sex totemism is a local specialization of totemism, confined, as far as we know, to South-East Australia and to the tribes on the Finke.

MOIETY, SECTION AND SUB-SECTION TOTEMISM

These forms of totemism have already been fully discussed. The first is the most important of the three, for it symbolizes a dual

---

[3] Roheim 1933: 221. *Worakililja,* the male sex-totem, means "boys' grass," and *nyukaranpa,* the women's totem, "girls' grass."

organization which functions in the social and ceremonial life of
the tribe. It expresses an opposition between the moieties, but an
opposition which is not disruptive, for each moiety is dependent
on the other, both in social and ritual life. Now, this dichotomy is totemic in that the moiety totem is not merely symbolical
of membership of a common grouping, but expresses a relationship of a kinship nature between all the members of a moiety.
Where this is matrilineal, as in South-East Australia and in a
small region in the south-western corner of the Continent, it
symbolizes the sharing of a common life based on the inheritance
of the one flesh and blood through the mothers. This, as we shall
see, is the fundamental significance of matrilineal social totemism. The patrilineal descent of the moieties, however, in Central
Australia, East Arnhem Land, Northern Kimberley and part of
Cape York Peninsula, is correlated with a strong local organization into patrilineal hordes combined with a theory of localized
human spirit-centres, and of localized cult totemism, which is
either patrilineal or tends to be so, and is ideally so.

But in either case, moiety totemism is a method of classifying
nature and man into two main divisions, based on a special relationship which is believed to exist between the human beings
and natural objects and species grouped in each moiety. Moreover, all the natural objects and species are in some degree or
other objects of ritual attitudes as far as the members of the
moiety to which they belong are concerned. This is true whether
the moiety is subdivided into matrilineal social clans or patrilineal cult clans, and whether these clans have multiple totems, as
is very common in North-West Australia, or subsidiary totems
as in some south-eastern and central tribes.

Section Totemism

Section totemism is a method of dividing the members of a
tribe into four groups, each of which is symbolized by, or associated with, one or a number of natural species. In some tribes
of Eastern Australia it is a system of classification of man and
nature on the basis of a kinship which is held to exist between
the human beings and the natural species belonging to each section. In such tribes a person adopts a ritual attitude towards his
own or even all the totems of his section, and expresses sorrow
when one of them is killed. Reciprocally, the section-totem is

frequently regarded as the mate or guardian of the human members of the section. The main development of this form of totemism is in the strongly marked matrilineal area of Eastern Australia, and, incidentally, it is always indirect matrilineal in descent.[4]

Sub-section Totemism

Sub-section totemism, which is also indirect matrilineal in descent, is primarily a principle of dividing man and natural species, at least, those of social and economic importance, into eight groups. There are two main forms of it. In one, the sub-section totems are associated with local spirit-children centres, as in Eastern Kimberley and the Mungarai and Yungman tribes. In the other form, which is found in East Arnhem Land, this association does not exist, and sub-section totemism is a variety of social totemism quite distinct from the localized cult totemism and spirit-children centres which may or may not co-exist in the same tribe. But, whatever be the reason for it, the sub-section system exists, and was spreading in part of the region of Australia in which cult totemism was highly developed, and though it may be primarily a form of social totemism, yet it has to come to grips with cult totemism. Indeed, until it does so, it does not become an important factor in social integration.[5]

Where sub-section totemism has been best studied, namely, Eastern Kimberley, there is the characteristic totemic bond of kinship, and a ritual attitude is adopted towards the totem. The totem, too, is the friend of the members of the sub-section whose totem it is.

[4] In some tribes, the Weilwan and others, the sections are only a factor modifying clan totemism, though this may only be a stage in the development or spread of section totemism. Little is known of this form of totemism in Western Australia. Elkin 1933c: 74–79.

[5] The spread of a form of sub-section matrilineal social totemism amongst the Nangiomeri and in East Arnhem Land probably means that the sub-section system is bringing with it the totems which are localized in the tribe or tribes from which it is spreading, but which do not belong to the cult life of the tribes who have only recently acquired it. Elkin 1933b: 59–60; 1933c: 67.

Totemic clans in Australia are either matrilineal, patrilineal or
else are a variety of local grouping which is based on the chance
association of conception or birth with localized totemic centres.
In any case, the members of a clan regard themselves as related
to one another, and also to some natural species or object, the
totem, toward which they usually observe some form of ritual
attitude, refusing to kill or eat it, or making it the centre of
organized ceremonies on which the life of the totem and of the
tribe is believed to depend. This relationship, which is expressed
in totemism, may be based on what are regarded as blood-ties,
on membership of a common horde-country, or, primarily, on a
mythological and "spiritual" ancestry.

Matrilineal Social Clan Totemism

In the first case we have matrilineal social clan totemism, which
is found in most of Eastern Australia, Queensland, New South
Wales, Western Victoria and eastern South Australia, and also
in a small area of the south-west of Western Australia. To understand its significance we must grip the aboriginal view of life
according to which a person receives or inherits his body, his
flesh and blood, from and through his mother, mother's
mother, and so on, that is, a series of women related matriline-
ally. This seems obvious to a people who ignore or are ignorant
of the physiology of reproduction. The persons so related,
mother, mother's brother, mother's mother, mother's mother's
brother, and others in the mother's line, are one flesh, for all
have ultimately received their body, their means of incarnation,
from and through the womb of the same matrilineal ancestress.
Now, it is this belief which the matrilineal social totem symbolizes
and which underlies the reference to the totem as flesh, as is the
custom in eastern South Australia. Further, because the totem
is one's flesh, in many tribes it is neither injured, killed nor eaten,
except on very rare occasions of hunger and after regret and
sorrow have been expressed. A person respects the symbol, the
"flesh," of his mother's line. Likewise, the exogamy of the matrilineal social totemic clan is observed, for it is based on the
fundamental aboriginal incest laws, which forbid marriage with

sister or mother, and all who belong to the one totem, being one flesh, are brothers and sisters, or children and mothers.

This is the human side of matrilineal social totemism; there is also the "nature" aspect. In the first place, it implies a belief in a common life shared by man and natural species, for the totem is more than a name or emblem; something of the life of man is in the life of the totemic species, and *vice versa,* and there is a causal relationship between the good or ill of the one and of the other.[6] The clan and its totemic species are grouped together because they share mystically in a common life.

This principle is also expressed in what may be termed the classificatory function of matrilineal clan totemism, meaning by this the classification of man and natural species in totemic clans. Reference has already been made to it in the discussion of moiety totemism. Each clan includes not only a matrilineal group of people and one species of nature, the totem, but also a number of other species and natural objects, often referred to as sub-totems. These are subsidiary to the clan-totem in that they are classified in the group named after it. It may be sometimes possible to detect a reason, such as association by similarity or contiguity, for the classification, but fundamentally, this is based on the oneness of life of nature and man, and on the necessity man feels to bring the former into his social as well as economic system.

Patrilineal Clan Totemism

This is found in several parts of Western Australia, in the Northern Territory, in Cape York Peninsula, the coast of New South Wales and the neighbouring part of the Queensland coast, a small area in central Victoria, north-eastern South Australia and the lower Murray district. It is distinguished from matrilineal clan totemism not only by its method of descent, but also by its relation to the local hordes and, in most cases, by its function. Matrilineal clans obviously do not coincide with the patrilineal local hordes, for members of a horde may belong to a number of different matrilineal totemic clans according to the totems of their mothers who, through marriage, have been brought into the horde

[6] Amongst the tribes of north-west Victoria, to kill a person's totem is to cause an actual injury to that person; and to dream about one's own totem "means that someone has done something to it for the purpose of harming the sleeper or one of his totemites." Howitt 1904: 145.

and its country. Further, the members of any one matrilineal horde may be distributed throughout several local hordes. In patrilineal clan totemism, however, the local horde is also a totemic clan, and a survey of the facts suggests that the patrilineal descent of the totem is a corollary of the patrilineal descent of the local horde. Likewise, the exogamy of the patrilineal clan is really the exogamy of the local horde (Elkin 1932b: 329–31; 1933a: 265–67), and in the regions where patrilineal clan totemism has been adequately studied, the clan-totem symbolizes the local solidarity which underlies this rule of exogamy. Further, this solidarity is based on the belief that the spirits of the members of the local horde pre-existed in definite spirit-centres in the horde-country, so that the bond between them and their "country" is a spiritual one. Again, the pre-existent spirits and the spirit-centres are by myths associated with, or related to, heroes or ancestors who belong to the same totem or totems as do the present members of the horde.

Now this brings us to the important distinction between matrilineal and patrilineal clan totemism in Australia. The former is social in function: it stands for social relationships—relationships of flesh and blood, and it is an important factor in marriage organization. Patrilineal clan totemism, however, does not add anything to the marriage rules associated with the primary principle of local exogamy, nor does it symbolize the physiological relationship between parent and child. It does, of course, symbolize the solidarity of the local horde, even where there is multiple totemism as in the Karadjeri tribe. But, with the possible exception of a few tribes like the Yaralde of the Lower Murray River, and the Yuin of the south coast of New South Wales,[7] this solidarity, in so far as it is totemic, is not primarily social.

This will be made clearer by referring to those totemic clans of Central Australia and western South Australia which are neither matrilineal nor patrilineal. Membership is determined in them by the totemic locality in which conception is believed to have occurred (Aranda), or in which the child is born (western South Australia). As a result of patrilocal marriage, this is very often

[7] A. R. Radcliffe-Brown 1930: 223, 230. Our knowledge is really insufficient to assert that the totemism of the Yaralde and Yuin was social only, and not also ceremonial. Nothing is known of the patrilineal clans which are said to have existed in some Victorian tribes.

in the horde-country of the father, and therefore, probably also in his totemic locality. Moreover, there is always a tendency, at least with the breakdown of tribal life, for the descent to become patrilineal. The point, however, is that fundamentally a person's totem is the totem of the locality to which his pre-existent spirit belonged. In these regions, too, the totem has nothing to do with marriage; it is not exogamous; marriage is controlled by considerations of kinship and horde-membership. Moreover, it does not symbolize the solidarity of the local horde, for members of the one horde who are "found," that is, conceived, or born in different totemic "countries" from their fathers, will belong to different totemic clans; there are, however, signs of this even in the Karadjeri and Waramunga tribes with their normal patrilineal totemic clan-hordes (Elkin 1933a: 266–68; 1933c: 70).

All this, however, shows what is the real significance of the variety of totemism with which we are dealing, whether its descent be patrilineal or according to some fortuitous principle associated with conception and birth. It is not concerned with everyday social relationships, but with spiritual beliefs and the cult life. The members of such a totemic clan are joint owners of a set of myths and rites which centre around a hero or heroes of their own totemic clan, and generally, too, around the species which gives them their totemic name. This species is one which is specially associated with the horde-locality and is of economic or other significance. The totem marks the share of a group of people, the totemites, in the secret and sacred life of the tribe. The term for the cult-totem means dreaming. In this sense it signifies that state of action which is beyond, and not conditioned by, the limitations of space and time, though it is expressed in these. It is the long-past time, in which natural features took on their present form and in which present-day customs and laws were instituted and made. It is the "eternal dream-time"—a time which is past and yet is present, for the great heroes still live in spirit; they are symbolized by sacred objects, both artificial and natural, and are commemorated in myth and ritual (Elkin 1932c: 119–38).

Now the cult-totem, called *bugari* (Karadjeri), *altjira* (Aranda), and so on, denotes the share of the knowledge, myths, rites and symbols which belong to the clan, and of which the clan is the custodian. For example, to have the kangaroo cult-totem, or "dreaming," is to have that share of the tribal secrets, its myths, rites, sacred sites and sanctions, which is denoted by the kangaroo, and which refers to the actions of a tribal hero who belonged to the kangaroo totem, and may also refer to actual kangaroos of the dream-time. It is the duty of the members of this clan to guard and hand on these secrets, to perform rites which, being enactments of the myths, ensure the preservation of the clan's share of the tribal history and sanctions, and in certain cases ensure the increase of natural species (usually the clan-totem) and the continuance of the normal functioning of nature. Thus, the cult-totem denotes membership of a secret and sacred cult-society or lodge, of which there are several in each tribe.

The question arises: why should the symbol of such a cult-society be a natural species or object, a totem? The answer is that the Australian is not only concerned with his tribal history and social and ritual sanctions, but also with the necessity of living in a condition of harmony and co-operation with nature. His life depends on its formal functioning, on the regular order of the seasons and the increase of its species. The life of nature and his own life are obviously bound up together; apart from the former he cannot exist, and so real is this fact that he expresses it in myth and rite, and in such a way as though it were also true, that apart from his ritual acts, nature would not be able to maintain its ordered way. Thus, nature is brought into the social and ritual pattern of life. Just as in matrilineal totemism, man and his totem are one "flesh," so in patrilineal and local cult totemism they are bound together in the common belief in pre-existence of spirits; man and natural species alike pre-exist in spirit-centres from which, usually as a result of ritual observances, the spirits go forth to be incarnated, and so ensure the maintenance and increase of both.

Again, in coming to grips with his environment, man brings nature into his social and religious life by a process of personification. Natural species often act in myth and ritual in a personal way, though in some cases they are mainly totemic symbols of human heroes. But in any case, they are closely bound up with the sanctions of moral and social life. The kangaroo hero ordained this, the wild-cat hero introduced that, the iguana hero instituted those rites, and so on. In other words, the Australian, the primitive food-gatherer who depends wholly, and indeed parasitically, from our point of view, on the unaided processes of nature, interprets on the one hand nature and its species as personal and as part of his own moral and social order, and on the other hand, he symbolizes his own individual social life under terms drawn from nature, a symbolism based on the unity of life which he believes exists between natural species and himself.

The cult-totem, then, is no mere emblem, but is the symbol of the aboriginal religious and philosophical view of life and the universe. It may be asked why there should be more than one cult-totem in a tribe. The reason is based apparently on the subdivision of the tribe into families, which are the fundamental units, and into hordes which are groups of families related in the patrilineal line and by ties of propinquity. Each horde is associated with a definite locality, and like the latter is symbolized by one or more of the natural species[8] which are found there. Such symbols are its totems.

This locality is the part of nature with which the local group concerned has to come into special relationship, and it does so not only by economic activity, but also by making the particular totem or totems which are its symbols and links with nature, the centre of a cult life—a life of myth and ritual, sacred sites and symbols. Further, as there are several human segments, that is, hordes or clans, in each tribe, each with its relationship to a particular part of nature, so there will be at least as many cult-clans, or cult-societies as they may be called. Incidentally, this implies a system of co-operation between the various cult-clans, each of which depends on the others to preserve those ritual relationships which exist between them and their respective sections of nature, especially as represented by their totems.

With regard to the taboo on killing and eating the totem, we find that it is widely associated with matrilineal social totemism;

[8] Patrilineal cult-clans frequently, as in the Karadjeri and the North Kimberley tribes, possess multiple totemism; each clan is associated with several totems, and any one individual may have more than one of them. In the performance of increase ceremonies members of the one horde, but of several totems, may combine, as in the Kariera tribe, or the headman of the horde may perform the ceremonies for several totem-species. Of course, the general custom is for the members of the totem to perform the increase ceremony for their totem, though they may be assisted by members of some other totems, according to moiety or other rules. Multiple totemism tends to be a system of classification of natural species, and there is even in one region in east-central Western Australia an intertribal system of classifying clans and their totems into totemic divisions. (See Radcliffe-Brown 1930: 214; 1929: 304–9.)

very little is known about patrilineal social totemism, but there was no taboo on eating the totem in the Yaralde tribe (Radcliffe-Brown 1918: 241); it is definitely absent in some regions of patrilineal cult totemism, as in north-east South Australia, while the evidence is conflicting for parts of the Kimberley, but Spencer and Gillen report that there is a strict taboo on eating the patrilineal cult-totem in the Northern Territory; this is also true of the local cult-totem of the Aranda and Aluridja tribes of Central Australia and western South Australia. As the restriction on killing or eating also prevails in at least some instances of moiety, section and sub-section totemism (Spencer and Gillen 1899: 326–27; 1927 I: 80–82; Elkin 1931b: 69; 1933a: 60; 1933c: 76, 83), we can say that whether the totem symbolizes the matrilineal physiological relationship or the membership of a cult society and a common relationship to a mythological ancestor or hero and spirit-centre, there is a very general tendency to regard it as one's relation, and, therefore, worthy of care and respect.[9]

DREAM TOTEMISM

In this form of totemism the totem represents the totemite in dreams, especially in the dreams of other people. So far, this seems only to have been reported by myself, but I have no doubt about its existence in the two areas in which my main work has been done, namely, North-Western Australia, and north-east and western South Australia and adjacent regions. These areas belong to the great cult-totem region of Australia; as that is the case, and as the cult-totem is known as "dreaming," we might expect it to perform the function of a dream-totem. Now, this is true for the Dieri and kindred tribes of north-eastern South Australia, the Macumba sub-tribe of the Aranda, the Aluridja tribes of western South Australia, and the Karadjeri and Yauor of the Southern Kimberley. But it is not the case with the tribes of the Great Victoria Desert, Western Australia, although they have cult-totems, and use the same term, *dʒugur,* dreaming, for them as do the Aluridja tribes in the north-west corner of South Australia. More-

[9] In north-east South Australia there is a strict taboo on the matrilineal social totem, but a person may eat his patrilineal cult-totem. In the latter case, however, there is a ritual eating after the increase of the species following on the increase ceremony.

over, in both areas the cult-totem is the totem of the locality in which a person is born. But the dream-totem is connected with the first sickness of pregnancy. If, after having partaken of some article of food, a woman becomes sick, and later on dreams of a spirit-child, she realizes that a spirit-child has entered her womb with, or in the form of, the natural species thus eaten. This species is the child's dream-totem. It is the symbol and, indeed, the sacrament, of its incarnation. Amongst the Forrest River tribes the father or mother dreams of the child's dream-totem and then informs him, while in the Wurara, and probably in the Ungarinyin tribe also, the dream-totem is the mother's brother's patrilineal clan-totem. Further research, however, would possibly reveal some further significance in both these cases. I was unable to discover that any ritual attitude was observed towards the dream-totem, unless it were already respected on account of its cult significance.

There are, then, several forms of totemism in Australia, namely, individual, sex, moiety, section, sub-section, matrilineal social clan, patrilineal social clan, patrilineal cult-clan, localized cult-clan and dream totemism. A number of them may be found in one tribe, that is, one person may have several kinds of totem; thus, in north-eastern South Australia each person belongs to a moiety, has a sex-totem, a matrilineal social totem ("flesh"), a patrilineal cult-totem which is related to localized totemic-centres, and which also functions as a dream-totem, and, in addition, he inherits for his life only, but not to pass on to his children, nor to his sister's children, a knowledge of his mother's brother's patrilineal cult-totem; this gives him the privilege and responsibility of assisting in historical and increase ceremonies connected with it. In the Northern Kimberley tribes a person has a moiety totem, a patrilineal local horde totem, and a dream-totem. In the Southern Aranda each man has his patrilineal cult-totem, which is also a dream-totem, and also a share in the cult of his mother's brother's (that is, his mother's) cult-totem, while in the rest of the Aranda the individual definitely has some association with his mother's cult-totem, as well as his own localized (conceptional) cult-totem.

MAN, SOCIETY AND NATURE

The various forms of totemism may be summarized into three
types: (1) individual totemism; (2) social totemism, which includes sex, moiety, section and, to some extent at least, sub-section
totemism, matrilineal and patrilineal social totemism; and (3)
cult-totemism, which is either patrilineal or else is organized solely
on some principle of locality associated with conception or birth.
Dream totemism may be a derivative of this, though its function
appears to be social, and in the Forrest River district it seems
to be individual in form.

The second and third types may be classified together as group
totemism, and so distinguished from individual totemism. But in
all the forms there is one basis, a belief in the oneness of life which
is shared by man and natural species. It is on this foundation that
the totem is the assistant, the guardian, mate, "flesh," "father,"
"ancestor," name, or emblem of the totemites, and that social
totemism enters into marriage organization. On the other hand,
for the same reason, man respects his totem, takes up ritual
attitudes towards it, and even, in many tribes, performs ceremonies for its increase. Further, natural species not only share
man's life, but also, because they and he are interdependent, they
are brought into his social and ritual organization. This is the real
meaning of the statement that totemism is a ritual attitude to nature. Again, the bearing of totemic names is not based merely on
the necessity for social groups to have emblems, especially emblems associated with social and economic life, for the name
stands for a community of nature between the group and its totem.
Further, the grouping of natural species and objects as subsidiary
totems, within the human totemic groups, moieties, clans or sections, is not merely a method of classifying nature and so bringing
it into the social order, but is an expression of the idea that man
and nature form one corporate whole—a whole which is living
and social.

Finally, the rites to increase the supply of the totem species
express this same kinship of man and nature. These rites are
performed by fully initiated members of the cult-clans at sacred
sites, usually at prescribed times of the year. The sites and the
rites are usually secret, wholly or in part, and they are sanctified

by myths. The purpose is to send forth and make available for the increase of the species the spirits which pre-exist at the totemic centre, or in some more vague way. The ritual is not an attempt to control nature magically, but is a method of expressing man's needs and his desire for the maintenance of the normal in nature, and a way of co-operating with nature at just those seasons when the particular species should increase. It is not an attempt to bring about the irregular and extraordinary, but, rather, to maintain the regular. It is a system of co-operation with nature, which is both economic and psychological in purpose; it expresses economic facts and needs, and also gives confidence in the processes of nature and hope for the future. And all this is brought about by a ritual relationship with the pre-existent spirits of natural species, by a ritual standardized by tradition and performed in religious manner and faith, and by preserving continuity with the long-past period of creative activity and institution founding.

We have still to wait for some thorough studies of increase rites and the beliefs expressed in them, by students versed in the tribal tongue. But evidence is already showing that in some cases at least, the spirits of culture-heroes and ancestors are intimately concerned with these rites, and are indeed the very centre of them (Elkin 1933a: 296; McConnel 1931: 41). In any case, the belief in the pre-existence of spirits which lies at the basis of these rites, as of the increase of mankind, shows that Australian totemism is definitely animistic in nature, and not pre-animistic, as Durkheim fain would hold. It is true that the Australian believes that there is a common life principle in man and nature, such as Wandjina in the Ungarinyin tribe, and that this may be regarded as a totemic principle, but even in social totemism this is expressed in definite human personalities, and in a personification of natural species, while in cult-totemism, not only are natural species personified in myth, but the belief in the pre-existence and incarnation of individual human and natural spirits is the very core of the philosophy of life. If we also remember the aboriginal view of the totem as "dreaming," and the belief in a dream-totem, we must realize that we are face to face with an animistic view of life and the universe.

TOTEMISM AND THE PAST

Finally, totemism is a mechanism for preserving continuity with the past, a principle which is essential for the cohesion of any society. It does this by its system of myths, rites and sites. This is especially the function of cult-totemism, though, of course, all important social ritual performs it, but we do not know to what extent the rites of tribes which apparently only possessed social totemism, were coloured by their totemism. The idea of continuity, however, is enshrined in the very term for the cult-totem, the "dream-time"; very often the question "what is your totem?" brings as a reply, not just the name of an animal or plant, or even of a human totemic hero, but a myth enshrining some chapter of tribal history, and some sanction for customs and rites. Cult-totemism claims to be history, and as far as the natives are concerned, is history, as any field worker knows who has heard and watched the old men explaining a totemic rite or myth to the young men who have seen or heard it for the first time.

Thus, totemism provides a link with, and a basis in, the past—a past which is still present, for its personalities are still concerned with tribal life, and indeed, in the belief of many tribes, still enter into it.

Totemism, then, is our key to the understanding of aboriginal philosophy of life and the universe—a philosophy which regards man and nature as one corporate whole for social, ceremonial, and religious purposes, a philosophy which is from one aspect pre-animistic, but from another is animistic, a philosophy which is historical, being built on the heroic acts of the past which provide the sanctions for the present, a philosophy which, indeed, passes into the realm of religion and provides that faith, hope and courage in the face of his daily needs, which man must have if he is to persevere and persist, both as an individual and as a social being.

8 JÍVARO SOULS

Michael J. Harner

T HE JÍVARO proper (*untsuri šuara*) of eastern Ecuador have
long been famous for their warlike practices,[1] but the assumptions about reality upon which they predicate such behavior
have not been systematically studied and analyzed. A very important series of these assumptions is to be found in the Jívaro
ideas concerning souls. Among these concepts has recently been
discovered a deep-seated belief that killing leads to the acquisition
of souls which provide a supernatural power conferring immunity

Reprinted from *The American Anthropologist* 64 (2), 1962: 258–72, by
permission of the author and the American Anthropological Association.

[1] This tribe (dialect group) dwells, roughly speaking, between the Río
Pastaza in the north and the upper Río Zamora in the south; and from the
3,500 foot contour elevation of the eastern slope of the Andes in the west
to the Río Panguí in the east. The *untsuri šuara* comprise the Jívaroan tribe
which is usually referred to in the existing literature as the "Jívaro proper,"
"Jívaro," "Jíbaro," "Ecuadorian Jívaro," or "Shuara." This last term,
šuara, does not mean "Jívaro," as often has been stated, but is used by
the Jívaro proper to refer to any Indian or group of Indians without regard to cultural or linguistic affiliation. "*Untsuri šuara*," meaning "numerous Indians," is the designation applied to this tribe by its close eastern
Jívaroan neighbor, the Achuara tribe (*ačuara šuara*). Most of the serious
anthropological information published on Jívaroan culture so far has been
on the *untsuri šuara* or Jívaro proper. The other Jívaroan tribes definitely
known to be in existence today are the Achuara (Achual), Huambisa, and
Aguaruna.

The following Jívaro orthography is partially based on that developed
by Glen Turner of the Summer Institute of Linguistics. He is not responsible, however, for oversimplifications presented here. These approximate values are assigned to the following phonemes:

Vowels
- a Spanish *a*
- ĕ English *i* in sit
- i Spanish *i* (nasalized when adjacent to *n*)
- u Spanish *u*

from death. The purpose of the present paper is to outline some
of the basic elements of these beliefs with the hope of providing a
greater insight into Jívaro behavior.[2]

The emphasis here will be on presenting new data collected
in 1956–57,[3] but the concluding paragraphs of the paper embody
a commentary on relevant statements in the major publications
dealing with this subject. At the outset it should be mentioned
that I took the two most useful works on the Jívaro (Karsten 1935;
Stirling 1938) into the field and went over them in detail with
native informants. Accordingly, points of difference between the
following material and that given by Karsten and Stirling should
definitely be taken by the reader to indicate modification or refu-
tation of the previously published statements, at least in regard to
the Jívaro proper.[4]

Consonants

č Spanish *ch*
h English *h* (palatized; labialized when preceded by *u*)
k English *k* (palatized when following *ë* or *i* plus a nasal consonant)
m Spanish *m*, but more palatized and labialized
n Spanish *n* (palatized when following *ë* or *i* plus a nasal consonant; voiced like Spanish *ñ* when *i* is adjacent)
ŋ English *ng* in sing (followed by a hard *g* sound when not the terminal phoneme)
p Spanish *p* (voiced like English *b* when following a nasal consonant; labialized when preceding *ë*; palatized when following *ë* or *i* plus a nasal consonant)
r Spanish *r*
s Spanish *s*
š English *sh*
ts English *ts* in cats
t Spanish *t* (voiced like Spanish *d* when following a nasal consonant; palatized when following *ë* or *i* plus a nasal consonant)
w English *w* (but voiced like English *v* when adjacent to *i*)
y Spanish *y*

Unvoiced vowels (restricted to ultimate syllables) are capitalized. Stress
is on the penultimate syllable unless otherwise noted. A tilde indicates
nasalization.

[2] A more detailed presentation is intended for inclusion in a future monograph.
[3] The fieldwork was sponsored primarily by the Henry L. and Grace Doherty Foundation, with supplementary grants provided by the Department of Anthropology and the Museum of Anthropology of the University of California, Berkeley; by the American Museum of Natural History; and by the American Anthropological Association (SKF contract grant). John H. Rowe of the University of California contributed greatly to the undertaking of the fieldwork through his encouragement and advice.
[4] I wish to acknowledge my debt to these two previous fieldworkers. Their material provided innumerable leads for investigation and made my own research much more productive than it otherwise would have been.

Field research providing the present data was conducted for ten and a half months in the following river valleys occupied by the Jívaro: the Río Upano and its tributaries, the Río Tutanangoza and the Río Sepa; the Río Chiguasa; the Río Macuma; the Río Cangaimi; the Río Cusuimi; the Río Mangosiza; and in a refugee Jívaro settlement near Bucay on the western slope of the Andes. Informants who contributed particularly to the information embodied in the present paper were: *MukuimpU, TsakimpU, Učičl Akaču, KugušI,* and *Unta Akaču* of the Río Tutanangoza; *Mašu* of the upper Río Macuma; and *Hintač* of the Río Cangaimi. Chief interpreters were *HwaŋA, Tuŋi,* and *Naita,* all from the Río Tutanangoza region.

The best information on supernatural concepts was obtained in intensive eight or nine hour daily interviews with single informants over periods of a few days to several weeks. This was an exhausting procedure for all involved: interviewer, interpreter, and informant, but was conducive to the elicitation of truthful detail. Informants' accounts were continually cross-checked and contradictions called to their attention individually. An informant, when thus confronted with a contradiction, and with his reputation for knowledge and veracity at stake, generally provided elaborative supporting detail which he might not have otherwise volunteered.

Reluctance of informants to talk about supernatural or personal matters was in part overcome by paying them well for the time they put in. Payment was commonly in the form of black gunpowder, percussion caps, lead shot, glass and metallic beads, and cloth. In localities of Ecuadorian and missionary settlements, money was used as well. In visiting strange households, I found that a gift of an ounce or two of gunpowder invariably resulted in a friendly stay, since almost all Jívaro men today possess firearms and continually need replenishment of their supplies of ammunition. Leave-taking in the more isolated parts of the tribal territory typically involved assuring the host of my future return and "taking orders" for additional types of trade goods to be brought on the next visit. Thus, my host viewed my continued friendship to his advantage and an amiable departure always occurred, despite the fact that I was often leaving directly (with gunpowder and other goods) for a household or neighborhood with which he was feuding.

The following summary of soul beliefs is presented with two major reservations. First, as a summary, it omits consideration of the high degree of personal variability which is so characteristic of this population; what is presented here is a consensus of the views of men who were looked upon as experts in the field of religious beliefs and practices by the other members of the tribe. Second, I do not claim to have completely mastered the intricacies of Jívaro supernatural concepts; what is presented here should be viewed as a progress report on our knowledge of Jívaro soul beliefs. I fully expect additional field research to result in refinements of some of the statements presented here.

The 4,500 to 5,000 Jívaro proper live in a dense tropical rain forest environment amidst the hilly terrain at the foot of the eastern slope of the Ecuadorian Andes. The main source of food is shifting horticulture, with sweet manioc the chief crop. Hunting and fishing also have important roles in the economy. The basic economic and social unit is the nuclear family which most commonly occupies a house by itself. Such houses are scattered throughout the forest in very loose-knit neighborhood groupings, the Jívaro preferring not to live close together for explicitly-voiced anti-social reasons. Except in time of war, formal political organization is completely lacking at the neighborhood level and is never found at the tribal level. Suspicion and hostility are characteristic of the attitude toward fellow tribesmen, including many close relatives. Sorcery as well as murder by means of physical violence and poisoned food and drink are prevalent in the society.

Jívaro soul beliefs constitute one of the four major autonomous systems of verbalized thought so far noted in their culture. The other three are the systems of crop fairy (*nuŋuí*) beliefs, of witchcraft beliefs, and the kinship system. On a conscious level, each of these systems derives from independent assumptions and can be described as a logical unit in itself, though these conceptual systems may be functionally interrelated as an expression of subconsciously existing needs. Since belief in one of these systems is not explicitly based upon belief in another, an adequate understanding of Jívaro soul beliefs can be achieved without recourse to the beliefs regarding nuŋuí, witchcraft, or kinship.

Three kinds of souls are recognized. The first type to be described is the *arutam wakanI*. This is an acquired soul and is believed by the Jívaro to be the most important kind. A man may possess up to two arutam souls at one time. The second type of soul is the *muisak,* or avenging soul. The third to be dealt with is the *nëkás* wakanI, the "true," "real," or "ordinary" soul.

THE ARUTAM SOUL[5]

Arutam wakanI is perhaps best referred to as the "ancient specter" soul. The term "arutam" alone refers to a particular kind of vision or apparition. "WakanI" alone simply means "soul" or "spirit." Thus, the arutam wakanI is the particular kind of soul which produces the arutam or vision. An arutam appears only occasionally and, when it does, is only in existence for less than a minute. The arutam *soul,* on the other hand, exists eternally once it has been created. It is in the system of thought regarding the arutam soul that the Jívaro seek security from the ever-felt menace of death.

The Jívaro believe that the possessor of a single arutam soul cannot be killed by any form of physical violence, poison, nor by sorcery, although he is not immune to death from contagious diseases such as measles and smallpox.[6] In other words, a person who has even only one arutam soul in his possession is relieved from daily anxiety about being murdered. A Jívaro who is fortunate enough to possess two arutam souls cannot die of *any* cause whatever, including contagious disease.

A person is not born with an arutam soul. Such a soul must be acquired, and in certain traditional ways. The acquisition of this type of soul is considered to be so important to an adult male's survival that a boy's parents do not expect him to live past puberty without one. Women sometimes obtain arutam souls, but it is not considered so essential for them. One reason is that intratribal killing, the most common source of violent death, is primarily directed at adult males rather than at women and children.

A boy begins seeking an arutam soul at about the age of six

[5] Arutam may also be pronounced *arutma,* since the final vowel and consonant are interchangeable, as is the case with many Jívaro words. See Turner (1958) for a discussion of this and some other linguistic aspects of Jívaro.

[6] Jívaro faith in the existence of arutam souls is so strong that all persons interviewed on the subject, even adolescents raised in mission boarding schools in the Río Upano valley, expressed a complete conviction in their reality.

years. Accompanied most commonly by his father, he makes a
pilgrimage to the sacred waterfall of his neighborhood. This is
always the highest waterfall within a few days travel. It is believed
to be the rendezvous of these souls which wander about as breezes,
scattering the spray of the long cascade. By night the pilgrims
sleep near the falls in a simple lean-to. Here they fast, drink tobacco water, and await the appearance of an arutam to the vision-
seeker.[7] They may keep up this fasting for as long as five days. If
unsuccessful, they return home to make an attempt again at a later
date.

If the arutam seeker is fortunate, however, he will awaken at
about midnight to find the stars gone from the sky, the earth
trembling, and a great wind felling the trees of the forest amid
thunder and lightning. To keep from being blown down, he grasps
a tree trunk and awaits the arutam. Shortly the arutam appears
from the depths of the forest, often in the form of a pair of large
creatures. The particular animal forms can vary considerably,
but some of the most common arutam include a pair of giant
jaguars fighting one another as they roll over and over towards
the vision-seeker, or two anacondas doing the same. Often the
vision may simply be a single huge disembodied human head
or a ball of fire drifting through the forest towards the arutam
seeker. When the apparition arrives to within 20 or 30 feet, the
Jívaro must run forward and touch it, either with a small stick or
his hand. This is said to require a good deal of courage, and sometimes the person flees the arutam instead. But if he does run
forward and touch the vision, it instantly explodes like dynamite
and disappears.[8]

Upon thus achieving success in encountering an arutam, the
person returns to his house, but tells no one that he has accomplished the purpose of his quest. Arriving home, he goes alone to
sleep that night on the bank of the nearest river. After nightfall,
the soul of the same arutam he touched comes to him as he

---

[7] One of the members of the party may drink an infusion of *maikua*
(*Datura* sp.) instead of tobacco water. Usually this is a person who
has never seen arutam and therefore takes the drug to increase his chances
of success. The other members of the group abstain from maikua in order
to be able to restrain and protect the delirious person under its influence.

[8] One exception is the fireball arutam which only vanishes silently when
touched.

dreams. His dream-visitor is in the form of an old Jívaro man who says to him, "I am your ancestor. Just as I have lived a long time, so will you. Just as I have killed many times, so will you." Without another word, the old man disappears and immediately the arutam soul of this unknown ancestor enters the body of the dreamer, where it is lodged in the chest.

Upon acquiring this arutam soul, the person feels a sudden power surge into his body, accompanied by a new self-confidence. The arutam soul is supposed to increase a person's power in the most general sense. This power, called *kakarma,* is believed to increase one's intelligence as well as simple physical strength, and also to make it difficult for the soul possessor to lie or commit other dishonorable acts. His newly acquired power increases his resistance to contagious disease to some degree, but most importantly it makes it impossible for him to die as a result of any physical violence or sorcery. Most of his relatives and acquaintances shortly know that he has acquired an arutam soul simply because of the change in his personality. For example, he especially tends to speak with greater forcefulness.[9] However, he must not tell anyone that he has acquired such a soul, or it will desert him.

When one has thus obtained an arutam soul, he generally is seized with a tremendous desire to kill. If the person is past puberty, it is ordinarily only a matter of a few months before he joins or organizes a killing expedition. The rare women who possess arutam souls kill primarily by means of poisoning food or manioc beer.

Jívaro killing expeditions usually attack the victim's house just before dawn. Late in the afternoon of the day prior to the attack, the expedition halts in the forest about a quarter of a mile from its intended objective. There, in their concealed location, the participants must "declare" what kind of arutam they had each seen. The younger men form a circle around several of the most experienced killers who then ask each man in turn to describe the arutam that he had seen. As each man, young and old, does this, the soul of his arutam leaves his body forever, to roam again the

---

[9] Persons who have seen arutam can be surprisingly well singled out by this trait alone.

forest as a wind, for arutam souls "are satisfied with one killing."[10]
The departing arutam souls reportedly generate winds, thunder,
and lightning. Eventually, at some time in the indefinite future,
each soul is expected once more to enter the body of another Jívaro.

The warriors, having made their declarations, are ready to attack the following morning. Although each of them has just lost
an arutam soul, the power of that soul remains in the body, only
ebbing away gradually. The complete loss of this power is generally believed to take about two weeks. Since the power decreases
slowly, the members of the killing party still retain enough of it
the next morning so that they cannot be killed by the enemy in
battle. If one of their number *is* killed in the attack, the other
members of the expedition simply consider the death to be evidence that the deceased had already lost his arutam soul without
realizing it. As soon as the expedition kills its intended victim,
all its members again become entitled to obtain the soul of a new
arutam upon their return home.

Sometimes the attackers fail in their assault on the intended
victim's house. When such a failure occurs, the expedition must
immediately choose a new victim and go after him at once, without
returning home. If these men failed to kill someone, they would
not be entitled to obtain new arutam souls, and without new
arutam souls they would expect to die within weeks or, at the
most, months. Since it is therefore a matter of life or death to
them, the members of the killing party invariably find an enemy,
or at least some stranger, to assassinate. When the killing is accomplished, they return home and each immediately seeks to en-
counter an arutam again and to get himself a new soul.

The acquisition of such a new arutam soul not only brings the
new power or *kakarma* of the incoming soul but also serves to
"lock in" the power of the previous one and thereby prevent it
from ebbing away from the body. A person is limited to the possession of not more than two arutam *souls* simultaneously, but
this "lock-in" feature of the new soul makes it possible for a person
to accumulate the *power* of an indefinite number of previous souls.
In other words, while the acquisition of the souls is consecutive,
the acquisition of the power is cumulative.

---

[10] There is also a rare super-arutam, *amuaŋ*, whose soul is not so easily
satisfied and does not leave the body of its possessor when such declarations are made.

By repeatedly killing, one can continually accumulate power through the replacement of old arutam souls with new ones. This "trade-in" mechanism is an important feature because, when a person has had the same arutam soul for four or five years, it tends to leave its sleeping possessor to wander nightly through the forest. Sooner or later, while it is thus drifting through the trees, another Jívaro will "steal" it. Accordingly, it is highly desirable to obtain a new soul before the old one begins nocturnal wanderings. This felt need encourages the individual to participate in a killing expedition every few years.

Since a man with an arutam soul cannot die as the result of physical violence, poisoning, or witchcraft, i.e., any interpersonal attack, a person who wishes to kill a specific enemy attempts to steal his arutam soul away from him as a prelude to assassinating him. This soul-stealing or capturing process involves drinking large quantities of an infusion of *natemA* (*Banisteria* sp.), beating a log signal drum, and repeating the name of the intended victim. Then if the enemy's arutam soul is wandering nocturnally, it may one night hear the would-be assassin's call and, "taking pity" on his need for such a soul, enter his body, never to return to the body of its former possessor.[11]

The Jívaro warrior desires to have personally—and thus definitely—stolen the arutam of his intended victim. This feat is often not possible, however, and the would-be murderer instead watches for signs coming to him through gossip or direct observation that the enemy already has had his arutam soul taken away by someone else. Such signs or indications, for example, would include rumors of physical weakness or illness on the part of the intended victim, or the firsthand observation that the enemy was lacking in forcefulness of speech.[12] In any case, an attack is made only if the raiders believe that the potential victim has lost his arutam soul. If they should fail to kill him, it is because the enemy still retains the soul or had a second one in reserve.

[11] The arutam soul resident in the body of a person is *not* his *own* soul in any permanent sense, but only the soul of some ancestral Jívaro dwelling there temporarily.

[12] Visitors to the Jívaro are usually impressed by the near-shouting which typifies conversations between Jívaro of different households and neighborhoods. The functional basis for this custom can be seen in the desire of the individual to advertise his arutam power by being forceful in speech and gestures.

It should be noted that the personal security which the Jívaro believe comes from killing has some social reality. A man who has killed repeatedly, called *kakaram* or "powerful one," is rarely attacked because his enemies feel that the protection provided him by his constantly replaced souls would make any assassination attempt against him fruitless.

Second arutam souls can be acquired in several ways. One method is to capture the arutam soul of an enemy by beating a log signal drum as previously noted. Another common technique is to walk alone through the forest night after night, without the usual illumination of a copal torch, in the hope of encountering an arutam in the darkness.

Shamans always possess arutam souls. Those specializing in bewitching try to steal their intended victim's arutam soul before attempting to kill him through witchcraft. If the intended victim is believed to have two arutam souls, the shaman asks a shaman "friend" or partner to steal the second one for him, since no one can possess more than two such souls simultaneously. A shaman, incidentally, does not lose his arutam soul when he kills by means of sorcery.

The arutam soul must leave a man before he dies, since he cannot die while he retains one (except in the case of contagious disease, in which case retention of the power of two is necessary for certain survival). Thus, at death, he does not have any of the arutam souls left which temporarily dwelt in his body while he was alive. Then, at the moment of death, his *own* arutam souls come into existence for the first time. The exact number of these completely new, freshly "born" souls equals the quantity which the deceased person had acquired during his lifetime. Thus, if he had acquired and subsequently lost five arutam souls, then at the moment of death he forms five new arutam souls. The formation of these souls is said to generate strong winds, thunder, and lightning in the locality. The newly-created arutam souls of the dead man will live eternally, drifting as breezes and temporarily entering into the bodies of future generations of Jívaro. At the same moment that these arutam souls are "born," the second type of Jívaro soul comes into existence if the deceased person was murdered.

THE MUISAK[13]

The second kind of soul, the muisak or avenging soul, is closely connected with the arutam soul. Only a person who has had an arutam soul is capable of forming a muisak. Furthermore, a muisak comes into existence only when a person who has seen an arutam is killed, whether by natural or supernatural means. At the time of death of such a person his avenging soul is created and leaves his corpse through its mouth.[14] If one simply dies of contagious disease or of old age (the latter believed to be a rare occurrence), no muisak is created.

The sole reason for being of a person's muisak is to avenge his death. This soul therefore attempts to kill the murderer, or if this is not possible (due to the murderer having an arutam soul), a son or wife of the murderer. The muisak is occasionally distracted from this objective, out of jealousy, to kill instead a new spouse of his widow. Because of this latter danger, young men who have not yet acquired much arutam power tend to avoid marrying widows.

Technically, the avenging soul is only called a muisak while it is in the corpse, subsequently in the shrunken head trophy (*tsantsa*), or its immediate vicinity. When the human head trophy is not taken and prepared, the muisak is able to travel as far as it likes from the corpse and to form into one of three types of *iwančl* or demons. These three demons are forms of the natural nonhuman world that can kill a man. One is a particularly dangerous poisonous snake (*makančl*). Another is the water boa constrictor or anaconda (*paŋi*) which can knock over the raft or canoe of the murderer and thereby cause him to drown in the rapid waters of one of the numerous fast-flowing rivers and streams of this hilly country. The third form is a large tree in the forest which falls on the victim and crushes him. These are the three traditional forms of death in Jívaro society which might be called "accidental" in other cultures. Since the introduction

[13] Muisak may be alternatively pronounced *muiska*.
[14] When a man does not cut off the head of a person he has murdered (i.e., when the victim belongs to his own tribe), he turns the corpse face down on the ground so that the victim's muisak is delayed in emerging through the mouth. Thus the murderer hopes to reach home before the avenging soul can catch him.

of the steel bush knife or machete and of firearms, a belief has been
growing that a muisak can enter into these items to cause an "accidental" fatal wound. The Jívaro view slight self-inflicted wounds
as true accidents, but grave or fatal self-inflicted wounds are
always believed to be the results, respectively, of murder attempts
or murders through supernatural mechanisms.

Before the avenging spirit or iwančI kills the murderer, it sometimes appears to him in the form of a man or a jaguar while he
is sleeping. The sleeper tries to seize his firearm or lance (which
he keeps on the bed beside him at night) to kill the apparition.
Failure to do so will result in the demon eventually succeeding
in killing the person. Sometimes this iwančI fails in its assassination attempt, only wounding or injuring the intended victim. In
such cases, the victim becomes a permanent invalid.

When the demon has performed its act of vengeance, it then
appears in a dream to a relative of the victim. In this dream the
avenging soul has a human form. Around its neck hangs the
shrunken head trophy worn by a killer in the tsantsa feasts. The
demon tells the dreamer, "I have killed an enemy. Now I am going far away, where my relatives are. I am going far away to have
a feast with them." The demon disappears and, since it never
kills more than a single person, will never murder again.

The widely publicized practice of the Jívaro in shrinking human
heads can be well understood only with a knowledge of the muisak
concept. A major part of the belief and ritual associated with the
shrunken head or tsantsa is a direct effort to thwart the muisak in
its mission of vengeance.[15] The Jívaro believe that the completion of the process of head-shrinking forces the muisak, hovering alongside the retreating war expedition, to enter the head
trophy. For this reason, as well as the practical one that the
removal of the skull and its contents makes the trophy much
lighter to carry on the mountainous trails, the expedition prepares
its tsantsa(s) as quickly as possible while fleeing the enemy
territory. One of the final steps in the processing of the shrunken
head before arrival home is to rub charcoal into its skin "so that
the muisak cannot see out," thereby making it difficult for the

---

[15] A rather astonishing amount of misinformation has been published
regarding the beliefs surrounding the tsantsa. I wish to re-emphasize that
any contradictions between the information presented here and previous
accounts indicates rejection of that material.

avenging soul to plan an "accidental" death in the vicinity of the tsantsa.

When the expedition arrives in its home territory, the first feast of the tsantsa is held immediately. This feast is later followed by at least one and sometimes two others. At all these feasts or dances great care is taken to prevent arguments and fights between the inebriated celebrants out of fear that the muisak might take advantage of such an interruption of the magically-binding ritual to slip from the head trophy to cause a quarrel to result in a murder. If the feasts are conducted properly, however, the muisak will be kept inside of the tsantsa until the end of the last feast. At that time, the celebrants expel it from the head trophy and send it back to its neighborhood of origin. This neighborhood is typically at a considerable distance because head trophies are normally taken only of members of other tribes. As part of this final ritual the women sing:

> Now, now, go back to your house where you lived.
> Your wife is there calling you from your house.
> You have come here to make us happy.
> Finally we have finished.
> So return.

The tsantsa is customarily later sold by the head-taker (although illegally in terms of Ecuadorian law) to a mestizo in one of the communities on the western periphery of the tribal territory. At that time, the head-taker silently repeats the exhortation to the muisak to return to its distant neighborhood as he hands it over to the trader. The head-taker goes through this act just in case there is a possibility that the ritual in the tsantsa feast did not succeed in its purpose.

During the three feasts the celebrants had been concerned with utilizing the power of the muisak as well as containing it. As in the case of the arutam soul, the muisak emits power, but it is believed that the muisak's power is directly transmissible to other persons. The man who took the head holds the tsantsa aloft in the ritual dance while two female relatives whom he wants to benefit, most frequently a wife and sister, hold on to him. In this manner the power of the muisak is believed to be transmitted to the women who, ordinarily, lack power-giving arutam souls. This power, transmitted from the muisak to the women through the "filtering" mechanism of the head-taker, is believed to make it possible for them to work harder and to be more successful in crop production and in the raising of domesticated animals, both of which being primarily the responsibilities of women in Jívaro society.

Tsantsa feasts are also held using the shrunken head of a tree sloth. The tree sloth is the only nonhuman creature thought to be capable of forming a muisak. Because the tree sloth moves so slowly, it is said to be very aged and therefore must once have acquired an arutam soul to have lived so long. At the same time, since the sloth moves so slowly, it is further believed to have lost its former arutam soul(s) and therefore can be killed. The feasting and ritual precautions are basically the same as in the case of a human tsantsa but generally somewhat less extensive.

THE TRUE SOUL

The "true" or "ordinary" soul, the nëkás wakanI, is born at the same moment as the person and is possessed by every living Jívaro, male or female. The true soul is present in the living individual primarily in the form of one's blood. Bleeding is therefore viewed as a process of soul-loss. This soul is passive during a person's real life and apparently is of relatively little interest to the Jívaro in terms of their total native belief systems.

When a person dies, this true soul leaves his body and, in invisible form, eventually returns to the site of the house where the deceased individual was born. There the soul lives in a spirit house identical to the one in which the deceased was born, except for the fact that the spirit house is invisible to the living. The true souls of other deceased members of the family are likewise dwelling in this house. Similarly, the true souls of former neighbors return to their original house sites as well. It is believed that the true souls conduct their household activities and visit each other just as they did when their possessors were alive. As the years pass, these souls move from house site to house site in the same order, and over the same span of time as they did when incorporated in living individuals.[16]

One significant difference should be noted between this hereafter of the true soul and the real life of its former possessor:

[16] The Jívaro practice shifting cultivation and move their house locations along with their gardens.

these souls are always hungry. Although they engage in subsistence activities and eat what appears to be food to them, it
never satisfies them because it is really just air. The "animals"
which these souls hunt in the forest are only the souls of the birds,
fish, and mammals which they killed in their former lives. Such an
existence of perpetual hunger is the fate of the true souls of all
persons, without regard to the kind of life they led while in living
persons. Needless to say, the true soul's fate of persistent starvation is dreaded by the Jívaro.

One can often see deer and owls lingering in the vicinity of
abandoned garden and house sites.[17] The Jívaro interpret the
presence of such creatures at these old living places as evidence
that the animals are temporarily visible embodiments of true
souls. The true souls, when they are in these visible forms, are
referred to as "human demons" (*šuar* iwančI). There is a moderate fear of them, particularly by women, and the Jívaro taboo
on the eating of deer meat is based on the fear that eating such an
animal might result in a deceased person's soul entering the body
of the living person with the result that he may subsequently die.
These "human demon" animals are often seen in pairs, a fact which
the Jívaro interpret as indicating that the two creatures are temporarily visible forms of the souls of a man and his wife.

When a true soul has thus repeated the entire life history of its
deceased owner, it ceases its existence as a "human demon" and
changes into a "true demon." As a true demon, its form is permanently visible and more or less human, although a good deal uglier.
The true demon roams the forest hungry, solitary, and lonely,
feeling greatly the loss of the company of its former family. When
Jívaro children wander into the forest and are not found immediately, it is said that a true demon carried off the child because
it was so lonely for human companionship. Although it may take
the Jívaro two or three days to find the lost child, they almost always succeed and therefore say that the true demon never harms
children, but only wants to play with them.

Then the true demon, after existing for a span of years equivalent to a human lifetime, dies and changes into a certain species
of giant butterfly or moth called *wampaŋ*. This creature has markings on its wings which lend it the appearance of an owl's face.

---

[17] Possibly this is due to the fact that the old clearings provide feeding grounds for these animals.

All the wampaŋ are believed to be souls and are said always to be hungry, as is the case with any of the forms which the true soul takes. When a wampaŋ flies into a house, one of the persons there tosses a small piece of sweet manioc or a few drops of manioc beer in its direction. The Jívaro believe that since the wampaŋ might be the soul of a dead relative or friend it would be wrong to neglect its hunger. They do not fear the creature, however.

After a length of time about which the Jívaro are uncertain, the wampaŋ finally has its wings damaged by raindrops as it flutters through a rainstorm and dies on the ground. The true soul then changes into water vapor amidst the falling rain. All fog and clouds are believed to be the last form taken by true souls. The true soul undergoes no more transformations and persists eternally in the form of mist.

Of the three kinds of souls in which the Jívaro believe, they seem to be least interested in the "true" one, the nëkás wakanI, which does little to help the individual survive in his insecure society. It is the arutam soul instead which seems to rank first in the Jívaro mind. The arutam soul possessor believes himself to be unkillable, thereby gaining a greatly-desired sense of security in a social context of continual physical violence and interpersonal sorcery, both real and imagined. Paradoxically, the arutam soul concept also endorses assassination as a necessary form of behavior in the society.

The arutam soul belief system contains a number of significant supernatural traits organized together into one internally logical complex. In this system the central idea of immunity from death is combined with such anthropologically well-known concepts as: a vision quest; a guardian spirit; eternal and multiple souls; a variety of generalized ancestor worship; reincarnation; soul-loss; soul-capture; nonshamanistic spirit possession; and a concept of personally-acquired impersonal power, kakarma, which resembles, but is not precisely identical to, the Oceanian mana.

The concept of the muisak furnishes the rationale for head-taking and shrinking, as well as explaining as supernatural murders those deaths which in many other cultures would be ascribed to accidental causes. In conclusion, one may observe that the Jívaro are so preoccupied with killing in real life that it seems only consistent that their two most emphasized types of souls, the muisak and the arutam soul, are supernatural devices, respectively, for murdering and avoiding being murdered. Beyond this, it is clear that these internally coherent and complex bodies of belief are an important part of the Jívaro view of reality and, as such, affect their overt behavior.

A COMMENTARY ON PREVIOUS REPORTS

A few brief comments seem to be due the reader to clarify the differences between the statements presented here and those of Karsten and Stirling, the chief contributors to the literature on the Jívaro proper. The souls will be considered here in the same order as in the preceding body of the paper, with the arutam soul first.

The "arutam" dealt with here is the "*arutama*" of Karsten (1935: 448–51) and the "*tsarutama*" of Stirling (1938: 115, 116). Karsten's term is a corruption of "arutam," found in a trade language used between the Jívaro and the Ecuadorian mestizos living in the village of Macas. As Karsten (1954: 25) has already pointed out, Stirling's term does not exist in the Jívaro dialect.

Karsten (1954: 25) has stated, "The word *arúta* or *arútam* in the Jíbaro language means 'old'; as a religious term *arutama* may be translated into 'The Old Ones.' . . ." Actually, however, while both words do have the same root, and *arutA* does indeed mean "old" or "used," the term "arutam" refers exclusively to the special vision which I have termed "ancient specter." My informants assured me that it does not mean "old ones." Also an arutam, however frightening it may appear, never kills anyone, despite a statement to the contrary by Karsten (1935: 450). Although Karsten (1935: 448–50) had some of the visions described to him, he was unaware of the souls responsible for them and the related system of belief.

While Stirling (1938: 115) recognizes a similarity between his "*tsarutama*" (arutam) and concepts of the mana type in other cultures, he is misleading in stating that "tsarutama" is the force itself or that "it gives supernatural properties to certain classes of animals, plants or natural phenomena." When an arutam appears to a Jívaro, it is actually recognized to be a vision, distinct from natural forms of life or other natural phenomena. Stirling (1938: 116) also errs in stating that "All of the principal nature gods . . . contain powerful *tsarutama*." In fact, it is highly questionable whether there are any supernatural figures whom the Jívaro could be said to view as gods. Stirling's candidates for gods are primarily "Piribri, the Rain God," and "Pangi, the great anaconda River God." Any such deities are not part of the supernaturalism of the Jívaro proper. Karsten (1954: 26) has already taken note of this situation, saying, "But the Jíbaros have no belief in a personal Raingod Piribri." Actually, *pirípiri* is the correct term and refers to a plant which the Jívaro use magically to cause rain to swell the rivers so that their enemies cannot cross successfully. But it is not a god. The actual supernatural role of "Pangi" (*paŋi*) is not significantly greater than has been indicated in the preceding descriptions of the arutam and muisak souls. Karsten (1954: 31) is also correct in rejecting a claim for a Jívaro deity named "Cumbanama" (see Steward and Metraux 1948: 626), a claim simply deriving from a casual statement by an early traveler in the Jívaro country. While on the subject of supposed Jívaro gods, it might as well be mentioned that Karsten's (1935: 125–26) candidate for an "Earth-mother" goddess really refers to a class of female spirits (*nuŋuí*) which can probably be best defined as crop fairies. She (or really, they) also has no husband, despite such a claim by Karsten (1935: 379).

In regards to the muisak, Karsten (1935: 430) was aware of the potentially harmful nature of the spirit of a slain enemy, but does not report some of the major beliefs surrounding it, nor is he apparently cognizant of this term for the avenging spirit while it resides in the tsantsa. He (1954: 21) is wrong when he states that the sloth shrunken head is not called "tsantsa." Nor can I agree with him when he says (1954: 16): ". . . I have indicated the real purpose of the tsantsa, and in my statements, founded on personal observations and most careful inquiries, there is nothing to add and nothing to correct."

Stirling does not mention an avenging soul or spirit. While he notes (1935: 74) that the tsantsa possesses magical power, he incorrectly identifies such power as "tsarutama," when it is really power emanating from the muisak.

Karsten fails to distinguish the nëkás wakanI and thus, since he uses the term wakanI alone, it is difficult to tell when his remarks apply to this particular soul. He is definitely wrong in his statement (1935: 372) that: ". . . animals, plants and inanimate objects . . . seem to be conceived simply as disembodied human souls." What is fact is that no plants or inanimate objects are believed to *be* souls (although a few specific plants *have* souls) and only a few animals (e.g., deer, owls) are believed to be such. All other creatures with blood are thought to *have* some kind of true soul. Stirling never mentions wakanI.

To the reader who wonders whether some of these conflicts are due to culture change during the intervals between fieldwork by the different investigators, I submit the fact that several of my most important informants were already raising families prior to Karsten's initial Jívaro fieldwork in 1916–18 and did not come into significant firsthand contact with Whites until 15 to 20 years later. Stirling's fieldwork came after Karsten's, in 1930–31. The informants were also aware that what was wanted was the traditional Jívaro view, with recent innovations in belief being recorded separately.

Finally, there remains the question of whether the contradictions between the several investigators' reports stem in part from the fact that both Karsten and Stirling visited other Jívaroan tribes (i.e., Achuara, Huambisa, and Aguaruna) in addition to the Jívaro proper. In order to assess this possibility, I queried linguists who had been making prolonged investigations among the Huambisa and Aguaruna, and also personally questioned several Aguaruna, Huambisa, and Achuara men.[18] As a result, it was determined that Stirling's term "tsarutama," for example, is completely unknown in all the Jívaroan tribes, "arutam" being used by the Achuara and Huambisa and *"ahutan"* by the Aguaruna. Likewise reported absent are any beliefs in Stirling's rain or anaconda "gods" or in Karsten's earthmother "goddess." In fact, these cursory inquiries suggest that the soul belief systems of the other Jívaroan tribes may prove to be basically similar to that sketched here for the Jívaro proper.

[18] Thanks are particularly due to Mildred Larson and David Beasley of the Summer Institute of Linguistics for providing information regarding the Aguaruna and Huambisa beliefs, respectively. I briefly interviewed several Huambisa and Aguaruna men on these points at the Institute's base in Yarinacocha, eastern Peru, in January 1961, and questioned an Achuara informant on the same subject in 1957 near the Río Cangaimi, eastern Ecuador.

9 AFRICAN RITUALS OF CONFLICT

Edward Norbeck

THIS PAPER presents a description of rites expressing social conflict among various African societies and offers suggestions concerning their functional significance. In doing so, it examines critically hypotheses and supporting data presented by Max Gluckman (1954b; 1959), who has provided the only substantial published writings on this subject. Gluckman discusses rites involving rebellion against authority among societies of southeastern Africa. The following discussion broadens the geographic area to Subsaharan Africa and enlarges the subject to include many ritual events not considered by Gluckman. Some of the rites to be discussed lack the element of conflict but are relevant in other respects.

The idea that social conflict may serve important functions in supporting and maintaining society is fairly old in sociology (e.g., Simmel 1908). The outstanding contemporary work on this subject from sociology (Coser 1956) mentions anthropological writings only peripherally, drawing from them chiefly examples of institutionalized expressions of conflict. Anthropologists have not failed to note social conflicts, but they have generally regarded the conflicts as socially disruptive and have directed their attention chiefly to attempts to understand causes and modes of resolution. Only in recent years has anthropological thought turned to serious consideration of the idea that conflict may have positive as well as negative functional aspects.

Gluckman's writings on customs of African peoples are among the earliest anthropological works that present hypotheses con-

Reprinted from *The American Anthropologist* 65 (6), 1963: 1254–79 by permission of the author and the editor, *The American Anthropologist*.

cerning socially integrative effects of expressions of conflict. Gluck-man's criticism (1949a: 10) of Malinowski for his "refusal to see conflict as a mode of integrating groups and to recognize that hostility between groups is a form of social balance" is perhaps the first explicit expression of this point of view by an anthropologist. Gluckman's interpretations are unusual in another respect. They are the first writings in the social sciences to set up as a distinctive class of events rituals that express conflict. Gluckman has called these customs "rituals of rebellion." He refers to rituals in which rules concerning behavior toward authority are seemingly abrogated temporarily. These are rites in which rulers and chiefs are reviled, criticized, and threatened by those subject to their authority, and men are similarly subjected to various ritual expressions of putative hostility enacted by women, who are their inferiors in authority.

Gluckman sees the ritual enactment of conflicts of interest as a form of catharsis that banishes the threat to disunity imposed by the conflicts. This is a familiar line of reasoning in sociological writings on the role of conflict. Gluckman, however, goes further. He holds that institutionalized rites of rebellion may exist only in societies in which the social order is established and unchallenged. Gluckman states (1954b: 21): "The acceptance of the established order as right and good, and even sacred, seems to allow unbridled excess, very rituals of rebellion, for the order itself keeps this rebellion within bounds." In these societies, fundamental conflicts are said to exist despite social stability. The interests of the ruled do not coincide with those of the total society as personified by the ruler, but the needs of the individual cannot be met unless he follows the legal and moral mandates of his society to insure peace and order. When kings are ritually reviled and threatened, the aim is never to subvert the institution of kingship; only the individual ruler is the target of hate. When women ritually abandon their normal feminine roles to express rebellion against males, their intent is not to reject the social order and their position in it, for they are said to make no organized protest except through these conventionalized rituals.

In the rituals which Gluckman describes and interprets, conflicts are symbolically enacted. The rites are essentially dramas of conflict, conducted in a presumably religious atmosphere. Gluckman (1959: 119) distinguishes between ritual and ceremonial on the following basis: "These rituals contain the belief that if people perform certain actions they will influence the course of events so that their group be made richer, more prosperous, more successful, and so forth. Some of us therefore call these actions 'ritual', and say that they contain 'mystical notions'—notions that their performance will in some mysterious way affect the course of events. 'Ritual' in this definition is contrasted with 'ceremonial' which consists of similar actions but has no such mystical notions associated with it." Gluckman's distinction seems useful, but it must often be made intuitively when dealing with specific examples because ethnological accounts give no information on native attitudes toward these rites. Since information to settle this question is not available, and since it appears useful to consider conflict in a wider context that embraces certain events lacking a religious aura, this unresolvable issue will be set aside.

The discussion that follows concerns principally "rituals" expressing conflict. It also considers certain institutionalized acts lacking any apparent evidence of conflict but otherwise resembling Gluckman's rituals of rebellion in varying degree. All of the customs to be discussed may be described as institutionalized departures from everyday practice, norms for special occasions that oppose year-round norms. Most of the practices may be interpreted as direct or indirect expressions of hostility toward individuals or social groups. Others are not easily seen as expressions of interpersonal or intergroup conflict. These are customs that allow or require certain individuals, social groups, or the whole society to violate sexual norms and other important rules of behavior applying at all other times. These customs have moral significance for the people of the societies in which they obtain. Other institutionalized deviations from customary practice included in this discussion have no such evident meaning. They are acts that constitute sharp departures from everyday norms but do not in any readily perceivable way "violate" rules of everyday behavior in a moral sense.

For convenience in description and discussion, the rites may be divided arbitrarily into two major groups, with a variety of sub-types:

1   Ritual Expressions of Apparent Social Conflict
    a   Between the sexes
    b   Between superiors and inferiors

    c   Between kin groups of bride and groom
    d   Between formally defined social and political groups
    e   General, between any persons holding grievances
2   Other Institutionalized Departures from Everyday Norms
    a   With apparent moral significance
    b   Without apparent moral significance

As may be inferred from examination of their titles, the sub-classes listed above are not wholly exclusive. Each of the categories will be discussed separately.

1   RITUAL EXPRESSIONS OF APPARENT SOCIAL CONFLICT

a *Between the sexes*

Gluckman's examples of the ritual rebellion of females against males consist of rites in which women's behavior contrasts sharply with that of their everyday lives. During ritual, women appear naked, sing or otherwise act lewdly, wear the clothing of males, and assume other male prerogatives. Gluckman discusses principally data gathered by himself on Wiko circumcision rites for boys (1949b). During these rites women are said to rebel by departing from their normal roles in a number of ways, among which are the singing of lewd songs and the wearing of men's clothing. Gluckman (1954b: 3–5) refers to similar "rebellions" against the female role among Zulu women in former agricultural rites, when women acted lewdly and performed acts that were normally male prerogatives. These consisted of planting in honor of a goddess a field that was subsequently neglected, and herding and milking cattle while wearing men's garments.

Among the three additional societies to which Gluckman refers in the context of female rebellion, women act similarly during girls' puberty rites of the Thembu, rites of the Swazi and Tsonga to drive away insect pests (1954b: 5–11), and in Tsonga rites observed when moving to a new village (1959: 116–19).

As Gluckman notes, ritual transvestism and symbolic assumption by women of some part of the roles of males are common customs in Africa. But other forms of transvestism are also common, and here we are faced with a problem of interpretation. Does transvestism on the part of women constitute resentment of males and symbolic rebellion against female statuses and roles, as Gluckman holds, or does it have other significance? Transvestism, often accompanied by some reversal of sex roles or parody of the behavior of the opposite sex, is by no means limited to women. Even in Wiko society, for which Gluckman himself has furnished the original accounts, adults of both sexes dance obscenely, and some men dress as women during the boys' circumcision rites in question (1949b: 153). Clearer suggestions of sexual antagonism if not rebellion appear in other Wiko rites, however. Men sing songs that insult the women (1949b: 156), and men and women "fight," when the women try to seize the boys (1949b: 158). Gluckman's interpretations of rites of rebellion (1954b; 1959) make no mention of the male counterparts of women's presumed rebellion against the female role. If transvestism, lewdness, and obscenity on the part of females in a given society constitute rebellion, what do the same acts on the part of males represent?

Interpretations other than rebellion are possible and Gluckman, in his original report on Wiko rites (1949b: 165), offers one: ". . . the transvesticism in the initial and final dances symbolizes their [men's and women's] ultimate unity of purpose." This interpretation is not, of course, incompatible with the idea of rebellion by females until the essentially identical behavior by males is considered.

Customs of transvestism of other African societies are relevant here. Many examples may be cited of transvestism by boys during rites of initiation to adulthood and induction into age-graded societies. Among the Turkana, boys from "conservative families" prepare their hair during initiation rites like that of girls (Gulliver 1953: 76). On the approach of puberty, Midobi boys let their hair grow long and plait it as women do; after initiation rites the head is shaved (Seligman 1932: 450). During the period of recovery from circumcision, the Masai youth wears the dress of a married woman (Huntingford 1953b: 116). Also among the Gisu (LaFontaine 1959: 42), Moro (Nadel 1947: 242), Nyima (Nadel 1947: 410), Nupe (Nadel 1954: 80, 113, 218), Kipsigis (Peristiany 1939: 23), and Nandi (Fehlinger 1921: 110; Huntingford 1953b: 30), boys at initiation to manhood or into age-grades wear the attire or some article of the attire of females. Wolof boys are dressed "practically like women" during puberty rites and are "not considered to be men" (Gorer 1949: 36). Dur-

ing festivals marking initiation into the N'tomo society for boys,
two little boys, one dressed as a man and the other as a woman,
fight in public [Bambara (Tauxier 1927: 386)]. The occasional
account (e.g., Nadel 1954: 82, 218 on the Nupe) describes
transvestite boys comically imitating the walk, gestures, and manner of dancing of women. In two of the societies cited above,
Nandi (Fehlinger 1921: 110, 112) and Kipsigis (Peristiany
1939: 25), both sexes wear the clothing or some article of the
clothing and ornaments of the opposite sex during their respective
initiation rites. Nandi boys and girls receive these clothes and
ornaments from their lovers. According to native interpretation,
the Kipsigis custom for boys serves to frighten away spirits. No
information on native interpretation is presented for the similar
rites of Kipsigis girls (Peristiany 1939: 23, 25). Although Nyima
boys wear borrowed bangles and beads of women, they are reported (Nadel 1954: 7) to deny dressing up as women.

Other instances of ritual transvestism are highly varied, and
they are sometimes accompanied by sexual license and obscene
behavior. Among the Nuer, women bear spears and dress as men
while men dress as women at rites conducted before the marriage of twins (Evans-Pritchard 1956: 237). Nuer custom also
calls for a sham marriage ceremony of twins to one person of
the opposite sex before the twins may be courted; mock brides
and grooms dress for the ceremony in clothes and ornaments of
the opposite sex (Seligman 1932: 227–28). Gorer (1949: 34)
reports the custom at Wolof weddings of transvestism by children
of both sexes of sisters of the bride and groom. These children are also allowed to take with impunity the property of others
and have "complete licence."

Zulu co-wives wear the clothing of their deceased husband during his funeral rites (Bryant 1949: 703), and some Zulu women
carry shields and assagais during wedding rites (Delegorgue 1847
Vol. II: 230). The Bakitara mother of twins wears bark cloth
in masculine style at rites marking their birth (Roscoe 1923a:
251). Ibibio custom at funerals of members of the Egbo society
prescribes that the eldest daughters of the principal families come
dressed as men (Talbot 1923: 160). In a Shilluk rite to save
millet from the depredations of birds, a woman with a cloth
knotted on the left shoulder in correct masculine fashion dances
with movements of masculine style (Seligman 1932: 83–84). In

the Lobedu girls' puberty rites, a girl dressed as a man acts obscenely (Krige 1950: 105). During rites of initiation into the Mawŭ, a Dahomean women's cult, the Legbá priestess dances with a wooden phallus, simulating sexual intercourse and masturbation (Herskovits 1938: 125–26).

Among the Masai, a new husband wears women's dress for one month (Huntingford 1953b: 114). Agricultural rites of the Lango require that a man wearing a woman's skirt and apron must ritually begin cultivation of the soil; observers who laugh are subject to a fine (Seligman 1932: 356). To the amusement of the women, rain rites of the Bolewa require that the men who are heads of compounds remove their gowns, grind grain into flour, and make mealies (Meek 1931b Vol. II: 303). Mende rites to avert floods similarly require that men rather than women cook foods (Little 1951: 224). Among the Chewa, four men dressed as women participate in girls' initiation rites (Hodgson 1933: 133–34). Galla pilgrims wore women's clothes (Huntingford 1955: 84), and Lotuko men wear women's dress at a dance when new skins are provided for the drums (Seligman 1932: 356). According to Igbira custom, the kings of Panda were disrobed and clothed in a woman's loincloth during installation rites (Meek 1931a: 126).

The foregoing examples indicate that transvestism may be a feature of almost any kind of ritual and that it is observed by both sexes. It appears to be particularly widespread in rites for boys and young men marking their achievement of adult status or initiation into age-graded groups, perhaps in part because rites of this kind are so common. To interpret the significance of the boys' transvestism it is important to know what it symbolizes to the native peoples. This information is seldom given, and when explanations are presented, it is sometimes difficult to judge whether they represent viewpoints of the natives or the ethnographers (e.g., Gorer 1949: 36; Prins 1953: 69). The interpretation most frequently offered is that assumption of women's clothing at this time symbolizes the status of the boys: they are not yet members of the world of adult males. Writing on Moro initiation customs for boys, Nadel (1947: 242) states that young men consciously dress as women and that everyone is aware of this meaning of their masquerade. His interpretation makes no mention of conflict. He states that the significance of the masquerade is abundantly clear from the context: ". . . its exaggeration serves to throw into relief the transition from immaturity to full manhood." Nadel (1954: 113) offers the same interpretation for a similar rite among the Nupe, wherein boys wear a piece of woman's cloth and imitate and caricature female steps and mannerisms: ". . . the temporary change of roles pointing to a more permanent one."

This interpretation follows van Gennep (1909), who saw any departure from conventional behavior during rites of passage as a dramatic statement of social transition, emphasizing the social importance of the event celebrated. If frequency of use is indicative, it is an interpretation that generally meets with acceptance by anthropologists. The interpretation seems acceptable for African customs of transvestism among girls in their rites of initiation, and it has been used by Gluckman for rites of Zulu women (1935: 266). As we have seen, transvestism is also a custom among adult men as well as women on various ritual occasions. It therefore becomes difficult to accept any general interpretation of female transvestism as signifying rebellion or even sexual antagonism.

To help decide whether or not female simulation of male roles constitutes protest, it is of course useful to have information on the relationships between the sexes. The Zulu rites in question ended long ago, and information on them used by Gluckman comes from the early observers Bryant and Delegorgue. Bryant (1949: 597–98, 602–3) states explicitly that Zulu women felt no dissatisfaction over their roles as women, subordinate to men. Rather than feeling resentful, they enjoyed and took pride in their roles as wives and mothers, and indulged in ". . . no hankering to encroach upon or curtail the recognized privileges and preserves of the males." Robert Samuelson, who was born and brought up among the Zulu, reports that Zulu women were quite satisfied and happy with their lot (1929: 356, 361).

A modern psychiatric report on the Zulu by Loudon (1959) relates to Gluckman's hypotheses concerning the cathartic value for women of these rites. Loudon reports a type of psychogenic disorder called *ufufunyana* to be common among the Zulu, particularly among women. Resembling conversion hysteria, this disorder seems to have appeared at the turn of the century, about the time the rites in question became obsolete, and it has increased in incidence since that time. Loudon notes that in an area of Natal far removed from the industrial towns which now provide employment for many Zulu males, the men are able to spend little time with their families in the villages on the reserves. As a consequence, many responsibilities normally assumed by the men fall on the shoulders of the women. Loudon states (1959: 362–63): "Now, what is most interesting is that many of the women in this district who suffer from *ufufunyana* trace much of their anxiety to the fact that they are forced into this reversal of social roles, whereas none of the women in my district [where men are able to spend considerable time with their families] has any anxiety on that account. While this contrast is most illuminating, I wish it could be established whether or not there is a greater incidence of *ufufunyana* in a district where migrant labourers are away from home for long intervals. At present this cannot be done." A report on hypertension among Zulu women (Scotch 1960) reports that its incidence is greater among widows and women separated from their husbands than among married women living with their husbands, and states (Scotch 1960: 1007) that most women "do not appreciate the role of family head."

Much of the foregoing may be reworded to state that writings on the Zulu fail to provide clear information of the existence of conflicts and tensions between Zulu males and females or of their resolution by means of these rites. Similar circumstances surround Gluckman's other examples of putative female rebellion.

Interpretations of nakedness, lewdness, and obscene behavior among women as rebellions against their roles or even as expressions of hostility are also questionable. These customs are perhaps more common among women than among men, but as later discussion will show, they exist plentifully among adolescents and adults of both sexes. We are rarely told what they mean to the native peoples. Bryant (1949: 664) does give native interpretation of the significance of nakedness during Zulu rites conducted during epidemics of disease; mothers of young children disrobe to shock and frighten away the fever fiend.

Doubt may also be expressed of the implication that the exclusion of men from certain rites conducted by women constitutes female rebellion against the social order. It seems uncertain that it is even an expression of antagonism toward males. Zulu rites to drive away the fever fiend resemble in some respects the Nomkubulwana rites of the same society, which Gluckman (1954b: 4–11) uses as an example of female rebellion. In both rites girls sing lewd songs and march around the kraals. Men are excluded from both rites, but *young married women* are also excluded from the rites to expel the fever fiend (Bryant 1949: 663).

It seems reasonable, nevertheless, to think that sexual antagonism does in fact exist in these societies. One could probably build a good case for the existence of sexual antagonism in any society. But the causes are doubtless varied, and antagonism does not necessarily imply tensions arising from differences in positions of authority of men and women. In order to speak with assurance of female rebellion against males it is necessary to have more information than ethnologists' accounts presently provide on the relationships between the sexes. It is also necessary to know the manifest significance of the rites in question, a subject to which this discussion will return.

b   *Between superiors and inferiors*

Gluckman gives pointed attention to rites in which subjects are said to rebel against rulers and chiefs. The *incwala* ceremony of the Swazi constitutes his major example. In this elaborate series of rites, the king, members of the royal clan, and subjects all participate. Gluckman (1954b: 18–19) summarizes the ritual events as: ". . . the acting out of the powerful tensions which make up national life—king and state against people, and people against king and state; king allied with commoners against his rival brother-princes, commoners allied with princes, commoners allied with princes against the king; the relation of the king to his mother and his own queens; and the nation united against internal enemies and external foes, and in a struggle for a living with nature. This ceremony is not a simple mass assertion of unity, but a stressing of conflict, a statement of rebellion and rivalry against the king, with periodical affirmations of unity with the king, and the drawing of power from the king."

The account upon which this interpretation appears to be based (Kuper 1961) provides inadequate information to support an interpretation of ritual *rebellion* against the king by his subjects, although Kuper now and then makes very brief allusions to conflict between king and subjects. The expression of conflict seems to take the form of a ritual drama portraying the many dangers the king must face in pursuit of his duties of office, especially the hatred and hostility of his rivals in the royal clan. The ceremony also expresses the sympathy of the people for their king, their loyalty to him, his seeming reluctance to serve in the royal role, and "unites the people under the king" (Kuper 1961: 224).

Gluckman emphasizes traditional incwala songs, sung by the people, that express hatred of the king. It is important to note that these songs do not express hatred of subject for ruler. Recurrent phraseology in them uses pronouns in the form of the second rather than first person. The reiterated phrase "You hate the king" clearly refers to the hatred of the king by his rivals and potential enemies—men and women of the royal clan, women made pregnant by men of the royal clan, and foreigners who do not owe allegiance to the king. A concluding part of a segment of the rites consists of the peoples' singing repeatedly (Kuper 1961: 205):

> King, alas for your fate
> King, they reject thee
> King, they hate thee.

(This song is also sung on other important occasions in the life of a king, when he marries his main ritual wife, when the ancestral cattle are brought back from the royal graves, and in rites conducted when a king dies.) The song of hatred is abruptly stilled by a priest shouting "Out, foreigners" (Kuper 1961: 205). The king's "enemies" are then sent away, and this part of the ceremony concludes with the singing by the people of the Swazi "national anthem."

Despite the apparent lack of passages clearly describing antagonism or hostility of commoners toward king, these acts may well exist in the Swazi rites. They appear to have existed formerly among the kindred Zulu and are abundant elsewhere in similar rites. But antagonism and hostility, it should be noted again, are not equivalents of rebellion.

Gluckman's second major example of ritual rebellion against

rulers consists of rites formerly observed by the Zulu. Accounts of these rituals seem to describe events closely similar to the incwala ceremony of the Swazi. Included among the elements are songs expressing hatred of the king. Bryant (1949: 517–18) describes one of these songs, which seemingly expresses the hatred of enemy tribes for the Zulu king. Samuelson (1929: 386) interprets in the following words the "national anthem" which the whole assemblage of Zulu warriors sings to the king at the Feast of First Fruits: "They hate him, they are arranging evil for him, all nations hate him and are arranging evil for him . . ." Delegorgue (1847 Vol. II: 237) refers to three days each year when "the nation itself has the right to ask of the king a strict accounting of his acts." Delegorgue gives some details of the events of these three days, which Gluckman (1954b: 30–31) cites. Ordinary warriors may leap from the ranks, denouncing the king, blaming his actions, calling them base and cowardly, obliging him to explain, questioning his explanations, and finally threatening and expressing contempt for him. Delegorgue also describes the intense expressions of hostility between "the king's party and that of the opposition," but does not clearly reveal the identity of these two groups. Again, no clear evidence of rebellion appears in these accounts.

As another example of ritual rebellion against authority, Gluckman mentions in passing the Yao custom in rites of installation for a village headman whereby he is knocked unconscious by a blow on the head and thus is ritually killed. Writings on the Yao (Mitchell 1956, 1959; Gluckman, Mitchell, Barnes 1949) appear to give no support to an interpretation of these acts as expressions of rebellion. A brief summary of the events in the accession rites may be given as follows: The dangers to which a headman, surrounded by enemies in the village, exposes himself are pointed out to him, and he is warned of the possibilities of conflict in the village. He is struck on the forehead by the fist of the chief of another village, who serves as one of the leaders of ritual, and is knocked to the ground. Dressed and regarded as a corpse, he is sprinkled with flour from a sacrifice basket and is ceremonially brought to life. During a period of seclusion he is given a series of lectures by other headmen on the duties of his office, and various of the people give speeches saying what they expect of him. He is subjected to and passes a test, apparently symbolic, whereby he is judged as good or bad on the basis of whether or not he vomits human flesh served to him. Finally, ritual leaders call on the people for loyalty to him.

Rather than constituting aggressive acts of rebellion, the blow on the head and the ensuing events may easily be seen as symbolic death and rebirth, a theme which appears recurrently in African rituals marking changes in social status. This is the interpretation given these events by Mitchell, the ethnographer reporting on the Yao. In a general way, this relatively simple series of ritual events marking the inauguration of a village headman of the Yao may be seen to parallel the incwala rites of the Swazi. The sources of conflict, the difficulties that the headman must face are pointed up; the headman is put on his mettle to serve his office well, and he is finally ritually assured of the support of his group.

Like the rites Gluckman interprets as female rebellion against males, it is difficult to see in the ceremonies of these three societies *rebellion* against authority. Both types of rites may be seen as dramas of conflict. As the following pages will show, these may be found in abundance depicting relationships between ruler and subject and also other relationships that are not hierarchical.

African societies not discussed by Gluckman provide many examples of rituals dramatizing conflict between figures of authority and those beneath them, and of subjecting kings and officials to testing, lecturing, and accusations of wrongdoing. A new chief of the Kilba of Northern Nigeria is given seven blows by an official who warns him to treat people fairly (Meek 1931b Vol. I: 184). The new headman of the Luapula receives from the people lectures concerning his duties, and is told that he will "break the village" (Cunnison 1959: 139, 141). At his installation, the Luapula king receives lectures on kingship from the aristocrats (Cunnison 1959: 172–73). The Lango chief is similarly admonished during his accession rites (Hayley 1947: 104–5). Among the Bari, the people "threaten" a new chief and "a mock fight ensues" (Seligman 1932: 294). The Ba Venda chief is ridiculed by young men during their initiation rites (Stayt 1931: 134). The new village deputy of the Ngoni is upbraided, told how ungrateful, miserly, and deceitful he and his wife are (Gluckman, Mitchell, Barnes 1949: 103). At the time of the girls' initiation rites, the headman of the Chewa must pass a test of sexual morality (Hodgson 1933: 134).

The new king of the Mpongwe-speaking peoples is lectured regarding proper conduct by an official, with the people chiming in. The king's personal faults are pointed out and social ills that he should cure are called to his attention (Nassau 1904: 221). A sham fight observed by the Baganda depicts antagonism toward the king, and another sham battle symbolizes that his rival princes have "settled down" (Roscoe 1911: 193, 204). Rattray (1955: 151–58) describes an old Ashanti custom at an annual ceremony that allows commoners to accuse the king of failings and express hatred of him for injuries received. During his rites of accession, the Bambi, an official of the Bangongo, kneels on one knee before the king after "performing a mock attack" (Torday 1925: 158). A drama of conflict between ruler and subject is acted out among the Kanakuru in a game of backgammon, in which five of the seven players represent the chief and two the commoners; the game is accompanied by a "continuous flow of mocking remarks" (Meek 1931b Vol. II: 314). Meek briefly and cryptically explains the symbolism of this game as having "a magical character, symbolizing the hunter and the hunted." A similar game is reported among the Akamba during ceremonies when the crops are ripe (Meek 1931b Vol. II: 314). The killing of kings when they were judged to be failures in their roles as monarchs because of senility or for other reasons is reported as a custom of the past among the Shilluk, Fung (Seligman 1932: 424–28), Nyakyusa, and Ngonde (Wilson 1959: 18–19).

In many societies court and village jesters informally call attention to social failings of members of the society and may even rebuke rulers (see, for example, Campbell 1922: 41). In other societies, great annual festivals and crisis rites provide the occasion for a general airing of grievances. Rites of this kind and other rituals which include expressions of hostility are discussed in the pages that follow.

c *Between kin groups of bride and groom*

The symbolic expression of hostility between relatives of brides and grooms is so common in African societies that it has been set apart as a special class (see Radcliffe-Brown and Forde, eds., 1950: 49). This custom takes many local forms. Very frequently the bride expresses reluctance to enter the marriage, acting out this attitude in the fashion that has become the convention for her society. She demurs against joining her husband before the actual rites are performed or at various points during the rites by holding back, hiding, weeping, rejecting food offered her by relatives of the groom, or by demanding payment of goods of some kind before she will continue with the rites of marriage and settle into domestic life with her husband. Occasionally the groom similarly acts out reluctance (e.g., Nandi, Huntingford 1953b: 28; Ba-Ila, Smith and Dale 1920 Vol. II: 56; Bushmen, Thomas 1959: 158).

The issue does not appear, however, to be one between husband and wife or one of male against female, even when the new husband or wife insults the other (e.g., Natal tribes, Shooter 1857: 74). These acts seem to be only scenes in a larger drama of conventional expression of hostility between kin groups of the bride and groom. Mock capture of brides is the most common of the regulated expressions of conflict between these two kin groups, but various other acts, often a part of the routine of "capture," express more directly the hostility between the two social groups.

Relatives of a bride and groom insult and threaten each other and conduct mock battles that sometimes become heated (e.g., Zulu, Hoernlé 1925: 488 and Gluckman 1954a: 69; Nuer, Evans-Pritchard 1951b: 65; Makhanya, Reader 1954: 74–75, 86–87; Zulu, Shangana-Tonga, Krige 1950: 115; Swazi, Marwick 1940: 128; Banyankole, Roscoe 1923b: 126). Aggressive acts sometimes focus directly upon the bride or groom, the outsider whose interests and emotional ties, at least up to this point, have not coincided with those of the aggressors. The prospective groom might be cursed or derided (e.g., Lotuko, Huntingford 1953a: 82; pygmies of Gabon, Trilles 1932: 418). Brides might be lectured on their future conduct as wives, reviled, or told that they are unfit as wives and are troublemakers (e.g., Lango, Hayley 1947: 84; Kafir, Maclean 1858: 51). Among the Gusii, a feature of the *enyangi* rite formalizing a marriage is that ". . . female relatives of each partner have license to express in unmeasured terms any grievance against the other—the husband's sexual inadequacy, for example, or the wife's failure to show due respect to her mother-in-law" (Mair 1953: 60). One of the recurrent dramatic themes, found in many other ritual contexts expressing conflict, is a mock theft by a member of one kin group and mock outrage and pursuit by members of the other.

It is noteworthy that these standardized dramatizations of antagonism are not entirely restricted to the period when marriage rites are conducted. As with other ritual expressions of conflict described here, they may be a feature of rituals marking various kinds of events. Among the Baganda, Bakitara, and Bateso, for example, ritualized hostility between the maternal and paternal relatives of children are a feature of rites at the birth of twins (Roscoe 1911: 70; 1923a: 255; 1915: 265).

d *Between formally defined social and political groups*

Ritualized expressions of intergroup tensions are also widely spread among societies of Subsaharan Africa. Any social relationship that produces tension may serve as a theme. As with other events already discussed, the ritual occasions for expression are highly varied, including birth and initiation rites, weddings, funerals, ceremonies of accession to high office, rites performed at times of illness, and grand annual festivals.

On various of these occasions rival clans and lineages may deride each other's members for moral failings (e.g., Namoos, Fortes 1936: 596; Lugbara, Middleton 1960: 202) or stage mock battles (Baganda, Roscoe 1911: 70; Bari, Huntingford 1953a: 42; Lango, Hayley 1947: 100; Bari and Kuku, Seligman 1932: 291, 302). Mock battles and other controlled expressions of hostility are common between elder and younger age groups (e.g., Teso and Jie, Gulliver 1953: 25, 46; Nupe, Nadel 1954: 218; Lotuko, Seligman 1932: 322–23). Youths may oppose the aged in mock battles in which taunts and insults are exchanged (BaVenda, Stayt 1931: 130), and political or other intergroup rivalry may be acted out similarly (e.g., Mandari, Buxton 1958: 94; Nupe, Nadel 1951a: 396–97). In Shilluk ceremonies installing a new king, moiety battles moiety in a symbolic statement of the balance of power (Lienhardt 1954: 153; Evans-Pritchard 1948: 27; Howell and Thompson 1946: 48–49). Expression of hatred for outsiders is also ritualized (e.g., among the Swazi and Zulu, previously noted; Bushmen, Fourie 1928: 96–97; A-Kamba, Hobley 1910: 70; Shilluk, Howell and Thompson

1946: 24). Dinka rituals conducted on various occasions—when someone is seriously ill, when women fail to conceive, and at other critical times—include mock duels with other tribes (Lienhardt 1961: 281). Funerals provide an occasion for the Tallis and Namoos, neighboring peoples, to taunt and challenge each other (Fortes 1936: 593). [At girls' initiation rites among the Ovambo, boys even conduct a mock attack upon mortars, for the arduous work they cause the girls who use them (Hahn 1928: 31).]

e *General, between any persons holding grievances*

Attempts are sometimes made to keep the expression of individual animosities on a group level, as among the Nuba, where stick fights are held on many occasions. Nadel (1947: 245) observes that even when the fights center on grudges, ". . . their aim is clearly to lift the personal dispute to the level of the dispassionate group contest." The general airing of grievances against other individuals is, however, permitted or urged in many societies on ritual occasions. It is important to note that differences of status do not seem to inhibit the expression of hostility; one declares his grievances against superiors, equals, and inferiors. The Lugbara speak out their grievances toward members of their group at a sacrifice for a sick person (Middleton 1960: 92–93). The Nuer similarly settle grievances at funerals and also on other very formal occasions (Seligman 1932: 236; Evans-Pritchard 1956: 209). During Bemba fishing rites, the priest in charge asks the people to express their grievances (Richards 1961: 339).

Rattray (1954: 122–26, 1955: 153–60) describes annual rites among peoples of the Ashanti federation, and cites (1955: 151) Bosman, the Dutch historian of the coast of Guinea:

> . . . a Feast of eight days, accompanied with all manner of Singing, Skipping, Dancing, Mirth, and Jollity: in which time a perfect lampooning liberty is allowed, and Scandal so highly exalted, that they may freely sing of all the Faults, Villanies, and Frauds of their Superiours, as well as Inferiours without Punishment, or so much as the least interruption; and the only way to stop their mouths is to ply them lustily with Drink, which alters their tone immediately, and turns their Satyrical Ballads into Commendation Songs on the good Qualities of him who hath so nobly treated them. . . .

Meyerowitz (1951: 153–54, 161) also discusses these customs among peoples of the Ashanti federation, describing "the great day of abuse" of the people of Takyiman, and speaking of "traditional vituperations" among the people of Wankyi.

Wilson (1959: 11–13) gives a succinct account of Nyakyusa customs of expressing grievances. Family quarrels are expressed at rites held at birth, marriage, death, and when someone is seriously ill. The expression of grievances between other people and between social groups comes when sacrifices are made to the founding heroes (Wilson 1959: 12–13):

> Quarrels between chiefs and people, between the divine king and his vassals, or the chiefdoms which acknowledge his overlordship; quarrels between villages, and personal quarrels between the leading men of the country, all these are brought up at the sacrifices to the founding heroes and in the chief's groves. The priests and village headmen and chiefs express and reject their anger against one another, the commoner leaders being particularly forthright in their criticism of the chiefs. On such confession is thought to depend the efficacy of the rituals, and so the weather, the fertility of the soil, the increase of the herds, and the health of the participants themselves.

The foregoing examples and others that might be cited seem to describe "rituals"; that is, the speaking out occurs on ritual occasions and is thought to have mystical benefit. Similar airing of grievances, however, is conventionalized for occasions that are secular or less clearly religious in tone. As previously noted, the Nuer expressed grievances at any "very formal occasion" (Evans-Pritchard 1956: 209). The airing of grievances between mother-in-law and son-in-law was permitted among the BaVenda after the beer drinking that follows group economic efforts (Stayt 1931: 324–25). Boloki village dances on moonlight nights included impromptu songs satirizing all human failings (Weeks 1913: 120–21; Hambly 1930: 34). Chopi songs, sung on many occasions, described social injustices and were often critical of those in authority, white or black; they are described as having a "highly social and cathartic function" (Tracey 1948: 3). Dahomean customs are similar (Herskovits 1934: 77–78; 1938 Vol. I: 218). The songs and acts of jesters, to which we have already referred, may be seen as vicarious clearing of the air.

2 OTHER INSTITUTIONALIZED DEPARTURES FROM EVERYDAY NORMS

a *With apparent moral significance*

The institutionalized violation on ritual occasions of important rules of behavior, rules that do not always or directly pertain to interpersonal relations, is a common practice throughout the world, and this custom prevails generally among Subsaharan societies of Africa. Evans-Pritchard (1929) has written on African customs allowing obscene speech and song, sexual license, and nakedness on many ceremonial occasions. He notes that obscene behavior may also accompany many collective economic enterprises, such as sowing, threshing, pounding mealies, smelting, fishing, and carrying roofs of huts, that are not "ritual" in the sense that they lack an aura of sanctity or supernaturalism. Ethnographic writings published since the time of Evans-Pritchard's account allow some expansion of the list of tribes among which these customs prevail and amplification of the occasions when the activities are allowed, but they do not alter his general observations on their nature.

Ethnologists writing on Africa have called attention to the danger of accepting freely the ethnocentric judgment in writings of missionaries and other early writers that native customs are obscene and licentious. Yet many accounts bring out clearly that the behavior so labeled there is viewed by the people themselves as improper and shocking except on these special occasions (e.g., Meek 1931b Vol. II: 65).

It is useful to note again that ritual license is by no means limited to females. Rites such as those already described in which girls and women remove their clothing or sing lewd songs are widespread, and they are sometimes a feature of cult ritual (e.g., Ekoi, Talbot 1912: 225). But boys also go naked during initiation and other rites of passage in some societies (e.g., Wiko, Gluckman 1949b: 148; Otoro, Nadel 1947: 143, 411; Zulu, Bryant 1949: 654; Kikuyu, Hobley 1938: 81). On these occasions, custom may call for boys and men to speak or sing lewdly or perform obscene dances (e.g., Basuto, Ashton 1955: 48; Wiko, Gluckman 1949b: 156). During iron-smelting operations, Bambala men sing lewd songs (Smith and Dale 1920 Vol. I:

207–9). Obscenity at female initiation rites sometimes has counterparts in male rites of the same society (e.g., Becwana, Brown 1921: 426–27; Basuto, Ashton 1955: 57). In some societies both sexes jointly indulge in obscene behavior on various occasions (e.g., Wiko, Gluckman 1949b: 153; Nanzela and Ba-Ila, Smith and Dale 1920 Vol. II: 113, 272; Nupe, Nadel 1951a: 396; 1954: 82–83, 218; Kafir, Maclean 1858: 98–99; Shangaan, Sachs, W. 1947: 49–50; see also Sachs, C. 1937). Obscenity by both sexes is especially common as an accompaniment to joint economic activities (see Evans-Pritchard 1929).

Numerous writings on Africa describe certain ceremonies as Saturnalias, referring especially to the temporary suspension at these times of rules governing sexual behavior. Some measure of sexual license on prescribed ritual occasions appears to be so common among these African societies that it may be described as general. The latitude varies, however, from sanctioned sexual play through promiscuity and adultery, and it may extend as far as the violation of incest prohibitions (e.g., Batwa, Campbell 1922: 105).

License as an accompaniment to ritual extends far beyond the sexual sphere. Many precepts may be broken by persons about whom ritual centers or by all members of society. Theft, assault, and damage done to the property of others may at these times go unpunished (e.g., Wolof, Gorer 1949: 34; Teso, Gulliver 1953: 25; Swazi, Kuper 1961: 200; Gisu, LaFontaine 1959: 45; Ashanti, Rattray 1954: 122; Bakongo, Weeks 1914: 166–67). Sometimes all or nearly all restrictions on behavior are said to be lifted during certain rituals (e.g., Thonga, Junod 1913: 297; Smith and Dale 1920 Vol. II: 113; Va-Nyaneka, Lang and Tastevin 1937: 160).

In summary, it may be said that a varying degree of license to violate on special occasions sexual and other rules of moral behavior seems characteristic of the societies of Subsaharan Africa. The occasions are principally ritual events, and they are often the same as those during which expressions of hostility are allowed or prescribed. Ritualized expressions of interpersonal and intergroup hostility may then be seen as a part of a larger scheme of the temporary suspension of ordinary restraints applying to almost any sphere of life.

b *Without apparent moral significance*

The practices so far discussed are striking because they seem to have important moral significance for the participants. Few European observers have failed to note them. Yet custom in these societies prescribes many other ritual departures from conventional behavior which appear to have no moral connotations, at least from the eyes of Europeans. These are customs ordinarily called taboos, restraints upon customary activities, against working, ordinary sexual relations, drawing water, talking, eating certain ordinary foods, and the like, that apply to some or all persons during part or all of ritual periods. Other customs during periods of ritual prescribe unusual behavior but do not proscribe. As in other parts of the world, prescriptions and proscriptions of these kinds are common in Africa.

From the viewpoint of a European, funeral rites in many African societies may well be described by Rattray's phrase (1954: 61) as the "deliberate antithesis of funeral rites," because they are occasions for jokes, horseplay, and hilarity (e.g., Bondei, Dale 1896: 237; Ba-Congo, Claridge 1922: 292; Tonga, Colson 1953: 54; Tallensi, Fortes 1945: 92–95; Chewa, Hodgson 1933: 156). Among the LoDagaba (Goody 1957: 91) the dead man is insulted and joking partners clown at the funeral to "counter the sense of loss felt by the close relatives." In Ashanti rites observing the death of an infant, parents shave their heads (a token of joy), dress in white (an insult at funerals), and eat groundnut soup (symbolic of a joyous feast) (Rattray 1954: 60).

Scratching, washing, sitting on mats, touching other people, and sexual intercourse were forbidden for the entire population during accession rites of the Swazi (Kuper 1961: 219). Features of the Ashanti Yam Custom, in addition to the extension of general license to the population, included the playing of discordant music, the king's appearing in humblest clothing, and the killing and eating of an ox, an act otherwise forbidden and defiling (Rattray 1954: 125, 134–36). During his accession rites, the king of the Bakitara was required to remain silent and was not allowed to defecate (Roscoe 1923a: 301–2). At a Lozi funeral, skin cloaks are worn with the hair outside, the reverse of normal fashion (Turner 1952: 46). For an interval during their wedding rites, the Basuto bride and groom must sit with legs straight instead of folded in the ordinary sitting posture and must observe various other prohibitions against customary behavior (Ashton 1955: 67). The Lovedu boy wears his loin-cloth backwards during initiation rites (E. J. and J. D. Krige 1956: 119). Custom sometimes prescribes that in societies where intergroup or personal hostility is normally expressed rather than repressed it come to an end during the ritual period (e.g., Lango, Hayley 1947: 69; Bagesu, Roscoe 1924: 3–4, 23; Ibo, Talbot 1927: 111). The many rites already noted in which women assume the roles of men and vice versa may also be seen as "reversals" of ordinary practices.

Ritual requirements of this kind have generally been interpreted, in line with the reasoning of van Gennep, as events that point up by contrast the social importance of the occasion. This interpretation seems reasonable and it also seems reasonable for many of the other ritual acts discussed earlier. This statement does not mean to imply, however, that the acts lack other functional significance.

SUMMARY AND DISCUSSION

This review began by examining institutionalized African practices, in ritual context, that appear to express intergroup and interpersonal conflict. The scope of investigation was then extended to cover other institutionalized practices on the same or similar occasions that likewise constitute departures from everyday behavior or ideals. Some of the practices have apparent moral import, and scholars in the social sciences have commonly labeled them "violations" of customs or "license." Other prescriptions and proscriptions have no readily apparent moral connotations and have not been described by these terms. All of these events share a common characteristic. All are sharp deviations from everyday practice. Following van Gennep, I suggest that all serve a common function of making memorable and enhancing the importance of the social occasions upon which they are observed. Beyond this, their functional significance is doubtless various.

Special attention has been given to certain rites appearing to express conflict which Gluckman has interpreted as rituals of rebellion. The term "rebellion" conventionally means opposition to authority or to control, and for this reason it seems inappropriate for the rites Gluckman describes. This examination of writings on Africa reveals an abundance of socially regulated expressions of resentment on ritual and other special occasions. They are conducted at certain times and are not allowed to get out of hand. In some societies "regulation" is strengthened by limiting the expressions to a group level so that more intense personal hostility is avoided. Interpersonal airing of grievances is also common, although it seems rarely to apply to specific dyadic relationships.

Serious question exists, however, regarding the interpretation of expressions of resentment and hostility as expressions of rebellion. Nakedness, lewdness, and obscenity during ritual are not limited to females. The widespread custom of transvestism by both sexes on ritual occasions casts doubt on a generalized interpretation that behavior of this kind by women constitutes rebellion against male authority and against female roles—unless transvestite males are also rebelling. Like wearing one's loincloth backwards and many other "reversals" prescribed by ritual, the symbolic assumption of dress or roles of the opposite sex are dramatic departures from usual behavior. Perhaps in some instances this unusual behavior also symbolizes unity of the sexes. When a requirement of male initiation rites, the return to male garments following transvestism may symbolize the end of the boys' identification with the social world of women and children. When transvestism is accompanied by exaggerated and comical parodies of the opposite sex, it seems more reasonable to regard the complex of behavior as including an expression of antagonism, although not necessarily an expression of rebellion.

Rituals clearly expressing sexual antagonism exist in some societies, but these are acts other than those described by Gluckman and the causes of dissension are usually unreported. Often antagonism is expressed by both men and women, in rites in which the opposite sex is insulted, derided, charged with faults, and "assaulted." In a few societies, rites exist in which the superiority of men over women is clearly asserted. The BaVenda girl undergoing initiation is switched by men ". . . to demonstrate the futility of her arrogance, and to show in the end the man will be the most powerful" (Stayt 1931: 119). Yakö songs during the first fruits ceremony vaunt the superiority of men over women

(Forde 1949: 8). It does not seem justifiable to regard any of these acts as forms of rebellion unless the meaning of the term is made to signify expressions of antagonism toward any other person regardless of cause and of relative positions of authority. Lack of information on relations between the sexes does not allow even assured statements for most societies that resentment of male authority exists.

This review of African rites also renders doubtful Gluckman's interpretation that seemingly antagonistic acts against rulers or other figures of authority constitute rebellion. The clash of interest between ruler or chief and subject may well result in tensions. Although the validity of Gluckman's specific examples of aggressive acts against king or chief has been questioned here, additional examples have been cited that leave no doubt of the existence of rites in which the people express *resentment* of their rulers and concern over the propriety of the rulers' behavior. These rites resemble in some measure customs of acting out hostility toward bride or groom and also the ordeals that young men and young women must often undergo at initiation to adulthood, acts which seem in part to be adjurations and dramatic assurances that husband, wife, and new adult will perform satisfactorily in their roles. Many of the apparently hostile acts directed toward rulers seem similar—the ruler is upbraided, accused of faults, threatened with dire consequences if he fails to meet expectations—and therefore it seems reasonable to think they have similar significance as well as serving a cathartic function. The ruler is also ritually assured of the support of those subject to his authority. Admonition and castigation are not always limited to the lowly against those above them. There is often a general clearing of the air for all members of society, regardless of differences in social status. In discussing rites of the Nyakyusa, Wilson (1959: 13) has expressed a similar opinion: ". . . I suggest that much of what has been cited as evidence of rebellion in rituals elsewhere in Africa is in fact the formal admission of anger, the prelude to reconciliation. The body politic is purged by the very act of 'speaking out'. . . ."

When rites seemingly hostile to rulers are conducted only in ceremonies of accession, it seems doubtful that they are even expressions of anger. Since they are conducted at irregular and sometimes great intervals, their value as safety valves for the expression of anger seems most doubtful.

Interpretation of the significance of rites apparently expressing hostility is seriously hindered by lack of information on their manifest meanings. Although Gluckman (1935: 264, 266–67) seems well aware of the importance of these data, his interpretation of rituals of rebellion proceeds without regard to native attitudes toward the ceremonies. Monica Wilson calls attention to the importance of having knowledge of the symbolism involved in a Nyakyusa rite of "cleansing the country" wherein there is a sham fight. She states (1959: 13), "Only if the symbolism of the rituals of kinship is ignored could this be interpreted as an expression of rebellion rather than a confession. . . ." It seems probable, as Durkheim states (1915: 381), that some acts of ritual lack symbolic meaning and merely fill the need for action. It is likely, too, that the symbolism of many ritual acts has become lost although the acts themselves are perpetuated and regarded as necessary. Knowledge of the meaning that symbolism conveys to the actors seems nevertheless vital to functional interpretation. Boulding's view (1962: 5) that awareness of conflict is an essential element in its definition seems appropriate. Nadel (1954: 108) states similarly: "In my view uncomprehended 'symbols' have no part in social enquiry; their social effectiveness lies in their capacity to indicate, and if they indicate nothing to the actors, they are, from our point of view, irrelevant and indeed no longer symbols (whatever their significance for the psychologist or psycho-analyst). But let us note that certain modes of acting may be significant for the actors without constituting symbols, merely because they represent a rule, a formalism of acting, that is, a *ritual,* and not accidental or random behaviour." Referring to the Zulu, Loudon states (1959: 352) ". . . it is not clear from Gluckman's account whether or not there is any evidence to show that either the men or the women were conscious of the symbolism involved in the ritual, insofar as it may be a catharsis." The original accounts also fail to settle this question.

When the participants are aware of conflict—between the sexes, between ruler and ruled, and so on—*and we are apprised of this awareness,* it seems in order to assign to the ritual the function of expressing and relieving, if not resolving, conflict. In some of the cases cited here, the ethnographers have clearly indicated that the rites convey this meaning to the participants (e.g., see Middleton 1960; Seligman 1932; Evans-Pritchard 1956; Richards 1961 in their discussion under classification *e*). In many other instances, including the examples of "rebellion" cited by Gluckman, this information is lacking, or, as previously noted in certain cases, ethnographic accounts tell us there is no feeling of conflict. Judgment that women feel hostile toward men seems assured when rituals allow or expect women to insult, deride, and find fault with men, and many societies of Africa follow such customs. Examples already given, however, indicate that the reverse also often applies. Men act out hostility in similar fashion toward women. There is no justification for giving the name rebellion to the acts of females only. On the issue of the cathartic value of the direct airing of grievances on ritual occasions, the record often seems clear. Many accounts state that "speaking out" is regarded by informants as necessary for their well-being and that harbored resentment is harmful.

The rites reviewed here make it clear that African customs allow periodic freedom from restraints of many kinds. At the same sorts of occasions and often the identical times that one is allowed to "speak out," he is often also freed from other normal restraints. He may violate rules of sexual behavior, indulge in lewdness and obscenity, commit theft, and take many other liberties. The customs of initial concern in this paper, Gluckman's rituals of rebellion, may then be seen as part of a still larger order of institutionalized practices which go beyond the freedom to express resentment or hostility and provide controlled, periodic relaxation of many or all rules. Still other practices followed at these times are somewhat more difficult for us to regard as elements of a common theme because they do not represent in any conventional sense violations of controlling norms. Nevertheless, I suggest that customs which seem to have no moral or ethical import—practices such as wearing one's clothing inside out, transvestism, and the reversal of sex roles—are closely related and, as departures from everyday norms, have in part common significance.

Some of the customs Gluckman discusses may also have cathartic value as forms of humor, but available descriptions of them permit no conclusions on this point. Writings on Africa contain many brief references to humor and laughter, and to village jesters, court jesters, and strolling entertainers who amuse by exercising license in pantomime, speech, song, or folktale. Hilarity at funerals, as we have noted, is a common custom, but in other contexts we are rarely given details on the nature and occasions for humor. Occasionally we are told that ritual transvestism and mimicking the behavior of the opposite sex are regarded as amusing. Gluckman's accounts of rituals of rebellion are silent on this subject. It is impossible to avoid wondering what cathartic role laughter might play in various of the customs we have discussed, and whether some of them do not function primarily as forms of humor rather than as direct expressions of antagonism.

Gluckman holds that rites of rebellion may exist only in stable societies wherein the social order is unchallenged and suggests that political ceremonies of modern England may not take the form of rituals of rebellion because "our social order itself is questioned" (1954b: 30). Various writers (e.g., Richards 1956: 117–19; Norbeck 1961: 212) have observed that this interesting idea cannot be verified because we lack objective means of judging whether societies are stable or unstable. In explaining the near absence of rituals of rebellion among the Lozi, Gluckman (1954b: 30) asserts that their governmental organization provides elaborately for the release of tensions between various components of the state, whereas that of the southeastern Bantu, the peoples of his principal concern, does not. The idea that ritual protests are but one of a large variety of safety-valve mechanisms is certainly worth investigating in connection with Gluckman's hypothesis. To gain a full understanding of the issue, we need to investigate for these societies such things as joking relationships, witchcraft, gossip, patterns of social fission and emigration, customs surrounding the use of alcoholic drinks, and legal procedures. Even then, as Loudon observes in discussing Zulu women (1959: 367), it is unjustified to think that tensions among the general population of these societies ever reach an intensity that *demands* release through these or other means.

Gluckman asserts that rites of rebellion do not exist within the family and explains their absence in accordance with his theory concerning the kind of society which can allow these rites (1959: 129–30): "The family is not such an enduring group: it breaks up with the death of the parents and with the marriages of the children. It has not the same sort of cohesion as the other groups.

And the basis of my argument is that the licensed ritual of protest and of rebellion is effective so long as there is no querying of the order within which the ritual of protest is set, and the group itself will endure." This review does not reveal an entire absence of "speaking out" against members of the family. Wilson's description (1959: 12) of the settling of "family" quarrels in this way refers specifically to mutual complaints between sisters-in-law and between younger and eldest brother. We have also seen that the BaVenda man and his mother-in-law may air their grievances against each other. Discussing Nuer funeral customs, Evans-Pritchard (1956: 150) states, ". . . any of the kin of the dead man who bears a grudge against a relative must now declare it. If he does not do so now, he must for ever keep silence. This is an occasion for amicable settlement of family and kinship quarrels." One of the Azande curing rites requires that members of the family "hurl the most abusive expressions at the head of the father and mother" (Evans-Pritchard 1958: 493).

Assuming that customs of mock fighting and mutual derision between men and women represent generalized protests against the opposite sex rather than hostility between husband and wife, I would amend Gluckman's statement to say that ritualized expression of hostility between members of conjugal families and other close relatives is uncommon. I suggest that the explanation of its scarcity in part opposes that put forth by Gluckman. The economic and emotional interdependence of members of the family, or any other small and closely knit social group, doubtless serves to inhibit strong intra-group aggression. At the same time, the very intensity of the bonds of close kinship may allow freedom rather than repression of the expression of grievances. I have previously made this suggestion in connection with accusations of witchcraft (1961: 195). A similar idea is advanced by Plotnicov (1962), who holds that the conjugal family, a "fixed-membership group," is an important source of cultural innovations in the new cities of Africa. Because of the strength of the idea that their relationship cannot easily be ended, members of the conjugal family are said to have considerable freedom of action denied to participants of "flexible-membership" groups.

Rather than attempting to determine whether societies are stable or unstable, it may be more feasible to judge whether they are or are not highly organized socially and politically. Expressions of hostility in ritual form, firmly regulated, are of course congruous with a social life that is otherwise highly organized socially and politically. Where other safety valves are inadequate, ritual expressions of hostility seem most expectable in societies that exercise firm control over the behavior of their members through formal social units and highly formalized institutions. Wallace (1959: 94) has presented a similar idea in discussing changed psychotherapeutic techniques among Iroquois Indians: ". . . in a highly organized sociocultural system, the psychotherapeutic needs of individuals will tend to center in catharsis (the expression of suppressed or repressed wishes in a socially nondisturbing ritual situation); and . . . in a relatively poorly organized system, the psychotherapeutic needs will tend to center in control (the development of a coherent image of self-and-world and the repression of incongruent motives and beliefs)."

The relative scarcity of ritual expressions of hostility in societies such as our own appears also to reflect a different view of the nature of the universe and changed religious conceptions. In culturally simple and scientifically unadvanced societies, supernaturalism is put to many uses for which it is unsuited in our society. Diamond (1963: 102–3) states: "Civilization represses hostility . . . , fails to use or structure it, even denies it. . . . Certain ritual dramas [of primitive peoples] or aspects of them, acknowledge, express, and symbolize the most destructive, ambivalent, and demoniacal aspects of human nature; in so doing, they are left limited and finite; that is, they become self-limiting. For this, as yet, we have no civilized parallel, no functional equivalent." Meyer Fortes (1954: 90–91) states similarly, ". . . in primitive societies there are customary methods of dealing with these common human problems of emotional adjustment by which they are externalized, publicly accepted, and given treatment in terms of ritual beliefs; society takes over the burden which, with us, falls entirely on the individual. . . . Behavior that would be the maddest of fantasies in the individual, or even the worst of vices, becomes tolerable and sane, in his society, if it is transformed into custom and woven into the outward and visible fabric of a community's social life. This is easy in primitive societies where the boundary between the inner world of the self and the outer world of the community marks their line of fusion rather than of separation." Perhaps there is merit too in the idea that the ritual enactment of conflict lends color and dramatic interest to the lives of primitive peoples, among which forms of self-expression are limited (Boulding 1962: 306).

Finally, I shall summarize by saying that this paper has questioned Gluckman's specific hypotheses concerning rebellion and expressed doubt as to the suitability of some of his supporting data. It has presented an interpretation of the rites of Gluckman's special interest that puts them into a larger category of ritual events and gives them a significance differing from that offered by him. Doubt has also been expressed of the validity of Gluckman's view concerning the kinds of social groups in which ritualized conflict may exist, and another interpretation has been suggested. The basic idea underlying Gluckman's hypotheses, that conflict may be seen to have positive functional value, seems nevertheless meritorious. Gluckman's efforts in applying this idea to ethnological data impress me as deserving wider attention than they have thus far received.[1]

[1] I wish to thank Robert Anderson, William R. Bascom, Harumi Befu, Stanley Diamond, Hugh Dalziel Duncan, Frank Hole, Stanley A. Freed, M. J. Herskovits, Pauline Mahar Kolenda, and Leslie A. White for providing information or making suggestions useful in the preparation of this paper. I, however, am responsible for the views expressed herein and for errors in information. I am deeply indebted to Mimi Cohen for invaluable assistance over a period of many months. She should properly appear as co-author of this paper. I am indebted for financial aid to Rice University, Social Science Research Council, and Wenner-Gren Foundation for Anthropological Research.

Data presented here were gathered by many months of laborious reading. Because the topic under discussion has heretofore received almost no attention from ethnologists, indices of books were of little or no aid. M. J. Herskovits (personal communication) suggests that some of my ideas might be altered if the data included more writings on areas of Africa controlled or formerly controlled by France, Belgium, and Portugal. This may well be so, but the moderate number of works in French that were reviewed have not changed my impressions. Many of them contained no relevant information.

10 DEATH AND FERTILITY RITES OF THE MAPUCHE (ARAUCANIAN) INDIANS OF CENTRAL CHILE

Louis C. Faron

AN ESTIMATED 200,000 Mapuche Indians live on approximately 2,200 small reservations, in an area of about one-half million hectares, distributed over several political provinces in southern central Chile. In spite of military conquest, pacification, settlement on reservations, marginal incorporation into a regional agricultural economy—all important accommodations to colonial status—they have maintained a cultural and social distinctiveness *vis-à-vis* Chilean culture and society.

The religious ceremonials and other-world notions held by the Mapuche would seem to be among the most stabilizing forces operative in their society. The ethnographic literature, most of which is listed by Cooper (1946), indicates that Mapuche supernatural beliefs have remained relatively intact for many generations and, as seems undeniable, have helped to shore up traditional patterns of social action—albeit in a changing social ambient. But is not this an expectable "function of culture" and an expectable consequence of the "weight of tradition?" Explicit or not in the following pages, this is my point of view.

During more than 400 years of contact with a white, colonizing civilization, Mapuche concepts of the supernatural have changed relatively little, although certain rituals have undergone significant modification. Regardless of accretions and losses in the area of ritual activity and belief, their symbolic value has been of enduring cohesive power, and changes which have occurred both in ritual and belief are consonant with the structure of Mapuche society (see Faron 1961a, 1961b, 1962). It is likely, however,

Reprinted from *Ethnology* 2 (2), 1963: 135–56, by permission of the author and the editor, *Ethnology*.

that only since the reservation system of 1884 brought the Mapuche into contiguous blocks of immobilized reservation communities in the indigenous zone has religion pulled them together in such large numbers and in such a complex manner. In this paper I would like to examine the rationale and the cultural dress of Mapuche ritual, the ideological and behavioral framework of the structure of religious morality.

Funeral observances and fertility rites account for the greatest assemblages of people among the modern Mapuche. The great *nillatun* (agricultural fertility rite) and the compelling *awn* (funeral observances) serve to unite the Mapuche before the Supreme Being (*nenechen*) and their ancestors. Death and burial services serve to intensify the kinship relations among the several patrilineages involved. They also unite in sympathy (a psychological expression of social obligation) persons of unrelated households, unrelated by either blood or marriage, and reaffirm family friendships which are rooted in long contact and local residence. In this sense, both *nillatun* and *awn* are parochial, their conduct based on trust and expressed in terms of mutual obligation. They serve to reinforce solidary relationships among reservation groups within a traditionally defined locality, even though their conduct rests on lineage-based rights and duties imbedded in the structure of religious morality. I hope to give some order to these beliefs and practices.

DEATH AND BURIAL RITES (*awn*)

Traditional Mapuche belief holds that death is caused by supernatural intervention, specifically, that *wekufe* (the forces of evil) cause death, usually at the behest of a *kalku* (sorcerer-witch).[1] This explanation covers all situations, and "accidental" death (caused by falling from a horse, drowning, etc.) is regarded merely as one manner in which the forces of evil operate and, therefore, not accidental at all. While all deaths are associated with evil forces, a "bad death" (*wesa l'an*) usually refers to the fact that a person died violently and far from home, with the

---

[1] The term *wekufe* is a generic concept under which are subsumed various forms of malevolent spirits who appear to the Mapuche as animals and birds, shooting stars and whirlwinds, and as contaminated ancestral spirits. *Kalku* control these forces and direct them against the Mapuche.

further implication that he might not have been attended by relatives.

A growing awareness of modern medicine has had little effect in weakening traditional beliefs in supernatural causation. The syringe and the aspirin tablet combat certain illnesses better than some traditional herbal remedies, but should the new methods fail, resort is made to the native curer or shaman (*machi*), and the patient is always, because of this procedure, brought to the threshold of the supernatural world.

Upon death, certain preparatory acts must be performed. These follow a ritual pattern, a pattern consonant with the basic features of Mapuche social structure. Since postmarital residence is patrilocal (i.e., a woman comes to live with her husband on his natal reservation, where his father and other male lineage mates reside), a married woman most often dies among neighbors on the reservation into which she has married, rather than among her own patrilineal kinsmen. Her husband and his closest relatives are responsible for the proper display and burial of her corpse. A man dies among his lineage mates and is cared for by his wife, grown children, and closest blood relatives. The same procedure is followed regardless of whether the deceased is single, married, adult, or a minor of either sex, although in the case of children there are fewer mourners and less ostentation. One important difference between the death services of an adult married man or woman and a child is that in the case of a child attendance of affinally linked groups is less complete and less important to the ceremony.

The dead person is referred to as *l'ayen* while still guarded indoors. The corpse at this time is considered dangerous to handle, thus imposing a heavy obligation on those to whom its preparation falls. Children are kept away from the corpse and are not even supposed to view it. The feeling about the newly dead diminishes once the wake is concluded and the burial ceremony is under way.

The body of the dead person is washed, usually by one or two of the adult co-residents of his household. No attempt is made to preserve the corpse by draining the body fluid, but the practice of smoking the body of an important person still exists, although it is uncommon. While it is possible that smoking the corpse was more common in the past than it is today—and the historical data are inconclusive on this point—smoking the corpse takes place today only if burial is not feasible, owing to frozen ground (a problem in the Andes) or because of unusual delay in assembling the relatives of the deceased. Andean Mapuche tell of the corpse being suspended over the cooking fire in the household or lodged in the rafters somewhere near the smoke-escape hole. Although I failed to witness this practice, detailed descriptions of the procedure and of the stench of the corpse during the early stages of "preservation," besides freely offered evaluations of the depression of household members under such circumstances, lend credence to accounts of this sort. It is said that in these cases the viscera are removed by a shaman who is well paid for the service. Removal of the viscera not only aids in the preservation of the corpse but enables the shaman to perform an autopsy to determine the exact cause of death. The Mapuche report that few autopsies are performed nowadays, which seems to indicate that smoking of the corpse is equally rare. It still exists, however, both in practice and as an ideal tribute to the dead, although apparently not commonly effected. In any case, the important aspect for this paper is that the corpse is in no case quickly disposed of, not immediately interred in its final resting place—even if not smoked—but is handled in a deliberate and temporary manner which may be singled out, for analytic purposes, as the first phase of the funeral ceremony. In effect, final burial is "secondary burial."

After the corpse is washed and clothed in its finest garments, it is placed for display on a *llani* or *mellel* (each signifying a bier or altar, likewise used for the burning of offerings in the *nillatun* ceremony). It is retained in the house for an ideal period of four days or a multiple thereof (four and its multiples being of magical significance among the Mapuche), a period which is said to be extensible, even nowadays, to several months. In the burials which I observed, however, the corpse was retained in the house for no more than eight days (in only one case) and usually for four days. If there is already a coffin (*huampu*) on hand, the deceased is placed in it, and the coffin is raised on the bier. Coffins are still sometimes made of a tree trunk, split and hollowed in canoe shape, but most people purchase simple pine boxes manufactured in nearby Chilean towns. There seems to be a very close connection between the preservation of traditional methods—delayed burial, canoe-shaped coffin, etc.—of displaying and interring the corpse and the ability of the family to afford the higher cost of a traditional funeral. It is difficult and time-consuming to provide the corpse with an oxhide wrapper and a canoe-shaped coffin. The skin of the ox or horse must be prepared and the tree felled and worked. When such burial takes place, the hide wrapper and the canoe have usually been prepared well in advance, kept in the house of the chief or *ulmen* (a wealthy and respected person), and have served as objects of display for the purpose of receiving acclamation and gaining prestige.

Immediately upon death there is a great demonstration of remorse on the part of the deceased's family, especially by the adult females, who alternately sob and wail their grief, tear their hair and clothing, and imprecate the evil spirits (*wekufe*) and the sorcerer-witch responsible for causing death. At this time promises are made to avenge the "murder," regardless of the circumstances under which the person died. Grief is obviously deeply felt. Demonstrations of sorrow at the loss of a kinsman and neighbor, and of wrath against the *wekufe,* are repeatedly and spontaneously made. All who maintain the death watch participate in extolling the deceased. The wake or *kurikawin* (black gathering) is a tearful and noisy affair, attended by much drinking and the performance of spontaneous *awn* or, specifically, *amulpellun,* an encirclement of the house which contains the corpse by horsemen who hurl invectives at the forces of evil who are felt to be lurking about to capture the deceased's lingering spirit. This, more than the washing of the body, is the ritually purifying act, the functional equivalent of the *awn* (the encirclement of the main altar during *nillatun*). Its purpose is to drive off the evil spirits. This central concept results in the entire funeral ceremony being called *awn.*

The tempo of activities during the wake increases with the arrival of more relatives. Drinking becomes heavier, and the wailing and maudlin songs more frequent. Most of the visitors who live nearby spend a respectful period of time at the wake, and may return on successive occasions, but once advised of the death they prepare themselves for the *awn* celebration, the major festive demonstration of the obligation of the living to the dead. Those relatives who have traveled some distance to attend the services remain in the house of the deceased or with relatives on the reservation. They take up the death watch on successive days and nights prior to the final burial. Except for this nucleus of kinsmen there is an ebbing and flowing of mourners.

The death watch, variously called *monetun* (curing, sustaining), *kurikawin* (black gathering), and the Spanish-derived *velan mán* (*velan: velorio* or wake; *mán:* right), lasts at least four days and nights. Its termination at the end of this ritually auspicious number of days tends to coincide with the arrival of late comers, usually relatives, who live some distance away. In the opinion of a few Mapuche, the reason for the delayed burial is simply to give distant relatives an opportunity to arrive. For the vast majority, however, the reason for the delay in final burial is stated differently and has to do with respect and proper attention due the deceased.

The body is displayed in an approximation to what present-day Mapuche consider the traditional manner, because in this way they are able to accord it the respect prescribed by *admapu* (customary law). Although on display, the corpse is not touched by the viewers, for it is dangerous. This is common knowledge. It is preserved in state for the ritually perfect number of days (if possible) because by so doing the well-being of the living as well as the dead tends to be insured. The notion of "curing" or "sustaining" the spirit of the deceased shows that this ritual delay in burial is a most necessary procedure during the transitional period in which the newly released spirit is in danger of falling prey to the forces of evil.

There is some evidence that the Mapuche formerly practiced urn burial (Cooper 1946: 734–35) and that this custom later gave way to the preservation not only of the bones but of the entire eviscerated corpse through smoking. Present-day informants know nothing of urn burial or of any special treatment of the bones of the deceased other than the general belief that their distant ancestors interred the bones of their dead in urns, derived from the discovery of such ancient receptacles in plowing their fields. The practice of smoking the corpse and wrapping it in a hide is described in oral tradition and is felt by some elders to be represented vestigially in the few cases which occur today—although whether or not it is appropriate to view this as a "vestigial" custom is certainly open to question. The historical sources certainly do not contain the answer.

Regardless of whether or not the corpse is handled in the traditional manner (by smoking, etc.), the Mapuche wake is nevertheless quite distinct from the Chilean *velorio* in that the Mapuche show a decidedly different emphasis in their concern over the state of the corpse. The departed spirit does not immediately rise to "Heaven," nor does it automatically descend to the underworld (which, in any case, the Mapuche usually view as a witch's cave or *renu* rather than as "Hell"). What happens to the newly released spirit depends on how the living (mourners) behave, on how the ceremony is conducted. For example, if the burial ceremony is conducted improperly, as is sometimes the case with the funeral of a child, the corpse itself may be used by a witch to create another malevolent spirit. This is the usual explanation given about the creation of *anchimallen,* child-sized ghosts fabricated from all or part of the bones of a corpse which has been literally "spirited away" by a witch. In all cases, the lingering spirit is in danger of contamination by the forces of evil. Death, therefore, is not viewed as a lightning-quick transformation in which the spirit is instantly wafted to its final resting place. Rather, death is a condition of transition for the spirit and, if properly handled, a step toward eternal comfort in the afterworld.

On the morning of the fourth day after death the corpse is carried out of the house and set up on a *llani* or bier which has been built to receive it in a nearby field. This concludes the wake (*kurikawin*) and initiates the second phase of the ceremony, which may be referred to as *weupin*. This term refers to the most important aspect of this part of the ceremony—a series of orations over the coffin in which praises of the dead are uttered to the living participants and to their most attentive ancestors, whose names are mentioned and whose memories are extolled during the oration.

The coffin is painted black, the traditional color of death and mourning, and is decorated with garlands of flowers (in season) and sacred leaves of cinnamon, apple, and *maqui* (*Aristotelia maqui*) and, if the most influential relatives are nominally Catholic, is sometimes surrounded by lighted candles. A large wooden cross or else a carved effigy-pole is placed at the head of the coffin, which faces toward the east. This emblem is later carried to the graveyard and is placed at the head of the grave. The display of the deceased in the open field, in conjunction with the eating and drinking feast that takes place on this occasion, signalizes the end of the wake. The spirit of the deceased has not yet departed for the afterworld, but the chances of its being captured by the forces of evil are considered to have diminished.

On this, the appointed day for final burial, relatives assemble in the early hours of the morning and begin the preparation of the ceremonial meal which will, at great cost to the family of the deceased, be offered to the full complement of relatives and neighbors who arrive before noon. A thousand or more people may be present. Most of the women and young people travel on foot or in oxcarts, but adult males usually arrive on horseback, dressed in their finest *huaso* costumes. There is an air of grave formality. The horsemen line up at the end of the field which contains the *llani,* or form a semicircle around the *llani* if their number is very large. As they line up, they are greeted by their host, a male of the deceased's immediate family. The host passes from one horseman to another, greeting the guests by appropriate kinship terms. Through the widest extension of these terms even nonrelatives are accorded kinship status on these occasions.

No condolences are offered at this reception, although they are freely rendered later and, indeed, have already been expressed at the wake by most of those assembled. The horsemen remain mounted and grouped during most of the morning. After they have all arrived and have been welcomed by the host, they dismount and begin to mill about, eat, drink, view the corpse, speak to their friends, and renew acquaintances.

The women, in their turn, assemble in the family oxcart or on foot near the dwelling of the deceased's family, and are likewise greeted by a woman relative of the dead person. These salutations are much less formal and, largely because of the presence of children, much less solemn. Women gather apart from the men at first. As more and more wine or chicha is consumed, however, the formality begins to break down, and the over-all aspect of the feast becomes one of confusion.

The elders among the relatives and friends of the dead person, together with visiting chiefs and elders from other reservations, congregate with the members of the deceased's immediate family, usually in the shade of a tree or under the eaves of the house, where a banquet table has been set up to receive them. The honored guests are diligently served by housemates of the dead person or by other relatives who have been asked to assist them. They remain here during most of the ceremony, except when formal orations (*weupin*) are being made at the coffin and when the coffin is later borne to the cemetery. It is from this select group that the official *weupin* (orators) are chosen, usually by prearrangement, on the basis of closeness or type of kinship bonds and familiarity with the deceased's personal history and family connections. There is always one *weupin* from the wife-giving and one from the wife-receiving group,[2] and in their case the selection is usually unanimous and perfunctory.

It is customary for all present to look upon the deceased as he lies in his uncovered coffin on the *llani*. Many persons fear to view the exposed corpse and are reluctant to approach the coffin until it has been closed or is about to be closed. Close relatives and some of the others drop coins and other small articles into the coffin, but the inclusion of the deceased's personal belongings (such as shoes, hat, ring, jewelry) is a formal and stylized matter (called *rokin*) performed by the surviving spouse or eldest sibling to whom the prized objects have been entrusted. Accompanying the usual possessions there is always a small packet of food—meat, bread, fruit, and the like. This token gift of food for his trip to the afterworld will, it is believed, induce the spirit to depart for the world of the dead rather than be tempted to linger near his house.

On one occasion which I witnessed, these items were not placed in the coffin, having been forgotten until it had already been lowered into the grave (*minchemapu*)—presumably because of the people's haste to bury the corpse, which was in an advanced state of decomposition. The coffin was therefore reopened and some food placed on top of the corpse. This event would seem to illustrate the importance attached to the inclusion of food for the journey of the spirit and for its protection from possible capture by the forces of evil. It underscores the notion of ritual precision or perfection involved in funeral ceremonies.

While the coffin rests on the *llani* in the ceremonial field, the

---

[2] This alludes to the Mapuche system of matrilateral alliance based on stable, localized patrilineages which stand to one another as wife-givers and wife-receivers. The wife-receiving groups have a social status relatively inferior to wife-givers (see Faron 1961b: 199–201; 1962).

mourners partake liberally of the food and drink supplied by the consanguineal relatives of the deceased or by his widow. There is always an abundance of wine or chicha and also of meat—sometimes mare's meat from the horse of the deceased, a Mapuche delicacy. The first helpings of food (especially of horsemeat) are served by the elders of the deceased's family in special portions to the matrilaterally related elders and the chiefs among the honored guests. These choice servants are reciprocated at some future date by the recipients, provided the organization of any future ceremony warrants such reciprocation.[3]

The *weupin* orations constitute the keynote of the burial ceremony. They are highly laudatory and recount in synopsis the exploits and good qualities of the deceased. The word *weupin* signifies any discourse on a serious note. Hence, all mourners who speak a few words over the corpse are delivering *weupin* and are themselves technically *weupin* or *weupufe*. However, certain male relatives are chosen as official *weupin,* and these utter lengthy encomiums over the deceased in formalized and somewhat archaic language. Each delivers an account of the noble qualities of the dead person, speaks of the loss to his family, his friends, and the community, and stresses the respectability and responsibility of the survivors, especially the obligations of the children of the deceased. The *weupin* trace the genealogy of the deceased to the founding ancestor of his patrilineage and extol the virtues of the principal male members of each generation back to the founder. Indeed, so important is this genealogical aspect that it limits the choice of *weupin* to those relatives who are most closely related to the deceased, regardless of personal friendship. These are usually the elders of the lineage, who are most likely to know best the genealogical connections or are responsible enough to determine them beforehand.

Genealogical reconstruction of this kind may take place at any point in the *weupin,* although it tends to come either at the end, as a summation of the person's good qualities and connections, or in the beginning, as an introduction to them. Through *weupin* one's linkage with important ancestors is brought into focus, called to the attention of both ancestors and the funeral assembly, and then

[3] A consideration of relative rights and obligations would take us too far afield from the theme of this paper. The reader may consult Faron (1962) for a closer examination of relative categorical status in Mapucheland.

disclosed or made explicit and public to many of the living for the first time. This is obviously an occasion on which genealogical manipulation takes place, sometimes inadvertently. Genealogies are weeded of inconsequential ancestors. Only those of most importance, especially in the direct line, are remembered with certainty. Even women are sometimes included in the reconstruction, to augment the status of the deceased by relating him to his matrilateral cognates with their relative superiority in social status. Sometimes, when an inmarried male (i.e., a man living in uxorilocal residence on his wife's reservation) or one of his children has died, the blood link to the resident lineage is especially emphasized. There is ample room here for manipulating genealogies, and the resultant modifications come to the anthropologist's attention in collecting life histories of the inhabitants of any reservation.

When the *weupin* are terminated, the time has arrived to transport the coffin on its bier to the graveyard, initiating the third and final phase of the funeral service. This may be done by pallbearers who go on foot to the burial ground or by oxcart; the latter is the usual means of transportation if the cemetery is distant and if roads are available. The burial place, *eltun* (cemetery) or less frequently *minchemapu* (grave), has already been prepared by relatives of the deceased. Closeness of relationship and comparative youthfulness are the criteria for selection of pallbearers and gravediggers.

The procession to the burial ground is usually disorderly, owing to the drunken condition of the pallbearers, who, indeed, usually have to be cautioned not to set down or "drop" the coffin. Only a handful of the closest relatives accompanies the coffin to the graveyard. By this time many of the participants are already in a stupor or are sleeping off the effects of wine and chicha. Those accompanying the coffin make additional libations of wine at the grave, drinking a good deal more at this time. The scene at the grave is characteristically maudlin.

Two or more of the men remain to fill in the hole with earth. The rest return to the house of the deceased, where family and friends continue to console one another and speak the praises of the dead, meanwhile finishing the remaining food and drink. The formal ceremony concludes with interment and final salutes to the dead. Ashes are sometimes scattered between the cemetery and the deceased's house or the ceremonial field. This is designed to

impede the spirit from returning to the familiar precincts of the
living, provided all other aspects of the ceremony have been
well executed.

Burial ceremonies vary not so much with region as with the
status of the deceased and his relatives. Age, sex, wealth, and
rank are the main determinants of variations in *awn* celebrations.
Mature persons all receive more or less the same ceremonial treatment as that described above, but chiefs and shamans are accorded
greater pomp. Children's funerals are generally much simpler than
those of adults, are attended with much less pomp, have many
fewer mourners, and are brought to completion in a shorter time.
It is apparent that the loss to their lineage and community is not
considered as great as the loss of a married adult member of the
group, since they are not yet full members of the society. Infants,
unless they die at the same time as their mother, are rarely interred in the communal cemetery but are buried near the house,
and with little ceremony. It is generally said that this is at least
partly to prevent them from being captured by *kalku* and converted into *anchimallen,* a feat which the Mapuche seem to feel is
more easily accomplished when infants are buried in the cemetery
at some distance from the house.

The funeral of a chief or shaman is more ostentatious and the
assemblage much larger than those of ordinary persons. In number of participants the ceremony may take on the proportions of
nillatun, with as many as 1,000 or more adults in attendance.
Wealth is a factor in the amount of display at funerals of shamans
and chiefs, but it is contributed wealth rather than the individual
riches of the deceased and his family. While any wealthy person
(*ulmen*) will have an expensive coffin and other trappings, the
wealth displayed at the funeral of a chief or prominent shaman
will consist of contributed food, drink, and garlands of flowers
brought not only by relatives but by friends, some of whom travel
great distances to attend the ceremony. Occasionally it happens,
to this day, that a chief's favorite horse is slain over his grave or on
the ceremonial field, later to be consumed by the people.

The most impressive features of a chief's funeral service are the
large number in attendance and the elaborate details of the numerous *weupin.* Members of his natal reservation turn out in full
force. In addition, there are representatives from other reservations
in the ritual congregation and beyond. The Mapuche speak of

their chiefs as "nobles," "men of pure blood," descendants from ancient families, and so forth. Any more or less friendly chief from another reservation will make an appearance at the ceremony with as many of his followers as he is able to muster for the occasion. A man who is merely wealthy in land and animals, but who is not in the direct line of chiefly succession, receives no such elaborate demonstration of respect. It is accorded to a chief, however, not only because of his political status or even because of his leadership in the ritual congregation, but because it is due him, regardless of wealth, as one who will shortly join the ranks of the most important ancestors and walk with the sons of the gods for eternity. Thus the three principal objectives of the *awn* are achieved: the remains of the dead are interred, the spirit is assured its proper passage to the afterworld, and the living have discharged their obligations of mourning, initiating another impulse in their life-long responsibility of ancestral propitiation.

THE FERTILITY RITE (*nillatun*)

The *nillatun* ceremony is the most elaborate Mapuche ritual in existence today. I suggest that it has attained this position and present complexity since the time the Mapuche have become immobilized on reservations and population density in the indigenous zone has increased.

A number of elements have probably been added to *nillatun* rites in the last few generations, and others dropped during the recorded history of the Mapuche. What appears today is a composite whole having some regional variation in trait content. Titiev (1951: 128) sums up his impression of the ceremony in the following words:

> Woven together into the great composite of nillatun rites are elements of machi lore, assembly customs, hockey games, curing and divination practices, and numerous other religious features, all of which are mingled in a two-day public celebration that is designed to give thanks for favors received or to ask for help in time of stress.

While this seems to me to be an empirically valid observation, I fear it may leave the reader with the impression that the ceremony is little more than a hodgepodge of assorted beliefs and practices having no more than a vaguely functional relationship in that they are "woven together" and "mingled" in a way which is "sort of"

propitiatory, adulatory, or supplicatory. I feel that a more meaningful analysis may be made.

In the following pages I present a generalized account of
nillatun rites as I observed them on five widely separated sets of
reservations in Mapucheland. Some regional variations seem partly
due to the fact that today's ceremonies are an ensemble of the
sort indicated by Titiev, but once this is recognized, and we look
below the surface phenomena, many such differences appear to
have little or no social significance.

The *nillatun* ceremonies are not held according to an exact
calendrical schedule, although nowadays they take place with regularity in the spring of the year or after the fall harvest. In the past,
according to historical documents and verbal accounts, they were
sometimes held for other than agricultural fertility purposes. The
principal non-agricultural motives seem to have been to ask
nenechen (the Supreme Being) and various of the minor gods for
success in war and deliverance from plagues and general disaster.
Today, concern is mainly with agricultural fertility and the general
well-being of the ritual congregation. But there still exists the
small, family-based *nillatun,* conducted mainly for non-agricultural
purposes, which seems to me to reflect the persistence of the traditional, multi-purposed ceremony which existed in the pre-
reservation era.

In the absence of a ritual calendar, *nillatun* ceremonies are
scheduled according to the inclinations of the leaders of the residential groups on each of the participating reservations within
any ritual congregation, according to how they view their responsibilities. Chiefs formally initiate the holding of a ceremony, but
other respected and important elders of the reservation help them
decide the matter. The concordance and participation of the chief,
however, are essential for a successful *nillatun.*

Members of each reservation in the ritual congregation provide
a conclave of elders, heads of lineages and sublineages, which
works out the arrangements for holding the ceremony. Decisions
are made about what to ask for (rain, sun, a favorable combination of both) depending on the season and the community's needs.
In the pre-harvest season, for example, dry weather might be asked
for, and a "promissory" *nillatun* held (perhaps by a single reservation in the ritual congregation) to propitiate ancestral spirits,
nenechen, and, perhaps, the old man and woman of the south

wind, in order to insure good growth and harvest. It is considered promissory if the people have not the means of staging a full-scale ceremony, owing to a scarcity of food, and if all the member reservations (some lineages of which might be in attendance elsewhere) do not participate fully.[4] In the post-harvest season, when food is at least temporarily abundant, a large, full-scale *nillatun* will be held to give thanks and to fulfill the promise.

Other decisions include the selection of officials for the ceremony, the "captains" (*awnkaman:* guardian of *awn*) and the "sergeants," as well as pennant bearers; the type of *rewe* or main altar to be used; the number of black and/or white banners, which symbolize, respectively, rain and sun; what shall be sacrificed; what shall be eaten and drunk; and many other important details of ritual arrangement.

A *nillatun* is sponsored by a single reservation, actually by the dominant or chiefly patrilineage thereof, and jointly participated in by several reservations which comprise traditional segments of the ritual congregation. The respective chiefs and *nillatufe* (ritual priests who, ideally, are chiefs) and the various lineage heads assemble to discuss the matter and do the major planning. The arrangement of the smaller, promissory ceremonies is not as complicated, decisions generally being made by the head of the dominant lineage after discussion with the elders of his reservation.[5]

Shamans (*machi*) are sometimes invited to these conclaves, but this is not common, even though it might be understood beforehand that a shaman will conduct some or most of the prayers of the forthcoming ceremony. Sometimes shamans are specifically excluded from participating in the ceremony although they are never excluded as spectators, and may even be honored guests. Sometimes, however, shamans instigate *nillatun* celebrations, as was clearly the case in a ceremony I witnessed near Angol in the northern part of Mapucheland, where chieftainship is weak and where the corporate structure of reservations is not strong. As I shall argue later, when shamans are called in to perform at *nillatun*, this represents a last-ditch expediency so that some sort of "religious"

[4] For a discussion of the structure of the ritual congregation, see Faron 1961b: 211–18.

[5] For a consideration of dominant and subordinate lineages on Mapuche reservations, see Faron 1961b: 99–101.

ceremony may be staged in the absence of a competent ritual priest.

The preliminary meeting ends with an agreement with respect to the details of the approaching ceremony. All *nillatun* I observed were held around the full of the moon, when the god of the moon (*kuyenfucha*) is especially receptive to human offerings.

Once agreement is reached, word is passed throughout the general region, formally to those people who are members of the ritual congregation and informally to others who live on the periphery of the congregation and may attend as spectators. The formal notice includes details concerning the exact purpose of the ceremony, the contributions which are expected from certain families, what shall be brought in the way of food and drink, and so forth. The people now begin preparations. They prepare large quantities of bread (of several kinds) and meat, chicha, and *mudai* (a beverage which becomes mildly alcoholic), mend or buy clothing for the occasion, polish their heirloom jewelry, repair oxcarts, clip and curry their horses, and so forth. There is often about a month's wait between the setting of the date and the staging of the ceremony.

Shortly before the date set, a select group of elders (the designated officials) goes to the *nillatun* field to make it ready for the performance. This constitutes a separate, secret conclave from which all women and children are excluded. The altar from the previous ceremony is very likely still standing, but it is in disrepair, as are the *ramadas* or pole-and-branch cubicles which serve as shelters for the assembled families and guests. If the altar pole is an ancient carved post, only the sacred boughs of cinnamon, apple, and *maqui* which have been stuck in the ground next to it are replaced. If it is simply a notched post, without any enduring significance, it too may be replaced at this time. The area for a number of yards around the altar is considered the sacred field and is not sown to crops or, theoretically, grazed.

The *ramadas* are erected or repaired by those persons who intend to use them. Sometimes they are constructed so as nearly to encircle the ceremonial field; sometimes they are aligned along one side or more of the field. The field itself, regardless of the appearance lent it by the arrangement of the *ramadas,* is considered to be circular, defined usually by the path followed by the *awn* riders as they gallop around the main and secondary altars chasing away the *wekufe* or evil spirits.

The renewal or rebuilding of the *rewe* (main altar) and the *llani* (secondary altar) is the final preparatory act before the public ceremony begins. Once this is accomplished, the people begin to assemble. They commence to arrive on the morning of the first day scheduled for the public ritual. The officials are among the first to arrive, for they must be on hand to direct the ceremony from the beginning and to greet the participants and guests as they appear on the scene. They attend to the last-minute preparations, such as tying the sacrificial sheep (sometimes cows) into place and seeing that enough firewood has been gathered and that the proper bowls of grain and libational offerings have been set in place near the main altar. Since so much of the success of the ceremony is in the hands of these officials, they attend to the most minute details of the ritual.

All participants, as distinguished from mere spectators, arrive at the ceremonial field fairly early to make ready their *ramadas,* start their cooking fires, prepare soup and other foods that take long to cook, and await the beginning of the ritual performance. Nearly all the people have arrived by noon, although there are some stragglers. The assemblage on the first day of the ceremony is generally much smaller than that on the second day. The first day is considered supremely sacred, and much time is given to the propitiation of ancestors of the host group and, in turn, those of the participating reservations which traditionally comprise the ritual congregation. Things change somewhat on the second day of the ceremony, and some profane activities are introduced. People tend to mix among themselves more freely on the second day, and there is usually a good deal of wine-drinking (although this is proscribed in certain parts of Mapucheland). On the second day, the spectators might well outnumber the participants, and the total assemblage may easily reach several thousand people. While this vulgarization of the ceremony is deeply regretted by the elders as a departure from "tradition," it is likely that it has been a feature of *nillatun* during most of the reservation period.

As the various participating family groups arrive, they take up positions sufficiently removed from the center of the field of ceremonial activity. If *ramadas* have been set up to receive them, their positions are predetermined. The officials (*kaman:* guardians) of the ceremony are responsible for the ordering of the crowd and do not hesitate to tell family heads to move to more suitable positions rimming the ceremonial field. There is a good deal of milling about among the assemblage before the ceremony starts, as people compete to obtain places of vantage from which to view the activities. At the first sign of ritual activity, however, the entire audience fixes its attention on the *rewe* and settles down to watch and participate in the ritual.

Ideally, each day's ritual is divided into four parts, each largely a repetition of the other. A full performance consists of early morning, midmorning, early afternoon, and late afternoon ritual activities. There are no nocturnal rites, although there is a good deal of visiting among the participants and guests if they remain the night on the ceremonial field.

Whether there are four, three, or only two ritual periods in a day, each closely duplicates the main features of the others. There is always this repetition, even if there is only a one-day ceremony having only a morning and afternoon session. If *nillatun* last two or more days, however, on the second day the regimen of the first day might be modified because of drunkenness and disorder, if the officials have not maintained proper supervision. The job of the officials, especially the sergeants, is to preserve order (and there are almost always a pair of Chilean policemen present to help insure this). The officials may strike at people with their long poles of office if their orders are not heeded. It is felt that the success or failure of the ceremony largely depends upon the smoothness with which it is conducted, and the sergeants and captains are consequently authorized to evict disorderly persons. Orderliness is a prominent characteristic, and certainly a traditional ideal, of *nillatun* ceremonies.

After the initial prayer has been offered in the special, archaic language to *nenechen* and the ancestors, the *nillatufe* or ritual priest signals for the performance of *awn* in order to clear the ceremonial field of any lurking forces of evil (*wekufe*). This act is so important to the successful conclusion of *nillatun* that, even where there are few horses available, I have seen it performed by men riding "stick horses." The altar is circled several times, ideally four times or a multiple thereof. The more horsemen there are available, the more effective the maneuver is believed to be. Some of the riders wear sheepskin masks, or have their faces painted, in order to enhance their ability to frighten away the ghosts (contaminated ancestral spirits) while hiding their own identity from them.

The front of the main altar, before which the head priest stands, faces east, a ritually propitious direction. It is around this and the secondary altar (*llani*), set up a hundred yards or so east of it, that the riders gallop. Starting from the right of the main altar, they ride counterclockwise in a number of complete circuits. Two or more of the horsemen carry standards, the rest follow them in a column of twos, and the rear is brought up by a sergeant carrying a long staff of office. The sergeant, who takes his cues from the captain or the priest, shouts commands to the riders. At regular intervals they raise a cry to chase away the evil spirits. All this is a duplication of the *amulpellun* ceremony, which takes place during the funeral services and is conducted for a similar purpose. The riders, who are the center of attraction as they race around the ceremonial field, finally dismount near the *llani* (secondary altar). Here they dance around the altar and then return on foot to the *rewe* (main altar), leaving their horses tethered some distance away.

Meanwhile, the *purun* (a dance) has begun around the *rewe*. The *awn* riders now take up their positions in the *purun,* the two sergeants assuming command of the dancers subject to orders relayed through the captains from the *nillatufe* (ritual priest). After a series of fast and slow *purun,* the dancing comes to an end. The men may dance a special *lonkopurun* to dramatize the relationship between the living and their dead chiefs and to show how the ancestral chiefs aid their descendants and help combat the forces of evil. All *purun* dancers, including women, who also are expected to perform, wear sprigs of cinnamon or *maqui*—and sometimes spikes of wheat or barley or a few kernels of maize which they carry from the *rewe* when they begin to dance, replacing them when they finish. This endows them during their performance, the dancers feel, with a sacred quality. As in the *awn* encirclement, the *purun* is also danced counterclockwise around the main altar.

After the *purun* is finished, the men line up on the right-hand side of the *rewe* facing the *nillatufe,* and the women participants line up on the left, forming two lines stretching toward the east between the *rewe* and the *llani.* The *nillatufe* then begins his second prayer of the morning which he utters in four stanzas, during the intervals between which the opposed lines of men and women dance in place. The words of the orations (or at least their sacred meaning) are incomprehensible to the ordinary assemblage. The details of this part of the performance are as follows. With the assistance of the captains and sergeants, the *nillatufe* kills one of the sheep staked out near the *rewe*. He does this with a long knife, slitting the sheep's throat. While the animal is bleeding to death, he cuts off its right ear and holds it aloft while uttering a prayer. He then opens the chest cavity of the dead animal, frees the heart, and withdraws it. He holds the heart aloft, again in his right hand, and utters a brief prayer to *nenechen* (the Supreme Being) and the generalized ancestors, the "hawks of the sun." Then he bites into the heart and passes it to one of the assisting *nillatufe* (i.e., chiefs from participating reservations) who stands on his right. Each official in turn offers the sheep's heart to the sky, utters a short prayer, and bites into the heart. The principal priest then places the heart in the crotch of the *rewe*. His arms and face being smeared with blood, he wipes some of this off on the *rewe* pole and some on the sacred leaves and branches surrounding it. The other officials do the same. A bowl of sheep's blood, collected from the throat incision, is placed at the right side of the altar, and from it the *nillatufe* occasionally asperses the *rewe* and the ritual fire (*llupe*) which burns near it. Some blood is also burned in the special fire ignited near the *llani* or secondary altar. When this is accomplished, the *nillatufe* commands that the first in-place dance begins.

Meanwhile, the carcass of the slaughtered sheep is carried to the *llani*, where it is skinned and quartered. The sheepskin is then brought back and laid beside the *rewe*. A black skin, which calls for rain, is placed to the left of the altar and a white one, for sunny weather, is placed under the bowl of blood on the right of the altar. Some of the meat from the sheep is burned on the fire near the *llani*. The head and feet of the animal are in most cases thrown into the fire, and, unless the people are extremely poor in animals, much of the rest of the meat may also be burned. Sometimes the entire carcass is thrown on the fire. If the people are very poor in animals, however, most of the meat is taken off the fire when it is cooked and is then consumed as part of the ritual meal. The smoke which rises from the fire to the sky constitutes the morning offering to the ancestral spirits. For this the *llani* serves as a special altar, whereas around the *rewe* concern is chiefly for *nenechen* and the pantheon of minor gods, and the sacrifices are of a somewhat different order.

After the first in-place dance is completed, the *nillatufe* starts the second stanza of prayer. This time he scatters grain (although the order of procedure in different *nillatun* ceremonies varies) and asks for abundant harvests. The grain is taken from one of several wooden bowls next to the *rewe,* and some of it is thrown on the *llupe* fire. As the smoke rises, a short prayer is again offered to *nenechen* and the pantheon. Ancestors may not even be mentioned at this time. Attention is directed mainly to the god and goddess of abundance, the *kapuka* (although there is some regional variance with respect to their name).

The second in-place dance is then performed to the commands of the sergeants, after which the *nillatufe* begins the third stanza of prayer. This time he usually casts kernels of maize only, or of barley or oats, depending on which crop has been sown in greatest amount, throwing some on the sacrificial fire as before. After a third dance, the *nillatufe* again prays, either scattering grain or asperging with *mudai* or chicha or blood taken from the special bowls near the main altar.

After the fourth stanza of prayer the *purun* is repeated, and many of the spectators now participate. They dance for ten or twenty minutes around the *rewe,* many of the older persons tiring and dropping out to return to their *ramada,* where the midmorning snack is prepared.

When the sergeants signal that the *purun* is over, the dancers leave the area of the *rewe,* replacing the sprigs of sacred branches with which they danced. They return to their respective *ramadas,* where libations of chicha are already being poured by the older folks, and everyone partakes of a light meal. There is a good deal of visiting between *ramadas.* Visitors are presented with food; the amount they receive usually indicates their importance and is often calculated to reciprocate exactly a gift of food made by them during a previous ceremony. Gifts of food are thus exchanged among the majority of families in attendance, and special *konchotun* exchanges (a sort of blood brotherhood) may also take place at this time.

Subsequent segments of the ceremony duplicate the early morning rites part for part. Ideally, the prayers and other activities must be repeated perfectly, but there seems to be only an approximation to this notion of ritual perfection, a broad interpretation of the ideal. A second sheep or other animal might not be sacrificed until the close of the ceremony, for example, but if animals are abundant (i.e., if the donors are wealthy), a sheep may be killed at each part of the ritual. It is said that there should be four sessions of sacrifices, dances, and prayers and one special *lonkopurun* on each day of *nillatun,* and that the ceremony should last at least two days, but again this ideal is only approximated. There may be only two main sessions on the first day, perhaps three on the second, and an ordinary *purun* may be called a *lonkopurun.* There are always at least two main prayer sessions each day, however, one repeating the main features of the other.

The *awn* (on horseback) and the *purun* (on foot) are accompanied by the playing of *pifulka* (whistles of clay, wood, or stone with one or several tones), the sounding of the *trutruka* (a long trumpet tipped with a cow's horn), and the continual beating of the *kultrun* (drum).

Clearly, a major aspect of *nillatun* is the offering of food to *nenechen* (the Supreme Being), the pantheon, and ancestral spirits. These are not first-fruits ceremonies, because they take place both prior to the ripening of grain or after the harvest is gathered, but they are nevertheless supplicatory rites associated with Mapuche agriculture.

I have stressed the priestly function of the *nillatufe,* the sacrificial offerings to gods and ancestors, and the supplicatory nature of the prayers, rather than the role of the shaman, the manipulation of her familiar spirits, and the more coercive aspect of her activities. This is because most of the ceremonies I witnessed and heard about were conducted in the manner I have described. Only once did I see a shaman assume control of a *nillatun*—although the chief, an ineffectual *nillatufe,* was present and responsible for part of the ceremony—and the difference in the shamanistic performance and the usual priestly ritual was considerable. As I shall try to show, the shaman has achieved her status (shamans are usually women) in *nillatun* largely by default. A growing scarcity of competent *nillatufe,* in the face of a rapidly increasing population and a continued need for *nillatun,* has forced the people to solicit the services of the only other "religious" functionary in Mapuche society.

THE SHAMAN AND THE PRIEST

In this concluding section I present what I consider a plausible historical reconstruction of a most interesting aspect of cultural and social change, which may be of some help in understanding the role of the shaman in public fertility rites. While it is not absolutely necessary to an understanding of the structure of contemporary Mapuche society, of the present importance of *nillatun,* or of the significance of the ritual congregation in the scheme of Mapuche morality, it nevertheless seems to be a *leitmotif* in the development of the modern ritual community. Concerning *nillatun* organization, Titiev (1951: 130) has written: "Even on so fundamental a point as the role played by a machi there was no agreement among early writers. . . ." The following discussion is offered as a hypothesis about the development of the role of the *machi* (shaman) on the one hand and that of the *nillatufe* (ritual priest) on the other.

There is always a headman at a *nillatun* ceremony. Ideally he is the chief of the host reservation, but, if not, he is always a lineage elder and almost always an elder of the dominant lineage of his reservation. He operates with the support of peers of the other lineages or lineage segments of his own patrilineage on his reservation and with that of elders from other reservations in the ritual congregation. In the vast majority of these ceremonies involving several lineages and several reservations the headman is always a chief, and the most important functionaries are chiefs from participating reservation communities.

If the chief conducts the ceremony, he is *ipso facto* the *nillatufe.* The host reservation feels strongly that its own chief should be the *nillatufe,* provided that he is a person who has been trained in the ritual and who has committed to memory traditional prayers in the archaic ritual language. However, at the larger ceremonies in which a number of reservations cooperate to hold *nillatun* it is sufficient that any one of the chiefs knows the ritual prayers and is able to organize the activities. Within the congregation there is always at least one chief or elder who performs as *nillatufe,* even though his reservation might not be host of the particular ceremony. It sometimes happens, however, that none of the chiefs is sufficiently capable in ritual performance and therefore cannot carry the entire burden of ceremonial responsibility. Sometimes—and this is a most infrequent circumstance—a *nillatufe* will be called in from another congregational unit. At other times a reservation chief will perform the best he knows how, relying on the services of a shaman to supplement his own lack of skill if he or his constituents are fearful of not staging a proper ceremony. This is always a communal decision, and it may vary from one occasion to the next, depending on current needs. Shamans do not characteristically officiate at *nillatun,* but sometimes they do. It is important to note that some of the earlier ethnographic reports describe shamans as playing a part in these ceremonies, while in others Mapuche specialists have stated flatly that shamans did not assist in *nillatun.* And so the issue is raised.

Félix José de Augusta and E. Moesbach were convinced that shamans did not participate in *nillatun* ceremonies. Guevara wrote that they sometimes participated. It is likely, I feel, that Félix José and Moesbach merely failed to witness such performances, perhaps because of the fairly remote regions in which they worked, but that shamans were nevertheless active in *nillatun* ceremonies at the time when these scholarly priests were compiling their ethnographic material. Guevara's testimony seems to indicate this. He writes (1898: 440):

> Con anterioridad han sido designado para ofrecer el sacrificio propiciatorio de los corderos, algunos hombres esperimentados, *caciques* por lo común, que en el ritual del ngillatun se conocen con el nombre de ngillatufe.
>
> Entra entonces en acción la *machi,* se es una, i todas si son varias.

What Guevara did not say in so many words is that there were also *nillatun* in which *machi* did not participate at all, although this is clearly implied in his remarks. He argued at length about the connection between *nillatun* and ancestor worship, as did Latcham, in the unfortunate vogue of his time, and failed to report some of the important ceremonial details which might have enabled his readers to make a clearer analysis of his ethnographic data. While none of his arguments concerning the development of ancestor worship is especially convincing or subject to verification, I feel that his observations about the inclusion of prayers to ancestors in *nillatun* rites must be taken at face value. This remains an important feature of *nillatun* today, but it is likely that it was the main theme and principal reason for its conduct around the time Guevara was in the field, that is, during the early reservation period.

We have the following statement from Guevara (1898: 440) which is illuminating: "Hasta pocos anos los indios celebraban un ngillatun particular, ordinariamente de una familia." In the celebration of this family ritual, ancestors were propitiated, but it is unclear whether or not the ancestors were particular, authentic ancestors of the family or generalized forebears of regional populations. I suspect the former was the case. I feel that generalized ancestors, as such, became venerated in this manner only after final military defeat and the formation of large ritual congregations under the present reservation system. As lineage depth increased, in my opinion, ritual congregations became defined according to participating reservation memberships, and local ancestor-gods emerged in a socially significant way as generalized congregational ancestors. It is strange that Guevara should have written that "hasta pocos anos" the Mapuche conducted small, family-based rituals called *nillatun,* for they do this to this very day and call them by the same term. It is possible that Guevara was merely emphasizing the fact that ceremonial assemblages had increased in size by his time and had become more complex than anything described for pre-reservation times. In line with this, Guevara (1898: 440) wrote:

> Aveces el ngillatun assume grandes proporciones, porque lo acuerdan i llevan a cabo tres o cuatro grupos, es decir, una zona entera.

This I take to be a description of the beginnings of the present-day formation of ritual congregations, an aspect of Mapuche social structure which is still undergoing development.

At the small, family-based *nillatun* there was no officiating shaman, nor is there one today. When describing the larger ceremonies, Guevara conceded that shamans might participate, but he never asserted that they dealt with spirits ancestral to the participating groups. Nor do they do so today—for reasons consistent with Mapuche ideas of religious morality.

Today a shaman always shares ritual functions with an authority, such as the *nillatufe,* on the occasions in which she is invited to participate at all. If there is no need for her services, she is not called upon to perform. A shaman is not extended an invitation to perform simply because she may be available, at least not the sort

of invitation which would entitle her to perform as a ritual specialist in the celebration of *nillatun*. In all cases, therefore, even when
the ritual skills of the *nillatufe* are wanting, there is a leader who
is called *nillatufe,* and, if a shaman is called in to perform, her
activities are always supplementary to his.

If a shaman is invited to participate in an official manner and
to carry out most of the ritual procedures, the ceremony takes a
shamanistic rather than a priestly turn. Titiev described two
nillatun in which shamans were the main functionaries (according
to his description), although chiefs were also present. I have nothing to comment on in regard to Titiev's description in general, but
I should like to describe here, and very briefly, the performance
of a *machi* I saw in action at a *nillatun* ceremony—mainly as a
contrast to the foregoing description of the priestly conduct of
nillatun.

In one instance, the shaman threw her voice with such success
that a large part of the audience turned away from the *rewe*, where
she performed, apparently expecting to see the spirit with which
she was supposed to be communicating. A second occurrence
which startled the crowd was the "stabbing" of the shaman by
her helper. The assistant made repeated thrusts with a knife and
finally appeared to drive it into the shaman's breast. The blade
merely got caught up in her flowing shawl, but the dexterity with
which the maneuver was accomplished was astonishing. This action was taken in order to drive out the evil spirits that might have
attempted to enter the shaman during her possession. It was a
theatrical performance of high quality by any standards, and it
served to distinguish sharply the shamanistic performance from
that of the ritual priest.

My feeling is that whatever prominence shamans have attained
in *nillatun* ceremonies, it is in proportion to loss of ritual knowledge in the community and is due specifically to the decline in the
number of competent *nillatufe*. Shamans have acquired importance in fertility rites by default, as it were. They are introduced
into this stately ceremony to compensate for gaps in ritual knowledge, and perhaps this has been the situation for many generations; but they act as shamans, as grapplers with supernatural
forces, not as priests who deal in studied ritual. While both shaman and priest deal with spirits, the shaman manipulates her
own familiars and is customarily possessed by them (on impor-

tant and difficult occasions), and is also attacked by evil spirits. The priest is the representative of a community before its ancestors, is not possessed, does not grapple directly with the forces of evil, and never manipulates ancestral or other spirits. The shaman is called upon to serve at *nillatun* mainly because she is considered a specialist who deals with the supernatural world. She does not know *nillatun* ritual and is not familiar with the special language used in *nillatun* orations (although she communicates with her familiars in unintelligible and apparently archaic language, but of a different order). She is, nevertheless, competent to drive away evil spirits, which is one of the central features of *nillatun*. She concentrates on the *awn* performance and adds her special knowledge of the supernatural, at which times her life is usually felt to be at stake in directly combatting the forces of evil.

A final point distinguishing shaman from priest is the matter of payment. A *nillatufe* is not paid for his performance but is, as a rule, a heavy contributor himself to the cost of the ceremony. He may receive gifts of food from most of the families present, but these he redistributes immediately, generally by asking people who visit his *ramada* to share them with him. The shaman is always paid. She negotiates about payment with the council of elders (if she has not an established price) before the ceremony is arranged. Most of her payment is in food and drink, although it may also include live animals and cash. She does not redistribute these payments but takes them to her home for her own use.

In a few instances I have heard "cynical" Mapuche mention that shamans instigate *nillatun,* when this is possible, so that they may receive rich payment; also that *nillatufe* are sometimes reluctant to hold *nillatun* as frequently as the people feel it should be staged because they do not want to make their customary large contributions. Be that as it may, the priest-chief or *nillatufe* is a deeply responsible person (not so the shaman, until she has embarked on her performance), one who operates within the well-defined framework of kinship rights and obligations as these are extended throughout the ritual congregation. The shaman, on the other hand, is a paid professional, brought in to compensate for gaps in ritual knowledge. She operates where chieftainship or ritual skills are weak, and outside the framework of kinship. While she certainly takes great pride in her ability, she is primarily interested in receiving payment for her dangerous services, and she in no case is able to deal successfully (by her special kind of manipulative techniques) with spirits ancestral to the group holding the *nillatun*. Her presence at *nillatun* is, therefore, essentially an anomaly.

11 THE GHOST CULT IN BUNYORO

J. H. M. Beattie

W̶HEN A NYORO[1] suffers illness, childlessness, or other misfortune, his traditional culture provides three broad types of explanation of why this should be, each with its associated pattern of cultural response. It may be due to sorcery (*burogo*) by some living person; it may be due to one or more of the wide range of nonhuman *mbandwa* spirits; or it may be due to the activity of a ghost. I have given some account elsewhere of Nyoro beliefs about sorcery (Beattie 1963) and of the Nyoro spirit mediumship cult (Beattie 1957, 1961). In this essay I consider Nyoro ideas about ghosts, the kinds of social situations in which their activity is diagnosed, and what is done about them (for a brief outline of the pattern of Nyoro attitudes to ghosts see Beattie 1960: 75–77).

A ghost (*muzimu*, plural *mizimu*) is the disembodied spirit of someone who has died. When a man is alive this vital principle

Reprinted from *Ethnology* 3 (2), 1964: 127–51, by permission of the author and the editor, *Ethnology*.

[1] I carried out field work in Bunyoro, western Uganda, for about 22 months, during 1951–53 and 1955, mostly under the auspices of the Treasury Committee for Studentships in Foreign Languages and Cultures, whose support I gratefully acknowledge. The Nyoro are, for good reasons, very unwilling to discuss their traditional cults, and much of the information given in this paper could not have been obtained without the help of my two Nyoro assistants, the late Perezi Mpuru and the late Lameki Kikubebe. The deaths of these two young men, one while I was in the field and the other last year, are a grievous loss to Nyoro ethnography.

In the Nyoro language (*Lunyoro* or *Runyoro*) one Nyoro is a *Munyoro*, two or more are *Banyoro*. In the interest of simplicity I omit these prefixes except in the name of the country itself, Bunyoro. I also omit initial vowels throughout, except in reproduced texts, for the same reason; thus I write *muzimu* (ghost) instead of *omuzimu*, and so on.

is called *mwoyo* (plural *myoyo*), which may be rather loosely translated as "soul," and it is believed to dwell in the breast or diaphragm. But a ghost is not just a person who has died; it is a being of quite a different order from the living. Though it possesses human attributes it is not human. A Nyoro who wishes to threaten another with posthumous vengeance for some injury does not say, "I shall haunt you when I die"; he says, "I shall leave you a ghost" (*ndikulekera muzimu*). Ghosts are left by people, but they are not people. This is implied also by the fact that the noun class to which the word *muzimu* belongs is not that of "people" (*muntu,* plural *bantu*) but that of a certain class of things, a class which includes in particular most kinds of trees and other plants.

Ghosts are thought of as somehow diffused through space, "like wind" (*nk'omuyaga*). An informant said:

> When a man dies, his soul (*mwoyo*), which dwells inside him [he pointed to his diaphragm], is spread all around, like water. Afterwards it goes and lives underground, in the country of Nyamiyonga, the king of the dead. There it meets all other people who have died, and lives for ever. A man's soul can go away from his body and visit other places while he is asleep. It is no good killing a man or an animal while he is fast asleep; he will not die, or at least not so soon, if his soul is not there. You must wake him up a little first; as soon as he begins to stir, then you can kill him.

Thus ghosts are particularly associated with the underworld, Okuzimu, and it is significant that the phrase most commonly used for spirit possession refers to the ghost's "mounting into the head" (*kutemba ha mutwe*) of its medium. Okuzimu is sometimes thought of as a real place, and Nyoro myth tells of an early king, Isaza, who was enticed away into the world of ghosts by its ruler Nyamiyonga, who sent him some beautiful cattle which vanished into a pit in the ground, whither the infatuated ruler followed them (Beattie 1960: 13–14). As in European belief, ghosts are also sometimes associated with particular places which they frequented when alive, and with their graves. The color black is appropriate to them; we shall see that a goat which is sacrificed or dedicated to a ghost should be black.

Unlike its European counterpart, a Nyoro ghost is never seen, although it may appear in dreams in the form of the dead person whose ghost it is. Rather it makes itself known to the living by causing them illness or other misfortune, and its agency can only be diagnosed by a diviner (*muraguzi,* plural *baraguzi;* a doctor-diviner who can treat as well as diagnose ghostly activity is called *mufumu,* plural *bafumu*), whom the victim consults. For the most part ghosts are inimical, but they are not always so, and the ghost of a man's dead father, especially, is thought to retain some concern for the well-being of his sons and his other descendants. We shall see that the Nyoro do not have a highly developed ancestral cult, but a person may look to the ghost of his father (and to other patrilineal ghosts) for support, as he does to his father while he is alive. Nyoro say that a man can call on the help of his dead father by sprinkling an offering of *nsigosigo* (a dry mixture of millet and sesame) on his grave and asking him for assistance. I was told that a girl whose brother was forcing her into a marriage against her will, to obtain the bridewealth for her, might call on her dead father's ghost in this way and ask him to thwart her brother's plans and prevent her marriage.

Here is a Christian informant's account of help given to him by his father's ghost:

> I dreamed that my father appeared up above, accompanied by an angel. They were surrounded by a very bright light, which got brighter and brighter. The angel said, "Don't be afraid." Then suddenly they disappeared, and there was intense darkness, out of which a savage lion approached to kill me. But my father again appeared and said, "Don't fear; I shall not let it hurt you." Then I woke up. Another night I dreamed that a neighbor of mine, who I knew hated me, was approaching me with a horn (*ihembe,* used in sorcery) held in his outstretched hand and pointed at me. I knew that he was making sorcery against me, and I was very frightened. But at that moment my father appeared and stopped him, saying, "Leave off bewitching my son." I then woke up feeling very scared. The next morning when I went out into my compound I saw something sticking in the ground, and when I went to see what it was I found that it was a horn. So I knew that my enemy had really come to make sorcery against me in the night. That day I burned that horn; while it was being burnt it cried out "eeeeh! eeeeh!" That same day a goat and two of my fowls died. Two weeks later that man died; my father's ghost had killed him for having tried to make sorcery against me.

On the whole, however, ghosts are thought to be maleficent, which is what we should expect, for like other spirit agents they usually become socially relevant only when illness or other misfortune strikes. Nyoro say that when a relative dies he ceases to think of his kin as "his" people; the ghost no longer takes a warm and friendly human interest in the welfare of his living kin, as his own flesh and blood. *"Amara kufu taba wawe,"* Nyoro sometimes say, i.e., "A person who is dead is no longer 'your' person." But they are not absolutely consistent about this, for there is another saying, "A ghost follows its own"—though of course the pursuit may not be inspired wholly by benevolence. We shall see below that just as people are dependent on the good will of ghosts, or at least on the suspension of their ill will, so ghosts are also thought to be dependent on people who, through rites of sacrifice and possession, provide them with what they need. Like most social relationships, Nyoro relations with ghosts are ambivalent. But for the most part ghosts are feared, not loved, and much of the ritual concerned with them is aimed at keeping them at a distance, rather than achieving closer relations with them.

Ordinarily the Nyoro do not like speaking of the dead. "A person who speaks the name of a dead parent or close relative feels unhappy at once," one of my assistants told me. He added that his mother refused to have a photograph of her dead husband on the wall of her house for this reason. If a man mentions the name of his dead father he should say, "I haven't spoken your name, father; when I die I'll see you." He means that he has meant no injury to the dead man.

Though a victim of illness or other misfortune may suspect ghostly activity, this is always confirmed by divination (*buraguzi*). The sufferer visits a local diviner (*muraguzi*), of whom there are still several in every Nyoro locality. Using one of the accepted techniques of divination—the most popular is the one which involves throwing nine prepared cowry shells on a mat (see Beattie 1960: 71–73)—the diviner determines whether his client's trouble is due to sorcery, to the agency of nonhuman spirits, or to a ghost. If ghostly agency is diagnosed, then further divination, combined with skillful questioning of the patient, may establish the ghost's identity.

This is not always very difficult, though sometimes it is. Like sorcerers, ghosts generally attack people against whom they have a grudge. So when ghostly activity is diagnosed, the ghost is usually that of someone who was injured or offended before he died —or in certain cases of someone whose ghost was neglected after he died. But the ghost may not confine its vengeance to the person who actually offended it; often, indeed, the offender may not be directly attacked at all. In eight out of fifteen cases on which I have details (see Table 1) where ghostly activity was diagnosed, the original offender was not attacked directly but through his children, and in two others he was long since dead and vengeance was wreaked on his descendants. The biblical reference to "visiting the iniquity of the fathers upon the children unto the third and fourth generation" makes good sense to traditionally minded Nyoro.

There follows an informant's account of a case in which a woman's miscarriage was attributed to the ghost of a household slave or servant (*mwiru rubale*) who had been a member of the household long ago. The ghosts of such persons, who in pre-European times were usually people who had been captured in war, probably as children, and were thus often members of other tribes, are thought to be particularly dangerous. I return later to the "social sanction" aspect of the Nyoro ghost cult, but it may be remarked here that this belief must have conduced to the reasonable treatment of such captives, who usually lived as for all practical purposes members of the family of their captors. Certainly the Nyoro say that it was always advisable for families which owned such domestic slaves to treat them well.

Case 1 When this ghost came into my house I consulted a doctor-diviner (*mufumu*), who said that it was that of a former household slave in my father's family. It was making my wife ill and had caused her to have a miscarriage. We did not know the name of that slave, and you know that it is very difficult to catch a ghost whose name is not known. First you have to sing songs to call that ghost. When it comes into the head of its medium you ask it what its name is. It generally refuses to say, and this is what happened in our case. So the diviner had to make special preparations. He made two pots and fired them on that very same day. I had to provide a black billy-goat and two red fowls. And the *mufumu* brought a number of special charms (*bihambo*), which were small pieces of various kinds of wood and other plants.

I remember the names of some of these. One was called *kiboha*, which means "that which ties up." It was a small, creeping plant for "tying up" the ghost so that it should not return to our house. Another was called *kinamiro*, which means "that which stoops," and another was called *kyombera busa*. This last means something that makes a lot of noise for nothing, and it suggests that the ghost should go shamefully away and not come back. Other charms were: a piece of wood from a tree called *mutatembwa*, which means that it cannot be climbed (its bark is very smooth); a piece of tree stump called *bahumaho* (so that the ghost should stumble on it); a plant called *ihozo*, "that which makes cool"; another called *ruhunahune*, "that which is silent" (so that the ghost may remain still and peaceful); and a kind of grass named *ntahinduka*, "I shall not turn round." The *mufumu* put all these charms into the pots he had made.

Then, when the ghost had mounted into my wife's head after the usual seance with singing, the shaking of gourd rattles, and so on, the goat and the chickens were shown to it and slaughtered. Then the ghost [through its medium] spat on the goat's head; the head of an animal sacrificed is always given to the ghost. After this the head was put into one of the pots, and the ghost was persuaded by the *mufumu* to leave my wife and go into the pot. Then we hastily took both the pots and buried them at the foot of a tree near the front of the house. This meant that if the ghost tried to return it would not get any further than the place where the pots were buried. After that we planted some of the grass called *ntahinduka* over the place, so that the ghost should not turn round and come back to trouble my wife. The *mufumu* then said that my wife would soon bear children. She has not borne any yet, but I hope that she will do so soon.

Although this text does not describe in detail the process of possession and ghost transference, it indicates one of the ways in which ghosts may be dealt with, i.e., by "catching" them and either destroying them or (as in the present case) insuring that they are kept away for good. Also it provides some interesting examples of the symbolism involved in ghost ritual. If it be accepted that ritual is a kind of language, it is plain enough what is being said in this case through the kinds of charms used and the Nyoro names given to them. Especially interesting is the symbolic "tying up" of the ghost. A brief text from another informant further develops the same notion:

When a ghost has caused a woman to have miscarriages, the *mufumu* may make a horn called *ruboha* as medicine for her. He takes a goat's horn and cleans it and puts special medicines consisting of pieces of wood and other plants in it. Then he smears it with the slimy juice of a plant called *rucuhya* [*Sida rhombifolia*, a plant with tiny white flowers].[2] When the goat provided for the ghost is being slaughtered, blood from its neck is allowed to flow over the horn. The horn is then given to the woman to keep. The *mufumu* names that horn *ruboha* because the ghost has been "tied up" (*kuboha*) by the medicine in it, and it will protect that woman from further attack by that ghost.

[2] I owe this and other plant identifications to Davis 1938.

TABLE 1 Cases of Attack by Ghosts

Case No.	How Manifested?	Relationship of Ghost to Victim	Who Had Offended Ghost?	How?	Did Ghost Attack Offender?		Action Taken	Successful?
					Directly	Through Relative of Offender		
1	Miscarriage	Household slave of patrilineal ancestor	Household head long ago	Cruelty	No	Yes, through descendant	Ghost caught and buried	Not yet
2	Epilepsy	Co-wife of mother's mother	Its co-wife	Practiced sorcery against her	No	Yes, through daughter's child	Victim's mother became ghost's medium	Not recorded
3	Ulcer on leg	Mother's father	Its daughter	Neglect	No	Yes, through son	Victim's mother became ghost's medium	Yes
4	Sudden seizure	Younger brother	Its elder brother	Retained property bequeathed to sisters	Yes	No	Younger sister became ghost's medium	Yes
5	Illness	Father's father	Its son	Prevented wife from taking food to father	No	Yes, through child and brother's child	Mediumship; sacrifice; brothers to live together	Yes
6	Miscarriages	Mother	Its husband	Deprived her of goat by refusing bridewealth for daughter	No	Yes, through daughter	Ghost-hut built, goat dedicated	Not yet
7	Leprosy, beaten by children	Wife	Its husband	Cruelty	Yes	No	Various means	No
8	Death and illness	Mother's sister's son	Its mother's mother	Refused goat for sacrifice to help sick grandchild (ghost)	No	Yes, through daughter's children	Victims' father became ghost's medium; sacrifice	Not recorded
9	Miscarriages	Household slave of father's father's father	Household head long ago	Cruelty	No	Yes, through son's son's child	Ghost caught and burnt	Yes
10	Property burnt	Husband	Its wife	Not recorded	Yes	No	Victim became ghost's medium; sacrifice	Yes
11	Miscarriages	Pat. half brother	Its parents	Not keeping its child at their home after it died	No	Yes, through daughter	Various means	No
12	Painful swellings	Father	Its daughter	Marrying against wishes	Yes	No	Sacrifice; probably possession	No
13	Epilepsy	Mother	Its husband	Accepting bridewealth for daughter against her last wishes	No	Yes, through daughter	Mother's wishes complied with (bridewealth returned)	Yes
14	Allergy to goat meat	Wife	Its husband	Keeping goat given to her	Yes	No	None	—
15	Epilepsy	Mother's mother	Its son and his wife	Neglect when ill	No	Yes, through children	Not recorded	No

Of interest, also, in Case 1 is the notion that nameless ghosts are especially difficult to deal with. An old man told me:

> Nameless ghosts generally come from outside the household, perhaps from very far away. They come especially from men who were killed with women [i.e., in war]; perhaps speared and thrown into pits. These increased very much in the time of king Kabarega, because at that time there was much raiding and killing. These nameless ghosts may make impossible demands. I once heard of one which asked for buffalo milk, a dog's horn, and the tendon of a *nkuba,* a fabulous fowl associated with thunder and lightning. It said that it wanted to drink buffalo milk in the dog's horn. If it doesn't get what it wants, it may kill off a whole settlement. One such group of agnates (*kika*) lived at Kiswaza, and now not a single person of that group remains.

However the ghost is dealt with (and, as we shall see below, not all ghosts can be destroyed or sent away), it must first be induced, through possession ritual, to "mount into the head" of the affected person, or sometimes—as, for example, when the person affected is a small child—into the head of someone who represents the victim. In this way it is enabled to enter into communication with the living, and they with it. This possession can only be brought about by a doctor-diviner (*mufumu*) who is an initiated member of one or more of the Nyoro spirit mediumship cults, as most *bafumu* are. There follows a text dictated to me by some women who were formerly pagan but had recently been converted to the revivalist branch of the Native Anglican Church known as the *balokole* ("saved"). It gives some account of the ritual of possession.

> When the *mufumu* comes to the house, food is cooked, and they eat. Then they cut some *ngando* wood [a wood which burns with a white flame], and special medicines are put on the head and body of the sick person. When the time for the possession has come, usually at night, the people sit around the hearth, where a fire is glowing. The *mufumu* begins to shake his gourd rattle (*nyege*) rhythmically, and everyone present begins to sing special songs. The words of one song are *Rwitakwanga araire omu rubale nagaranga omunaku wabu* [meaning roughly "Rwakitanga died, and his body was left among the rocks; on account of his poverty there was no one to bury him"]. Another song is *Karota Karota ija turole,* which means "Karota, Karota, come so that we may see you!" Karota is the name of a magic horn which the *mufumu* may put in the initiate's hands; it is then called upon to bring the ghost (*Karota leta muzimu!*). The singing may go on for a long time.

If the ghost does not come, they may take the sick man "to search for the ghost" (*kusera muzimu*). First the *mufumu* takes a torch of burning grass and thrusts it in all four directions. Then he takes the sick man outside, and he and the other *bafumu* present ask him if he has ever been initiated as a spirit medium. If he says "No," they explain to him what he has to do, and he agrees. Then they bring him into the house again and put the horn Karota in his hands, and they go on singing the appropriate songs. Soon the sick man begins to weep bitterly, without words but noisily. The *mufumu* says, "The ghost is coming!" Then they sing another song, the words of which are *Lira muno, tiguli muzimu, idomora* ("Weep much; this is not [just] a ghost, it is a terribly powerful thing"). Soon the patient falls forward on his face; he has been in a sitting position. Then the *mufumu* addresses the ghost, which is now in the patient's head: "What would you like to eat?" The ghost answers through the sick person "meat." But he uses the special vocabulary used by ghosts and calls it *kanunka* instead of the usual Nyoro word *nyama*. The *mufumu* also asks the ghost who it is. The ghost may give the name of someone who has died long ago.

Then the *mufumu* goes on to ask, "And what was it that annoyed you?" The ghost replies: "They refused to give me meat," or "They killed me," or "They didn't take proper care of me so I died," or gives some other reason.

If the ghost asks for a goat, they bring a black one (*kibogo*) and present it to the ghost. And the *mufumu* says, "The matter is finished; here is your goat. Now leave off killing people." Then they cut the goat's throat, and they cause the blood to flow into a new winnowing basket (*rugali*), which is sound and without holes. They order the patient to drink some of the blood. He drinks as well as he is able. Then the goat is skinned and divided up, and a small part of it is cooked; most of the meat is taken home by the *mufumu*.

Different *bafumu* have different techniques for inducing ghosts to mount into the heads of their clients, but always the use of medicines, singing special ghost songs,[3] and the rhythmical shak-

---

[3] I give below the words of four such songs. Like *mbandwa* songs (Beattie 1961: 33–35), they contain a good deal of repetition as well as unverbalized humming and ululation. They are sung to the accompaniment of the gourd rattles of the *bafumu* who are present. I was unable to get a clear account of the meaning of all of them (if indeed they all have clear meanings), but they may be worth putting on record nonetheless.

1   *Tiguli muzimu idobora ahaha idobora:*
    It is not a ghost, ahaha, it is a very very big thing.
2   *Tete alemere balete nyamukanura ahaha ehehe Tete alemere:*
    Tete has been overcome; let them bring the sudden destroyer; ahaha, ehehe, Tete has been overcome.
3   *Eihembe karondoza, ihembe karondoza; alire enaku, ihembe:*

ing of gourd rattles form part of the ceremony. Usually the sick person who is to be the ghost's medium is completely covered in a barkcloth, and often special medicines are burnt or infused and the patient required to inhale the fumes. Medicines, one of which is an infusion of chalk, may be rubbed on his body. An informant's account of one way of inducing possession follows.

Case 2   When I was a small boy about seven years old, one of my half brothers, who was about four, started having fits. So one day my father brought a *mufumu* to the house to catch that ghost. The diviners had told him that was the ghost of a co-wife of the child's maternal grandmother, who was said to have practiced sorcery against that co-wife long ago. The ghost was now avenging this injury by attacking her co-wife's daughter's child.

The ghost was made to come into the head of that child's mother, Nyezi, as the boy was too young to be a medium. When the *mufumu* came, we had our evening meal, and then, after it was dark, we gathered round the fire inside the house. The *mufumu* took a rope, of the kind used for tethering goats, and he tied one end of this to the center pole of the house. Nyezi was made to hold the other end with both hands by means of a stick to which the rope was tied. The *mufumu* sat beside the rope; he draped certain kinds of leaves over it and held others in his hand. He also had various medicines spread out on a mat in front of him. Then he started rhythmically shaking his gourd rattle and singing; other people who were present and knew the songs joined in. Nyezi did not sing, but she gradually started swaying backwards and forwards with the rope in her hands. Suddenly she cried out in a loud voice: *Mawe! Mawe!* ("Mother! mother!"—a cry of distress). Then we knew that the ghost had come into her head.

Soon after that I fell asleep, and I do not know how the ghost was eventually caught. But I was told afterwards that it was caught in a pot and thrown away. *Bafumu* often do this; they put dry banana leaves in the pot and sometimes a small lizard, which makes little rustling sounds in the pot and also itself makes a funny little noise, almost like a person.

Another technique is to make a hole in the roof of the house and to pass a rope through the hole. To the end of the rope is attached the flower sheath, called *nkonombo* in Nyoro, which

---

The Horn which Searches Things Out, the Horn which Searches Things Out; he may cry poverty, the Horn.

4   *Kahembe ruiragura tema enkorra nonaga; bwoya bw'atorogo terebukire:*
The Small Black Horn, cut bean leaves and throw them away; the hair of *atorogo* [?] has slipped away [i.e., has escaped].

grows at the end of a bunch of bananas. The rope, with the *nkonombo* at the end, hangs down inside the room where people have assembled for the seance, and as it proceeds a close watch is kept on the rope. As soon as the *nkonombo* is seen to shake, the *mufumu* leaps up and says that the ghost has come and is shaking the rope. He may then persuade it to pass, via the medium, into a pot prepared for it, and so encompass its own destruction.

Alternatively, the *nkonombo* may be suspended outside the house, as in the case recorded in the following text, written by one of my assistants:

The ghost of a person outside the family or lineage (*kika*) can be burnt, but not that of a close relative. Ghosts of slaves or other unrelated persons may be burnt. For example, if a thirsty traveler were refused a drink of water at a certain house, and then died of thirst on his way, his ghost might attack the members of that household and could be burnt.

Such unrelated ghosts are caught at night. They may be caught with the help of certain *mbandwa* spirits [for an account of these see Beattie 1961]. The *mbandwa* spirits that I know of which can do this are Irungu, the spirit of the bush, and Kapumpuli, the spirit of smallpox; both of these spirits can divine when they are in their mediums' heads. After rattles have been played and the songs of *kubandwa* sung, the *mbandwa* spirit comes into the medium's head, and it begins to talk to the ghost. In this way the ghost may be persuaded to leave the sick person and to come into the head of the doctor-diviner, who is already being possessed by the *mbandwa* spirit. Then the spirit and the ghost talk while both are in the medium's head.

Here is a new way of catching a ghost that I observed. The *mufumu* came with his assistant, called *ow'ensaho* (bag carrier). In the bag were many kinds of medicines, plants, cowries, and other things; also a knife for cutting meat. The patient's family were told to find six strong people, who had to stay outside the house to catch the ghost. Inside, where the seance was being held, a rope had been attached to the patient's wrist and passed through the roof, so that it hung down over the edge of the thatch. To the end of the rope the *mufumu* had tied an *nkonombo* [banana flower sheath]. An opening had been made in this, and the *mufumu* had spat in it. He then told the people outside that if, after the rattles and singing had gone on inside the house for some time, they should see the rope shaking, then they must seize the rope firmly and not let it go; if they released it, the ghost would escape and might throw some of them down and kill them. The people were very frightened of the *mufumu*, and they did as they were told.

Indoors, the *mufumu* began to talk to the ghost, which was now in the patient's head: "What is it? What is it? You shall not kill this person. What is the trouble between you?" The ghost replied: "Now I shall really destroy this man. Why did they leave me alone in the house to die?" It was using the ghost vocabulary, not everyday Nyoro. The *mufumu* pleaded with it: "Leave off, my friend [literally my 'blood-partner']; please leave off!"

Then the *mufumu* took some dried wood of a kind called *kitimazi*, literally "dungwood," which has a smell like human ordure, and he fumigated the patient with this, in order to drive the ghost out of him. [He probably burnt some of it and caused the smoke to penetrate the barkcloth wherein the patient was swathed.] He also rubbed other medicines on him. And the rattles were shaken hard and fast. Then the ghost left the patient and passed along the rope to the banana flower sheath which was hanging outside.

When the people who were outside saw the rope shaking violently, they seized it very firmly, as they had been told, and the people came rushing out of the house. The *mufumu* quickly sealed the hole which he had made in the *nkonombo* and untied it from the rope. Then he ordered the people to cut firewood early in the morning and to make a big fire. The next morning this was done, and the *mufumu* threw that thing on the fire. He did not allow anyone else to approach the fire while he did so, and after he had thrown it in the fire he ran away very quickly. As he did so we heard a shriek; I think that this noise was made by a friend of the *mufumu* who was hiding near the fire, but I did not see anybody.

A further brief account tells in more detail how a ghost may be induced to enter a pot, and how it may be disposed of:

When the ghost is in the medium's head, they may burn a little meat for it. They take the ears of the goat that has been slaughtered and char them so that there is a smell of burning. Then the *mufumu* throws these into a pot which has been smeared with clay; the pot is shaped rather like a water jar (*nfumbi*). With them he puts into the pot a certain kind of reeds (*busagazi*); while he is doing these things the people are singing, and gourd rattles are being shaken. Then he takes hold of the head of the person who is being possessed and looks closely into his nose and mouth. [Then the ghost passes] into the pot, which the patient has been given to hold. The pot is taken from him quickly. If they hear the reeds rustling inside the pot, they close it with mud as quickly as they can, for now the ghost has been captured. Then they put the pot on one side, and everybody is pleased, because the ghost has been caught. Next someone who is very strong takes up the pot, holding it very carefully so that it won't burst. He has to hold it very firmly, for the whole pot may be shaking and its contents churning about (*kucundacunda*). In this way they know that they really have caught the ghost. Sometimes some of the people there may say that the man is just pretending, and they take hold of the pot too. In this way everyone may confirm for himself that the ghost is truly there.

Then there is a discussion as to how they should destroy it. Some say that it should be burned; others that it should be buried. If they agree to bury it, they dig a hole about five feet deep. And if they decide to burn it, they cut firewood and burn it in the bush some distance away from the house, perhaps two hundred yards away. If the fire is not strong enough, so that it just burns the plantain-fiber ropes with which the pot is bound, the ghost may suddenly escape. If it does, it may there and then kill the people who have caught it and go on to kill others. But if the fire is a really strong one, it doesn't matter when the rope is burnt; the ghost will not be able to escape from the flames and will be consumed. Then the patient will recover, and that ghost will never return to do more harm.

As well as being destroyed, a ghost may also be, as it were, kept permanently at bay. After the sacrifice of a goat and the performance of the possession ritual the *mufumu* may "keep" that ghost in front of the homestead. He does this by burying the goat's head in front of the courtyard; on the goat's head he has placed a small quantity of saliva procured from the ghost when it was possessing its victim. This will satisfy the ghost that it has eaten its goat, and so it will not want to come into the house and injure people. A speckled cock (*rusanja*) may also be buried with the goat. On top of these things the grass called *ejubwa* is planted.

But not all ghosts can be finally disposed of in these ways. Ghosts which can be burned are those of domestic slaves (*bairu rubale*), of blood partners (*banywani*), and of parents-in-law. The ghost of a close relative, or of a spouse, cannot be destroyed, but must be enabled to enter into an enduring relationship with the living by means of the possession cult. Here is an informant's account of what happens:

The *mufumu* and others present play their rattles and sing the songs which are sung to raise ghosts. The fire is dim and glowing, not blazing. When the ghost comes into the medium's head it makes a small fawning noise, like a dog welcoming someone it knows, before it starts to talk. Then it begins to speak in a small, far-away voice, like a dying person. It may say: "We have died; we live in the country of Nyamiyonga [the king of the ghosts] far underground where the termites live". The *mufumu* asks it, "Who are you?", and the ghost replies, "I am so-and-so". The *mufumu* continues, "What do you want?", and the ghost answers, "I want to eat". The ghost is now using ghost words instead of ordinary Nyoro; thus *kwehila* (to eat) is *kulya* in everyday speech. The *mufumu* then asks it, "What do you want to eat?", and the ghost replies, "I want to eat meat and millet porridge".

Then the *mufumu* explains to the patient's relatives what the ghost has said. A black goat is produced; this is the meat which ghosts eat. If the ghost is a man's, the goat should be male; if it is a woman's, it should be female. But if a man who has been caught by a man's ghost cannot obtain a male goat, then they take a female goat and kill it. But first they tie 25 cents, or perhaps 5 cents, on to its head, and so turn it into a male goat. When they have done this they cut the meat up, and they give the ghost the goat's head with these cents tied to it. The cents are buried with the goat's head; the *mufumu* says that he cannot take them himself, for if he were to try to cheat the ghost he would die.

Thus in the course of the initial possession the ghost states what it wants. Almost always this involves the immediate provision of a goat. But it may also involve the making of periodic sacrifices to it (entailing further mediumistic ritual), perhaps the dedication of an animal to it, often the erection and maintenance of a special ghost hut for it, sometimes the carrying out of specific obligations or commitments which have been neglected. In the fifteen cases of ghostly activity which I recorded in some detail, six ghosts were quite close maternal kin of their victims, four were quite close paternal kin, three were spouses. In none of these cases could the ghost be destroyed or sent away. There follows a long account, by a young man who had had some secondary education, of how a ghost, avenging neglect by a daughter when it was alive, attacked that daughter's child. The account is of some interest also as showing that the conflict between modern Western ideas and traditional ones arises in the context of the ghost cult, as in many other contexts.

Case 3 When I was at school in Hoima [the capital of Bunyoro] I used to stay in the home of a woman called Kabasika. I called her my *nyinento* [mother's sister, literally "little mother"] because she was born in the same clan as my mother. She lived about two miles from the town, and I used to walk in to school every day.

In May, 1954, her son Turumanya, a boy of about seven, became affected (*yakwatwa*, literally "was caught") by a big ulcer on his leg. It hurt him very much, and when medicine was put on it it would not stay there but fell off at once. After about two weeks the ulcer was enormous; I used to treat it myself with powder which I got from the hospital, but it got no better. One afternoon my *nyinento* said to me: "This child of mine is being made sick by a ghost, perhaps by a ghost of this very household (*eka*)." Early the next morning when I went to greet her I found that she had left the house. After a while my cousin Turumanya and I saw her returning. As soon as she came in, and before I had time to ask her where she had been, she called me aside. "Come behind the house with me, Apuli" (a pet name), she said, "I want to tell you something." We went out behind the house and sat down. She was holding a small bunch of a special kind of grass (*etete,* lemon grass) and *rweza* (literally "that which whitens or purifies," a small herb with a pretty white blossom, perhaps a celosia). Then she said to me: "Atenyi—this is my *mpako* name[4]—do you know what has made that mother's child of yours sick?" I said "No," and she went on: "He's been made sick by the ghost of his grandfather Kahanda, my father; it wants to eat. And if it is given meat to eat and can then be persuaded to spit on Turumanya, so conveying its blessing to him, then that ulcer will get better. This is what took me out so early in the morning; I have been to the diviner Karoli to find out what the matter was."

Then she said: "Now, Atenyi, let me start with a prayer (*kambanze ndame*). Then I must prepare millet porridge and meat for the ghost, so that my child may get well." Then she went into the house. I stayed outside, but I could hear what she said when she prayed at the *ihangirro* (shrine or sacred place) in the corner of her room. This is what I heard her saying, after she had knelt down: "Ai, father, I know that it is you who has made this child of mine sick, because a long time has passed without my cooking anything for you to eat. Ai, all you good people who have died, release this child of yours so that he may be all right again. I am just going to prepare a meal for you so that you may eat."

After this my *nyinento* prepared millet, and she sent me to buy some beef at Hoima market; I bought just two pounds. When I got home I wanted the meat to be cooked at once so that I could have some of it. But she refused, saying, "That meat is not for you, or for your brother either; no, this is my private affair!" So I left it. That evening she prepared our evening meal for us as usual and we ate; but we did not have any of that meat, no! And after we had eaten, she started cooking food for that ghost. She cooked it like any other food, but when she had finished dishing the millet porridge she called me to carry that food into the house. I did so.

Soon after this a neighbor, a married woman who was a friend of my *nyinento* and a kind of interpreter (*muhinduzi*) for the world of ghosts [i.e., she was an initiate in the Nyoro spirit mediumship cult] came to the house, to tell the ghost that its food had been prepared for it. She sat down on the ground by the hearth. My *nyinento*

---

[4] Every Nyoro child is given one of the eleven or so special *mpako* names, which are supposedly of Nilotic origin. Their use in everyday discourse implies friendly intimacy.

went to her room and took a barkcloth. When she returned she called me and my young brother (who was also staying there at that time) into the house, but we refused and went to sit on the verandah. But the boy Turumanya was with his mother; he sat beside her while she was being possessed by her father's ghost. However, we did come into the house a little later, and these are the things which I heard and saw.

My *nyinento* was sitting in the room near the *ihangirro;* she was stooped over and completely covered by the barkcloth. She was quite silent for some minutes. Then she started to make little grunting noises (*kuhuna*): "Nnn, nnn." Then she began to speak, but her voice was quite changed; it was small and high-pitched. She said, "I have come back!" (*ntarukire*); this is the ghost's way of saying *ngarukire*, "I have returned." And the neighbor who was there to speak to the ghost said "Return!" (*taruka!*). Then the ghost greeted the people present: "Are you all right there? And I'm here, all right. [This is a usual form of greeting in Bunyoro.] I died, alas! alas! So it's you people, well! well!"

The woman replied and told the ghost that its food was ready for it: "I have called you; come and eat. I have cooked a little millet for you and some meat; help yourself and eat with your children. Because I know that it was you who made this child of mine sick." And the ghost answered, "You, is the child there? Bring him so that I can have a look at him". Then the boy was brought forward to be spat upon by his grandfather's ghost. And the ghost spat lightly on him and said: "Apuli, recover from your ulcer; grow strong; do a man's work!" While the ghost spat on him, it moved him about by his head, shoulders, and arms. And it gave him a small morsel of millet porridge, which it had spat on, and a piece of meat, which the boy ate. Then the ghost wanted to spit on me as well, but I refused and ran out into the kitchen with my young brother, and stayed there.

Then I heard the woman explaining to the ghost: "These children are schoolboys (*basomi*, literally 'readers'); they are people of the Europeans, outsiders (*balimwoyo*, a term used to denote people who have not been initiated into the possession cult). That is why they are not able to come near." Then she shouted to us: "You there! Take care of yourselves in matters like these. You could easily die or be caught by a terrible disease!" And she called to us again to go in. But we refused because we were attending school, and they had forbidden us there to have anything to do with things of this sort or to eat such food. They are absolutely forbidden by the Catholic religion.

After my *nyinento* had finished being possessed by her father Kahanda's ghost, she put the barkcloth back in its place. Then she came back and said to the other woman: "My dear friend, hunger is killing me; give me some of that millet which is there to eat." I said to her: "But you've just been eating millet porridge and meat!" She answered, "My child, do you think it was I who was just eating?" I said "Yes," and she went on: "It was the ghost that was eating, not I. Well, perhaps I was eating, but I do not know where the food has gone. These are things of the devil (*Sitani*)."

From that time the boy Turumanya began to recover, and after one month his ulcer was quite gone.

There are gaps in this account. Possession is usually induced by singing and the shaking of gourd rattles, but there is no mention of this here; also it is not stated whether the ghost required a ghost-hut to be erected for it. Nevertheless, the account illustrates some points already made. We noted, for example, that a ghost may attack the person who has offended it not directly but indirectly, and in the account it was not Kabasika but her child Turumanya, who had never done anything to annoy his late grandfather, who was inflicted with a painful ulcer. Although individualism has increased in Bunyoro, as elsewhere, with the coming of Western influence, the bonds of family and lineage are still sufficiently strong for an attack on one member of the lineage or domestic group to be thought of as an attack on all.

It is significant, moreover, that Kabasika was not thinking of her relationship with the ghost world solely in interindividual terms. It is true that her direct concern was with her father's ghost, which was supposed to be offended because she had neglected it, but she also expressed her concern with "all you good people who have died," that is, with the ancestral ghosts as in some sense a collectivity. Furthermore, in this case the possession was by proxy. The usual pattern is for the victim himself to be formally possessed by the ghost which is afflicting him, but where the victim is a small child, and hence presumably incapable of understanding and memorizng the quite complex pattern of behavior required, the ghost may be induced to possess his mother or another close relative as a substitute.

Finally, the case reveals the conflict which prevails between traditional Nyoro ritual practices and the new Christian-inspired ideas being disseminated by both church and state. My informant and his young brother had attended a mission school [almost all education in Bunyoro is in mission hands, and the Protestant Church Missionary Society has had much influence on the native rulers]. The missionary attitude to traditional religious and magical practices in Bunyoro has, I believe, been exceptionally repressive. This has created, at least during the present period of transition, a painful dilemma for many schoolchildren from traditional homes. Strong pressures may be put on them by their parents and relatives to participate in traditional rites, and refusal may be regarded not merely as a regrettable indifference to the old customs but as an act of deliberate injury to family and kin.

Another detailed text, related by a Christian informant with a secondary education, also involves possession by proxy, though it is likewise of interest on other grounds. Mission influence, though not directly mentioned, may well have been reflected, directly or indirectly, in the chosen medium's reluctance to participate.

Case 4 A neighbor of ours called Yowana died. He had several brothers and sisters, and when he was dying he said that his goats should be given to his eldest sister, except for a few which should go to a younger sister. But his older brother Isoke was a greedy man, and as soon as Yowana was dead he took those goats into his own house. He did not trouble to obey his brother's wishes; he said to himself, "He's dead and will never know." But Yowana's ghost said to itself: "Ma! Shall I not say God forbid that you should steal my property! You have shown your hatred for me, and now that I am dead you flatter yourself that you can help yourself to what is mine! You cheat!" And the ghost caught that man Isoke and threw him on the ground in a fit. People cried, "What is it? What is it? What is killing him?", and those who were near rushed to help him. And they called to his relatives, "Go quickly to the diviners and find out what is killing him!" So his mother went to a diviner, and the diviner threw his shells and said, "It's his brother's ghost; this man has taken (*akalya*, literally 'he has eaten') what was refused to him and given to his sisters."

His mother asked the diviner, "What shall we do?" He said that first the property should be divided up as the dead man had ordered. Next they should find a doctor-diviner (*mufumu*) to come and arrange for the ghost to possess someone (*kutendeka*); otherwise her son would die. The mother replied, "But my son is as good as dead already; it is finished; shall I go and help him when he is already dead?" The diviner threw his shells again and saw that they had fallen in a straight line (*muhingo*). So he said to her, "He's not dead yet; but if you don't do as I have told you he will not eat again until he has seen the gateway of the pit".

The woman wept, and after she had wept she gave her son medicines to calm him, rubbing them in his armpits and groin. Then he began to come to his senses, and she explained to him that it would be well to give the goats to their proper owners; if this were not done he would die. So Isoke softened and agreed to divide up the property. She went on to tell him that the diviner had said the ghost should be enabled to possess a member of the family, after which it would cease to trouble him (*guraculera*, literally "it would calm down").

So the young man called a *mufumu* to arrange for the possession. He came, summoned everybody in the household, and spread out his medicines. He had told them to collect the wood called *ngando* and to make a fire in the house, so that he could call the ghost into the sick man's head and talk to it. He threw some medicine on the fire, and other medicine was put in a potsherd which was placed on the embers and the patient made to inhale it. After this the *mufumu* took the potsherd in his hands and circled the sick man's head with it. While he did this he called upon the ghost to cease making him ill. Then he asked it what it wanted and whom it wished as its medium. But that day the ghost refused to explain what it wanted done. So that night after dark he continued to talk to it, and at last it said that it wanted to have its youngest sister as its medium.

When that sister heard about this the following morning she was afraid, for she knew that possession by a ghost sometimes entails rough handling, and she ran away and hid herself in a neighbor's house. But the mother set out to track her until she found her. When she caught her she beat her very much, bound her legs so that she should not run away again, and tied her arms behind her back. That night the *mufumu* continued to talk with the ghost, and the ghost said that it wanted a black goat killed for it and that it would eat the meat while it was "in the head" of its medium. The next evening, after the evening meal, the *mufumu* ordered that the girl who was to be the medium should be prepared. Her legs and arms were untied, and she was made to sit near the fire. The goat was brought and slaughtered, and one leg was cooked at once. The *mufumu* rubbed medicine on the girl, and he put other medicine in the potsherd which was by the fire; this he then moved in a circle round her head.

Then the ghost descended (*kusirimuka*)[5] into its medium. When it had entered her [*kumugwera*, literally "fell upon her"], it began to hurl her about and choke her. She knew nothing of this; others explained it to her later. But the next day her throat was so sore that she could not even swallow her own saliva.

As soon as the *mufumu* saw that the ghost had seized her and was choking her so fiercely, he began to talk and plead with it and to put more medicine on it [i.e., on the medium], until it calmed down. Then he fed it with the meat which had been cooked for it, and the others present ate as well. There was also millet porridge. The *mufumu* gave the ghost pellets of food by putting them into its

[5] The use of this word seems to contradict the idea that ghosts "rise" into the head of the medium, but the implication here is of violent attack.

[i.e., the medium's] mouth, and the ghost also began to give the
people who were there morsels of food in the same way, and told
them to eat.[6] When the meal was finished, the *mufumu* released the
ghost to go back to its own place, and it was all finished. Then the
ghost's strength left the girl. From that time the ghost has been
quiet and has brought no more trouble.

My informant told me that he afterwards asked the girl what it
felt like to be possessed by a ghost. She replied that it had made
her feel strange and unwell; she had felt impelled to weep, that
she was being moved by some power outside herself, that she
was being strangled and knocked down; she did not remember
anything more.

This case well illustrates the sanctioning aspect of the ghost
cult. When Isoke fell ill, the diviner's diagnosis and advice were
powerful incentives for him to carry out his dead brother's wishes
and give the goats bequeathed to his sisters to their rightful
owners. It may be presumed that Isoke's meanness and dis-
honesty in this matter were common knowledge in the neighborhood; it is very unlikely that the cheated sisters had kept silent.
It is possible, too, that Isoke felt a certain uneasiness at having
defied the wishes of his dead brother. So the diviner's findings
can hardly have been unexpected.

Belief in the power of ghosts also served as a powerful sanction
for conformity with accepted social norms in the following case.

Case 5 An old man called Yozefu was ill, and Mariya, the wife of
his second son Yonasani, cooked some food for him and took it to
him to eat. She was intercepted by her husband Yonasani, who an-
grily threw the food away, saying abusively to Mariya: "Why do you
want to cook for him? Hasn't he got a wife of his own?" A day or
two later the old man Yozefu died.

Shortly afterwards Yozefu's ghost appeared in a dream to Rumondo, his eldest son, and said that his [Yozefu's] daughter Eseri
should become its medium. Also, at about the same time, Rumondo's
small daughter became ill, and the diviners said that this was due to
Yozefu's ghost. So Rumondo called a doctor-diviner to deal with the
matter. The *mufumu* spoke with the ghost through the sick child,
and the ghost said that the child would get better, but that unless
the possession were arranged quickly it would find another victim in
the family. A day or two later Yonasani's son, a lad of about
twenty, fell ill; he seemed to be going out of his mind and kept

---

[6] This rite of putting food into another's mouth is called *kubegera*. It
symbolizes amity and close attachment, as between a mother and her child.

falling down. The girl Eseri was duly initiated, and various *bafumu* were consulted, but the young man remained ill for several months.

Then Yozefu's ghost again appeared to Rumondo in a dream and told him to call an old friend of his [Yozefu's], who was also a medium. This man came, there was another seance, and at last the ghost spoke through its medium Eseri. It said that a sheep should be bought and slaughtered for it, a feast held, and a small ghost-hut erected for it in the courtyard. It also said that Rumondo's two brothers should come back and live together with Rumondo at the family home (at that time they were living far apart, and only Rumondo was living at his father's place). All these things were done as directed. At once the sick boy got better, and that was the end of the matter.

Here again the actual offender was not attacked directly but indirectly, first through his brother's child and then through his own. A man is especially vulnerable through his children, and particularly through his sons. The Nyoro, like other peoples with a classificatory kinship terminology, think of a brother's sons as being, in a real sense, one's own sons too. In predominantly patrilineal Bunyoro a man looks to his sons to continue his line and perhaps, after his death, to provide his ghost with the attentions it needs. This case is interesting also in its sanctioning aspect, as vividly expressing the traditional value of agnatic solidarity, which is nowadays giving way before the new individualistic values of contemporary Bunyoro. In traditional times adult brothers often lived together in large compound families, which formed real corporate agnatic units in relation to other similar units. Though this is no longer the norm, many brothers still do live near one another and look to one another for co-operation and support. Even though many do not, the story of Yozefu's ghost shows that the belief that they ought to do so is still an important value for some Nyoro.

In the cases just quoted, the action taken at the ghost's behest is reported to have been successful. But this is not always so. Kiboko had a ghost-hut (*kibali*) under the eaves of his thatched, mud-and-wattle hut to the right of the doorway; in it was a small piece of a kind of ant-mound called *mpike*. I asked him for what ghost it had been erected, and he replied:

Case 6 My wife had many miscarriages and failed to give birth to a live child, so I went to the diviners, and they said that the trouble was due to the ghost of my wife's dead mother. She had been annoyed before she died because she had not received "the goat of the bride's mother" when her daughter was married. This was my wife's father's fault; he had refused to accept bridewealth for her. Had he done so, then one of the goats which I would have paid would have gone to her mother. When I consulted a *mufumu* and made contact with the ghost, it told me to make a ghost-hut for it and dedicate a black goat to it. I did all these things, but that wife has not yet had a child.

When I asked Kiboko whether he thought that it was still possible that the action he had taken might be effective, he replied skeptically, "Will a woman of forty begin to bear children?"

Ghost-huts are of standardized pattern, usually untidy-looking conical huts of sticks and grass about eighteen inches high. Here is an informant's description of a *kibali*.

The frame is made of sticks of a tree called *bijegejege* or *ebosa* [I have not been able to identify these]. The sticks are tied together in the shape of a small cone about a foot or eighteen inches high; they are tied with the bark of *ebosa* or with *esojo* grass. On the floor of the hut they spread *esojo* grass, not *etete* [lemon grass], which is used in huts for *embandwa* spirits only. If the hut is for a male ghost a stick of a tree called *rusinga* is placed upright in the hut as a spear is in a real house; this stick is the ghost's spear. [Real spears are made of *rusinga* wood, which grows strong and straight.] All the bones of the goat which was eaten at the possession feast are buried in a hole dug beside the entrance to the ghost-hut, except the lower jawbone, which is placed on top of the hole after it has been filled in. Sometimes a black goat is kept in the household permanently for the ghost, and when the ghost says it wants to eat they may kill it and replace it with another goat. In this case only the bones of the first goat that is killed are buried in this hole. A piece of a special kind of anthill called *mpike* [these are small, hard, dome-shaped mounds, sometimes used as cooking stones] is brought and may be put on top of the jawbone. This is the ghost's stool, for it to sit on when it comes there. The *mufumu* also puts a small piece of barkcloth in the ghost-hut; this is to provide clothing for the ghost. The tail of a chameleon may also be put there; this is because a chameleon can look in all directions at once, so that the ghost may not approach unseen.

Some ghosts are believed to be so inimical that none of the measures described above are effective against them. Here is an informant's statement about the powers of different kinds of ghosts:

The ghost of a sister's child (*mwihwa*) does not have a hut built for it, nor can it be "caught." If a *mwihwa's* ghost attacks a family it finishes off the whole household; this is something about *baihwa* which causes them to be very much feared.[7] The ghost of a person's mother's brother (*nyinarumi*) or mother's sister (*nyinento*) is also very strong; such ghosts are stronger than those of parents (*bazaire*, literally "those who have begotten or borne one"), which may have huts built for them.

The ghost of an infant (*nkerembe*) is stronger than that of an adult, but it is not as strong as that of a sister's child. An infant's ghost cannot be burnt; they simply do what it wants. It can cry like a real infant. An *nkerembe* can leave a ghost for three reasons—perhaps because they have thrown it away (*kunagwa*), perhaps because they have left it in a burning house and run away, perhaps because it has been killed by its mother. Those ghosts which have huts built for them are usually those of the father's side.

Particularly dangerous is the ghost of a person who has committed suicide because of some injury or slight. The following text illustrates the fate of a man attacked by the ghost of his late wife, who had killed herself because of his unkindness to her.

Case 7 Tito left his wife at home in Bunyoro looking after his home and farm while he went to Kampala to work. He stayed away for six years, and during this time his half brother by the same father, Asafu, came to his house and helped his wife with the farm, giving her presents of clothes and other things and, eventually, a child. When Tito returned, he was very angry about this. He had no right to be so; it was not as though his wife had taken up with a stranger. The child was of his clan and house, and the blood was the same. In Nyoro custom, if a man sleeps with the wife of his brother by the same father, there is no adultery. Also it was unreasonable to expect a woman to remain faithful through six years of separation. In fact, the Native Government had recently made a law that if a man left his wife for two years or more he would have no claim if she went elsewhere or had a child by another man, and he would have no right to compel her to return to him.

However Tito did not see things in this light. He never left off reproaching his wife, and he constantly abused and beat her. After some time she went off into the bush and hanged herself on a tree. She left a very powerful ghost. The first thing that happened was that the child who had been born during Tito's absence died, a week after her own death. Then the children of Tito and his dead wife began to fight with their father and beat him. A year later he

---

[7] This may reflect the fact that the relationship between mother's brother and sister's son in Bunyoro is an ambivalent and highly institutionalized one, with specific ritual obligations on both sides (cf. Beattie 1958: 17–22).

contracted leprosy, and he has suffered from this ever since. He does not die, but he is weak, cannot walk, and is wasted away. Sometimes he seems to get a bit better, and then he relapses and seems about to die, and then he recovers a little again. This is because the ghost wishes him to suffer as much as possible. Even now, in his present state, his eldest son beats him from time to time when he is drunk. Tito has tried every means to get rid of that ghost and has bought many medicines, but they could never succeed in catching it.

Where it is suspected that a dying person is likely to leave a ghost to afflict the living, the Nyoro say that the danger may be averted by premortem treatment (though I have never heard of an actual case).

If a man who is always cursing people and threatening to leave a ghost to injure them falls sick, sometimes when they see that he is just about to die they find some clay, and they suffocate him by putting this in his mouth. They also put some in his anus, and after that they bury him. Thus that man cannot leave a ghost, because they have "caught" it before he died.

In three of the seven cases cited above the ghost was a relative on the victim's mother's side, in two a patrilateral relative, in one a spouse, and in one a domestic slave (*mwiru rubale*). In all these cases the ghost was an individual believed to have been offended before death by the victim or by a near relative of the victim. And in all of them, except that of the old man Yozefu whose ghost first announced itself in a dream, illness or other misfortune was the first intimation that a ghost might be active. Even in Yozefu's case, illness in the family followed hard on the heels of this announcement. Is there, then, any sense in which we can say that the Nyoro have, or traditionally had, an ancestral cult, in which the ancestors are "worshiped" and sacrificed to as a collectivity? Or is the ghost cult simply an individual and *ad hoc* reaction to illness or other misfortune, like sorcery and certain other kinds of spirit possession?

It is plain, I think, from the cases already given that it is mostly the latter, but there is a little more to it than this. It would be misleading to say that the traditional religion of the Nyoro was ancestor worship. In fact, their traditional religion centers on the Cwezi spirits, which are associated with a wonderful race of people supposed to have come to Bunyoro many centuries ago, to have ruled the country for a couple of generations and performed many wonderful things, and then to have vanished as mysteriously as they came. These spirits, of which there were traditionally nineteen, are linked with the Nyoro clan system, one or more of them being specially associated with each of the local agnatic descent groups in which the Nyoro are said to have been traditionally organized. The cult of these spirits was also a mediumistic one (Beattie 1961).

Nonetheless, there are traces of an ancestral cult in some parts of Bunyoro. Although in most of the country it is either not practiced at all or is of negligible importance, everybody knows what it is and that it is, or was, practiced by some Nyoro. We noted, in Case 3, that Kabasika was concerned with her father's ghost not solely as an individual but also as associated with a collectivity of ancestors. It is significant that the region where the ancestral cult is still much spoken of and practiced is the Lake Albert littoral—an area which is largely isolated from the rest of Bunyoro by a steep escarpment and where the inhabitants, unlike those of upland Bunyoro, live in compact settlements of villages which are territorially organized on a lineage basis. The large settlement of Tonya, for example, consisting of about 130 households, comprises four distinct subdivisions or wards, each named after one clan of which practically all the adult men in the ward are members. In this lakeshore region membership in a group defined by agnatic descent is very much more important than it is for the members of the more dispersed communities of upland Bunyoro, where residence is comparatively little determined by descent.

To perform a special rite of prayer and sacrifice for the father's ghost is called *kubembeka*. It can be carried out only by a son, and, if there are several sons, by the father's heir. In Bunyoro there is only one heir (*mugwetwa*); the patrimonial authority is always transmitted undivided. In the *kubembeka* rite, remoter patrilineal forebears are always implicitly or explicitly associated with the father's ghost; the Nyoro say that other ghosts of the father's line are always present. A special shrine is constructed and maintained by the man who has authority to perform the rite. This is quite different from the ordinary ghost-hut, which, as we have noted, is a flimsy conical construction of sticks and grass. The *ibembo* shrine consists of four short stakes stuck in the ground in a straight line so that they stand about four inches

above the surface and about two or three inches apart. Each stake
is neatly bound with grass. Usually they are placed under a flimsy
rectangular stand made of sticks. I could obtain no explanation
of the form of the *ibembo* shrine, but it is relevant to note that
in a number of ritual contexts in Bunyoro the number four is
associated with men, three with women. The stakes are said to
be made of the wood of a tree fern (called *mulere*) and are called
bikondo or *bibibi*.

Though one informant told me that in Tonya and other lakeshore communities prayers are addressed to the patrilineal ghosts
at every new moon, my impression is that *ibembo* is likely to be
performed about once a year. Even then, my informants agreed
that it would very often be neglected until the man responsible
for arranging it was reminded of it by seeing his father in a
dream, or by an illness in his family which the diviners attributed
to his neglect of the *ibembo* shrine. The ceremony would be
attended by all the brothers of the dead man and their families.
It could also be attended by wives and sisters' children (the
latter being "children" of their mothers' clan), but not by more
distant affines or by mothers' brothers (*nyinarumi*). The rite
might or might not include possession; if it did not, it probably
amounted to little more than a prayer and the placing at the
shrine of a little millet or beer. I was told in Tonya that an offering of fish could also appropriately be made; when this was done
the fish offered should be the species called *ngasa* (tiger fish).
Unlike most Lake Albert fish, this species is equipped with extremely sharp teeth. It may be that, like Tallensi totems (Fortes
1945: 145), this implied aggressiveness makes them particularly
appropriate to represent the ancestors, but the Nyoro to whom
I suggested this, though amused, were unwilling to confirm it! The
following is a Tonya informant's account of what takes place at
ibembo:

> Yowasi is the head of all the Basaigi clan in Tonya, and he performs
> the *ibembo* ceremony for his dead father on behalf of them all. The
> *ibembo* is for other ancestors of the Basaigi besides Yowasi's father;
> the names of some of these ancestors are Karasi, Rwemera, Karongo,
> Miigo, and Kiiza. The members of the Basaigi clan gather at
> Yowasi's shrine (*bikondo*). They do not do so at regular intervals,
> only when there has been some kind of misfortune (*bujune*), like
> someone being sick, a woman failing to bear children, or a man
> becoming impotent. In such a case the victim would have consulted

the diviners first, and they would have advised that *ibembo* should be held. It might occur once a year or more often.

At this ceremony a goat is killed, and fish and millet porridge are also prepared. When the goat is being brought to be sacrificed, it is a good thing if it urinates on the way. This shows that there is no evil ahead, that the ghosts will do no harm to anyone in that house, that they wish them to give birth and to have good health, and that the ghosts are pleased with the goat that is being brought for them. But if the goat defecates, that is a bad sign and shows that the ghosts are not pleased. Beer may or may not be provided.

In the ceremony different ancestral ghosts enter into Yowasi and speak through him. Yowasi speaks in his ordinary voice, but it is the ghosts who are speaking and not he. He is dressed in a barkcloth. While Yowasi is in a state of possession members of his group may ask him for what they want. Thus women may say, "We want to give birth," and the ghost which is possessing Yowasi says, "You will give birth"; it spits in the outstretched hands of the suppliant women, who then wipe the saliva [which conveys the ghost's blessing] on their faces and heads. Or a person may say, "I'm sick, cure me," and the ghost may reply, "You will recover," and convey its blessing in the same way. After this the food is brought and the ghosts eat, being still in the head of Yowasi. Sometimes a goat is not slaughtered there and then but is kept for the ancestors; it may be eaten at a later *ibembo*.

This ceremony is usually carried out in the early afternoon. Yowasi had to be initiated into the possession cult in order to receive these ghosts. Initiation takes place in the bush at night and is carried out by old men of the Basaigi clan who are members of the possession cult.

To the question whether Nyoro have an ancestral cult, then, the answer must be that they know what is meant by such a cult and that some of them practice it. But the presence or absence of such a cult is very much a matter of degree. Most Nyoro, although they know that their fathers and their fathers' fathers left ghosts behind them when they died and that these ghosts can injure them, are little concerned with their ancestral ghosts as such. Ghosts, whether ancestral or otherwise, are for the most part thought of as individuals who can injure the living when they are offended. At least outside the sparsely populated lakeshore region, where residence is still largely based on unilineal descent, there is in Bunyoro little idea (though there is some) of "the ancestors" as a kind of unindividuated power, a collectivity—an idea which is still strongly held by some neighboring peoples such as the Lugbara (see Middleton 1960).

In the foregoing pages I have set out, with some ethnographic illustration, how the Nyoro think about ghosts and what they do about them. Let me recapitulate the principal stages in the ghost ritual. To begin with, a person (or someone close to him) falls ill or suffers some other misfortune, e.g., repeated abortion in the case of a woman. He or she consults a diviner, who is likely to diagnose one of three possible causes of the trouble: sorcery by some living person, the activity of nonhuman *mbandwa* spirits, or the action of a ghost. If ghostly activity is diagnosed, two broad types of action may follow, depending on the nature of the ghost and its relationship to the victim. First, it may be destroyed or otherwise permanently got rid of; second, an enduring relationship with it may be entered into, expressed through periodic sacrifice and prayer, the dedication to it of an animal, and the erection of a ghost-hut for it. But in either case the ghost must first of all be induced, through the spirit mediumship cult, to mount into the head of either the sick person or his accredited representative. When there, it may be either removed or disposed of, or propitiated, depending on the kind of ghost it is.

In some parts of Bunyoro an enduring relationship of this kind may be entered into especially with patrilineal ghosts, and to this extent the Nyoro may be said to have an ancestral cult. But in by far the greater part of the country, and in most respects in all of it, the ghost-victim relationship is an individual and interpersonal one, supposed to derive from some real or imagined slight, injury, or neglect either by the victim or by one of his close relatives. When all the culturally prescribed action has been properly carried out, the sufferer should recover. Some do; in six of the fifteen cases which I have recorded the victims are said to have recovered, in five not to have done so, and in two (both cases of repeated miscarriage) the victims had still not given up hope that the treatment would be effective.

I conclude by considering a little further the social and psychological implications of the Nyoro ghost cult. Functionally, like the other institutionalized forms of Nyoro spirit mediumship which I have discussed elsewhere, the ghost ritual is effective on two levels. First, it provides one way of thinking about and dealing with situations of stress and anxiety, and, second, it embodies an effective social sanction against certain kinds of socially disapproved behavior.

In Bunyoro, as in other relatively underdeveloped countries (though here as elsewhere the situation is rapidly changing), there is still much ill health, especially in infancy and childhood, and miscarriage is common. In rural areas access to modern means of dealing with these misfortunes is not yet easily or readily available. But the traditional culture provides a means of coming to terms with them, and even though these means are not (or at least not wholly) satisfying clinically, they do nonetheless provide emotional relief for the sufferer and his relatives. It may be, indeed, as I have remarked elsewhere, that the length and complexity of the ritual involved is psychologically beneficial rather than the reverse. In situations of stress what is important is to have something to do; to be compelled to remain inactive and impotent in the face of illness or other misfortune is psychologically unendurable.

But like the other Nyoro mediumistic cults, the ghost cult does more than offer its practitioners something useless to do merely for the sake of doing something. To begin with, it is by no means to be assumed that it is wholly useless. Subjection to treatment through ghost mediumship, whether the supposed medium's attitude to it is credulous, wholly skeptical, or a mixture of the two—I return to this point below—is a vivid and traumatic experience. Even for a man in the pink of condition, the darkness, the close group of people in the small warm hut, the monotonous but exciting rhythm of gourd rattles shaken close to his ears, the singing, and perhaps the fumes from burning or boiling herbs and other medicines can hardly fail to have a powerful physical and emotive effect. On a person who is sick and impressionable the effect must be very much greater. High excitement, profuse perspiration, and perhaps final collapse may afford a kind of shock therapy which, at least in some cases, may well relieve certain kinds of symptoms.

Even where dissociation is not achieved or is incomplete, the dramatic, cathartic effect of the performance is important. As in other Nyoro possession ritual, the medium takes on the voice and gestures of the ghost which is supposed to be possessing him, and it is plain from some of the cases recorded in this paper that professional mediums may possess considerable histrionic talent. Whatever else it is, a mediumistic seance is evidently a thrilling dramatic performance. It is "expressive" rather than, or at least as much as, it is "instrumental." Or perhaps it would be more accurate to say that it is thought to be instrumental precisely because it is expressive. It is not a practical technique like pottery or basket-making, to be varied and improved in the light of experiment and experience. It is a symbolic procedure, to be understood rather by reference to what is being said than just by reference to what it is being sought to achieve. And it is the whole rite, not the instruments or techniques used, taken by themselves, which is believed to be effective.

When I was investigating the *mbandwa* possession cult in Bunyoro, an informant told me that she knew even before she was initiated into the cult that possession was not genuine, but simulated. But even so, she told me, she thought that it was a good thing to go through with the prescribed ritual. For her, although it involved pretence, it was not just pretence. If it is thought that ghosts, like other spirits, exist and can harm the living (and this is still widely believed in Bunyoro today, as it is in many other countries), then it may be supposed that these ghosts are gratified, and may be appeased, by the rituals which are performed on their behalf. This is so even though these rituals be regarded not as scientific procedures (and therefore "true"), but rather as symbolic ones. As among the ancient Greeks, it is held appropriate to approach the spirit world through drama, through vivid symbolic statements of what is feared and desired, not through empirically tested, practical techniques. To suppose otherwise is to fall into the Frazerian fallacy of interpreting religious behavior as though it were a kind of inferior and misguided science.

The Nyoro ghost cult, then, like the other Nyoro spirit cults, is a drama. At the same time, in some of its forms (as in *kubembeka*) it is an expression of worship and piety toward beings whose existence is still widely acknowledged.

I turn now to a few comments about the cult's aspect as a sanction for good behavior. Obviously the belief that ghosts can injure and even kill living people, and that they are likely to do this if they are ill-treated or neglected while they are alive, is a powerful incentive to treat one's fellow men properly. Every one of the cases quoted in this paper exhibits this aspect. Cruelty, neglect, cheating, and failure to maintain good brotherly relations are socially disapproved modes of behavior. And in every case some such delict was diagnosed as having given cause for ghostly punishment. Thus, in its traditional form, the cult was essentially a moral one. For the Nyoro, as for members of many Western European societies not so long ago, illness and other misfortune are thought of as often being somehow "deserved." And just as orthodox Christianity threatened wrongdoers with hell fire in the afterlife, so the Nyoro ghost cult threatens them with illness or other misfortune in this life.

It is of interest that it is the kind of relationship between ghost and victim, even more than the degree of enormity of the precipitating offense, that is held to determine the severity of the ghost's attack. A man's closest ties are with his father and his kin, but although the father's ghost can and sometimes does punish his children, its attack is rarely fatal, and often it is thought (unlike other ghosts) to be benevolent. This is not surprising, for a man in a sense lives through his children, who will remember him and honor his name, and a Nyoro thinks of himself as "of one blood" with his father and with the surviving members of the agnatic descent group to which he belongs. Here also other and more pragmatic sanctions come into play. Even after his father's death, a man probably has—and certainly would have had in traditional times—other agnatic kinsmen with whom in his own interest he is bound to maintain friendly and cooperative relations.

This is less so in regard to one's mother's people, who belong to a lineage and clan other than one's own (though here, at least as regards the mother, the relationship is usually tempered by close affection). Thus a mother's brother's ghost, and even her sister's, are said to be more dangerous than paternal ghosts. But the most dangerous of all related ghosts is that of a sister's son, who is an "outsider" as no other relative is; "a sister's son is outside" (*omwihwa aheru*), say the Nyoro. Though a man's mother's brothers are all members of the same clan or descent group, his classificatory sisters' children are likely to be scattered in many groups and so to be widely dispersed. His relationship with them is consequently ambivalent; though he is their "male mother," and they are his "children," they are also in some sense strangers, "outsiders," for they are not members of his own or his mother's clan but of "outside" clans whose members have married women of his own clan (see Beattie 1958 on the ambivalence of the relationship between mother's brother and sister's son).

The more "outside" a ghost is, the more dangerous it can be. Thus unrelated ghosts, as we saw earlier, may be among the most dangerous of all. The ghosts of former domestic slaves, of blood partners (who are by definition of separate clans), and of wandering unnamed ghosts are among the most difficult to deal with. Outsiders are feared, and they must therefore be treated with special care and consideration. This fear is expressed in the ghost cult.

There is yet another aspect to this way of distinguishing between ghosts in terms of their potency. In Bunyoro most social relationships are hierarchically conceived, so that in any relationship one partner is thought to be superordinate, the other subordinate. In several contexts, it seems that occupation of a role of social or political subordination may be, as it were, compensated for by the ascription to the inferior of a kind of ritual superiority. Thus the Nyoro say that a sister's son has ritual (though not of course secular) power over his mother's brother, whom he is said to "rule" (*kulema*), even though he stands to him in the subordinate and inferior relationship of "child." And it may be supposed, as was noted earlier, that the ascription of a special ritual potency to captives used as household slaves (who of course had no secular means of enforcing any claims against their owners) must have operated as a strong sanction against maltreating them.

An effect of culture contact, and especially of the advent of a cash economy, on Nyoro possession cults and on the techniques of divination with which they are associated has been to increase the profits available to ritual specialists, and so to further the proliferation of many such cults. All Nyoro believe that some diviners and mediums are charlatans, but few believe that all of them are. But although Western influence has led to a great proliferation of cult activity in the context of the spirit (*mbandwa*) cult, it seems to have had no comparable effect on the ghost cult.

This is simply explained. It follows from the nature of the ghost cult that it should exhibit less structural modification under the influence of Western contact than either the *mbandwa* spirit cult (which has readily assimilated many new and inimical forces deriving from the contact situation by turning them into *mbandwa* spirits) or the complex of sorcery beliefs, in which some *mbandwa* spirits play a significant role. For ghosts are personal powers, they are left by people with whom one has had dealings when they were alive, and for all practical purposes these are now, as they have always been, other Nyoro. Unlike other kinds of spirits, therefore, ghosts cannot proliferate into a variety of new kinds any more than people themselves can. Ghosts are, as they always were, spirits of the dead; they cannot be anything else.

Consistently with this, it is my impression (though one that in the nature of the case it is difficult to confirm) that, although recourse to spirit mediumship has certainly not declined in recent years, and may even be increasing, explanation by diviners of illness and miscarriage as due to ghosts is decreasing and is giving way to explanation in terms of the now very extensive Nyoro pantheon of nonhuman spirits. Certainly I have recorded many more cases of possession by *mbandwa* spirits than of possession by ghosts. Further, as we have noted, except in one small and distinctive region of Bunyoro the cult of the patrilineal ancestral ghosts, regarded as in some sense a collectivity, is no longer practiced. I have, indeed, no firm evidence that it was more widely practiced in the past than it is now, but the Nyoro say that it was, and the term for the ancestral cult, *ibembo,* is known throughout Bunyoro. Such a decline would be consistent with the breakdown of an older type of residential grouping in which, even if residence was never wholly in lineage terms as it is among some neighboring peoples, local groups were firmly centered on patrilineal descent groups, and solidarity among a group of close agnates was a primary social value at the community level.

12 THE ASCETIC BUDDHIST MONKS OF CEYLON

Nur Yalman

THE MORTIFICATION OF THE FLESH

TAPAS, THE MORTIFICATION of the flesh, has always held considerable fascination for religiously inclined people everywhere. Asceticism, the attempt to break the links with the world of men, is one of the approaches to the world of the deities. It is remarkable how the problems confronting all those groping toward the deity, or deities, are similar in essence. The many ascetic orders of Christian monks, the Trappists, the Whirling Dervishes of Islam, and the ascetic hermits and wanderers of India and Ceylon, with all the varieties of doctrinal differences between them, are attempting to devise means of approaching the threshold between men and gods. The flesh ties one down to this side of the threshold (like all other wordly interests). The approach to the "threshold" (which is probably the state of ecstasy so often described by the mystics) requires at least a subordination of the flesh, but the crossing of the doorway must probably be paid for more painfully.

There are startling descriptions of these attempts in India. Carstairs (1957) writes of the Hindu *sannyasi* who, having withdrawn from the world in most respects for many weeks, announces that he will reach union with the deity at a particular time, sitting under a particular Bo tree. Great crowds of pilgrims are gathered. The holy man exhibits complete tranquillity and dissociation from the world around him. Not a muscle moves as a grave is solemnly dug in front of him and he is lowered—still alive—into the hole and the earth is closed over him for all time.

Reprinted from *Ethnology* 1, 1962: 315–28, by permission of the author and the editor, *Ethnology*.

Less fatal examples of the mortification of the flesh are often to be seen in the annual festivals in Ceylon. In Kataragama, the enigmatic shrine in the eastern jungles of Ceylon, a favorite method of fulfilling vows to the gods is to drive hooks and skewers through the flesh. Tamils in particular, as a result of pledges of fulfilled wishes, will sometimes hang themselves on great trees by large hooks biting into their naked flesh. Those less ardent may join in the fire-walking ceremonies held annually.

The Tapasa Bhikku, who are the subject of this essay,[1] are a group of ascetic Buddhist monks who have reappeared in the last decade in Ceylon (Anagarika Ananda 1955). They profess to practice complete withdrawal from the world, and in doing so claim to be returning to the original teachings of the Buddha. They reject the established institutionalized forms of monastic and temple life which the ordinary Buddhist priests lead by arguing that this has preserved the form but has extinguished the mystic spirit of true Buddhism.

While working in the eastern provinces of Ceylon in September, 1955, I was told that some pilgrims from Pelmadulla had come to visit a community of Tapasa Bhikku in the vicinity. The monks inhabited some historic caves near Selave, 20 miles south of Pottuvil, on the coast of the Indian Ocean in a very isolated spot. Being interested in the new movement of ascetic monks, and not having realized that they had communities, I decided to visit them.

The locality inhabited by this community of nine monks is grandiose in its beauty. The ancient caves are approached by a long and arduous walk near the ocean, among tall trees which filter the sunlight. Here and there the foliage opens up to reveal huge, dark gray, single rocks sitting in the middle of the jungle like pebbles on grass. One crosses open spaces, sandy, dried-up torrent beds, and meets a great variety of tropical animals—peacocks and flamingos, alligators and huge iguanas.

The first glimpse of the community enhances the impression of

[1] The field work on which this essay is based was carried out in the Dry Zone of Ceylon between August, 1954, and January, 1956. It was supported by the Wenner-Gren Foundation for Anthropological Research and the University of Cambridge. I am indebted to Dr. E. R. Leach for many suggestive discussions on Sinhalese Buddhism and would also like to record my gratitude to the Director and staff of the Center for Advanced Study in the Behavioral Sciences, Stanford, California, where the essay was written.

strangeness. Immense buffalo skulls with their horns intact hang on trees, making a fence on the path leading to the caves. There are heaps of large elephant bones strewn in various places. The caves themselves have been inhabited, in the first centuries A.D., and contain Prakrit inscriptions. There is even a concession to comfort since the upper parts of the caves have carved "drip ledges" to keep the rain out of the sandy interior. There are lotus ponds here and there among the rocks.

The ascetic monks reject the appellation *tapasa* for themselves. The term implies the application of extreme pain, hunger, and discomfort to mollify the body. It is recalled that the Buddha, too, tried *tapas;* according to legend he joined a community who were engaged in painful and extreme practices. He is often depicted in Indian sculpture as a ghostly, shrunken figure at this stage of his career. He rejected these sensational methods for a less frenetic but more balanced and complete withdrawal from the world. But the term is used by the ordinary villagers in referring to these ascetic monks. I shall continue to use the term, but the objection should be recorded.

The ascetic monks regard themselves as true Bhikku (lit. "beggars"), in contrast to the orthodox clergy who are described below. The main tenets of all orders are similar and derive from almost the same sources (see Sarma 1930). The goal of Buddha's teaching is the attainment of Nirvana, a state of perfect being without any contradictions or change. To attain Nirvana, the Buddha preached a complete withdrawal of all desire and hence a nonattachment to the world. Without desire there could be no sorrow. There would also be no sin (*pau*), and merits (*pin*), which are necessary to be reborn in a higher state in the next life, would be easier to collect.

The main formulas which express the teaching as it is accepted in Ceylon are contained in the five precepts (*pan sil*) symbolizing the renunciation of certain forms of desire. All Buddhists are expected to conform to them, and the formula is frequently heard on all occasions involving Buddhist priests. In the five precepts the Buddhist renounces the taking of life, stealing, adultery, lying, and alcoholic drinks. The promise not to take life is more than a denial of murder, for here the protection of the lives of all beings (*ahimsa*) is implied.

The priests themselves are expected to conform to some additional precepts. One of these enjoins the Bhikku not to eat solid food after twelve o'clock noon. The second, by implication, involves the renunciation of high office and honor, and the third the renunciation of amusement, gratification of the senses, wealth, and the like.

THE ORTHODOX CLERGY

The ordinary Buddhist priests of Ceylon do conform to these and other rules, but they are not particularly ascetic and live, often in considerable comfort, in their residences (*pansala*) in temple grounds (*vihara*).

The priesthood is highly organized. The individual joins one of the various priestly orders in Ceylon.[2] He first remains a novice and is later promoted to full priesthood. He usually receives a living in a village temple about this time and finds himself a member of a very highly respected order and the holder of a secure and definite position in Sinhalese society. His way of life is closely regulated by the rules of the priesthood. There is intense concern with his "purity." He must avoid all pollution and in particular the pollution of the body. In his initiation he repeats the *taco pancake,* "a list of the 32 foul and despicable elements of the body" (Coplestone 1892: 457). The ceremony of initiation is similar to the Tapasa (see below), and he formally renounces his family ties and receives a new name. His head and all bodily hair are shaved, and hereafter he may not commit sexual intercourse and may not marry. He will wear the saffron robe and will do some preaching (*bana*) in Pali. He will often be invited to special services (*pirit*) in the neighborhood. When he becomes an incumbent of a temple, he will officiate in the daily food offerings to the Buddha (*dana*) and may play a role in annual celebrations. He will be well taken care of by the people.[3]

A temple often has extensive lands dedicated to it by the villagers. Indeed the desirability of a living is precisely the wealth of the *vihara* concerned. Some temples are wealthy enough to own

[2] Siam Nikaya, Amarapura Nikaya, and Ramanya Nikaya. For a further discussion of these orders see Ryan 1953: 32 ff.; Coplestone 1892: 427 ff.

[3] Sometimes villagers in their irreligious moods will refer to the Buddhist priest as a *mudu mahana* (bald priest) who "kills rice" (*bat maravana*), i.e., is useless.

cars. Others may have radios, quite elaborate furniture, and even sewing machines. The Bhikkus, however, are supposed to be mendicant monks. In orthodox Buddhist ideology, they should have no possessions other than a robe (*siura*) and an alms bowl (*patara*), and they should beg their food. But the usual Bhikku who lives in the ordinary, pleasant villages of the Kandyan districts, leads a life which, with all its solemnity and limitations, is by no means an unpleasant one. In some respects the food supply is more secure than that of the normal villager. In the village of Terutenne (see Yalman 1960: 81), the priest of one of the temples had a considerable amount of cash always available from the sale of the produce of temple lands. He had always been a very shrewd money-lender.

THE TAPASA BHIKKU

In recent years there has been a sudden growth of interest in ascetic monks. I am told by the villagers that their numbers have grown and that they are seen more frequently around villages. The reasons for this revival of interest in asceticism are not entirely clear. Two points may be indicated. First, it is quite possible that the growth of interest is only illusory and that the Tapasas represent simply one of the periodic attempts to return to the pristine, pure, otherworldly, charismatic aspects of Buddha's teaching. Second, if the growth in interest and numbers is genuine, then it may well be related to the increasing economic difficulties that individuals have to face, both in the small villages and in the overcrowded towns, with serious unemployment in Ceylon.[4] In either case, I found considerable interest in these Tapasa Bhikku in 1954–56 in the Kandyan villages in which I worked. The inhabitants of even the distant villages had heard of them. One had come to stay a while in the jungles around Terutenne (Yalman 1960) a few months before I arrived in the village. I used to see them

---

[4] In a study of 89 sibling groups in Terutenne, a Walapane village, I found that 25 per cent out of a total of 217 men had left the village to migrate to towns and tea estates for work, and that 10.6 per cent of the 228 women had done likewise. In the other two villages, which were more remote from towns, the exodus was less: 3 out of 47 men and none out of 39 women in 28 sibling groups in the village of Udumulla in the Wellassa jungles, and 3 out of 54 men and none out of 54 women in 29 sibling groups in Vilawa in the Wanni Hatpattuva.

walking through the jungle in single file, looking down at the ground, bedraggled but impressive figures in their brown, humble attire.

How are the Tapasa distinguished from the orthodox priesthood (*sangha*)? Why has the priesthood taken a violent stand against them? How do they derive their support from the villagers, and how is the community organized?

The Tapasa are outside the established orthodox Buddhist orders. They wear soiled brown robes, in striking contrast to the resplendent saffron robes of the ordinary priesthood or the brilliant saffron orange colors of the Amarapura order. They cover both shoulders with their robes when walking to prevent the right arm from swinging.[5] They refuse to carry umbrellas or wear sandals as the ordinary priests do. They do not ride in buses and allegedly will only walk four miles a day. They do not carry the traditional alms bowl and, again allegedly, will not request food but will only take seven handfuls in the traditional manner.

The Tapasas have incurred the hostility of the established church in particular on two doctrinal points. The first is that they deny the validity of the formal organization of the orthodox Buddhist orders. They claim that the clergy has no right to live in comfortable temples, to draw secure incomes from the lands dedicated to these temples, and to own worldly objects. In this manner they assert that their way takes them back to the mystic and otherworldly traditions of Buddhism. In other words, their claim is that the charisma of the Buddha has been lost in the formal edifice of the church.[6] An attempt must therefore be made to return to the original source of charisma, the denial of the world and its institutions.

A second and even more significant doctrinal point which differentiates them from the orthodox clergy is that, while almost all the formal relations between the ordinary Buddhist priests and the laity are conducted in high Pali or Sanskrit—which ordinary people cannot understand—the Tapasa speak normal Sinhalese, and when they preach they attempt to communicate their ideas di-

[5] In speaking to a Tapasa on these topics, I asked why the arm should not be swung. He replied that this gave sensual pleasure. I am not sure whether this was an oblique reference to masturbation, which can be referred to as "shaking the arm." The covering of the right shoulder is an important doctrinal point which differentiates the Amarapura and Ramanya orders from the Siam Nikaya order, which does not cover the right shoulder.

[6] For a brilliant analysis of this point see Weber 1947: 358 ff.

rectly to the villagers. In both respects the intention is to break through the traditional formal channels of the Buddhist church.

The attitude toward the ascetic monks has its roots in the place of the individual in Buddhism. Even though the role of the Bhikku in the community is highly formalized (the villagers will place their heads almost at his feet to salute him), he is not a shepherd. The individual is responsible for his own spiritual efforts. On Poya days (the quarters of the moon), many villagers are seen wearing white, visiting the temple and taking *ata sil,* that is, following for the day the eight precepts obligatory for Buddhist monks. The Tapasa would, I think, claim that this conscious individual effort to follow the *Dharma,* the body of the Buddhist code, is the only correct one, and hence ought to be the code of the Buddhist church as well.

The established clergy has repudiated and vigorously denounced the Tapasa. They have even claimed, both in their sermons and in furious letters to the press, that the Tapasa are communists. Considering the highly critical tenor of the Tapasa's teaching with regard to the orthodox priesthood, this attitude is hardly surprising. The conservative elements in the population have, on the whole, also taken a critical stand toward the Tapasa. But in the villages, interest in the movement persisted in 1954–56.

The visit of a Tapasa to Terutenne village (Walapane) was related to me with, I suspect, considerable embellishment. The Tapasa in question lived for a few days in a cave near the graveyard. He had not enough food, and the villagers say that they saw him closing his eyes and plucking leaves from the jungle here and there for his morning meal. Large numbers of people from surrounding villages apparently came to see this hermit in the jungle, "worshipped" and respected him. It is said that the reason he stayed in the graveyard was not only to have peace and quiet but also to demonstrate that there are no *pereteya* (dangerous spirits), *yakka* (demons), and *deviyo* (deities) hanging around there. He preached in Sinhalese, speaking very slowly and looking only at the ground.

The villagers of Terutenne appeared unanimous in claiming that the movement was started as a reaction against the established clergy. It was said that the first Tapasa was the son of a rich businessman who left his home, wife, and children and became a monk all by himself. There are now, they claimed, more than 500

Tapasas. The story is no doubt apocryphal, and the figure exaggerated, yet to those who know the mythology of the life of the Buddha—how as Prince Siddharta he left his home, wife, and children—the modern reinterpretation of the story may sound familiar.[7]

THE ORGANIZATION OF THE ASCETIC COMMUNITY

I turn now to a description of the community of Tapasas at Selave. The original site of this ascetic group was in Ambalantota, near Hambantota, in the Low Country. The originator of the movement is now respected as a Nayaka (head priest in the Selave group). They had moved to a new site for greater isolation. Their numbers in the community were nine, of whom two were novices. There were apparently others who were on their own or in small groups of two or three in other parts of the island. Even though the Tapasa criticized the orthodox clergy for their formalism, the economic aspects of the ascetic community were well taken care of. A lay benefactors' society (*dayakaya samitiya*) has been organized with connections in the Low Country as well as in the small villages around Selave. Contributions were made to the society, but the food of the community was provided by the villagers in the vicinity.

The community was rigidly and hierarchically ranked. Seniority went according to order of ordination. The hierarchy was manifested every day at mealtime. Food would be passed along from the junior members to the next senior, and the junior would ceremonially "worship" (salute) the senior. The two novices did all the menial work of the community; they swept the grounds, cooked, and cleaned the pots for the entire group. Apart from the reading of hallowed Pali texts on Poya nights, there was no collective activity in the community. The monks each had a separate cave and spent most of their time meditating in the cave or in the jungle around. Some would go down to the deserted seashore for their meditations. It was expected that they would be com-

[7] In fact, the structure of the modern story and the ancient myths appears the same (see Lévi-Strauss 1955). Note also that, as King Wessantra, the Buddha gives his wife and children to be servants to a beggar who asks for them. The theme of renouncing the family reappears in many myths.

pletely silent three weeks in the month. This was, apparently, not
a rigid rule, but an ideal to be lived up to. They were also expected
to be silent during most of the day, but allowed themselves to
communicate with each other and with visitors briefly after mid-
day.

The Nayaka head priest, who had the largest cave, was an impressive person. A handsome man of about 35, he appeared highly
intelligent, serious, and obviously better read and educated than
the ordinary Bhikku or the other members of his community.
He had a heap of books in one corner of the cave, an alms bowl,
a sleeping mat, and two twigs used as toothbrushes; this seemed
the extent of his possessions.

In front of each cave there was a path a hundred paces long,
traced out with pebbles around it. At either end of the path bones
of large animals had been heaped. Some skulls had been placed on
top. Around these paths, too, horned buffalo skulls were hung
upon trees as somewhat eerie ornaments. Sometimes, during
meditation, the monks would pace up and down this path marked
by bones at either end.

The Symbolism of Bones

I was told that the bones were intended to remind the monk of
death.[8] For, it was said, everything loses its importance when
faced with this inescapable fact. If one keeps thinking about death,
all social customs, all objects and people who are thought important in ordinary life, all desires become meaningless. And when
every aspect of human society becomes unimportant, one loses
one's attachment to worldly matters. This is why one loses desires
and hence banishes all sorrow. And again, it was claimed, this is
why, when someone asked the Buddha for his wife and children,
he readily gave them away. He also cut a piece of his body for
food for a hungry person who was Maraya—his enemy, the symbol of death—testing his strength.

Even though the heaps of bones and skulls around the community were explained consciously in this manner, one must draw
attention to the symbolism of bones (*atta,* bone, also seed, also

---

[8] In contrast to the monks who are reminded of death, the explanation
for the food offerings to the Buddha is that they remind him of "life."
For an analysis of the two aspects of the Buddha and the priests, see
Yalman 1962b.

testicle) in other contexts among the Sinhalese. I think bones are associated with the body (*sarira*) of the Buddha. It is well known that all the most important shrines in Ceylon contain one or another of Buddha's "relics." The most famous of these are the *danta dhatu* (tooth relic), the *nyepata dhatu* (nail relic), the *khesa dhatu* (hair relic), as well as the forehead (*lalata dhatu*) and the jaw bone (*hakuru dhatu*) of the Buddha.[9] These are the *dhatu*, "small pieces of bone like seeds" (informant) which remained behind after the Buddha was cremated. The relics are thought to be powerful (*saraya*). The tooth relic in Kandy produces rain when shaken. All relics increase the fertility of the lands around them. The supernatural potency of bones was probably uppermost in the minds of the ascetics since, when asked about them, they emphasized that they had collected the bones of dangerous and powerful leopards and wild elephants for their heaps.

The Priestly Robe

If the bones were associated with death and kept the concept alive in the minds of the Tapasa, their robes had a similar implication. The traditional form of the elegant garment (*siura* or *chivaraya*) has not altered, probably, since the sixth century B.C. The robe is a large, square piece of cloth made up of smaller squares sewn together. The traditional view is that the priests acquire their robes from cloth they find in graveyards. Indeed it is significant that at the end of the Sinhalese funeral ceremony a white piece of cloth is ceremonially left over the grave. I say ceremonially because the act is associated with the recitation of *pansakulaya* and is intended as the offering of an earth-soiled cloth to the priesthood.

This is not the only explanation of the special patches of the *siura*. Another explanation is that the Buddha on his way to the sky saw the paddy fields of his father from above. He liked their pattern (they are, in the plains, often formed of rectangular patches—*liyadda*—with ridges—*niyara*—around them) and wanted his robe to look like them. Hence the traditional rectangles and

[9] The word *dhatu* also has other important conscious associations in the minds of the Sinhalese peasants. It means life force, or semen or seed, as well as relic. The peasants speak about *sikura dhatu*, the "semen" associated with *sikura grahayo*, one of the planets in the horoscope which controls sexual life. They also speak about *djiva dhatu* (life semen). For further elaborations of this concept, see Yalman 1962a.

the stitched ridges on the Buddhist robe.[10] The saffron color of the ordinary robe, too, invites association with the ripened paddy fields. If this kind of statement is meaningful, one might also draw attention to the dark, soiled brown of the ascetic monks in contrast to the splendid saffron of the ordinary clergy. The villagers do assert that the ascetics wear "mud-soiled robes," and I would hazard the suggestion that the robe, too, associates the Tapasa with death. There is clearly an ambivalence in the symbolism of the sacred robe. For just as it is to some extent associated with grave-yards and pollution, and yet also stands for the paddy field, so also the explanation of its patches is that it is made in 108 pieces like the 108 kinds of sin (*dos*). I have argued elsewhere (Yalman 1962b, 1962c) that this ambivalence is a reflection of the positive and negative aspects of the Buddhist priest.

Initiation

The initiation of Tapasas appears to be similar to the ordination of orthodox Buddhist priests. I was told that it would be possible for an ordinary person to take to the Tapasa way of life alone, without a community. But since there is a community, those who are interested in the life of ascetics prefer to go through the period of training with other Tapasa groups. They therefore become novices for a time before turning into full monks.

The initiation ceremony is intended to break the initiate's connections with his immediate position in society. Three important ritual acts take place. First, the person is completely shaved, including the eyebrows.[11] Second, he is smeared with mud for the *gihiganda* (lit. *gihi:* lay householders; *ganda:* smell, explained as "human smell") to disappear. Third, he is given a ritual bath.

---

[10] The *siura* is named after the number of verticle lines of rectangles, known as *atta* (branches), of which it is composed. Each line has about three rectangular patches (*mandala*) along it. Thus there are *siuras* with five, seven, nine, eleven, and thirteen "branches." The dividing lines are referred to as *gäba*. The central "branch" is always named *vas attu* (i.e., "rain" or "poison" [?] branch); on either side are *ela attu* (i.e., "leaning" or "adjacent" branches); next, in a "five-branch" *siura*, are the *nava attu* (last branches). The *mandala* are said to be the same as *liyadda* squares of the paddy fields, and the dividing *gäba* lines are believed to be water lines of the fields.

[11] This, again, is a doctrinal point which is disputed among the orders. The Siam Nikaya order, in contrast to the rest, do not shave their eyebrows.

Only after this is he dressed—to the singing of the *gata* scriptures—in the *siura*.

The initiation of the monk is thought of as a rebirth. Perhaps the most explicit evidence of rebirth is the assumption of a new name and the renunciation of all kinship connections. One ex-ascetic told me that he was known as Herat Mudiyanselage Hinguruwela Uda Gedara Punchi Banda when he was a man (*miniha*), but that when he became a priest he received the name Punyananda Thero (*thero*, priest). After he has taken the robe, his parents and kinsmen would never speak to the priest by kinship terms. He would always be spoken of respectfully as *hamuduruvo*. When his parents and kinsmen meet him, they do not fail to salute him in the customary humble manner, prostrating themselves on the ground and raising their arms, palms joined, above their heads.

The initiation effects a complete break in the social relations of the priest. He moves sharply from the world of ordinary men to the realm of sacred beings. Social distance between men and priests is wide, and contacts between them follow formal channels. While such is the theory, the practice does not always attain these standards. In the Walapane village of Terutenne, a Tapasa who had come on a visit to the Maluvegoda temple turned out, upon investigation, to be the son of the wily old priest who was the temple's incumbent. Before taking the robe, the Tapasa himself had had three wives and numerous children. When the chief priest of Walapane discovered that a Tapasa was staying in a Siam Nikaya temple, he swooped down one day and, after remonstrations, initiated him into the Siam Nikaya order. Thus it happened that, during my stay in this village, one temple had a father and his son as incumbents. I was assured by the priests in question that they never used kinship terms between themselves but always referred to each other as *swamin vahanse* (learned priest).

THE PLACE OF ASCETICISM IN A RIGID SOCIETY

The main theme in the sermons of the priests of all orders is that ordinary life is full of sorrow (*duka*). Buddhist ideology is an attempt to escape from sorrow. Its solution, as we have suggested, is negative—the renunciation of desire—for desire attaches one to the world. It is worth pausing here to inquire: Why must one detach oneself from the world? Why is this world full of sorrow? Why should the individual renounce worldly attempts to remedy the situation?

Let us admit that some individuals who find it difficult to lead and organize their lives may well take this attitude. Let us also admit that all attempts to revive religious feeling must of logical necessity take the form of detaching the soul from its connections in this world to allow it to come closer to the "other world." Hence the receptacle of the soul must be broken—or mortified. All mystics at all times must face the dilemma that, while the soul may be thirsty for what lies across the threshold, the body cannot be taken across as well. A logical solution is provided by the trance states and the forms of religious possession which are often used as devices by Whirling Dervishes, European and Eastern mystics and prophets, and certain types of priests (*kapurala*) in Ceylon. The prevalence of trances and possession for a heightened religious experience in the rituals of many peoples probably springs from this logical necessity of a threshold between the world of humans and the world of sacred beings. The temporary loss of consciousness in heightened mental states, and the visions and hallucinations which appear to mystics in these trance states or states of ecstasy, probably support the impression that one is on the threshold between this world and another (see Huxley 1954; Wirz 1954). It should be observed that communication between the two realms takes two forms. In some cases spirits and deities come down and actively "possess" the intermediary; in other cases, with mystics and prophets, deliberately controlled "meditation" brings the person nearer to the "other world" (see Yalman 1962c).

Even if these points are accepted, it is still significant that certain societies accord great prestige to those who do turn in other-worldly directions, whereas other societies do not do so. It is also noteworthy that those societies which are highly and rigidly strati-fied appear to accord greater prestige to asceticism and other-worldliness in their religious ideology, whereas this does not appear to be so in societies with considerable mobility. Such hypotheses would be difficult to prove but the evidence is worth considering.

In India and Ceylon, although a rise in ritual status is sometimes possible in the caste system (Yalman 1960: 108), in fact the only legitimate path open to the individual is the shedding of all social affiliations—caste, kinship, and others—the breaking of all social bonds to assume the "high status" of a *sannyasi* (mendicant ascetic).[12] Hence mobility is allowed, but only with a complete denial of all secular interests. In both societies a rise in economic status, though theoretically possible, does not necessarily bring in its train a rise in social status and it is the latter which is relevant. It must also be said that in most of the traditional communities in India and Ceylon, the number who can successfully rise in economic terms must still remain extremely small.

If the emphasis on otherworldliness is associated with rigidly stratified societies, medieval Europe and its great elaboration of ascetic orders becomes highly relevant. Here again society was rigidly divided into strata, into orders in which membership was acquired by birth. And here again the emphasis was on the other world. The Protestant ethic appears on the scene and is elaborated only after the feudal superstructure is already broken up.

We may well note that the Protestant ethic with its emphasis upon acquisition here and now would be a threat to a rigidly organized and stratified society. It preaches high individual mobility, which must in the end break through the traditional patterns.[13] Conversely, emphasis on the other world turns attention away from the society in which the individual lives. Much more hardship can be accepted and those who are ambitious or sensitive or both can fulfill their cravings by rising in status and becoming ascetic monks.

We cannot claim, of course, that no other outlets are provided. Even in the Middle Ages, humble men could rise in the church and elsewhere, but the practice was difficult and was kept to a minimum. The safety valve of the "other world" was, in contrast, utilized to the full.

Note also in this connection that even members of the lowest castes are accepted both as ascetics and as ordinary priests in modern Ceylon. In no other respect in Sinhalese society would the individual be able to escape from the strictures imposed upon him by birth. While the Tapasa leave the door fully open to the lowest caste, the acceptability of low-caste persons into the orthodox or-

[12] The mechanism of breaking all social bonds is utilized not only in the legitimate pursuit of asceticism but also in illegitimate attempts to falsify and alter one's birth station in life (Yalman 1960).

[13] On the point of the Protestant ethic I follow Weber (1958).

ders does have an acrimonious history behind it (Coplestone 1897; Ryan 1953: 39-45). Some orders, like the Amarapura, were created to accept the low castes. But it is evident that caste still looms large in the well-established orders like the Siam Nikaya, and even this single factor may well account for the interest and significance of the Tapasa order of ascetics.

While further research may substantiate the association between asceticism and highly stratified societies, it seems unlikely that monasteries can also be correlated with similar social conditions. In some respects monasteries are organized groups of ascetics, and we would expect to find them in the same context, but the presence of elaborate monasteries in Burma and Thailand—societies which are not particularly stratified—suggests that a distinction should be drawn between individual asceticism and monasticism. It is still true that even monasticism assumes a fairly elaborate social structure in which there is some hierarchical dimension—hence monasteries are conspicuous by their absence in Africa—but individual asceticism may be a response to particularly rigid structures. India is a good example in this respect. The caste system of India is more elaborate and rigid than in Ceylon, and, although in contrast to Buddhist countries monasteries are not common, individual ascetics, *sannyasis,* and *yogis* continue to flourish.

MOTIVES FOR ENTERING THE ASCETIC COMMUNITY

For the mystic who turns to the other world, or for the individual who hankers after the protection and certainty of the deities, the bonds that tie him to society become irksome. The Buddhist priests in Ceylon do not specifically mention caste as a source of sorrow in their sermons. But one's position in Sinhalese society and one's status in the caste are determined by kinship. Hence it is kinship, with the attendant troubles between kinsmen, the difficulties which beset the family, and the uncertainty of getting a living, which is always emphasized in the religious utterances of the priests. The theme of King Vessantara giving away his wife and children and of Prince Siddharta leaving his palace and sensual pleasures reflects the present.

The villagers also speak in this vein. They emphasize the delight of cutting oneself off from all relatives and turning to the

peace of the life of the Buddha. I recall, when speaking to some
educated villagers, being impressed by how dangerous they considered the world in which they lived to be. The discussion concerned the subject of horoscopes. I wanted to know why they
considered it so important to know the future. The answer was
that the future had to be known so that the dangers it contained
could be averted. These dangers were partly supernatural—you
could be killed by *yakkas*—and partly social—the girl you marry
might turn out to be low caste—or they might be economic—the
world was an insecure place (cf. Wirz 1954: 1 *et passim*). The
formal denial of emotional attachments by the assumption of
the robe was, in Sinhalese villages, acceptable both as orthodox
theology and as a practical insurance against sorrow.

The question arises: Why do individuals take to the robe, and
how do they choose between the orthodox priesthood and the
ascetic orders? Most of the membership of the orthodox orders is
drawn from boys who have been handed over to the church from
an early age. The giving up of children to the church earns merit
(*pin*) for their parents and reduces the number of mouths to
feed in the family. In these circumstances there is little point in
seeking ulterior emotional motives behind the recruitment of children to the Buddhist order.

Those who join in later life are in a different predicament. Many
appear to be somewhat more unstable types of individuals. The incumbent of the Maluvegoda temple mentioned above had twice
given up the priesthood to return to his ordinary existence, and
this was his third attempt. Another ex-priest I came to know in
the Monaragala area had taken the robe as the result of a family
quarrel but had returned to his village after five years. For this
type of individual, the priesthood is a socially approved method
of escape from family obligations.[14]

The members of the ascetic Tapasa community were also
men who had made a deliberate decision to become mendicant
monks. One of them had been an engine driver in the Ceylon rail-
ways. Another had been a shopkeeper in the Low Country and

[14] In the three villages I studied the numbers who had taken the robe
were as follows:
Terutenna (Walapane): 6 (or 2.9 per cent) out of 217 men;
Udumulla (Wellassa): 1 out of 47 men;
Vilawa (Wanni Hatpattuva): 1 out of 54 men.

had left his wife and children to join the order. Yet another had been a mason in Kandy and had enough money to start a shop himself. He heard of the Tapasa and made his choice to join them. In this fashion the Tapasa community provided an acceptable outlet for these persons and one which at the same time gave them great prestige among their people.

CONCLUSIONS

The first point to be made is that the Tapasa, much to the chagrin of the established clergy, are a revivalist sect and express some of the dissatisfaction with the state of the Buddhist church. It has also been suggested that the renewal of interest in the more ascetic forms of monasticism could be related to the increasing economic difficulties on the island.

Apart from a description of the organization of the ascetics of Selave, we have also considered the motivations of the individuals for entering the community. Two categories of explanations were suggested. First, we noted that asceticism and otherworldly communities provide alternative safety valves to compensate for the rigidity of the social order. In a lesser sense, the monasteries of the modern world still provide havens for individuals in difficulty, but they no longer enjoy the prestige or the general interest which is expressed in societies where otherworldliness is made the central tenet of the religion. Lastly, we noted that the breaking of kinship ties is an essential aspect of turning to the other world, providing an explanation for the presence of some of the monks in the ascetic order.

13 INDEPENDENT RELIGIOUS
MOVEMENTS IN THREE CONTINENTS

L. P. Mair

I THE CASES TO BE DISCUSSED

IT APPEARS to be characteristic of a very large number of societies that from time to time movements arise in opposition to
the established religious institutions, offering either new means of
attaining the benefits offered by the established religion or new interpretations of its dogmas. The leaders of these movements often
claim to have received direct revelation from supernatural sources,
and for that reason are frequently called prophets, though this
name is of wider application, embracing also such persons as the
Hebrew prophets, whose chief function appears to have been that
of moral criticism, and also the givers of oracles who have a
recognized place in some established systems. There is no reason
to suppose that the movements of this kind which appear among
non-European peoples subject to European rule form a class by
themselves, but, owing to the circumstances in which ethnographic information has been collected, the bulk of this refers to
subject peoples, and among such peoples religious movements are
largely concerned with the relations between subject and ruler.

Millenary cults, again, are sometimes treated as if they belonged
to a class by themselves. I do not believe that a sharp distinction
should be drawn between them and movements which attest religious autonomy without promising the immediate coming of the
millennium, or between them and the cults which limit their
activities to healing and the detection of witches. It is common
for the prophets of millenary cults to offer these limited benefits

Reprinted from *Comparative Studies in Society and History* 1 (2),
1959: 113–36, by permission of the author and the editor, *Comparative
Studies in Society and History*.

in addition to the promise of the final regeneration of the world; sometimes they fall back on healing practices when the promise of the millennium is discredited; in any culture area millenary, healing and witch-finding cults will be found to have common elements of miracle, revelation and ritual.

I propose to discuss religious movements which have been recorded in three ethnographic areas—among the Indians of the American North-West, the peoples of the South Pacific, and the Bantu of southern and central Africa. In each of these regions a particular form of religious movement has been held to be typical: in the case of the American Indians this is the Ghost Dance, in that of the Melanesian peoples the "cargo cults", and in that of the Bantu various reinterpretations of the Christian religion as presented by missionaries.

The Ghost Dance gained its widest popularity during the period of westward expansion when Indian tribes were being confined to reservations, cut off from their accustomed hunting grounds, and subjected to various kinds of pressure to induce them to settle as farmers on holdings allocated to them by the Indian Administration. The second and more famous Ghost Dance movement, which began in 1889, followed the extermination of the buffalo by white hunters, which reduced the tribes that had not been willing or able to take up agriculture to a state of complete dependence on government rations.

Wovoka, the prophet of this movement, promised his followers that a millennium was imminent in which "the whole Indian race, living and dead, [would] be reunited upon a regenerated earth, to live a life of aboriginal happiness, forever free from death, disease and misery" (Mooney 1896: 654).

A volume describing all the recorded cargo cults was published by Worsley in 1957. There are records of such movements from 1892; their prevalence increased steadily during the inter-war period, and they reached their climax at the end of the Second World War. After this they began to give way to movements in which the political content predominated. From the time of the "Vailala madness" of 1919 all the movements have had the three themes of the return of the dead, the arrival of a miraculous cargo of trade goods, and the destruction of the European population.

The Koreri movement of the Schouten Islands (Netherlands New Guinea) resembled the Ghost Dance in that it was based on a myth of world renewal and took so much of its content from Christianity that it almost deserves to be classed with the African syncretic religions. An admirably detailed account of this movement, based on the statements of participants, has been given by F. C. Kamma (1954).

The most obvious contrast between the cargo cults and the Ghost Dance is that, whereas the latter idealizes the world of past tradition, the millennium of the former consists essentially in the possession of the material wealth of the modern world. Both types of movement look to freedom from alien domination, but the cargo cult believers envisage a world where they will live as Europeans appear to them to do, enjoying wealth without working for it. The imitation of European behaviour (the District Commissioner writing in his office), organization (lining up after the manner of police or plantation labourers), and mechanical contrivances (wireless, rifles) is characteristic of the cargo cults. Some have gone beyond mere superficial imitation and have created functioning political organizations. The Koreri movement, which reached its climax under the Japanese occupation, developed into an organized resistance with political aims, though still relying on magical sources of strength. This opposed its own version of Christianity to that of the missions. The accounts which we have rarely make it possible to follow the process of transition, and the relation to it of the offer of political models by the European administrations. This is a subject that would repay further study; again there is a contrast with the American Indians, who were offered American-style political institutions on their reservations, but do not seem to have drawn from these any inspiration to develop organizations opposed to those of their rulers. Some cargo cults—notably Yali's among the Garia of New Guinea and the John Frum movement on Tanna, New Hebrides—involve the express rejection of Christianity after an initial acceptance. In the Ghost Dance by contrast, as far as one can tell from the records, the identification of Wovoka with the messiah was held to be consistent with the doctrine received from missionaries.

In Africa the syncretic or separatist churches have been discussed at length by Sundkler (1948) in his *Bantu Prophets in South Africa* (for the Union) and by Balandier (1955) in his *Sociologie Actuelle de l'Afrique Noire* (for the Kongo on both sides of the Congo river). An instance in this area of the link be-

tween witch-finding movements and those of wider scope is the
fact that the messiah of the new African religion described by
Balandier, Simon Kimbangu by name, was in his brief period of
activity the leader of a movement largely concerned with the detection of witches. The witch-finding movements which spread
into Northern Rhodesia and Nyasaland have been described by
Richards (1935) and Marwick (1950).

The movements in South Africa to which Sundkler has given
the name of "Zionist" are largely concerned with the detection of
witches; those which he calls "Ethiopian" are not millenary in
character. The Kimbangist religion, or *Mission des Noirs,* is significant in that it expressly rejects Christianity and offers its own
prophet as the counterpart for Africans of Moses for the Jews,
Mahomet for the Arabs and Christ for white men. It has its own
scriptures, in which a close parallel is drawn between the mar-
tyrdom of Kimbangu and that of Christ.

II SURVEY OF THEORETICAL COMMENTS

Most theoretical discussions of these movements have considered
together only those which have appeared in a single region, though
the explanations offered are usually assumed to be of general application, and may well be so in fact. It is assumed that we agree
on the question of what are to be regarded as their essential distinguishing features. Mooney, who quoted parallels to the Ghost
Dance from various other places and historical periods, describes
them as "religious abnormalisms based on hypnotism, trances and
the messiah idea", and his parallel instances are marked in some
cases by dancing as an element of ritual and in others by "paroxysms of twitching and trembling" (1896: 930–45). To Williams
(1928) the paroxysms were the most significant feature of the
Taro cult, which he regarded as pernicious for this reason alone.
Stanner (1953) also attaches importance to "the tendency to rap-
ture and paroxysm", which he ascribes to "the influences of psychic
suggestibility, voluntary imitation, and the excitements of charismatic leadership with its new theorem of action". The phenomena
of dissociation mentioned in this paper are a feature which many
of the movements discussed have in common with religious cults
over a much wider field. Detailed study of these phenomena are of
interest rather to the psychologist than to the anthropologist. To

the latter it would be valuable to know much more precisely, in many of the cases recorded, what was their place in the movement, and, where they were not a feature of prescribed ritual, how and at what stage they became associated with the cult. It is perhaps worth recalling that, in the account given to Berndt (1952) of the cargo cult among the Kogu of the New Guinea Highlands, fits of trembling were said to have seized individuals before anyone appeared with a message from the spirits; while on Manus the seizures, as described by Mead (1956), were not passed on from one village to another by a process of imitation, as in the Vailala madness (Williams 1923), but began spontaneously after the arrival of the spirits had been reported.

We can at least reject Williams' interpretation of the hysterical symptoms as an outlet for the superfluous energy accumulated when labour was lightened by the introduction of steel axes, and a substitute for the excitements which disappeared with the suppression of head-hunting and pagan ritual; and the applied anthropologists of today would not follow him in recommending football as a therapeutic. Nevertheless, Berndt, though he does not seek to explain the shaking fits in this way, considers that the cargo cults as such reflect a development of interest in non-native activities which to him requires explanation; this he too finds in the suppression of indigenous outlets for energy and aggression.

Haddon (1917) remarked that "an awakening of religious activity is a frequent characteristic of periods of social unrest"; and both he and Williams found in the earlier New Guinea movements evidence against the theory of the essential conservatism of native peoples. Williams likened the Taro cult to a biological mutation. One might ask in this connection what is to be regarded as a significant social change, and whether a new prescription for restoring a state of affairs consonant with traditional values should be so described.

Yet another explanation was offered by Williams when he ascribed the Vailala madness to mental indigestion caused by the presentation of Christianity to intellects not ripe for it.

Lowie, while following Haddon's view that social unrest is the predisposing factor for the appearance of new cults, is more specific. He contrasts the relatively slight extension of the Ghost Dance in 1870 with its widespread adoption in 1890, and after enumerating the hardships endured by the Indians in the later period, con-

cludes: "The intense emotional stress predisposing a people to
yearn for deliverance from their ills is amply accounted for. In
1870 all these conditions were either lacking or much less acute,
and the soil was therefore but indifferently prepared for the reception of a Messianic faith" (1936: 184). This comment raises the
question *how much* dissatisfaction does it take to create a new
religious movement—a question which has been discussed by Firth
(1955) with reference to the cargo cults.

Elsewhere, however, Lowie argues, as do other American
anthropologists, as if he considered that "the sudden contact of an
aboriginal and a Caucasian population" was enough in itself to
produce the religious reaction. Discussion in terms of "acculturation" and "contra-acculturation" is peripheral to the interest of
this paper. One might, however, mention the distinction drawn
by Linton (1945) between "nativistic" and "non-nativistic" messianic movements, as recognizing the significant contrast between
the backward-looking Ghost Dances and almost all other movements of this type.

Philleo Nash interprets "nativistic" movements as a reaction to
deprivation in the psychological sense, taking it for granted that
such deprivations result from the situation created by conquest.
He points out, however, that they may include not only the loss of
satisfactions found in the traditional way of life but also failure to
attain expectations aroused in the new situation. "Skills were introduced which brought no rewards and values were introduced
without appropriate skills for attaining them" (1955: 441). He
considers that the significant predisposing factor is the failure of
expectation and not the rejection of domination or of an alien culture as such. From an examination of the different forms which
the Ghost Dance of 1870 took in different parts of a single reservation, he shows how its fantasy content was most aggressive
among the sections which had suffered most at the hands of the
whites.

During the period at the end of the Second World War when
cargo cults were springing up in every part of New Guinea,
various persons who were concerned with the interests of the New
Guinea natives, whether as administrators or as anthropologists,
sought an interpretation in terms of attitudes which need not seem
to a European to be wholly absurd. The present writer summed
up the view of this group in the phrase that the cargo cults were

an expression of the natives' "hopeless envy" of the material wealth of the European, and suggested that "there is no way to meet them except the slow one of increasing the native's economic opportunities and giving him a reasonably devised education" (Mair 1948: 67).

Firth, recognizing that there is always and everywhere some incompatibility between wants and means of satisfaction, has considered more fully than other writers the question in what circumstances this will give rise to a movement in which, as he puts it, satisfaction is sought in an imaginative projection. "Cargo cults", he writes, "tend to arise as a resultant of several factors in operation together: a markedly uneven relation between a system of wants and means of their satisfaction; a very limited technical knowledge of how to improve conditions; specific blocks or barriers to that improvement by poverty of natural resources or opposed political interests" (1955: 130). They tend to arise in groups where the sense of communal responsibility is so strong that it is not felt to be adequate for individuals to be able to meet their wants by leaving the group. "Education on the one hand," he says, "and the provision of avenues of employment and political expression on the other would seem to be important alternatives to cargo-cult development" (1951).

Stanner, in rejecting what he calls "the hopeless envy theory", must be taken to reject also this elaboration of it. "It is not easy," he remarks, "to see increased 'economic opportunities' or 'reasonably devised' education as the simple panaceas." This type of cult he considers as "a redemptive act of faith by which what is 'realized' as pragmatically difficult, or impossible, of attainment, is 'seen' under charismatic leadership as becoming possible by the 'grace' of the spirits or ancestors" (1953: 68–71). This interpretation is in line with that of Keesing, who calls such movements an "authoritarian way of salvation amid the uncertainties of modern experience" (1941: 77). Kamma (1954: 224) also objects to the idea of "imaginary satisfaction", but he appears to think that this is offered as an explanation of myth in general.

Balandier (1955) in his massive study of the contemporary messianic movements in the French and Belgian Congo makes a number of comments, not all of which would be applicable to the earlier movements in North America or to the less sophisticated cults in the Pacific. He finds the treatment of the subject by

"Anglo-Saxon" anthropologists wholly inadequate, but after a careful reading one gets the impression that his strictures are directed mainly against those who regard these phenomena simply as examples of "acculturation", on all fours with the "borrowing" of a technique or a magical process from a neighbouring tribe (he does of course recognize that not all exponents of acculturation theory are as naive as this). This would account for his insistence on the colonial situation as something *sui generis;* in the field of "culture-contact" it certainly is, though it may well have points in common with other situations which have given rise to religious movements. It would also account for the emphasis placed upon his interpretation of these movements as a "total reaction".

Balandier advances a number of different reasons for the emergence of the *Mission des Noirs* and its offshoots: it represents an assertion of the African's ability to evolve a "civilized" religion; it is a reaction in the field of fundamental beliefs, that in which the people feel themselves most gravely threatened (is this so?); it is a reaction in the only field where any resistance is practicable; it is a reaction in the field where defense against insecurity was traditionally sought. In his view, movements of opposition to the established order in primitive society have always taken a religious form. Finally—agreeing on this point with Sundkler—he remarks that the new social classes which colonial rule has called into existence have no other field than this in which to pursue their struggle for power (1955: 477–79).

III   RELIGIOUS MOVEMENTS AND THE STRUGGLE FOR POWER

To the sociologist one of the most interesting aspects of these movements is their relationship with this struggle. It is recognized that established religions validate the political structure of the societies in which they are found. But new religions are by definition in opposition to the established religion: if the latter gave to its adherents all that they expected of it, new religions would not arise. In the field covered by this paper all the messianic religions are in some way concerned with the distribution of power. But their adherents belong to the section of the total society which has the least power, and in so far as we accept the explanation of these cults, or any of them, as offering a fantasy compensation for practical disappointments, we see in them, not a reinforcement of political action but a substitute for it. Not all, however, have operated wholly on the plane of fantasy. How far, then, do the prophets under our examination provide their followers with opiates and how far with stimulants? The answer in any given case has naturally depended to some extent on ideas about the prospects of successful recourse to political action, including in this term rebellion as well as legally recognized forms of pressure, and the ideas held by the subject group will be modified by their experience.

Some American Indian prophets have led or inspired armed rebellion: some have supported war leaders, others have provoked aggression against the war leaders' will. Many have offered recipes for invulnerability, but the demand for these is just as likely to arise in response to fear of attack as from a desire to initiate aggression. Perhaps the attitudes are necessarily combined. At the time of the 1870 Ghost Dance the resistance to the whites which eventually led to the Modoc War of 1872 was encouraged by a shaman in what Nash calls "the traditional association of shaman with factional leader", but the Ghost Dance prophet among the same people had no war-like message. Nash, however, correlates the abandonment of the Ghost Dance with the resort to direct aggression, and thus implies the hypothesis that the fantasy and the practical reaction are mutually exclusive.

Can this be asserted as a general proposition in the cases where events set in motion by a religious revival have culminated in an armed conflict? It might have the support of Balandier, who comments on one of his African examples that Utopian beliefs encourage passive rather than active resistance, and that they are accompanied by "verbal" rather than "direct" opposition, in which the weaker party can indulge at little cost in a violence which could not be translated into action without serious risk. He therefore discounts even explicit threats as simply verbal outlets for aggression; he draws attention to the fact that such threats, in the form, e.g., of formal curses, are held by Africans to be practically efficacious by themselves. Mooney, however, does not suggest that in 1890 the Sioux lost interest in the dance at the moment when they decided to leave their reservation and so incur the intervention of the troops, though they obviously could not hold five-day dances while on the march; and in their

final ill-judged aggression the (defensive) magic of the Ghost
Shirt was invoked.

But it is of course not possible to evaluate the content of these
movements as if their aims were stated once for all, and remained
fixed; nor is it possible to follow out the history of a wholly
Utopian movement to its natural conclusion, whatever that may
be, since these cults among subject peoples do not operate in
sealed compartments but in the presence of the persons against
whom their aggression, verbal, fantasy or other, is directed. People who are aware that their destruction is being promised to
enthusiastic audiences are not often calm enough to derive re-
assurance from their own disbelief in miracles; knowing that they
are objects of hostility, they demand the protection of the forces
of the law. This commonly takes the form of attempts to crush
the movement by the removal of its leaders, and arrests are often
effected without meeting resistance. Where they are resisted, it is
impossible to say what the progress of the movement would have
been had there been no such intervention; perhaps it would not
even be safe to say that movements which meet force with force
must have been initially more disposed to resort to physical
force than those which "go underground" or peter out. It may
be that the intervention itself changes the character of the movement, and matters of historical accident such as the nature of
the weapons in the possession of the resisting group must affect
the course of events.

The fact that the Ghost Dance ideology involves a complete
rejection of the alien way of life places it in a different category
from the other movements we are considering, in all of which the
ideal world is conceived as in some way involving access to advantages associated with the dominant group. In the case of the
Ghost Dance, the question of the relation between religion and
politics can be reduced to the question of its relation to armed
rebellion. Of the African religions, those of "Ethiopian" type can
be placed at the opposite pole; they are a direct means of pursuing power, though not in the formal political sphere, and they
have their own internal political organization. The earlier New
Guinea cults may be said to represent a transition stage in which
the overt behaviour of the dominant group is imitated without the
structure of relationships in which political power actually resides.
One might put it that the symbols of power are grasped before

the reality. The use of military titles, "General" and "Captain", is on record as far back as the "German Wislin" of Saibai in 1892; Haddon thought this "evidently a reminiscence of the old native word *kuiku-garka,* headman" (1917: 460). The prophet of the Taro cult in the Mambare valley in 1914 bade his followers go to their gardens in line, like police, and encouraged them with shouts which are obviously those of the parade-ground (Chinnery 1917: 453).

On other occasions an illiterate leader has established himself in an "office" imitating that of the local official, or has appeared in public going through the motions of writing. The John Frum movement had its "militia" commanded by captains and lieutenants, which "exercised daily", its guard posts at which persons entering the village were questioned and the purpose of their journey entered in a register, and even its traffic regulation signs (Guiart 1952: 170).

Such actions may be viewed as part of a wider complex of imitation of European behaviour, and the whole complex might be interpreted either in terms of "sympathetic magic"—behaving like the dominant group in the belief that this will raise the subjects to a status equal to theirs—or as a symbolic *assertion* that the subject group has in fact qualified for this status by adopting the behaviour appropriate to it. As the culture of the dominant group is more fully understood the grounds offered for this assertion become, by its standards, more valid. Balandier instances the importance attached by the *Mission des Noirs* to their possession of a corpus of scriptures as setting their adherents on an equality with those of the recognized great religions. Yet even in the *Mission des Noirs* we find what is perhaps an analogue of the cargo cults in the wearing of khaki as a "uniform of hope and victory" (1955: 449).

Particularly interesting, though not surprising, is the part played in all these movements by the recognition of the technical superiority of the dominant culture. To the cargo cult adherents the consumer goods which they hope to possess and enjoy, and understand how to manipulate, and the types of capital goods that are familiar to them, are, as Balandier remarks, symbols of power even if not necessarily instruments of authority. These are associated with the ancestors, who are expected to use them for the benefit of their descendants, bringing the desired goods not by what we should call supernatural means but by steamship or aeroplane (sometimes even lorry). To the same order of ideas belong the imitation wireless installations that have been set up in some cases, and perhaps too the "heavenly telephone" used by one of the Bantu prophets described by Sundkler.

Although the cargo prophets seem to offer no more than a fantasy solution of their followers' problems and thus an alternative to political action, some of them have actually envisaged an armed struggle as a necessary means to the attainment of the cargo, and others have set up a temporal authority of their own which does more than imitate the behaviour of their rulers. It seems that in the period during which we have records of these movements there has been a steady development towards a more realistic type of organization. It is not always clear what has been the relation of practical modernization movements to cargo cults. In some cases the leaders of the former have been different men from the cargo prophets, who may have either used the latter's support or been opposed to them altogether: in one at least, a practical movement developed into a cargo cult, and this has a parallel in one of the Kongo religions.

The general impression derived from the literature on the Pacific cults is that, as in the case of the Ghost Dances, the destruction of the Europeans is expected to be the automatic concomitant of the return of the spirits and the arrival of the cargo. But in two cases of which we have full accounts, this is not so. The Kogu expected that they would themselves kill the Europeans when, on the arrival of the spirits, their dummy weapons were changed into real ones, and the Garia expected to have to fight the Europeans and not necessarily defeat them without losses. Even in the Vailala madness there were some reports that the cargo would include rifles.

In the Garia case we have also a feature which appears again in the *Amicaliste* movement among the Kongo; a primarily rational attempt by a native leader to raise the status or the material condition of his people is re-interpreted in mystical terms by his followers, and he is treated as a prophet without having himself made claims to supernatural inspiration. Yali, the Garia leader, was a discharged sergeant-major who was encouraged to further "community development" by building a model village: the favour in which he was held by the missions and government

contributed to the popular belief that he was supernaturally fa-
voured also, and his followers assumed that his instructions were
preparations for the millennium. André Matswa during his lifetime was concerned solely with the rational political demand for
citizen status for Africans: after his arrest for subversive activities the popular imagination made of him a messiah.

In the African movements one may again see different types of
connection between religion and politics. The founding of a new
sect may be a means of asserting the autonomy of a tribal group
vis-à-vis its African neighbours, without reference to its relations
to the European authorities. A religious organization may become
a pressure group making claims on the base of the ethical assumptions of the Christian faith which is ostensibly common to rulers
and ruled. It may, as Balandier suggests, be deliberately made a
cloak for a political movement, or immediate political aims may
be interpreted in millenary terms by adherents too unsophisticated
to conceive them otherwise. It may lay foundations for political
unity by combining social groups which in the past had no common
ritual.

In the case of the South African separatist churches Sundkler
has taken the first step in the analysis of the political and religious
elements by distinguishing between the "chief-type" leader associated with the Ethiopians and the "prophet-type" leader associated with the Zionists. He also notes that it is the Ethiopian
churches which aim at obtaining a fuller share for their members
in the European world, while the Zionists, though claiming to heal
sickness by virtue of a more powerful spiritual force than that
commanded by the old-style diviners, are little interested in political advancement or the improvement of African status. The
difference is of course correlated with the fact that the Ethiopian
churches are mainly urban and the Zionists largely rural. The
importance for either type of the apocalyptic message is here
reduced to almost nothing; occasionally a new leader wins a following by announcing an imminent judgment at which only his
adherents will be saved, but we do not find large bodies of people seeking a way out of their discontents in fantasy constructions.

Sundkler has studied these movements largely from the point
of view of the personality and social status of the leaders. He
remarks that in South Africa the religious field is the only one in
which there is any opportunity for the ambitious African to exer-

cise leadership, and also that the pattern of kingship characteristic of Zulu culture determines the way in which this is exercised. Leaders of Ethiopian churches have some of the traditional functions of chiefs, including the settlement of disputes; they are expected to be the spokesmen and champions of their followers in relation to the government; they sometimes claim and are sometimes expected to hold their position for life and pass it to their sons. Students of social structure might add that the creation of churches with membership limited to a single tribe or smaller unit may correspond to a desire to express the autonomy of the group through the only available form of organization; though of course there is no church extending its authority through a *whole* tribe. At the time when Sundkler wrote, Ethiopian churches had accommodated themselves to the South African situation to the extent of valuing the advantages to be derived from recognition by government and so of refraining from making demands of a type that might bring them into disfavour. It would be interesting to know what line they are taking in view of the increasingly repressive nature of government in South Africa. Dr. Sundkler recently revisited that country with a view to revising his book.

Matswa, as an example of the politician made a prophet by his followers, has already been mentioned. It remains to discuss the political aspects of the *Mission des Noirs*. This neither has overt political aims nor does it offer a means of hastening the millennium. It simply asserts the promise of an eventual second coming at which the African leader will be the king. It appears, however, that before the Kimbangist religion had been systematized by Mpadi, its adherents expected the new kingdom to arrive every Christmas for several years, and that on one occasion it was believed that on New Year's Day a flood would engulf all Ba-Kongo who had been hostile to the movement.

The organization of the *Mission des Noirs,* however, is almost as much political as religious. It is modelled on that of the Salvation Army, itself a church of military type. According to Balandier, it is tending to arrogate to itself all the basic social functions, religious, political, and in a very embryonic way, military and police. Further, it has political significance not in virtue of any direct opposition to Belgian authority but because it appeals to all the Kongo tribes whether in French or Belgian territory. This it is enabled to do by its doctrine, taken from Christianity, of a universal god transcending the divisions which are emphasized by the ancestor cult.

IV   HOW THE MILLENNIUM IS ENVISAGED

The chronological relationship of the movements in the three regions under discussion is not of very great significance. As it happens, the first Koreri movement of which we have knowledge preceded the Ghost Dance, and this in turn preceded the earliest recorded instances from Africa and Eastern New Guinea. The first independent African church and the first recorded cargo cult are almost contemporaneous. The syncretic religions described by Balandier are the most recent in origin, but they exist side by side with new secessions in the Union and new cargo cults in the Pacific. But one can relate the characteristics of the different types of movement to an evolution in the attitudes of subject peoples towards their rulers and towards the civilization of the latter. One can trace this in two ways: by examining the nature of the millennium as it is represented at different times and by asking what happened to the cults in which millenary promises are specific. Under the first heading we have to consider not only the way in which the ideal world is pictured, but the way in which it is expected to come into existence and the explanations that are offered for the differences between the world as it is and as it ought to be. Neither aspect of the cult ideology is, of course, open to the free play of the prophets' fantasy. The ideal world must be what most people desire, and the explanation must be in line with current explanations of misfortune and disappointments. It seems that before the appearance of a specific millenary prophecy there must be in existence a generally accepted myth to which the prophet may appeal. Firth mentions that on Tikopia, which has never had a cargo cult, rumours of a world cataclysm and of a promised cargo circulated while he was there. He concludes that there can be "a cargo cult type of behaviour" without a cult. Surely this is far too narrow a category. His instances illustrate the much more general proposition that I have just referred to, which might be put in the form that in any society there will be found to exist stereotyped expectations, corresponding no doubt to certain basic hopes and fears, which can be activated either when the hopes and fears become pressing or when actual events conforming to some part of them occur.

Some of these stereotypes are found in such widely separate peoples that one would like to ask psychologists for a more convincing explanation than that offered by Jung's archetypes, and one that would marry psychology and anthropology in a happier way than that attempted by Freud. They must in some way be traceable to a limited number of common human experiences.

The myth of world renewal characteristic of the Ghost Dance is one of the best known; a catastrophe will destroy the existing world and all those in it who have not deserved to survive, and a new more perfect world will take its place, in which living and dead will be united and all the ills of real experience will be eliminated. This is common to so many mythologies—including the Christian—that its absence is of more note than its occurrence. It does not appear, however, to have been characteristic of New Guinea peoples, with the one recorded exception of the Koreri myth on the Schouten Islands.

What is interesting for our purposes is the way in which the perfect world is envisaged by subject peoples, experiencing at the same time forced changes in their own way of life and contact with another which claims superiority and both offers and denies new opportunities.

There are several records of the messages of American Indian prophets. Some were recorded by Europeans who were present when they were delivered, some written down by themselves. That received by the Delaware prophet of 1763 and conveyed by Pontiac to a gathering of Algonquin tribes was taken down by a French priest. It appears to have been uncompromising in its rejection of the English, though more tolerant to the French; though even they were not to be imitated. "Before those whom you call your brothers [the French] had arrived, did not your bow and arrow maintain you? You needed neither gun, powder, nor any other object. . . . When I [the Great Spirit] saw you inclined to evil I removed the animals into the depths of the forest that you might depend on your brothers for your necessities, for your clothing. Again become good and do my will and I will send animals for your sustenance" (Mooney 1896: 665). As regards "those who come to trouble your possessions"—the English—the message is explicit: "Drive them away; wage war against them;

they are my enemies; send them back to the lands I have made for them."

Smohalla's views were recorded by MacMurray, an emissary of the United States army who spent a year on the Upper Columbia enquiring into Indian grievances. MacMurray's unpublished manuscript is partly digested and partly quoted by Mooney. In Mooney's summary, Smohalla told his people that "their present miserable condition was due to their having abandoned their own religion and violated the laws of nature and the precepts of their ancestors". To him the settlement of Indians on agricultural holdings was itself a violation of these laws of the earth mother, and competition for control of land (hunting grounds and fisheries) was the root of all evil since it led to fighting. God had ordained that all land should be held in common. Mooney's information from this and other sources does not ascribe to Smohalla any explicit prophecy of the destruction of the white man, though MacMurray wrote that at the same period "some of the wilder Indians to the north have more truculent ideas as to the final cataclysm which is to overturn the mountains and bring back the halcyon days of the long past. As the whites and others came only within the lifetime of the fathers of these Indians, they are not to be included in the benefits of the resurrection, but are to be turned over with all that the white man's civilization has put upon the present surface of the land" (Mooney 1896: 723).

Wovoka, the prophet of the 1890 Ghost Dance, delivered his message to a delegation from the Cheyenne and Arapaho tribes who came to learn his doctrine, and it was taken down by one of them—according to Mooney, from dictation—at the time. Here too the prophet himself is not on record as foretelling the elimination of the white man. The essence of his message is: "Jesus is now upon the earth. He appears like a cloud. The dead are all alive again. I do not know when they will be here; maybe this fall or in the spring. When the time comes there will be no more sickness and everyone will be young again. Do not refuse to work for the whites and do not make any trouble with them until you leave them. When the earth shakes [at the coming of the new world] do not be afraid. It will not hurt you" (Mooney 1896: 178).

Naturally the message was developed by the apostles, and it seems to have taken divergent forms, a few holding that in the ideal world all races would live peacefully side by side—though separated—others that the whites would be destroyed by fire or flood, or, as in the case of the Pawnee, by a great wind.

In all these cases the ideal world represents a complete return to the past, a rejection even of those material objects which have aroused the envy of most peoples of simpler technology, and of course of many Indians also. The Ghost Dance ideology is generally regarded as representing a fantasy compensation for the loss of all hope in the real world, and it was certainly most popular among the tribes which had been reduced by the extermination of the buffalo to the condition of helpless dependents of the United States government, and least so among those which were obtaining a reasonably satisfactory living as farmers.

The characteristic feature of the cargo cults, in contrast, is an intense interest in the material possessions of the dominant group. Although, as has been mentioned, the cult activities reflect an equal interest in the rulers' ability to exercise power, it is the goods that play the central part in the ideology. In this case the very roots of the myth seem to lie in the "colonial situation", since its theme is the misappropriation by Europeans of goods destined for the natives, goods of which they had no knowledge until Europeans appeared in possession of them. The cases quoted by Haddon indicate that it was in existence from a relatively early period of European activity in New Guinea. If we ask why, in this case, European possessions excited cupidity instead of the aversion to everything European manifested in the Ghost Dance, the answer may be that the New Guinea natives were not forcibly cut off, as were the Indian tribes, from their accustomed way of life. They were not moved from their traditional homes to a different environment, nor deprived of their traditional mode of subsistence. Thus their desire for European goods was not countered by that longing for a lost way of life which gained the upper hand among those Indians who adopted the Ghost Dance, and who, of course, up to that time had not rejected foreign goods.

The longing for reunion with the dead, which is a universal human experience, does not seem to have given rise to a myth in New Guinea apart from the Koreri story. But the belief that they remain in touch with the living is, of course, characteristic of New Guinea as of most other societies; and it might be regarded as a "natural" reaction of people living in what they suppose to be a self-contained world to interpret the appearance of human beings unlike any seen before in terms of a return of the dead. It is on record that members of exploring parties have been welcomed with great emotion as returning ancestors. Nor is there anything logically outrageous in the assumption that the new goods, some of which are in fact usually given as presents to smooth the explorers' path, have been brought expressly for the benefit of their descendants. It is of interest to note that an identical reaction was met with among Amerindians in British Guiana.

By the time experience has proved this explanation to be false, the hopes built on it have become too dear to be abandoned, and there now comes into existence the myth of the gift from the ancestors diverted from its rightful owners by the Europeans. This is a simpler analogue of the belief in a false version of the Christianity propagated by the missions which has gained so much ground in Africa; and indeed the theme of deception by the missions is also current in New Guinea, though it there takes a cruder form than in Africa, being concerned primarily with cargo and not with the brotherhood of all the children of God. Once a myth of this kind is current, it is easy to see how events are interpreted in the terms which it gives; Firth's example from the Tikopia, who had had no such belief on his first visit twenty-five years earlier, is interesting here.

Lawrence's (1954) reconstruction of the history of Garia attitudes towards missions and cargo traces a sequence which may well be typical. Believing as they did, he tells us, that their own gods could be constrained by the appropriate actions to give them what they desired, the Garia saw the rites of Christianity as a means of constraining a more powerful god, and readily abandoned the "heathen practices" which missionaries condemned. Since missionaries have frequently urged their converts to destroy their "idols", it is not surprising if the latter sometimes actually do so: nor is the association of a large-scale public exposition and destruction of magical objects with a cargo cult as remarkable as Williams thought it, if we see this as symbolizing a transfer of allegiance to the source of greater benefits. In the case of the Garia a mass baptism held in 1937 was preceded by such a public demonstration of the rejection of idols, and this seems to have been the model imitated by Yali's followers. In other parts of the world, too, this is a recognized symbol of conversion, of the making of a new choice or the rejection of some accustomed practice; it has been mentioned as an element of the Kimbangist religion, and is necessarily prominent in the cults which are primarily directed against witchcraft.

Among the more impatient Garia converts the idea became current that, just as some of them had secret prayers which gave them compelling power over different deities, so the missionaries had a secret prayer which they had not revealed; in fact they had deceived the people with false promises. At this stage arises the search for a direct means of communicating with the sources of cargo or a more effective way of coercing them. The prophets who attached themselves to Yali put their faith in a traditional god, but Yali himself was on good terms with the local missionaries at first. When he turned against them, he—unlike the more sophisticated African prophets—reverted to the traditional god instead of developing his own version of Christianity; it has been pointed out that Yali is one of the few prophets of any note who have been illiterate.

The New Guinea millennium, then, is seen in terms primarily of the possession of material goods but also of an enhancement of status for the subject group. Several myths refer specifically to the latter point. The returning dead are expected to be white-skinned and the living natives to become so; or the world is to be literally turned upside down, and black become white and white black; in the Koreri movement there were incidents when the reversal of roles of the natives and Indonesian officials was actually effected (Kamma 1954: 167). The John Frum millennium combines fantasy and practical aspirations, in an engaging way. John Frum will supply all material needs, so that work will be unnecessary; he will also provide schools giving a better education than that of the missions and pay salaries to chiefs and teachers (Guiart 1952: 166).

On the millennium in Africa the most succinct comment is that there is none. The African churches represent a stage of development beyond that at which an immediate solution of all difficulties is expected. They may be said to embody the answer to the question what happens to millenary movements when they fail, as they must, to come up to expectations.

V MORAL TEACHING OF MILLENARY PROPHETS

Before going on to this point, however, we should consider some other themes which will be found to be common to most of the movements.

In the first place, the coming of the millennium is rarely to be brought about by ritual alone. A moral code is often part of the prophet's teaching; and there is often, as well as the rejection of certain kinds of conduct which this implies, a symbolic rejection involving the destruction or abandonment of some material objects. These two features can be seen as expressing the idea that obstacles to the coming of the millennium have to be removed. The first, however, taken by itself, demonstrates the concern of the prophets with the ills of everyday life, such as sickness, and tension within small groups, which they share with the humbler healers and diviners.

In the case of the American Indian prophets the moral message is part of a consistent whole; the believer must please God by conduct as well as ritual, and it is often asserted that existing misfortunes are a punishment for breaches of his laws. This theme has no place in the New Guinea cults, emphasizing as they do coercion rather than placation in their relation to their gods. Yet New Guinea prophets are on record as condemning such acts as theft, adultery and quarrelling. The African religions tend to emphasize traditional practices, such as polygyny and the levirate, which are not permitted by the missions.

Among the cases mentioned by Mooney, the Delaware prophet of 1762 was instructed by the Master of Life to tell his followers: "Let them drink but one draught, or two at most, in one day. Let them have but one wife, and discontinue running after other people's wives and daughters. Let them not fight one another. Let them not sing the medicine song" (Mooney 1896: 665). The Shawnee prophet of 1805 began his "earnest exhortation" by denouncing the "witchcraft practices and medicine juggleries of the tribe". He threatened torments after death to those who drank "the firewater of the whites". "The young must cherish and respect the aged and infirm. All property must be in common" (Mooney: 672). The Kickapoo prophet of 1827 told his followers "to throw away their medicine bags and not to steal, not to

tell lies, not to murder and to burn their medicine bags"
(Mooney: 695). Wovoka, the initiator of the 1890 Ghost Dance,
was told by God to "tell his people they must be good and love
one another, have no quarrelling and live in peace with the whites,
that they must work, and not lie or steal; that they must put
away all the old practices that savoured of war" (Mooney: 772).
How one longs to have been able to investigate such a statement
at the time. Was Wovoka really a pacifist, or was he merely urging
the Indians to keep the peace among themselves? It does seem
to be clear that he told them to cease from internal war.

In New Guinea we learn that the prophet of the Kekesi cult
forbade his followers to carry weapons in the gardens, and (as
translated by Chinnery) said: "The people are to hear and obey
the government. The people are to observe the moral code of the
tribe. Food is to be properly cultivated, and no wastage is desired
by me." Later he announced that Kekesi was angry with a man
who had stolen his brother's wife (Chinnery 1917: 452–53). The
Taro cult prophet told Williams that God had given him commandments "against 'swearing' [i.e. abuse, wrangling], theft,
adultery and anger, and two positive injunctions—to be like the
missionaries and like the white men" (Williams 1928: 75). In
the Vailala madness various people claimed to have received direct ethical instructions from God. According to Williams, "Thou
shalt not steal, commit adultery, nor break the Sabbath, are the
three commandments most frequently heard" (Williams 1923:
25). Mead (1956) lays great emphasis on Paliau's injunction to
refrain from quarrelling or giving support to a kinsman involved
in a quarrel; she interprets this as part of a rational policy which
he adopted after repudiating the local cult. Such commands, bearing as they do on the unity of the group, have a dual significance;
they relate to the ideal of internal peace which is part of every
tradition, and also to the need for union in the face of external
pressure.

Sundkler mentions various rules of dress and behaviour which
serve to identify the members of different churches, but does not
indicate that their leaders appeal for any kind of moral reform.
He notes, of course, as does Balandier, their insistence that
polygamy is not contrary to religious teaching. In the latter's view
this is prompted not only by practical reasons, but also by a
nationalist determination to maintain a distinctive institution

which the foreign rulers have treated with contempt; one calls to mind reports of the recrudescence of suttee in India.

Examples comparable with those from the other two regions can be found elsewhere in African material. Gluckman has noted in the Mau Mau movement, along with insistence on the sexual freedom permitted by Kikuyu tradition, a puritanical attitude to indulgences learnt from Europeans which condemns smoking and prostitution with equal severity. I might also quote the commands given in a recent Ashanti witch-finding cult: "Do not commit adultery; do not swear against thy neighbours; do not steal; do not harbour evil thoughts against anyone" (Ward 1950: 53).

We can perhaps draw from these injunctions the conclusion that millenary dreams, concerned as they all are, in one way or another, with rejection of an inferior status, never entirely displace the everyday wish for peace and good will within the small community, to be attained by respect for the rights of others and by eliminating causes of quarrelling such as drink, and the dreaded concomitant of quarrels, sorcery.

VI   OTHER CHARACTERISTIC THEMES

In addition to their strictures against socially disruptive behaviour, the prophets' teaching often involves the renunciation or destruction of specified material objects, either because they are conceived as obstructing the coming of the millennium or because they symbolize something which is in contradiction to the new doctrine. The destruction of symbols of a religion which is abandoned of course has an obvious significance, as has that of objects used in sorcery. In South Africa the Zionist churches reject European medicine, claiming that they possess the only true means of healing. The Ghost Dance adherents "discarded everything they could which was made by white men"—though they had to make their invulnerable shirts of cotton cloth. The John Frum movement is unique in that it required its followers to get rid of all European coinage; two reasons were given—that when there was no more money the traders would have to leave the island, and that John Frum would supply a new currency. The "Noise" which preceded the Paliau movement on Manus called for the destruction of all native-made goods, but in the excitement which broke out when it was reported that the magical ship had actually arrived, it appears that people exceeded their instructions and also threw away some of the possessions that they had acquired from the American troops. The taboos imposed by Angganitha, the latest Koreri prophet, do not seem to have had any symbolic meaning of this type.

Another recurrent theme is that of a human rescue by the action of Europeans of another nationality than that of the current rulers; this of course can only arise if there are circumstances which make the idea plausible. I suggest that there is a very early example in the "German Wislin", with its suggestion that help will come from the other European nation installed in New Guinea, and that it is paralleled by those cargo cults which include the return of the Americans in their myth. In Africa, again, the followers of Matswa believed that the German advance in Europe in 1940 was a prelude to his "vindication" and establishment as their king. One may associate these ideas with the notion that is so widely encountered in Africa, and no doubt elsewhere as well, that, however dissatisfied people may be with those in immediate authority over them, there is always, at some higher level, a just ruler who "loves us", and, if he knew what was going on, would intervene to put things right. And this again has something in common with the belief that new and strange objects of wealth must be destined for the people among whom they appear, and must be intended as a gift for them from some being who is interested in their welfare.

The idea that the prophet himself has returned from the dead, and has originally received his message not by the recognized process of possession but by direct speech with its supernatural giver, is also widespread enough to deserve mention.

Something should be said too about the very common belief that when the millennium is at hand there is no need to go on with normal economic activities. How far is that the "act of faith" to which Stanner refers, involving a practical expression of confidence in the benevolence of the spirits? Occasionally, though not always, the dogma is that all consumable goods must be used up or got rid of before the millennium can arrive, but this does not by any means always involve sacrificing the enjoyment to be derived from them. In some cargo cults the people threw their pigs into rivers, but in others they ate them in a succession of feasts. This could not be described as a hard way to salvation.

If the data from the three regions are compared, the theme of guilt—of having brought about one's own misfortunes—seems to be explicit only among the American Indians, while the theme of deception—of having been misled as to the means of commanding supernatural power—is absent there. No doubt the difference can be correlated with the Indian lack of interest in any advantage to be gained from participation in European culture. The theme of peace and good-will—for I suggest that this is the essence of the moral teaching of these religions wherever it is recorded—is common to the millenary movements, but in Africa is replaced by a nationalist insistence on rules of conduct which differentiate the subject from the dominant group. The theme of symbolic rejection is found in all three regions, though in the case of the *Mission des Noirs* Balandier emphasizes that it rejects material symbols in favour of a more abstract kind (Balandier 1955: 451).

VII THE SEQUEL TO MILLENARY MOVEMENTS

What is the fate of religious movements which hold out specific promises that they cannot in the nature of things make good? In the majority of cases they are not put to the test, since their activities are usually suppressed by authorities which are either afraid of subversion or concerned at the consequences of the destruction of property or cessation of work, or both. There is thus usually open the explanation that the actions necessary to produce the millennium were obstructed by *force majeure*. But this is not always enough to maintain the faith of the believers. I suggest that there are two main reasons for this. One is that after a period of extravagant collective expectations people lower their sights and return to preoccupation with personal problems of sickness or failure in their own enterprises: the other that, as their understanding of their situation increases, they see it in more realistic terms, and look to solutions in which supernatural intervention plays a smaller part or no part at all.

It is important for the first type of development that the cults usually combine healing and sometimes also the detection of sorcerers and witches with the preparations for the millennium. Hence there is a way out for the prophet in reversion to traditional practice in this field. For example, Doctor George, the prophet of the 1870 Ghost Dance in the Klamath Reservation, had a long and successful career as a shaman after the failure of his specific for invulnerability brought his Ghost Dance message into disrepute. What is more interesting in this case, however, is the character of the new doctrines which took the place of the Ghost Dance among the same people. Nash's reference (1955: 424 ff.) to the shift in religious interest "from a world event to the self" expresses, I think, the point made in the preceding paragraph. The first successor to the Ghost Dance was the Earthlodge cult. This too was concerned with the return of the dead, but without reference to any specific event such as the earthquake associated with the Ghost Dance. The Earthlodge cult gradually merged in the Dream Dance, in which all kinds of individuals had dreams giving them personal instructions, and this in turn into shamanism of more or less traditional type.

The 1890 Ghost Dance, according to Mooney, continued to be performed for a few years, but without the conviction that the performance would immediately bring the ideal world into being; it had become an expression of hope for an indefinite future.

The information collected by Kamma shows that the Koreri leaders found various lines of retreat. One took service with the Japanese, and was beheaded by them when they guessed that he was planning to go over to the Americans. Another withdrew into the interior and there organized the revival of the traditional ceremonial dances. Their followers returned to the mission churches, from whose teaching they did not consider that they had ever departed.

In Australian New Guinea we have seen the appearance of leaders offering practical betterment schemes, and organizations directed towards the autonomous control of local affairs. The relation of these to the cargo cults is by no means clear from available descriptions, but Yali's case shows that actions which are advocated on practical grounds may be given a mystical interpretation. However, one might guess that, as the leaders of any community develop a better understanding of practical possibilities and familiarity with means of exercising political pressure, legally or extra-legally, they themselves will cease to rely on mystical solutions, and the cargo myth will decline to the status of folklore. Naturally this process will be assisted by the present policy of the Australian administration of introducing representative local councils. Of course these will not remove all grounds for discontent, but the discontent will be expressed in demands for a fuller share in the political system.

In South Africa we can see the two possible developments that I have suggested following parallel streams in the Ethiopian churches and *Mission des Noirs* on the one hand, and the Zionist churches on the other. The former place their hope in a vague future: their rites assert their solidarity but are not conceived as means to bring about a direct result. The latter offer immediate results, but only on the personal plane. In the data given by Balandier we see how these two attitudes can be combined in what is ostensibly the same religion; the less sophisticated adherents, and those less exposed to indoctrination by the leaders, introduce into it the magical beliefs and extravagant hopes that might have given rise to independent religions had not a single organization made itself dominant in a wide region.

There are, of course, Christian sects which believe in the imminence of the millennium, and the best known of these, the Watchtower movement, is at work in two of the three regions that I have discussed and very likely among American Indians as well. In comparison with local cults it, like the *Mission des Noirs,* has the prestige derived from the possession of its own doctrinal writings, which re-interpret the dominant religion in a manner favourable to the aspirations of the subject group. As a proselytizing body it has the immense technical advantage that it can produce literature on a large scale in a language understood over a large part of the world. We may guess that it will come to supersede the cults which appeal to local myths.

VIII   CONCLUSIONS

The similarities between events in such widely separated regions will not occasion any surprise to readers who are accustomed to recognize the same social processes at work wherever small-scale societies have been drawn into the orbit of industrial civilization. It has been remarked that the similarities in fantasy interpretation of the new situation would repay the attention of psychologists.

As regards the general characteristics of these movements, the Ghost Dance, with its complete rejection of the new world,

stands in sharp contrast with the eagerness for participation in
it represented by the cargo cults. I have suggested an explanation
in the fact that the South Pacific peoples, whatever disturbing
experiences they may have had in the early days of European
contact, were not, as social groups, forcibly detached from their
accustomed environment and whole way of life. Obviously those
Indians who welcomed the Ghost Dance belief eventually accommodated themselves to their new circumstances as other
tribes already had.

In the information from the South Pacific and from Africa we
can see a development which corresponds to an increase in rational understanding of the situation. The naive belief that the
solution of material problems depends on control of supernatural
power can be seen giving way, in New Guinea, to an understanding of political forces which may still be naive but is at least
more realistic. In Africa, where external trade gradually penetrated the continent through long centuries, there was no sudden
appearance of a wealth of material goods to be accounted for
only in terms of a miraculous source, and we know of no parallels
to the cargo cults. Here the fact of political subjection itself is the
theme of the independent religions, and they look for their ideology not to traditional myths but to the Old Testament. In the
examples we have studied the millenary element plays a relatively small part; the relegation of the idealized world to a remote and indefinite future corresponds to an acceptance of reality
such as we find also in the final phases of the Ghost Dance.

It has been remarked that syncretic religions tend to flourish
in colonial territories where the direct expression of opinion on
political questions, and the formation of organizations for this
purpose, are not allowed. This is only a part of the story, however.

Sundkler's explanation of the South African churches is conceived largely in these terms. He almost seems to invite us to
see them as coming into being to satisfy ambitions for which there
is no other outlet. One can, of course, understand the desire of a
subordinate in a mission church for a wider field of authority,
and recognize with him that it has led to many a secession—but
would *the same men* have founded political parties if these had
offered equal opportunities for leadership? One may more readily
assent to the proposition that religious *organizations* will be

formed in circumstances where other types of organization are liable to be suppressed; their significance then is as much in the expression of internal solidarity and differentiation from other social groups as in the emotional appeal of their doctrine. But the suggestion that there is a quota of some kind of energy which will come out in religion if it cannot come out in politics is almost like Williams' interpretation of the Vailala madness in terms of the need for excitement. In this case it is relevant that Christianity does make specific promises which colonial rule does not implement. The discrepancies between its teaching and the actual standards of governments which profess to uphold it have led in Europe to the formulation of atheistic ideologies; in Africa they lead more readily to the elaboration of rival theologies. In those areas where Christianity has not been identified with a dominant group, because there is no settler population belonging to that group, alternative religions have not gained importance. As it happens, political activity has latterly had freer rein in those territories, again because there is no settler population seeking to preserve its dominant position. But the need for a *religion* that corresponds to widely held aspirations is surely as important in the creation of the new sects as the need for a means of expression of some kind or other, or for an instrument for the activities of ambitious men; one can see this in the presence of millenary sects alongside the religions of hope deferred, and alongside such organizations as political parties and trade unions. Looking into the future of those territories where the dominant African group are the orthodox Christians and dissident sects are not prominent, one may ask whether one day new religions of the under-privileged will arise there too.

14 MILLENARIAN MOVEMENTS
IN MELANESIA

Peter M. Worsley

M ILLENARIAN movements have been reported from many parts of the globe in the anthropological literature of the last few decades. The movements among the North American Indians, such as the famous Ghost Dance,[1] and those in Africa, are especially well known. But there is an immense literature of these movements extending back into remote historical times, for China, Europe, Indonesia, and many other parts of the world.

For Africa, much of the literature has been skilfully marshalled by Katesa Schlosser in her work, *Propheten in Afrika* (1949). A wide variety of movements of this kind will be known to most Africanists: the Murimi movement among the Tsonga (Junod 1927, Vol. II, Appx. V); the Mwana Leza movement among the Ila (Smith and Dale 1920: 197–212); the episode of the cattle-killing and the rise of Makana and Nongqause among the Xhosa (MacMillan 1929: 294–95), as well as a number of allied phenomena such as the Bemba anti-witchcraft movements (Richards 1935; Marwick 1950) and the development of native separatist churches among the Southern Bantu (Sundkler 1948). In addition, these movements have inspired two of South Africa's finest novels, Sarah Gertrude Millin's *The Coming of the Lord* (1928) and Jack Cope's *The Fair House* (1955). Unfortunately we still lack an adequate theoretical analysis of these African movements.

In lieu of such analysis, I wish to present some tentative con-

Reprinted from *The Rhodes-Livingstone Journal* 21, 1957: 18–31, by permission of the author and the Rhodes-Livingstone Institute.

[1] Especially James Mooney's classic study (1892–93). Cora Du Bois, Leslie Spier, and other American anthropologists have also filled out our knowledge of this movement.

clusions drawn from a study of similar movements in Melanesia. My interest in these Melanesian movements was first stimulated by their resemblance to the well-known African movements; I believe that the conclusions about the Melanesian cults will help to shed some light upon those which are recorded for Africa, and may perhaps stimulate comparative research.

I define millenarian movements as movements in which the imminence of a radical and supernatural change in the social order is prophesied or expected, so as to lead to organization and activity, carried out in preparation for this event, on the part of the movements' adherents. There are minor variations: in some cases, the millennium is expected to occur soon, on this earth; in others, the people are expected to enter an abode of heavenly bliss in the future; in yet others, there is only an expectation of relatively minor improvements of life on earth, though these usually develop quickly into one of the more radical forms.

In Melanesia today, millenarian movements present more than a theoretical challenge to the anthropologist; they present also a practical challenge to the administrator.

The characteristics of such movements are these. Commonly, a prophet announces the imminence of the millennium. A complete upheaval of the social order is expected: liberators, who may be the spirits of the dead ancestors, American soldiers, or, in one case, the Communist Party of France, will appear, bringing all the material goods the people desire so strongly. Hence the name 'Cargo Cult' is applied to many of these movements.

In order to prepare for the Day, organizations are set up; new insignia, forms of dress, etc., are adopted; and new codes of morality and of law are drawn up. Often airstrips are cleared in the bush, and huts and stores are built to house the expected goods. (Sometimes the buildings associated with the cults are built in the shape of an aeroplane.) The injunctions of the Administration are generally ignored, and economic life may be disrupted by such actions as abandoning gardens, throwing away money, killing stock, etc., since all these activities will be pointless in the conditions of abundance of the millennium. Money, moreover, is a European introduction in many parts, and the anti-European tinge of many such movements is here manifest.

In order to present the picture more vividly, I will describe one movement in more detail.[2] On Buka, in 1932, a pagan native named Pako who had travelled outside his home-area, and learnt something of the outside world, built himself a European-style house, and renounced paganism in favour of Christianity. He began to have dreams, as a result of which he told people that the Cargo was going to arrive: storehouses were therefore set up to receive it. Natives, he prophesied, would become the equals of Whites, and the ancestor-cult was to be revived, focused on the village burial-grounds. In-law taboos, magic and monetary wealth were all to be abolished; the women were to be given the secrets of the initiation ceremonies.

The Administration acted vigorously, and exiled Pako and two others to Rabaul, where Pako and one other man later died. There was little further disturbance until 1935, when missionaries reported that cemetery-worship was being revived. The natives, they said, did not believe the report of Pako's death, and insisted that he had been hanged by the Government. He had then risen from the grave and returned from Rabaul as a spirit to his old house at Malasang.

Spirit-meetings were held at this place; a plan was said to have been mooted to attack Rabaul in order to kill the Europeans there; later Buka was suggested as an objective. The missionaries also were to be killed. Drilling commenced with sticks which were to be used until better arms were brought to them.

The official dogma of the movement asserted that Europeans were not the all-powerful beings they appeared to be, but that their power really derived from their secret knowledge of a hidden portion of Christian doctrine which they kept from the islanders. It was, in fact, the spirits who made the goods the Europeans imported: confirmatory evidence was that the Europeans were unable to repair mechanical contrivances when these broke down, but had to send them away. It was said that the Germans would bring the people the secret knowledge they lacked, but before the movement developed very far, the Govern-

[2] The Buka movements are described in the Reports to the League of Nations on the administration of the Mandated Territory of New Guinea by the Australian Commonwealth Government for 1933–34 (pp. 22–23), 1935–36 (pp. 21–23), 1937–38 (p. 30). There are several non-official sources, notably Paul Montauban, P. O'Reilly, and J-M. Sédès (1949); and various short notes in *Pacific Islands Monthly*.

ment attacked the movement, burnt down the house of Pako, and made numerous arrests.

This show of force was followed by the exit of the officers of the Administration themselves at the point of Japanese bayonets. On the departure of the Administration, Government stations were looted. The Japanese were welcomed with the greatest joy, since they were clearly the bringers of the long-awaited Cargo. Moreover, the Japanese ancestor-cult fitted well into the ideology of the developing millenarian movement.

By December 1942, a military organization was set up, in which each village had its soldiers and police-boys, armed with wooden guns or spears. There were guards of honour for the chiefs, who were given special greetings, including the Japanese bow. Messengers were used to maintain communications and control, and rigid discipline was exercised over the members.

The continual activity of the Japanese was taken as a sign of the proximity of the Coming of the Cargo. Many visionaries sprang up, some of whom predicted the coming of a 'King'. However, friction broke out between the natives and the Japanese, the details of which are somewhat confused. Two Japanese planes landed in the Hahalis and Malasang area and arrested the leaders; after being tortured, three of the leaders were executed at Sohana; the rest were put into prison. A far more tragic end to one of these movements occurred at Biak in Dutch New Guinea, where the millenarists attempted to attack a Japanese vessel, their only arms being wooden mock-rifles, and their only protective device a holy-water drink of invulnerability (the same charm gave the famous East African Maji-Maji Rebellion its name) (Sayers 1930). The natives at Biak were mown down in scores (Pos 1950; ten Haaft 1948).

If we look back in the records, we find references to such movements in Melanesian history occurring as far back as the last century, shortly after the occupation of the region by European powers. In Fiji, in 1885, appeared the Tuka movement (Brewster 1922), from Milne Bay 'prophetism' was reported as early as 1893 (Thomson 1895). Although few detailed studies of particular movements exist, other than those by F. E. Williams on the Vailala Madness and the Taro Cult (1954, 1955) and contemporary studies by Lawrence (Williams 1923, 1928), and Berndt (1952–53, 1954), there are innumerable short accounts of such movements for almost every year from the turn of the century onwards, a quite extraordinary number when taken together. They range in distribution from the western 'Bird's Head' of New Guinea to the islands of eastern Melanesia, and from the Admiralty Islands in the north to the Torres Straits Islands in the south.

Even among the Highlands of New Guinea, which have only been opened up since the 'thirties of this century, millenarian movements have already developed in areas which have only been under the control of the Administration for a very few years. Indeed, movements have been found already in full swing by the first White people to enter some areas. They arise from contact with millenarian movements in controlled areas.

The problem then arises of classifying the different movements, and of trying to distinguish the processes of development which seem general to them. There is clearly a great difference between two types of movement which may be taken as opposite ends of a single process of development. In the first type, the link between the ideology of the millenarian movement and the traditional ideas and beliefs of the people is a very close one, for the activities of such movements principally relate to magical practices designed to secure well-being in the daily life of the people. There is little attempt at organization of the movement's adherents, and usually no expectation of, or preparation for, a violent upheaval in the social order. The agencies of this amelioration are the indigenous ancestral cult, fertility cult or possession-mechanisms. Such movements are essentially passive in nature, although they are a response to changed conditions.

A typical example of such a movement was the Taro Cult, so ably described by F. E. Williams in his book *Orokaiva Magic* (1928). This movement swept through the Orokaiva people in the 'twenties and centred on the performance of various rites designed to 'ensure an ample crop in the gardens'. 'The new cult came into existence through the visions of an individual who believed himself actually possessed by the spirits of the taro . . . he received their instructions as to the various rites which would ensure an ample crop in the garden.' At a later stage in the development of the movement 'the various rites are expressly meant to ensure, through the medium of the spirits of the dead, a prosperous taro crop. It is thus at once a fertility crop and a cult of the dead' (p. 9).

The traditional element here is very clear, and, in fact, if this were all, there would be little ground for calling this a millenarian movement. (Williams himself seems to have underestimated the full social significance of this development, since he tries to interpret the cults in terms of individual and social psychology at some length.) However, the novel features of the movement, as Williams pointed out, were, firstly, the development of what he called 'an elementary tendency towards cohesion' (p. 96) of the Orokaiva tribes, and the emergence of an 'elementary hierarchy' (p. 95). This integratory function of the movement has particular significance when related to the new conditions under which the movement developed, conditions which Williams describes as indirectly 'unsettling and repressive. Whether intentionally or not, they have a destructive effect upon old belief, and they are not always able to provide an adequate substitute for what they destroy . . .' (p. 80).

At the other end of the scale of development of millenarian movements, we have the type of movement which is almost qualitatively different, and which is clearly passing into an orthodox political movement. Such a movement was the Marching Rule of the Solomons. Here the island of Malaita was divided into nine districts roughly corresponding to the administrative Districts. Each district had a 'head chief' who was assisted by 'full chiefs', in charge of sub-districts. The villagers were concentrated into 'towns', headed by a 'leader-chief', and, in large towns, each clan had its 'leader-chief'. Chiefs of all levels had 'clerks', who carried out administration, drew up lists of members, and codified custom. 'Leader-chiefs' had a bodyguard of 'duties', who were drilled when off duty by 'strife-chiefs'. Work in the newly-organized communal gardens was directed by 'farmer-chiefs', whilst the 'duties' also carried out the task of rounding up people for this work (Allan 1951).

Plans were developed for improved social services, schools, and improved farming. 'Courts' were set up in charge of 'custom-chiefs', whilst revenue was to be obtained by the imposition of fines for breaches of the new custom and from taxation, and the leasing of land to Europeans as the movement got under way. Wages of £12 per month were demanded instead of the pre-war 10s.

Here, plainly, there is little of the traditional in the organization and ideology of the movement. The organization of the movement cuts across traditional boundaries, and sets up an entirely new political and economic framework. It has little of the magical in it, but attempts to control and alter the environment by orthodox means. The millenarian emphasis is minimal; the benefits are to be obtained in the here-and-now by the actual organization of the people; and the familiar Prophets, expectations of the end of the world, and the passivity characteristic of the primitive type of millenarian movement, were but lightly emphasized in Marching Rule and then only in its early stages. This movement, indeed, brought the work of the Administration to a standstill and produced such a condition of chronic nervousness amongst planters and other Europeans that they tried to find in the title of the movement a corruption of the word 'Marxian'. Actually, this seems to be derived from an Ariari word *masiza* meaning 'brother' or 'young shoot of the taro'. Southern Malaita served as a base for the extension of the movement to Northern Malaita, Guadalcanal, Ulawa, and San Cristoval by 1945, whilst by 1947 Marching Rule embraced Gela (Florida) and Ysabel. Deported leaders started up the movement in the areas to which they were deported.

Many writers have discussed these movements as if they were solely reversionary, regressive, flights from the present into the past. Few analyses could be more superficial. The generally-accepted label 'nativism' embodies this attitude in the word itself.[3] These criteria of classification, however, prove valueless as analytical tools when one attempts to use them.

It is quite clear that magical practices and other features of the traditional order are strongly marked in the Taro type of movement. In the Marching Rule movement, however, all the organizational procedures I have described were entirely unconnected with the traditional political order, and the content of the aims and ideas of the movement has far more in common with orthodox political movements in colonial countries than

---

[3] Professor Linton, for example, described the movements as either 'revivalistic' or 'perpetuative', the former stressing the past, and the latter the continuity of the present existence of the society (1943).

with the use of ancestor and fertility-cults to gain limited ends. To label such movements as Marching Rule or the Paliau movement of Manus, as 'nativistic', to regard them as focused on the past and the traditional, is to caricature them. The 'taro' type of movement plainly derives most of its cultural material from the traditional order, but even here it is incorrect to overweight the reversionary aspect of the movements. What is really important about the *re*-adoption of *certain* of the old customs is not so much their revival, as the positive break with European ideology that itself replaced the ancient beliefs. It is this aspect of a sharp break with the ideas and activities imposed by the Europeans that is important. Since the people reject the teachings of the Europeans, they have no other ideological material on which to draw except the traditional: but, as the movement develops, ideas rapidly change also, and experience teaches the ineffectiveness of many of the traditional notions. The stages in the transition from a magical type of movement to the most advanced are fortunately discernible from several areas in full sequence. There are records, for example, from Espiritu Santo in 1908, 1923, and 1947–48, and from Biak there are accounts relating to 1884–85, 1906, 1911, 1921, 1925, 1942 and 1943–44. The later stages of the movements show that familiar political themes find increasing expression at the expense of the magical: on Biak, liberation from alien control (Japanese or Dutch, Indonesian or Chinese); on Santo, refusal to work for Europeans, hostility to missions; on Malaita, demands for improved social services, a higher degree of self-rule, higher wages, etc. The elimination of magical elements is almost complete.

Yet it would be incorrect to regard even the magical type of movement solely as creating an ideology on the basis of the traditional. There are examples in all millenarian movements of the revival of old ideas with a totally new significance in the changed social setting; they are shot through with dissatisfactions, and must be appreciated in their total social context as a reaction to foreign dominance. In addition, one finds new ideas which are not part of the traditional corpus of beliefs and knowledge, and neither is the whole of the old ideology resurrected. We have already shown the integratory function of the Orokaiva Taro movement, a movement which superficially differed little in ideological content from the pre-White ritual beliefs and activities. Whilst these ideas look little different, therefore, in the given sociological setting, they have a changed significance: they are no longer attempts to modify the environment within a tribal boundary, but are attempts to modify a White-controlled social order. Similar effects were observable in the Buna area, in Mambare district later, and in other parts. Under such conditions, the notion of a millennium is usually quickly added to the original beliefs of the movement.

Professor Linton speaks of 'nativistic' movements in general as 'frankly irrational flights from reality'. As a means of effecting a particular end, a millenarian movement is an inadequate appreciation of reality. But such movements do not represent flights from reality: indeed, they represent desperate searchings for more and more effective ways of understanding and modifying the environment. This is clear if we consider some of the more obvious impediments to such an understanding which Melanesians have to face.

Firstly, we must remember that the process of production of European goods is quite unknown to most of the natives of Melanesia. To them, 'cargo' merely appears brought by ship or plane from parts unknown. In addition, the existence of wants greatly stimulated by the war creates an enormous unsatisfied demand for trade-goods. The stress on cargo, from this point of view, is a perfectly understandable feature of the movement. But these goods are all consigned to, and pass into the hands of, Europeans, who merely hand over pieces of paper in return and do no work. Hence it is clear that they must possess some secret, which is denied to the Melanesians, of the source and mode of acquisition of the cargo; and much of the Cargo symbolism concerns 'letters' and 'passes'.

Again, the vagaries of the world economy appear mysterious, fortuitous and uncontrollable to the native who receives say, £2 per ton for his copra one year, £8 the next, and possibly in other years may be unable to find a buyer at all. Wages and prices of trade-goods are subject to similar fluctuations. And due to the expatriation of profits, the island territories received little of the benefit of increased exports (Stanner 1953). In the post-war era, moreover, wartime destruction and other dislocation left plantations ruined. This has produced a crisis in areas which have become dependent on the earnings of wage-labourers (for example, Malaita the seat of Marching Rule).

Political changes paralleled these economic fluctuations. Government authority has been seriously weakened by the events of the war years, which showed that sudden upheavals and radical changes in Government were indeed possible, as Australian, Dutch or British administration gave way to Japanese, only to be again replaced by the old authority or by an entirely new authority in the shape of the U.S. Army.

The reinterpretation of Christian doctrine found in Cargo thought, and the religious form of expression in which the programme of the movements are cast, are further conditioned by the extent to which the Missions control education. Theoretical understanding of European society, therefore, is coloured by an educational system which lays special stress on the religious elements in European culture.

Even the familiar myth that the European withholds the secret parts of the Bible (the secret of the Cargo or the supposed part favouring the Melanesians) reflects not merely the general contrast in levels of knowledge and power as between Whites and natives, but also the limitations of native education in its more formal aspects. Making a judgment which is representative of the views of most anthropologists who have worked in this region, Read remarks that education given by one mission (in the Central Highlands) is 'largely an adjunct of its primary aim to secure converts to the Christian faith . . . the instructions received aims little higher than a sufficient literacy to increase the pupils' understanding of the Scriptures' (Read 1952). Education is almost entirely in mission hands, and the stress on the Bible as the key to the Cargo secrets is thus clearly linked with this monopoly. Also, there are in fact many fields of education in which the natives do not receive any instruction, but of which they are aware.

Finally, religious activity is one of the few fields of European culture open to native participation, a fact which many writers on the sociology of the American negro have stressed, and which has also been emphasized by Sundkler in his study of South African separatist churches.

How this conditions native reactions to European culture may be seen from an examination of the different stages through which the movements usually pass. At first, the Whites are treated as spirits bearing gifts, in terms of traditional conceptions of spirits. Then there develops the notion that it is, in fact, the ancestors of the natives themselves who create these goods.

In the indigenous order, natives recognized fully that it was necessary to do real work in order to obtain material benefits. One had to plant seed-yams in order to get a crop. But in addition, they performed magical rites to protect their work against the vagaries of hurricane, disease, and so on. The Europeans, on the other hand, did no such work to obtain their material goods. They only used magical pieces of paper to obtain ready-made 'cargo'. In order to obtain these things, the natives too had to acquire this secret knowledge of the Whites. This knowledge seemed to lie in the Christian religion. Consequently, natives joined the Christian missions in large numbers. After some years, they became disillusioned and dissatisfied when their 'faith' produced no material reward. Some asked their missionary how long it would be before they received the cargo. Finally, they turned their backs on the mission, and created their own millenarian cults on the basis of a syncretic mixture of indigenous and Christian dogma.

While the actions taken in the magical type of movement are ineffective as a means of effecting changes in the environment, nevertheless they represent attempts to solve real problems of everyday life, even if the means adopted to secure these ends be incorrect. The people set themselves real tasks, though instead of changing the environment, they only effect changes in their own psyches. In relation to the knowledge and techniques at the disposal of the people, these actions are clearly not irrational, whether from the point of view of the people or of the observer. They make a logical interpretation of an irrational social order, given the facts at their disposal.

We have noted that one of the functions of these millenarian doctrines is to weld together previously disparate social groups. Wherever we look in the literature, we find these movements occurring among primitive 'stateless' people, or amongst the peasantry or urban plebians of feudal or predominantly agrarian societies. In all these kinds of society, the movements have served to give political integration to social groups which have developed new common interests, but which have no traditional political units which are capable of organizing these separate groups, or whose political integration has broken down. Such groups include separate tribes, localized groups with a common culture but no political unity, peasant communities isolated from each other not merely spatially but also by lack of any organization *qua* peasants, uprooted and disoriented urban plebians, and so on. Most writers have recognized this aspect in the case of the specific movement about which they have written, but it would appear to be a principle of more general significance which illuminates the whole meaning of the millenarian movement. We have already shown how the Marching Rule entirely cut across traditional divisions and united tribes which had never before acted in concert. Similarly, the Mansren movement of the Biak-Numfoor-Maokwari region involved the abandonment of existing villages for a large stockade where tens of thousands of adherents awaited the Coming. In other parts of the world, the Taiping movement in China brought into association the peasants who had previously no common organization (Chesneaux 1953); the Ghost Dance of America was distinguished by the way in which it swept through a large number of Indian tribes; in New Zealand, the Hau Hau movement 'banded together unfriendly tribes', and endured from 1864 to 1871 (Cowan 1910).

Such communities, then, united by common interests, but without any political forms through which to express and utilize this unity, must perforce *create* suitable political forms. Any leader who wishes to unite these divided social groups must dissociate himself from narrow allegiance to any one of them.

To unite them, he must stand above them; he cannot afford to be identified with any one village or any one clan. One of the most effective ways of doing this is to project his message on to the supernatural plane. He brings a message from God or the ancestors, and appeals to the people to join the movement on the basis of a common allegiance to a religion and an organization which stands above the separate units and unites them all. Such unity can, of course, be effected by quite secular devices, but in the context of a situation in which the key to the acquisition of European wealth and power appears to lie in obtaining secret magical knowledge the fantastic-religious type of organization is most likely to emerge.

We are now in a position to appreciate the significance of the emphasis upon the new morality, the adoption of new codes of behaviour, the smashing of the old custom (as in the giving of the initiation secrets to the women), the adoption of flags, uniforms and other symbols of group identity. The new moral and legal codes are brought into being because the relations between the members of the movement are of a new kind; the older morality and jural institutions limited to the boundaries of small social groups are inadequate for a movement which goes beyond these limits and cuts across tribal limits. Moreover, it is necessary for the adherents to break sharply from the moral and ideological domination of the Whites, just as they are to be delivered, or are to deliver themselves, from the material domination of the Whites. By breaking from the existing ideology of their rulers as well as from the old traditional and European-imposed forms of political organization, they are thus obliged to substitute new codes. The constant themes of millenarian movements—purification of the heart; the Brotherhood of Man; the abandoning of witchcraft, of both pagan and Christian religion, of taboos, and avoidances, etc.—all these emphasize the radical break with the past. The positive side of this break, the creation of new codes, is seen in the Book of Ritual among the Maori Hau Haus, the return to the sources of the Islamic faith in the Mahdiya of the Sudan, the 'custom' of the Marching Rule, the religious and secular codes of the Taiping revolutionaries in China, and the millenarian left-wing in Reformation Germany.

It is in this context of radical reorientation of secular and religious life that the more bizarre concomitants of millenarian movements must be set: trances, speaking with tongues, twitching and other motor habits, dreams, possession, etc. The general atmosphere of emotionality in an allied type of movement has been most successfully captured in Manzoni's vivid picture of the hysterical 'witch-hunt' in Renaissance Milan during the time of a major plague (Manzoni 1951). This hysterical and compulsive-obsessive behaviour occurs in situations of severe social crisis, when the routine of life is disturbed, and when there is confusion and ambiguity about hitherto-accepted moral and other norms. Men now reject the old order, but this very rejection involves the overcoming of ingrained habit; they accept the new, but resent its forcible imposition and their inferior position in the new order. It is from this ambivalence, from the incomprehensibility of the White economy, from men's desperation in the face of ever-growing wants which they cannot satisfy, and from their consciousness of their own ignorance and impotence, that the high emotionality of the cults springs. Motor symptoms are by no means unusual accompaniments of this psychological state.

Such elements of the old ideology, or of the ideology of the Europeans, as are taken over, are given an entirely new, and generally anti-European, content. Instead of the entire rejection of Christianity, for example, we find the familiar theme that the Whites are keeping a certain part of the Bible from the native people (often the first page). Often, however, the Bible is reinterpreted to favour the interests of the people themselves. Thus the leaders of the Tuka movement in Fiji evolved a new dogma in which traditional myths and excerpts from the Bible were intertwined in a new synthesis, the essence of which was an anti-European and pro-Fijian doctrine, justified by appeal to both indigenous and Christian dogma. It is not a question of the borrowing of separate cultural elements and fitting them together into a jigsaw, the separate parts of which can be pigeon-holed as 'traditional' or 'European', but of the development of an entirely new social movement and corresponding dogmas, doctrines and charters. In this framework, the elements of old ideas or of European teaching incorporated in the new doctrine have a quite different significance from that which they possessed in their original social context.

Such combinations of doctrine may well contain certain contradictions in terms of formal logic, but the millenarian doctrine is an interpretation of a reality which is itself full of contradictions. This interpretation goes deeper than formal logic. The fantasy in the millenarian doctrines arises not from alogical modes of thought, but from lack of adequate knowledge on which a sound analysis could be based. And the logical contradictions are of little concern to people whose major interest in the movements is in achieving certain political and social ends.

These movements are particularly common in situations where divisions of caste, class, and often nationality between rulers and ruled are marked. This may appear to be contradictory, since we have already categorized the movements as typical of backward communities. There is no real contradiction, however, for the movements only embrace the ruled, who have under such circumstances to evolve their own independent political organization. Millenarian movements are thus particularly characteristic of colonial and plural societies where a sharp division exists between the native people and the foreign administration. Previously divided and isolated groups now have to find forms of expressing and putting into effect these common interests. It is precisely this function that the millenarian movement serves, and it is for this reason that they are so common in the early phases of the development of colonial societies. Under such conditions, it is clear that the label of 'nativism' is singularly inapposite; such movements are a response to the demands of a totally new social situation, in which the native people are only one part. They therefore create new political forms, and do not revert to the past, regress, flee from the present, and so on. This view, of course, has already been strongly stated by Gluckman in his analysis of social change in Africa, when he opposed to Malinowski's metaphysical scheme of cultural 'compartments' the conception of the 'Rand mines [and] the African tribe which supplies their labour [as] both parts of a single social field' (Gluckman 1949: 7).

I link these movements with the *earlier* phases of colonial development advisedly, for it appears to me that they show a definite directional trend towards more orthodox political organization, whether violent or non-violent in method. There is little dividing such movements as the Marching Rule from ordinary nationalist movements. Certainly, the expansion of most movements appears to be limited; since national groupings have as yet hardly emerged in many colonial areas, this is hardly surprising, though the wide territorial expansion of the Mansren, Paliau and Marching Rule movements indicates the possibility of further development. But the Cargo cult cannot maintain a steady organization, for it must inevitably fail to bring the satisfactions their adherents desire. The ancestors, in fact, will never come with the Cargo. This accelerates the transition to ordinary forms of political organization.

There is probably little direct organizational legacy from the millenarian movement which can be handed on to the political movement proper. What the millenarian movement does is to break down tribal divisions, establish wider fields of common action, and prepare the way for the political movements which may well adopt quite different forms. For example, it would seem probable that a centralized pan-New Guinea political organization might develop, rather than a series of local political movements arising from the ashes of millenarian movements. And in the long run, when it fails to satisfy the wants of its members, the active, 'immediate' millenarian movement nearly always turns into a passive cult which puts off the millennium to a time which grows more and more remote. They become 'safety-valves', as one writer has remarked, rather than organs of radicalism and revolt (Shepperson 1954: 245).

A major difference between the orthodox political movement and the millenarian movement is that leadership of the former generally comes from the towns, from the educated and detribalized (I use this word in no deprecatory sense), and from the industrial and agricultural employees rather than from peasant cultivators. Such people can of course convert the more advanced type of millenarian movement into an orthodox political movement. It is significant that most of the leaders of millenarian movements have some record of White contact, whether it be through education in government or mission school, through government or Army service, or, more commonly as migrant labourers on plantations, etc. Nevertheless, such political leaders will have to rely for their support on the rural population in countries which are dominantly agrarian. Amongst this rural population, millenarian movements are already at work laying the foundations of future nationalist movements. It was with considerable felicity that M. Jean Guiart recently described these movements as 'Fore-Runners of Melanesian Nationalism'. They are not yet Melanesian nationalism, for the national groupings have not yet emerged, but they are steps on the road to the formation of such nationalities.

15 CHRISTIANITY AND ISLAM AMONG THE MOSSI[1]

Elliott P. Skinner

THE TWIN forces of Christianity and Islam are both seriously contending for the conversion of the pagan masses of the Western Sudan. Islam first penetrated this region during the 11th century and succeeded in converting many people to its faith. Christianity arrived on the scene only 60 years ago, and has not had the time to win many converts. However, there remained many societies in this area which were largely pagan until European conquests exposed them almost simultaneously to the influences of both Christianity and Islam. One such society, the Mossi, has been described as the principal island of resistance to Islam in the Sudan (Gouilly 1952: 52). André (1924: 31) states that the Mossi "offered to the Animists an irreducible rampart against the invasion of Islam." And Delafosse concurs that the Mossi "seem to have been particularly hostile to Islam which has made no progress among them since the Hegira. And although an appreciable number of Moslem strangers (Yarsé) lived among them, they have almost all remained pagans" (1912, vol. 3: 187).

The first Christian Catholic missionaries arrived in Mossi ter-

Reprinted from *The American Anthropologist* 60 (6), 1958: 1102–19, by permission of the author and the American Anthropological Association.

[1] This article is an expanded version of a paper read at a meeting of the American Anthropological Association in Chicago, 1957. The field work on which this analysis is based was conducted among the Mossi of Ouagadougou from November 1955 to January 1957, and was made possible by a Fellowship from The Ford Foundation African Studies Program. Needless to say, all ideas contained herein are my own. During these months among the Mossi I lived both in the predominantly Moslem district of Nobéré, and in the district of Manga, which has a fairly large Catholic population. I am indebted to Conrad Arensberg, Joseph Greenberg, Marvin Harris, and Ben Zimmermann for many helpful suggestions.

ritory in 1900, just four years after French conquest. These missionaries were kindly if fearfully received by the people, who gave them land for building a mission and for cultivating crops. The Mossi helped the Christians cultivate these crops and willingly allowed the children to attend the mission school. Nevertheless, when the missionaries tried to convert the children to Catholicism, the parents objected and withdrew the children from school (Socquet 1956: 62). The Protestant American "Assemblies of God" mission first worked among the Mossi in 1926, and in 1931 they reported that the outlook for conversions was "hopeful" (Cooksey and McLeish 1931: 215). But from 1926 to date, the Protestants have made negligible progress in their conversions. There are today about 155,000 Moslems, 26,000 Catholics, and 1,760 Protestants in a Mossi population of over 1,500,000. These figures attest to the fact that despite a long history of resistance to foreign religious systems, many Mossi are now abandoning their traditional religion. But the figures also show that while Islam is gaining many converts, the Catholics are making only slight progress, and the American Protestants hardly any at all. There are obviously many reasons for the differential advance of these three religious systems. In this paper I will examine and analyze the processes by which these religious systems attempt to gain converts, and delineate the reasons for their differential success.

The Mossi who are now feeling the impact of external religious influences represent the unique example of a Sudanese group which has preserved its ethnic identity and political autonomy through all the vicissitudes of Sudanic history until French conquest in 1896. Tradition records that the first Mossi rulers left the Dagomba region in the Gold Coast (present-day Ghana) during the 11th century and moved into the bend of the Niger River, carving out three large kingdoms and smaller principalities in the process. At the head of these still extant kingdoms are rulers (*Moro Nabas*) who hold feudal-like control of the provinces, districts, and villages which comprise their domains. A complex hierarchical administrative apparatus extends the power of the rulers into the smallest village, and funnels taxes and tribute back to them. French conquest modified this highly efficient system but did not greatly change it. The Mossi state apparatus rests on an economy which produces cotton cloth, horses, sheep, cattle, and goats, but the main support of this large population—one of the densest in the Sudan—is grain agriculture. Today, some Mossi districts still have as many as 70 persons per square mile.

The Mossi are divided into stratified royal, noble, and commoner patrilineages. Characteristic of this lineage system is a process by which royal sublineages descend serially until they merge with the mass of commoner lineages. Below the lineages there were once large non-Mossi groups of serfs and slaves, but these people have now been grouped into lineages and have become Mossi. Patrilocal polygynous extended family households, grouped into villages, form the basic Mossi settlement pattern. Marriages are arranged between unrelated persons through the agency of lineage members who establish "friendly" relationships. The two friends might ask their lineage heads for women to exchange as wives, or the "friend" who has received more gifts from his opposite number will give over a wife. Because only the older men have women and goods at their disposal, they are usually the ones who receive wives. The result is that most young men have no wives and must content themselves with occasional lovers until they inherit wives from lineage members. The Mossi have a great fear of incestuous relations which bring down the wrath of the ancestors (the *Keemsé*).

Ancestor veneration is at the core of Mossi religious behavior. The recent ancestors are notified, through sacrifices, of the important events in the lives of their descendants, and they are expected to aid in solving everyday problems. The ancestors also invoke their sanctions against antisocial behavior among their descendants. Once a year the Mossi people, in concert with the Moro Nabas, appeal to their individual and collective ancestors for good crops, large families, and for the preservation of the dynasty. Often associated with the ancestors as propitiatory agents are local deities called *Tengkougas* (sing. *Tenkougre*) or earth shrines, visibly manifested by clumps of trees, mountains, rocks, or rivers. *Tengsobas* or earth priests appeal to the Tengkougas on behalf of the local populations for help in sickness, for rain and good crops, and for children. When proper sacrifices are offered to the Tengkougas, their spiritual agents, called *kinkirsé*, enter the wombs of women and are born as children. Twins and children who die young are regarded as "evil"

kinkirsé who entered a woman without being invited. Nevertheless, many persons consider twins as special gifts to parents in
favor of the earth deities.

The earth itself, *Tenga,* is one of the principal deities of the
Mossi. Tenga is considered the wife of a male deity called *Winnam, Windé,* or *Naba Zidiwindé.* The true nature of Winnam
is not clear. The Mossi say: "Winnam is the sun, and Winnam
is God"; he is considered a sun god as well as a supreme deity.
Winnam is venerated but he is not feared, because it is the dead
ancestors who chastise evil-doers by affliction or death. When
wicked people die they face the wrath of the ancestors in
Keemsétenga, or land of the ancestors.

The Mossi have several concepts of the spiritual essence or
animating principle of man. First there is the *seega* (pl. *seesé*),
an entity found in all living beings; it leaves the body during
sleep, and its adventures provide the dreams of men. The seega
can be captured during its nocturnal wanderings or in places
where large crowds congregate. If the seega is captured and eaten
by a sorcerer, its owner will die. A man's shadow is also called
his seega; persons about to die have no shadows, since their
seesé have either been stolen or have left on their own account.

Another principle called the *keema* (pl. *keemsé*) is associated
with the dead or with persons about to die. The keema of a dying
man wanders around and often frightens people; as soon as he is
dead, he is no longer referred to by name but is called the
"keema." Keemsé is also the word used for the generalized ancestors who sanction the behavior of the living and who must be
placated if people wish to have enough food, wives, children,
and good health. A man's own keemsé take a vital interest in his
affairs, in return for which they receive nourishment in the form
of the seesé (animals do not have keemsé) of sacrificed animals.

The breath, called *vousem,* is also considered an animating
principle by the Mossi and, since it leaves the body through the
nose at death, they believe that a man's nose is the first thing to
die. It is not clear how the seega is disposed of when the body
dies. Some people say it remains forever about the haunts of
man; others believe that it goes to a mountain called Plimpikou
and disappears into a cavern. Still others believe that the seega
becomes the keema and goes to Plimpikou, from whence the
keemsé come to visit their descendants. It is difficult to deter-

mine whether the Mossi have always been vague about their traditional religious concepts or whether this uncertainty is the result of the influx of such foreign creeds as Islam and Christianity.

The first recorded contact between the Mossi and Moslems took place around 1328 when the Yatenga Mossi attacked, burned, and sacked Timbuktu, then held by the Dia dynasty of the Songhoi (Dubois 1896: 251). For more than a century afterward, the Mossi pursued a turbulent and aggressive policy in the region of the Niger bend, pushing as far as Gourma, Walata, and Banku (ibid: 127). They were finally defeated and routed by Sonni Ali in 1477. In 1499, when Askia the Great (El Hadj Mohammed ben Abou Bekr, usurper of the Songhoi throne from the Sonni dynasty in 1494) returned from his pilgrimage to Mecca, he launched a *jihad* or holy war on the Mossi who had rejected his ultimatum to adopt Islam. Askia defeated the Mossi, "devastated the towns and countryside, took men, women, and children as prisoners, and forcibly converted these captives to Islam" (Dubois 1896: 127–28). The pagan Mossi and the Moslem Songhoi fought several other battles until Songhoi power was broken by the Moroccans, who conquered Timbuktu in 1590.

The Moslems made no further attempt to convert the Mossi by force, but Moslem pressure did not stop; it now came in the peaceful guise of Moslem merchants and Yarsé Moslem refugees from the Mandingo cities such as Timbuktu and Djenne, who received permission from the Mossi rulers to settle in the country. However, judging from the reports of the first Europeans to reach the Mossi, the Moslems lived under many restrictions and were forbidden by the Moro Nabas to recite their prayers in public places (Tauxier 1912: 585–86). Despite these restrictions, the Moslems were able to extend their influence through conversion of the cadet sons of the rulers and conversion of at least one ruler of the Ouagadougou Mossi dynasty.

About 1780 Naba Kom, the son of Zombré and a Yarsé Moslem woman, permitted the Yarsé to live in the villages and sent one of them to the Gold Coast for religious instruction. His son, Naba Sagha, was involved in a civil war and replaced some dissident pagan district chiefs with his Moslem sons. The present ruling lineage of Nobéré (where I worked) is descended from

Ngado, one of these sons.[2] But although the rulers permitted their younger sons to adopt Islam, they themselves and the heirs to the thrones remained pagan in order to maintain the bonds with the ancestors. The exception to this rule was Doulougou, the grandson of Sagha, who was elected Moro Naba despite being a Moslem. Now the spread of Islam was given new impetus: Yarsé proselytizing increased, mosques were built in Ouagadougou and in the villages, and many Koranic schools were founded. But with Doulougou's death the rulers reverted to paganism and Moslem influence declined. Nevertheless, the learned Moslem Imams continued to serve at court and used their knowledge of the outside world for the benefit of the rulers.

The Moslem Mossi showed the greatest hostility to the first Europeans who arrived in the country. The Imam of Yako, under the influence of his Tidjani son (who had made the pilgrimage to Mecca), refused to have any dealings with Europeans. Furthermore, he convinced the Moro Naba that death awaited any ruler who granted an audience to a European. When the French attacked the Mossi in 1896, an Imam from Béré, a former pilgrim, told the ruler to flee and not depend on his ill-equipped soldiers to defeat the gun-bearing invaders. Lamberth reported that the Moslems told the defeated and demoralized Mossi that "as soon as all the blacks become Moslems, the whites will leave" (Tauxier 1912: 792).

No one knows how many Moslems were in Ouagadougou when the French arrived. Delafosse (1912, vol. 3: 193) records that around the turn of the century there were about 42 Koranic schools with 230 students scattered around the country. Tauxier (1912: 793), writing about the same period, states that there were 33 Koranic schools with about 358 students. No Koranic schools were reported for the Nobéré and Manga districts, but I know that there were several in the neighboring district of Béré. In 1926 there were 70 Koranic schools and 4,000 Moslems in Ouagadougou (seven percent of whom were non-Mossi). By 1944 there were about 240 schools and approximately 25,000 Moslems. The last census, 1954, did not record the number of

[2] Tauxier (1912: 792) reports that when he visited Pirigui village, situated to the north of Ouagadougou, he was surprised to discover that almost half of the nobles were Moslems. It is highly probable that here, also, were the descendants of a son of Sagha who replaced a dissident chief.

Koranic schools but gave the figure of 60,000 Moslems in the Ouagadougou region.[3] The 4,000 Moslems of Nobéré comprise 42 percent of that district's population. With the exception of one Catholic school master and the Catholic catechist who came to the district during 1956, the population is pagan. It might be relevant to point out that Nobéré has the highest percentage of Moslems in Kombissiri, an administrative unit (a subdivision) which has 152,000 pagans, 23,000 Moslems, 3,000 Catholics, and about 100 Protestants.

As noted above, Islam first came into the Nobéré district with Ngado, who replaced a dissident pagan chief, but Ngado's lineal descendants reverted to paganism until a few years ago when the present district chief became a nominal Moslem. The cadet sons of Ngado did not revert to paganism, and today all the noble sublineages of the district are Moslem. We may note here that one of the main aspects of Islamic proselytization in this district, as elsewhere among the Mossi, has been the conversion of persons who do not hold strategic positions vis-à-vis the ancestors. The present chief is no exception to this rule, because he is only a nominal Moslem. His eldest son is the only one in the family who is not a Moslem—a status which is becoming increasingly difficult to maintain in a growing Moslem population. The chief himself became partially converted to Islam in gratitude to a Moslem Hausa trader who cured his illness. He recites the five daily prayers and observes most of the prescriptions of Islam, but he still drinks European beer, subscribes to many pagan rites and beliefs, and supervises the annual Péléga or sacrifice to the ancestors. This dual allegiance is politically expedient because the chief can function as the head of the Moslem community as well as the traditional head of all the people. He does have occasional difficulty with intolerant Moslems who wish him to become a devout Moslem, and with the traditionalists who claim that today the crops are smaller, the people sicker, and the women barren because of the neglect of the ancestors. However, with the approach of holy days, these differences are resolved in the interest of community harmony.

The chiefs of the villages under the overall command of the

[3] These figures are only approximate since many thousands of persons are unreported. Again, many persons listed as Moslems are pagans who have taken Moslem names for ritual purposes.

district chief are mainly pagan, since they are descended from
the district chief replaced by Ngado. Yet they command villages
inhabited by the noble Moslem sublineages of the ruling house
as well as by commoner lineages. The village chief cannot become a Moslem because he too is responsible for sacrifices to
the ancestors, without whose help his people would suffer. He
does not take an active part in Moslem festivities, but receives
the homage due a chief from the Moslems on these and other
occasions. However, most village chiefs show an interest in
Moslem affairs, and one of them, the chief of Vooko, built a
prayer-circle (*misseri*) for Moslems who came to pay homage.

The pivotal role which the village chief plays in the exchange
of wives between Moslems and pagans has led indirectly to the
increase of the Moslem population. Before the French conquest
he gave the Moslems more wives than he received from them.
This unequal exchange, plus the nobles' prerogative of seizing
the wives of pagans, contributed to the increase of the Moslems.

The conversion of Mossi to Islam is sometimes accompanied
by a rupture in the relationships between persons involved in
"friendships" with a view of obtaining wives. A great quarrel developed in the district between a pagan chief and a recent convert who refused to give the chief a daughter promised as a wife.
The chief became furious and claimed that the Moslem had
broken a promise made years ago, but the Moslem claimed that
it was against his new religion to give his daughter to a pagan.
It is not true that Moslems in the village do not exchange wives
with pagans, but the Moslems often try to convert their pagan
friends so that the brides will not have to revert to paganism.
The chief's difficulty was that he could not become a Moslem because of his ritual and ceremonial relationship with the ancestors.
The Moslem men do not have such difficulties with their pagan
wives because most women follow their husbands' dictates in
religious and other matters. Many Moslem men attempt to prevent their wives from having sacrifices made to the ancestors,
but if a woman really wishes such a sacrifice she can easily have
it arranged through her pagan relatives. If a woman married to a
Moslem refuses to observe Islamic practices, she is liable to
divorce and runs the risk of having her children taken away.

Mossi anxiety over children is often instrumental in converting
them to Islam. When a woman is barren or her young children

die, she consults a soothsayer (*barga*). She is either told that
her Tengkougre benefactor was not amply rewarded and recalled
the children, or that her "Moslem" children (children who
wished to be Moslems) were angry because they were given
pagan names. In the latter case she is advised to make a gift to
a Moslem and to ask her husband to build a Moslem prayer-
circle outside his hut so that when her children "return" (are
born again) they will see it. Finally, she is advised to give all her
children Moslem names. I could discover no reason why the
pagan soothsayers advise these anxious parents to adopt Islam,
except that they hope that complicated prescriptions will be more
efficacious. Nevertheless, so effective is this technique for gaining converts to Islam that even members of the family of the
chief pagan priest are not immune to it. Furthermore, once a
woman has a Moslem child, all her other children must be Moslems or they will die. A man whose children are all Moslem has
no recourse except to adopt Islam if he wants a funeral, because
his Moslem sons may not give him a pagan funeral.

Every Mossi, whether Moslem or non-Moslem, wishes a
proper funeral, and now that travel has increased, the fact of being Moslem or pagan is of great importance. Many young migrants to Ashanti have reported that their dead pagan comrades
were unceremoniously disposed of, while the local Christians
and Moslems took care of their dead coreligionists. But despite
this fact, and the belief of administrators and missionaries, I
found no evidence that the seasonal and other migration of
Mossi youth to Ghana and the Ivory Coast have contributed very
much to the spread of Islam. It is true that some of the thousands of Mossi who fled their homeland to escape forced labor
or military service ultimately returned as Moslems, but the majority of seasonal migrants do not have enough contact with
foreign populations for them to become Moslems. Most of the
Mossi who migrate to Ghana work on cocoa farms far removed
from large centers of population. It is also true that even those
Mossi who worked for Moslems on the farms and found it expedient to "pray" (as the Mossi refer to conversion to Islam)
soon reverted to paganism on their return in order to escape the
displeasure of their lineage members. I have recorded several
cases of pagans who became Moslems only when they returned
from abroad to find their relatives all converted to Islam.

Today there are obvious rewards for those Mossi who embrace Islam; besides such tangible rewards as getting wives and children, there are the intangible ones of upward social mobility and greater prestige. It is important to note that most liberated slaves and serfs are now Moslems. Formerly these non-Mossi had low status, but today those who have been to Mecca bear such proud titles as *Hadji*. On the night before Ramadan, one of these men gave a talk before the Nobéré chief during which he chided the chief for his impiety and voiced the hope that the next chief would be a true Moslem. He admitted that the chief might interpret such a speech from a former serf as impertinence, but he begged him to accept the censure as coming from the servant of *Nabiyama* (the prophet). This same man had refused to pay homage to the chief at the annual sacrifice to the ancestors, and when admonished returned the daughter which the chief had given him as a wife. In earlier days a chief would not have given a daughter to a serf, and moreover, a disrespectful serf could be killed instantly.

Many French administrators and Christian missionaries allege that Mossi youth embrace Islam because they like the beautiful robes and red fezzes of the Moslems, but this is a naive explanation for the conduct of a highly sophisticated people. Most young men in Nobéré wear Moslem-type clothes because such clothes are the mode. Now that sun helmets, dark glasses, and women's raincoats with hoods are in vogue, pagans as well as Moslems wear them. What is of interest, however, is that when pagans become Moslems they wear cleaner clothes and affect a different style of life.

The local consensus is that Moslems are much better behaved than pagans because they do not swear, fight, or get drunk in public. The man chosen as Imam is required to have such characteristics as mercy toward evil-doers, benevolence, magnanimity, physical beauty, and virility. Yet many Mossi say that the Moslems can be worse than any other people. They accuse them of being charlatans, of selling Koranic verses as charms, and of committing murder by the use of magical formuiae. Neither pagans nor Moslems believe that a man is necessarily good because he recites his daily prayers or goes to Mecca.

Moslems in the district follow most precepts of their religion: they recite the five daily prayers according to the rites of Tidjani (there are only two Moslems of the Hamada sect in the district and no members of the Hamallist sect), give alms to the poor, observe the month-long fast (called by the Mossi the *Karême*), celebrate the great festival of Ramadan and the lesser festivals, and aspire to make the pilgrimage to Mecca. Most of the Moslems can lead prayers, but only about one-tenth of their number can read and recite the Koran. However, today the masters (*karasambas*) of the 32 Koranic schools in the district are endeavoring to instruct the many boys and few girls in reading the Koran and understanding Moslem theology.

The Karême is observed by most adult Moslems in the community with the exception of invalids and working men. Moslems say that the fast is intended to turn the minds of the people to God, and they distinguish between the Moslems "of the mouth" who break the fast and those "of the heart" who fast until Ramadan. The crescent moon of Ramadan is greeted with guns and general rejoicing and the following morning the Moslems gather at the tomb of Ngado to give praises to God; during the rest of the day they pay homage to the chief and visit their friends. However, a change in the traditional observance of Ramadan is expected, because one of the Moslem leaders objects to the ceremony at the tomb of Ngado. He feels that some Moslems are beginning to regard the tomb of the first Moslem as an earth shrine or Tengkougre.

So far, only five of the more prominent Moslems in the district have made or are making the pilgrimage to Mecca. The first man made the voyage about seven years ago, and is now conducting a Koranic school in a neighboring district. His brother went to Mecca about two years ago and is now the senior *El Hadj* in the district. Of the two men who were on the pilgrimage when I arrived in the district, one has since died near the Red Sea and the other is still away. One other man left for Mecca and returned to the district during my stay. Most of the pilgrims now fly to Mecca; only two men followed the traditional route through Ghana, Kano, Lake Chad, the Anglo-Egyptian Sudan (now Sudan), and on to Mecca. In general, all pilgrims have used their own resources for the trip, but they receive some help from their lineage brothers and from the other Moslems in the district and in Ouagadougou.

The pilgrimage to Mecca represents the greatest event in the lives of the district Moslems. When the last pilgrim left, a great crowd gathered at his house and prayed for his safe journey, and some even accompanied him to Ouagadougou and remained there until he left. The Moslems and many pagans of the district, under the command of the district chief, cultivated his fields during his absence. And when the new El Hadj returned, a large crowd accompanied him to his house with shouts of joy. There he killed a sheep in thanksgiving, sprinkled the crowd with holy water from Mecca, and recounted his experiences. His listeners were impressed by his airplane flight and the description of Mecca, but they showed the greatest interest when he said that Mecca women covered their faces and that most Meccan men were monogamous. The local Moslems smiled when they heard this bit of news from one of their members, but I have seen them scowl when discussing the monogamous practice desired by the Christians.

The attitudes of Moslems differ very little from those of the other Mossi as regards children and polygyny. They say that they do not believe in the efficacy of ancestor veneration and do not "kill chickens" to the ancestors, but they maintain that it is a man's duty to have many wives so that he may have children to succeed him. Furthermore, since Mohammed himself decreed that his followers may keep four wives, provided they treat each with the same degree of kindness, there is no conflict between Islamic tenets and Mossi practice of polygyny. The average Moslem has two wives, but even the few men in the district who have more than four wives do not appear overly concerned about transgressing the tenets of their faith. Mossi Moslems have not adopted the paternal parallel cousin marriage so common among other Moslems, and show surprise when told that Islam permits such marriages. However, they have modified their marriage behavior to harmonize with what they consider an Islamic tenet that "a man should not marry the widow of his father." The Moslem Mossi profess to look with horror on these marriages among their pagan brothers, preferring the levirate instead.

The Moslems' attitude toward the low status of women in Mossi society has not changed, and in one respect it can even be said that this attitude has been strengthened. Many Moslem wives now cover their faces, and many El Hadjis have attempted to place their wives in purdah by preventing them from going to the market for fear they would come in contact with pagan men. The development of this practice is running counter to the growing emancipation of Mossi women, who have just begun to leave their villages for periodic visits to the larger towns. Nevertheless, the important fact is that the Mecca pilgrims have the opportunity to see Moslem women playing roles which are forbidden or unknown to Mossi women. And while it is true that the Mossi pilgrims would not easily adopt and foster monogamy, their receptivity to new Islamic beliefs and customs might have a liberating effect on their treatment of women. Once institutional and cultural changes have been accepted by the El Hadjis, they are likely to spread quite rapidly throughout the society because men who have visited Mecca are believed to have returned filled with wisdom and understanding.

Christianity came to the Mossi on January 24, 1900, shortly after French conquest. As noted above, the first missionaries were well treated, but the Mossi balked at the attempts at conversion. Nevertheless, by 1919 the White Fathers of the Catholic missions had established several centers, among which was the district of Manga where this study was conducted. Manga is considered a Catholic district, but there are only 3,000 Catholics out of a population of 124,000—which also includes 9,200 Moslems and five Protestants. Thus, in contrast to Moslem Nobéré, which has no Catholics or Protestants, Manga, like most districts in Mossi territory, has a Moslem community.

The conversion of the Mossi in Manga to Catholicism follows the classical pattern of missionary proselytization in the country. Monsignor Socquet (1956: 62) states that the Mossi always react to attempts at conversion with the statement: " 'We are looking at our chief,' that is to say, 'We will follow our chief in conversion as in all other matters. If he is favorable to it, then we will not go against his will.' " Socquet concludes: "It is thus understandable how important is the conversion of the chiefs, or, at least, their sympathy for our religion, in the spread of Catholicism." The missionaries may have been successful in the village of the Manga district chief because he was sympathetic to them, but they made few converts in the villages far from the district center or in the neighboring districts. In the Béré district, a few miles from Manga, the Catholics have made only 22 converts despite more than 15 years' work. In Manga, however, they were

able to "recruit" most of the young children for their church and
school. When an old man was asked why his children became
Catholic, he tried to evade the question but finally replied that
he did not control the minds of his children. Knowing the nature
of administrative practice in the upper Volta before 1946, and
the nature of Mossi family structure, we looked further for the
answer.

Paradoxically, it comes from a Catholic missionary, André
Dupont, who, seeking to discover the reason for the decrease of
patients in the Catholic-controlled maternity clinics, asked:

> Why have the maternity clinics which in 1942 served more than
> seventy mothers a month now serve only two or three? "We are no
> longer forced to go," reply the villagers. Was it the fear of sanction
> which accounted for the unanimous use of the clinics? Alas! It would
> seem to be so. The use of force and sanction have rendered odious an
> institution of charity. It would have been better if the mothers were
> only encouraged to use the clinics. "These natives do not under-
> stand," I am told sometimes. But how does one expect them to un-
> derstand? (Dupont 1949: 4).

Fear was certainly one of the reasons why the people in Manga
embraced Catholicism. Before 1946 (the Brazzaville conference
in 1944 abolished forced labor), men and women were recruited
for work on the roads and on Ivory Coast plantations, and children were recruited for the schools. The district chiefs often
gathered orphans and the children of their former serfs and sent
them to the mission to fill the quotas, but many children and
whole families voluntarily attached themselves to the missions.
The reasons for so doing are legion, but in some cases it was
simply the desire to accept the new religious faith.

Once at the mission the children were taught French and the
tenets of Catholicism. Many of the boys later became catechists
or priests and several girls went into the nunnery. However, the
largest group of educated youths became the clerical personnel
of the administration and were lost to missionary activity. Because the administration lacked French-speaking Mossi, the
young people received good jobs. This desertion to the administration has become so serious that the missionaries at Manga
have ceased to teach French to their catechists and now use the
vernacular.

Conversion to Catholicism, bringing with it the knowledge of

French, was formerly one of the sure roads to upward social mobility. Most Catholic teachers at Manga (and at Nobéré) are individuals who were recruited as unwilling school-boys but today are the highest paid members of their lineages. Other gains have accrued to persons who become Catholics. For example, the people at Manga believe that the missionaries used their influence with the administration to have one of their converts, a younger son of the late chief, elected to the district chieftainship over his elder brother. This belief is probably unfounded, since the Moro Naba seems to be electing the literate sons of chiefs to their fathers' positions so that educated chiefs, and not educated commoners, can serve as members of French parliamentary bodies. Unfortunately, the people of Manga do not understand modern political problems, and have accepted the new chief only because of their traditional respect for the chieftainship.

The conversion of the Manga chief to Catholicism has not engendered many problems for his pagan subjects. The chief's primary duty—to begin the yearly ceremonial cycle of sacrifices to the ancestors—has been taken over by his father's brother, who is now considered the ritual head of the chiefly lineage. Nevertheless, to the chief still accrue the gains of this ceremony because his followers pay him homage and bring him gifts on his birthday, which comes at this period. Moslems in the community also pay their respects at this time, and they prefer his Catholic birthday celebration to the bloody sacrifices of chickens to the ancestors. On the other hand, the chief shows little of the common Catholic disapproval of Moslems and sends gifts to their leaders on the Moslem feast days. He also entertains the district Moslems when they come to pay him homage.

The Catholic chief does not act as a pivot in the exchange of wives between pagans of his lineage and the other lineages. This task now falls to his father's brothers. Nevertheless, as district chief he is constantly involved with the marital problems involving pagan parents and their Catholic children. The main source of the difficulty is that Catholic girls are encouraged to refuse to join their pagan husbands when so ordered by their parents. The mission not only insists that the girl freely choose her own husband, but encourages her to reject a polygynous union. Catholicism thereby interposes itself between the girls and their society, not only impairing the prestige of their fathers and lineages but also giving the girls more freedom than they would ordinarily possess.

The pagans claim that by encouraging girls to choose mates without parental consent, the Catholics are really taking the opportunity to obtain wives for young Catholic men. Paradoxically, there seems to be some truth in this, since Bouniol, a White Father, states:

> A Mossi who is unable to acquire a wife by [traditional] means must either remain unmarried or seduce another man's wife . . . they must choose between celibacy and immorality.
> Such a state of affairs creates many problems for the missions, especially as the system is recognized and sanctioned by the colonial authorities. . . . Young native Christians are obviously placed in a very awkward position. Their conversion angers their parents, who refuse to give them a wife; neither will their friends bestow a daughter upon them, because they know that they will not receive one in return, since a Christian may not give a daughter in marriage to a pagan. . . . *Consequently, unless the missionaries help them to find a wife, they must remain unmarried—a very discouraging prospect!* (1920: 160 italics mine).

When a young Catholic receives a wife through the mission, he may visit her father and pay the customary respect by giving him kola nuts and brass coins. The father of a mission girl may accept or reject his son-in-law as he sees fit, but formerly he could not defy the power of the missions.

A pagan youth who wishes to marry one of the mission girls has to discuss the matter with the priests and swear publicly that he will become a Christian. Before 1946 the young man had to fulfill his promise or be intimidated by the chief and the missionaries until he relented or fled the district. Today, however, the priests usually abandon their efforts to obtain the conversion of the young men after three months have passed. In some cases the young men take their wives and move to other districts, and return only after the girls have given up Catholicism. Despite the lure of wives from the mission, not many young men become Christians on this account because the Mossi are still concerned primarily with family relationships and the effect that conversion would have on these relationships.

The church's prohibition of polygyny is by far the most serious bar to the spread of Catholicism. Many men do not adopt Catholicism simply because they fear that monogamous marriages would not produce children. Father Paternot (Considine 1954: 103) has cited a study purporting to show that Christian Mossi have more children than the pagans, but the ordinary people of the district would not accept the facts he presented. They cite their personal experience to the contrary. Dim Delobson (1934: 136), a Mossi converted to Catholicism, states:

> A certain number of Christians of my acquaintance whose wives did not have children during the first years of marriage had recourse to magical practices in order to get children. These simple people thought that although they had an omnipotent God beside them, they could impudently—after all the good priests will not know about it—ask the little, but also powerful gods to grant them some material favors here on earth. When the gods given children were taken for Holy Baptism, they were given Christian names instead of the names of the earth shrines, and they did not wear magical charms which would have indicated to the priest the real state of affairs. Nevertheless, the children were bathed in water to which magical potions were added, and when the mothers went to visit their parents, sacrifices of chickens were given to the benevolent Tengkougas.

The Mossi's strong desire for children is admittedly one of the main reasons for leaving the Catholic Church so that they can take other spouses in addition to barren ones. The church has now belatedly recognized this problem and, knowing that it cannot prevent men from taking plural wives, allows them to come to church but prohibits them from taking the Mass.

Many cultural factors besides the desire for children make polygyny important for the Mossi, and make conversion detrimental to the functioning of their family system. Because of lineage opposition to their conversions, some converts are forced to establish nuclear households—a practice out of harmony with the normal rhythm of Mossi life. The reason for this disharmony is that Mossi women married to Catholics must work alone instead of with co-wives and other women of the extended families. Even the Catholic husbands would not help their wives with household tasks requiring more than one person, nor would they violate tradition by chatting with their wives except at night in their huts. Another factor is that after the Mossi Christian woman has given birth to a child, she follows the traditional custom and goes back to her parents' home to remain there during the two or three years' lactation period. This imposes a

great hardship on a Catholic husband because during this time
he is left without wife or helpmate. In the extended family household there would have been women to take care of a man's material needs, and his mistresses would have taken care of his
sexual needs. The Catholic can and does ask the mission for a
young girl to take care of his material needs, but of course she
is not expected to satisfy his sexual desires. Obviously this arrangement is not satisfactory, and many Catholic men, with the
acquiescence of their wives, keep mistresses. Dim Delobson comments:

> Ouagadougou has a large number of Christians, but does this mean
> that these people in their love for the church respect all her rules?
> Alas! there are a large number of Christians who oblige their lawful
> wives to leave the conjugal couch and make way for the accommoda-
> tion of mistresses . . . in conformity with the old custom. But this
> is a subject which is too delicate to discuss further. I only note it in
> passing: *Noli me tangere* (1934: 169).

Despite the influence of tradition on Mossi Catholics, I feel it
would be a mistake to say that the complexity of Catholic dogma
is one of the drawbacks to missionary success in this country.
One Mossi has already been made a bishop of the Catholic
Church, and most of the proselytizing in Manga falls on the two
Mossi priests and the five Mossi nuns. Under the supervision of
two White Fathers, the Catholic children and adults are acquainted with the dogma and rituals of the church. The festivals
are well attended and celebrated with as much pomp as possible.
Although the Mass is sung in Latin, the Mossi have adapted
some of their traditional tunes to the Mass, and use their own
language for prayers and hymns. Catholics observe all the sacra-
ments including Confession—a sacrament which is hazardous from
the Mossi point of view, because man must lay bare his innermost
thoughts to the priests, who, in the final analysis, are Europeans
and thus administrators.

It is true that even the staunchest Catholics in Manga have not
abandoned all belief in traditional rituals and religious credos.
For example, many Mossi Catholics believe in the existence of
sorcerers, but the Catholic Church does not recognize the existence of sorcerers or such evil forces (I have met White Fathers
who believe that there are unexplainable psychic and physical
phenomena in Africa), and moreover has no way of dealing with

them. "But," says Dim Delobson (1934: 136), "the Mossi believe so strongly in the power of such entities, that even those converted to Christianity cannot always escape the action of malevolent practitioners." The result is that many Catholics desert the church when they believe that only traditional specialists can help them with personal problems. Catholic families easily abandon Christianity when told by shamans that to do so is necessary in order to have children. Unfortunately, the panoply of saints in modern French Catholicism does not seem to be able to syncretize with or displace the local deities, and thus come to the aid of the Mossi. This weakness of modern Catholicism in West Africa appears to make it unable to deal with many of the insecurities which arise in the daily lives of its adherents.

The American Protestant missionaries were never able to establish stations in either Manga or Nobéré because of the relative strengths of Catholicism and Islam in these two districts. However, they do have stations in Po and Koubri, 30 and 50 miles away. The 1954 census lists five Protestants in Manga, but I could find only one family head who had been a Protestant and that during the period when he worked for missionaries. It is interesting to note that when he returned to his native Manga he did not become a Catholic but embraced Islam instead. Although Protestants among the Mossi are trying very hard, they are working under three handicaps: (1) the opposition of the local administration, (2) their own explicit cultural bias, and (3) the puritanical nature of their brand of American Midwestern Protestantism.

The first Protestant missionaries to arrive in 1926 reported: "There has often been opposition to the preaching of the Gospel in the district, and there is a continual under-current which has hindered many from accepting Christ" (Assemblies of God Mission 1934: 14). Americans who wished to train the young Mossi to read and write found official opposition to the use of the vernacular for such purposes, and were obliged to receive French teaching certificates. When one recognizes that in those days less than one-tenth of one percent of the Mossi children were in schools (today the number is just over three percent) one cannot help feeling that any kind of education would have been useful to the Mossi. During the war the Pétain-oriented administration restricted the movements of the Americans and frightened off their converts. And finally, the Americans come under the general disapprobation with which the Mossi view most Europeans.

American Protestants are fairly well insulated from the Mossi population, and have only now begun to show any interest in Mossi culture and problems. Geoffrey Gorer, who visited the Mossi in 1935, wrote:

> There were some American missionaries in this village, a whole family living in a house filled with texts; I do not know what creed they preached, or with what success; they looked more like American missionaries than I had thought anyone could have done off the films . . . they spoke with a dispassionate "none of our business" disapproval of the ill treatment of the negroes, who they said were ruled entirely by fear (1935: 149).

Many of the Protestant missionaries who are now working with the Mossi are still inclined to agree with the first missionaries' ethnocentric judgment of their customs:

> Moral standards are very low. Nothing is wrong until it is found out. Chastity is unknown . . . we questioned in vain many natives in search of a suitable Mossi word for "virgin." They all declared there was no such word in their language. . . . Many horrifying and degrading customs of theirs, we would not dare to put in print (Assemblies of God Mission 1934:12).

Given such reactions, it is not surprising that the Protestants take no opportunity to use "heathen" beliefs and practices to further their own work. When they do take an interest in village affairs, it is usually to aid some young woman having marital difficulties with her lineage members (Sanders 1953: 43). Since most Mossi problems are ultimately concerned with women, one can take it as a general rule that they are not in sympathy with any religious system which aggravates this problem.

The American Protestants have the most puritanical religious regime of all the proselyting religions in this country. The Catholics forbid polygyny, and the Moslems prohibit the use of alcohol, but the American Protestants forbid polygyny, drinking native beer, smoking cigarettes, and chewing kola nuts. The result is that the Protestants find it difficult to gain converts, and are constantly weeding out "rice Christians" from their mission stations. One young Catholic informant said that he was very impressed with the Americans who drove up in their big cars and straightway "cried out the Evangelists." Asked why the missionaries did not get converts, he said that the Mossi were afraid of whites. This response, while true, is inadequate, but as one former Protestant said to me, "With the Americans one can do nothing." So far the American Protestants have made little progress and it is safe to predict that the puritan brand of American Protestantism is not going to make much headway among the Mossi.

The old pagan priest, seeing the steady advance of the new religious systems, tells the visitor that the traditional ways of the ancestors are disappearing and that now the Mossi must follow one of three ways: Allah (Islam), Péredamba soré (Catholicism), or Americadamba soré (Protestantism). He is sad to see this happen, but even his grandchildren are now Moslems. In the struggle between Catholicism and Islam for adherents it is the general consensus that Islamic conversions are on the increase. Islam is gaining, not only because of the reasons already cited but also because the political situation, which has greatly changed since the Brazzaville conference in 1944, is still rapidly changing. Today the Moslems are gaining twenty converts to every Catholic convert, largely because the Mossi do not now fear official sanctions. For example, the Manga mission installed a Mossi catechist in Nobéré with the avowed purpose of gaining converts among Moslem and pagan children enrolled at the new state-run school. The people of the district initially refused to give their land for such a station, but were overruled by the administration through the chief. Although the teacher is a Catholic, he has not dared to encourage any of his students to join the church. The one pagan child who showed an interest in Catholicism was immediately ostracized and beaten by the other students. Shortly afterward, many Moslem parents attempted to withdraw their children from the school, claiming that the children could not attend Koranic classes and the public schools at the same time. But the teacher, realizing the source of their fear, told them that the school would remain entirely secular in nature. The Imam at Nobéré is positive that now the White Fathers do not have "force" behind them, no conversions will be made in the district. He said that the Moslems here do not rely on force to convert the pagans, and leave them alone if they resist persuasion to embrace Islam.

Mossi politicians who, for the most part, were trained by the Catholics and are still supported by the church, are careful not

to offend their pagan and Moslem constituents. One inter-
nationally-known Mossi politician told a Nobéré audience that
he had a Moslem name in addition to his Catholic name, and that
he even attended a Koranic school. Although this admission did
not help him gain the votes of the Moslems, he carried the district
because he was supported by the chief and received the votes of
the pagans. The politicians are now under pressure from the
people to expand the system of public schools so that the road to
social mobility, through education, would be open to pagans and
Moslems as well as Catholics. Even in Manga, where the
government-supported parochial school is adequate for the school
population, there are plans to build a public school. The special
prerogative of the mission schools to use noncertificated personnel on their teaching staffs is now being attacked by teachers
who themselves were trained in these schools. These teachers
are demanding that the government either cease paying salaries
to the unqualified teachers in the mission schools or else employ
similar persons in the public schools. Thus one of the most important channels through which the Catholics obtained converts
is being consciously narrowed.

CONCLUSION

The spread of Islam in Africa south of the Sahara is one of the
significant cultural events in this area. Islam is not only spreading
at the expense of the indigenous religious systems, but is taking
precedence over Christianity brought to Africa by the conquering
Europeans. The reasons cited for the success of Islam over Christianity are legion. They include: the adaptability of Islam in contrast to the rigidity of Christianity (Greenberg 1946: 70; Goilly
1952: 173; Marty 1917: 283); the simplicity of Islamic doctrines,
as opposed to the complexity of Christianity (Delafosse 1931:
236; Quellien 1910: 38–39); and the "imponderable factors"
brought about by European conquest (Goilly 1952: 261–66).

In this paper I have shown that Islam has made greater progress
than has Christianity among the Mossi because:

1. Christianity has a negative appeal to the Mossi because it
was brought by their conquerors. For the proud Mossi, Christianity is intimately linked with their first real invasion, defeat, and
occupation by aliens in their long history. In contrast, Islam has

penetrated the country by peaceful means after its initial failure at proselytization by means of the jihad.

2. In the early period of this century, the European administration recruited Mossi men and women for forced labor at home and in the Ivory Coast, and recruited children for the mission schools. But as soon as forced labor was abolished and the Mossi could do as they wished, mission school and church attendance declined, and the Mossi mothers even refused to attend the Catholic maternity clinics. During this entire period, the Moslems were propagating the ideas that recruitment for forced labor and other injustices would cease only when all the Mossi embraced Islam.

3. Catholicism attempted to break down the Mossi social system during the period when their political system was rendered practically impotent. But while the Mossi could not forcibly oppose the effects of French policy on their political system, they effectively neutralized the church's attempts to disrupt their social system. In contrast to Catholicism, Islamic practices and tenets harmonized with many aspects of the Mossi social system, especially with regard to polygyny and the status of women. Many Mossi converted to Islam in order to fulfill the prescriptions of pagan shamans, who linked conversion with the acquisition of children to continue the lineage. Christianity did not admit the existence of the traditional supernatural forces, and evolved no techniques for dealing with the Mossi's belief in the efficacy of such forces. In the sphere of social mobility, Islam permitted the most illiterate emancipated serf to make a pilgrimage and return an honored El Hadj, while only the most brilliant scholar is able to become an official in the Catholic community.

4. More of the young men who leave their homes to serve in the armed forces or spend long periods away as laborers return as Moslems than as Christians. There is, however, no evidence that the increased Islamization of the Mossi is due to the heavy seasonal migration of young men to Ghana and Ivory Coast.

5. American Protestantism, although not associated with French administrative policy, was negatively received because its missionaries were Europeans (whites). Furthermore, the extremely intolerant Protestant attitude toward the traditional Mossi religion and the puritanical nature of their religion made their efforts at conversion highly unsuccessful.

6. The increase of public schools is lessening the importance of Catholicism and the Catholic school as the only means of social mobility through education. The newly emancipated pagan and Moslem masses are forcing the Catholic-trained Mossi politicians to act in the interest of their constituents, even if at the expense of the missions and Catholicism. The Catholics have consecrated the first Mossi bishop and have installed him in his see, but the return of each plane-load of Mossi Hadjis from Mecca spreads Islam into the remotest villages.

16 THE BIRTH OF A RELIGION

Audrey J. Butt

THIS PAPER DEALS with the origins of 'Hallelujah', the semi-Christian religion of the Carib-speaking peoples of the borderlands of British Guiana, Venezuela, and Brazil which adopted from both direct and indirect sources certain elements of Christianity which fused with the indigenous system of beliefs so successfully that they formed a new and flourishing religion: the Hallelujah religion of the Akawaio to-day.

These traditional beliefs (an outline of which I have published elsewhere), did not include any knowledge of a supreme, all-powerful God. Although the Carib-speaking tribes all have legends relating to culture heroes, brothers who were children of the sun and creators of the tribal environment and social order, these heroes finished their work and left the peoples on earth to their own devices and ceased to have any contact with them. Prayer and worship had no part in the traditional ritual. Instead, the system of beliefs was more a philosophy of life, giving expression to ideas concerning the nature of spirit, or of the strength which is thought to exist in all living creatures and things. The culture heroes, because of their origins, merely had more of this strength than other beings.

Among the Akawaio the core of their beliefs is expressed in three words which are in regular use among them. These words have a common root, the meaning of which is modified by the addition of two suffixes.

The first word is *akwa,* which means 'light', 'brightness' or

Reprinted from *The Journal of the Royal Anthropological Institute* 90 (1), 1960: 66–106, by permission of the author and the Council of the Royal Anthropological Institute.

'life' which is 'in the sun's place'. *Akwa* is not a person or a spirit, nor is it the sun itself; it is an abstraction, a force, which manifests itself as 'light'. The sun is the symbol of it. The Hallelujah Indians sometimes translate it as 'glory' (*gölori*), 'Heaven' (*ebun*) and 'light'. For them, God lives 'in light' (*akwayau*).

The second word is *akwalu*. This is a word made up of *akwa* and the suffix '-*lu*'. It is used to express the concept of spirit, which is the life or vitality in all living persons, creatures and nature spirits. The suffix -*lu* means 'a sort of' or 'a kind of' and is a regular termination for modifying a noun. *Akwalu* therefore, literally means the 'sort of light' or the 'sort of life' which is in a person. Hallelujah Indians use the word regularly as 'spirit' and also talk of '*God Akwalu*' 'God's Spirit'.

The third word is *akwalupö*. This word is made up of *akwa* and the suffix '-*lupö*' and is used to mean ghost spirit, shade or shadow. It refers to something which is dead, cast off, gone or past. The suffix -*lupö* is a regular termination which literally means 'deprived of' or 'without'. *Akwalupö* therefore means 'without light or life'. Whereas the living spirit is thought to be light, the ghost spirit is thought to be dark.

Many of the Hallelujah chants can be understood only in terms of these traditional beliefs. Various funeral customs, traditional stories and other aspects of the society reflect them, as well as indicating the traditional belief that the origin and destiny of all life on earth is *akwa*, 'brightness and life in the sun's place in the sky.'

The beliefs did not, and do not, have any close connexion with the general social or political organization of the people.

'Their pattern of thought is an attractive one and certainly not without truth either from the scientific or the Christian points of view; for, with its suggestion that all forms of earthly vitality are derived from and return to that great abstract principle of life which exists in the sky, it approaches Christian teaching; while, with the derivation of this earthly vitality and the general location of life in the light which is the sun's place, it approaches the scientific view that life on earth is dependent on light and energy from the sun' (Butt 1953).

It was from Christian teaching that these Indians first acquired the concept of God and the worship of and prayer to a Supreme Spirit who was concerned with people on earth and their deeds.

God was put in the sun's place (*akwa*). His Son became their Elder Brother (*U'Wi*). The Holy Ghost (*Oli Go*) was God's Spirit (*God Akwalu*). The traditional feast songs and dances were combined with a Christian form of prayer to become a ritual of worship and the village dance hall became a church (*sochi* or *churchi*). So, with similar ingenious adoptions and adaptations —mostly minor ones if we are able to take a broad view of the meaning of religious beliefs—the traditional system was modified by the incoming Christian concepts and the combination gave birth to a new, semi-traditional and semi-Christian religion which the founding prophets called 'Hallelujah'. This paper is concerned with the story of the birth of Hallelujah and its spread among the Carib-speaking tribes.

In the literature of the Guianas in the nineteenth century there is interesting information concerning the state of religious excitement among the interior tribes which was a consequence of the spread of mission teaching among them from the eighteen-sixties onwards. Although the accounts all show that these religious movements had much in common, only one can possibly be regarded as an historical record of the beginnings of Hallelujah. This is contained in Sir Everard im Thurn's description of the last night he spent at Roraima, on the occasion of his celebrated climb to the top of that famous mountain, hitherto regarded as the unscalable heights of the 'Lost World', in 1884.

> 'The closing day of my stay there was last Christmas day,' he wrote a year later, 'which we spent at Teroota, the Arecoona[1] village at the foot, and from which is the most astoundingly magnificent view of the twin mountains of Roraima and Kookenaam. . . . Then, when night fell and hid this, the Indians around us, under the influence of a most remarkable ecclesiastical mania which had just then spread in a wonderful way into these distant parts, raised—as they kept Christmas with much drinking, without intermission from sunset to the next dawn—an absolutely incessant shout of "Hallelujah! Hallelujah!"'

Whether this in fact was the 'Hallelujah' of to-day, or just one of the many religious manifestations of the period preceding it, I have no means of proving, although it must have been about the time when this particular Indianized version of certain Christian

[1] The people in the neighbourhood of Roraima belong to the Taulebang tribe which has frequently been confused with the very similar Arekuna tribe to the North.

doctrines began to spread from the Rupununi peoples northwards and westwards. Whichever may be the case, the Akawaio still preserve the origins of the present-day Hallelujah religion in their memory.

I collected seven complete versions of the story of the origins of Hallelujah, from widely-scattered villages, during my first period of research (1951–52) and three complete versions, from different sources, during the second period (1957). Most accounts are derived from the religious leaders of the villages or from elderly and knowledgeable men and women of the tribe. I do not include in these numbers the repeated confirmation which was obtained on certain aspects of the story. Many of the versions have some interesting and individual descriptions and interpretations of events—one might almost say that they have an accumulation of myth—but, taken broadly, all ten versions are very much the same and present a consistent, if telescopic, account of how the Carib-speaking peoples 'got' Hallelujah. An outline of the story is best obtained by considering all the versions together.

I   MAKUSI HALLELUJAH: THE STORY OF BICHIWUNG

Everyone agrees that the original founder of Hallelujah was a Makusi from the Kanuku Mountains[2] of the Rupununi Savannah. He had three names. His English name was Eden (pronounced variously as Idam, Dam and Idang); his Makusi name was Bichi-wung (pronounced variously as Pichiwung, Bisiwung, or Pisi-wung). Another, Makusi, name he is said to have had was Ara'opö but this is not generally known. Some say that Kara'apo (or, Kala'apo) was the name of one of Bichiwung's followers. The story runs as follows:

The Makusi first had Hallelujah. A man called Bichiwung and other Makusi men went to work for a parson. They went to his house somewhere behind Georgetown and worked for him and they were taught by this parson at his mission school. Now the parson was a white man from England and he took Bichiwung

---

[2] The Kanuku Mountains extend east-west, dividing the northern Rupu-nuni Savannah, where dwell the Carib-speaking Makusi, from the Southern Rupununi Savannah which is inhabited by the Arawak-speaking Wapisiana. Some of the Makusi gardens and villages are situated on the northern slopes of the mountains.

back with him to England and took him to stay at his home there.

Bichiwung had learnt some English, so that when the parson spoke to his relatives about him he listened and understood what was being said. Bichiwung understood that the white people were preaching to him and giving him God's message and he also realized that God gave the parson good strength to give to everyone else. Yet when the white men talked to his family in England

Figure 1. The Upper Mazaruni District. Approximate distribution of Akawaio villages in the 1950s.

Bichiwung heard him say that he would like to fool the Makusi he had brought home with him and he was not going to show him God immediately and let him take God's Word. They therefore hid God's Word from Bichiwung.

Eventually, the white people told Bichiwung that they wanted

to give him some water and 'he got a good thing from God' for
he was baptized with water. After his baptism the white people
left Bichiwung alone while they went off to other villages. Before
going, they told him that he must stay in the one place and look
after the house and the great wealth which was in it and go no-
where else. Left on his own Bichiwung felt sad and lonely. He
thought, and he wondered why he had been told to stay in one
place. It was at this time that 'he saw God and got Hallelujah'.

He began to think about all he had been told and he wanted to
see God for himself to find out for sure that the white man had
told him the truth. The white people had shown him a trail to
God and he went off that way on his own. He met God. When
Bichiwung met God he wanted to get into heaven but God said
that he could not go in and He asked Bichiwung why he had
come. When Bichiwung said that he wanted to make sure that he
was being told the truth by the white man God let him into
heaven and showed him round the place. God spoke to him and
said that the white people were deceiving him and that it was
Hallelujah which was good. So Bichiwung got Hallelujah from
God then, and God also gave him a bottle of white medicine and
words and songs and also a piece of paper which was the Indian
Bible. These things Bichiwung was told to lock in his canister
and only to take out on his return to his homeland. Bichiwung
liked heaven and wanted to stay there but God said that he could
not stay because he had not yet died. God told him to go back
the way he had come, to continue guarding the white parson's
things and then to return home to help his family and to teach
Hallelujah.

Bichiwung returned to the parson's house taking the things
that God had given him and remembering what God had told
him about the white man's deceitful teaching and about Hallelujah being good. 'Through that he left off what the white man had
told him and he stopped reading the book. Instead, he took Hallelujah, which he had got *on his own,* from God.'

Bichiwung returned with Hallelujah from England. He also
returned with much wealth—a gun and several canisters full of
things. When he was back in Georgetown he sent a message to
his Makusi friends and relatives, asking them to come and fetch
all his new possessions and to carry them to his home in the far
interior. He also told them to come bringing tame parrots, bas-

kets and various articles which they could sell in Georgetown as curios and so earn money there to buy trade goods. This they did and obtained much wealth and Bichiwung returned home with them to the Kanuku Mountains with all his goods.

When he had returned to his wife and family Bichiwung began to tell people how he had got Hallelujah and he started teaching it to them. He opened his canister and produced the Indian Bible which God had given him. At first, however, he taught only his family. He told his wife not to work or go to the gardens on the Sabbath. She, wanting to get food for her family, would not listen to him or believe him and went to the garden as usual. While she was away Bichiwung locked the door of his house and went to sleep and his spirit went to God again while he slept. When his spirit was in heaven Hallelujah became apparent to him. His wife, returning from her gardens with food, found the door of the house fastened. She called on her husband to open the door but he was asleep and his spirit was away so that he could not. Eventually, he woke up and let her in. His daughter was inside the house with him on several such occasions, for Bichiwung was teaching her about Hallelujah and they both prayed together.

Because of these strange occurrences Bichiwung's wife became suspicious of the relationship between father and daughter and accused him of interfering with her. Bichiwung denied the allegations of incest and told his wife how he had got God and how they had slept in the house in order to go to heaven. His wife became converted to Hallelujah too, and also went about preaching.

Soon the Makusi people who heard Bichiwung and his family preaching wanted to get Hallelujah from them. Some people thought he was telling lies but many people believed them. Amongst these were Bichiwung's helpers (*baidoludong*), called Plegoman, Enewali, Pratalu, Wakowyamu, and Jesik. Those who believed in Hallelujah prayed continually until they got the right words from God.

The fame of Bichiwung and Hallelujah spread. People came from all parts to visit the Makusi, to hear Bichiwung preach and to get Hallelujah from him, 'for he was getting good Hallelujah.'

Bichiwung's gardens had plenty of cassava, plantains, bananas and all the garden produce and what with this and his knowledge

of Hallelujah bad people became jealous of him. *Edodo*[3] attacked
him when he was returning from his garden one day. He died but
his wife took the medicine he had received from God when he
first went to heaven and she rubbed him with it, so that he came
back to life again. A second time *edodo* killed him and cut him
into two or three pieces. His wife gathered the pieces together and
smeared the medicine on him and he again came back to life. A
third time Bichiwung was killed and his attackers cut him up into
small pieces and scattered them. Because of this some of the
parts were lost. His relatives could not put Bichiwung together
again so that the medicine was useless.

So Bichiwung died and went to live in heaven. His helpers
carried on his work but the original good Hallelujah words were
lost. The people Bichiwung had danced with kept Hallelujah but
began to forget what he had taught them and they started singing
tugoik and *palishara,* the old traditional songs and dances, getting
them and Hallelujah mixed up.

Then Abel, the founder of Akawaio Hallelujah, came and
found the right words and gave people good Hallelujah.

This is the main outline of the story of Bichiwung and of the
origins of Makusi Hallelujah. There are many points arising out
of it and also out of the elaborations which some of the other
versions have but which I have not yet quoted. These I now propose to consider for they help us to understand what actually
happened, what the nature of the Christian influence was which
gave rise to Hallelujah, and what the Akawaio to-day think about
these events.

THE LOCATION OF BICHIWUNG'S PARSON

As I have already described, it became the custom from the mid-
nineteenth century onwards for small parties of Indians from the
interior tribes to visit the Christian missions on the middle and
lower reaches of the main rivers of British Guiana. There they
stayed, often for some months at a time, to work and earn money
and also to hear what the missionaries were teaching and perhaps
to attend their schools. A few settled permanently near the mis-

[3] *Edodo* is the Akawaio word for *kanaima* (the better-known Makusi
and Arekuna equivalent) which refers to a secret killer or sorcerer.

sions but the majority from the interior returned to the main body of their tribe.

The first part of the story relates how Bichiwung, in the manner of many of the Makusi after the failure of Youd's mission at Pirara and before the foundation of Makusi missions in the first decade of the present century, went with companions to work in or near the coastal belt and attended and worked at a mission there. Enquiries relating to the exact place of the mission do not give much additional information. One account vaguely says that he was taken far from his own country, another that he went to Georgetown, yet a third, that the parson was somewhere 'behind' Georgetown.

Although I was at first highly sceptical of the assertion that Bichiwung went to England with an English parson, several details in the Hallelujah tradition as well as the frequent assertions as to its truth, have caused me finally to accept it as being true. 'Bichiwung went to England side with some white men and he stayed there a long time,' was one version. 'A white man carried him to England, so he got Hallelujah from England' was another. There would be nothing intrinsically strange in the fact that an English missionary should have decided to take one of his mission Indians back with him to England for a time. American Indians have been taken to Europe from time to time ever since the first occasion, when Columbus paraded a party of them before the Court of Spain after his first voyage of discovery in 1498. Sir Walter Raleigh was attended by two Guiana Indians during thirteen years in the Tower. Nearer to the time of the beginnings of Hallelujah, Robert Schomburgk took a Makusi, a Paravilhano, and a Warrau with him to London for a nine-month stay. Clad in native costume they delighted visitors to an Exhibition in 1839 by shooting with bows and arrows and blow-pipes up and down the hall.

The truth of present-day Akawaio assertions appears to be confirmed in the words of several of the Hallelujah chants which the Akawaio sing. One of these goes as follows:

Engiland,	Engiland	tawina	u	maimugong	u	yebu
England,	England	side	my	words		come

U	maimugong,	sochi,	bazigo.
My	words,	church,	sisters.

Engiland,	Engiland	tawina	Aleluya	yebu
England,	England	side	Hallelujah	comes

Aleluya	sochi,	bazigo.
Hallelujah	church,	sisters.

This might be translated:

My words come from England,
My church words, O Sisters.
Hallelujah comes from England,
Hallelujah Church, O Sisters.

The following Hallelujah chant is also sung:

Engiland	tawina	u	maimukong,	Papa
England	side	my	words,	Grandfather (i.e. God)

Engiland	tawina	Aleluya,	Papa
England	side	Hallelujah,	God

Engiland	tawina	u	yebu,	Papa
England	side	I	come,	God.

Translation:

My words are from England, O God,
Hallelujah is from England, O God,
I come from England, O God.

Finally, the fact of Bichiwung's journey to England appears to be confirmed in a chant sung by the Akawaio to-day but which is said by them to be an Hallelujah song obtained from the Makusi and to have been one belonging to Bichiwung himself.

Inungelan	göbödöbong	Gadö,
Earth	Maker	God,

u yönöbök mang,
   is coming,

Uraianda	göbödöbong	Gadö,
Mist	Maker	God,

u yönöbök mang.
   is coming.

Translation:

God Who made the earth is coming,
God Who made the mist is coming.

Uraianda is a Makusi word and not an Akawaio word, said my informants;[4] it means 'a sort of cloud which comes low down from the sky and is seen on approach to England'. *Uraianda* in this song undoubtedly refers to a thick sea mist or fog which Bichiwung saw towards the end of his voyage.

According to other accounts of Bichiwung's adventures, 'when Bichiwung went to England the skies came down to the sea and Akawaio call this *kak bragon*'[5] (literally, 'sky base' and therefore 'horizon'), 'and there was like a door and the steamer went through this' (presumably the narrow harbour entrance). 'The parson used to live there, beyond the *kak bragon,* the horizon, and he used to teach Bichiwung who began to understand English.'

There is therefore, little doubt that Bichiwung was taken to England. All accounts imply that he alone was taken, except one which mentions a Makusi companion. More difficult is the problem of whether the clergyman in question was Roman Catholic, Anglican, or of some Protestant sect. Akawaio do not usually bother to distinguish between the various Christian sects in their speech, even to-day when they have had direct and practical experience of several in their own territory. They use the English words 'priest' and 'parson' or 'pastor' quite indiscriminately. Certainly years ago, when much of the Christian influence was short-lived and of an indirect nature, they were less likely to have taken into account, or even to have realized, any significant differences. Since the great majority of the missions in the nineteenth century which the Carib-speaking tribes of British Guiana were likely to attend were Anglican it is not unreasonable to suppose that Bichiwung's parson, like the majority of others, was an Anglican. Only one fact might possibly suggest otherwise, and that is

[4] *Uraianda* is a word also used by the Taulebang and Arekuna. A thick mist is frequent in the valleys of the Gran Sabana and at the foot of the mountains during early mornings and late evenings. The Indians, living in their settlements on high land, see this about them frequently and call it *uraianda*. The forest Indians, like the Akawaio, rarely have an extensive enough view over the forest and mountains to look at a sea of mist. In the forest highlands it takes the form of a succession of clouds suspended over the trees or hovering at the base of a mountain. Sometimes it is like a light, white ground mist, rising up from the forest like smoke from a fire. The Akawaio use the word *kaburök* (cloud) to describe it.

[5] *Bragon* is also used in the phrase *wuk bragon,* i.e. 'mountain foot' and *yei bragon*, 'tree foot'. Since the Akawaio word for the foot of a person or animal is *ta*, this is not a literal translation. Probably the nearest English equivalent is 'base'.

the use of the words 'Mama Mary' at the end of some of the Hallelujah prayers. However, a knowledge of the Mother of Christ, which is confined entirely to the fact of her kinship relationship to Him, could also come from the Biblical teaching of the Anglican clergy, or it might perhaps have been an effect of Roman Catholic influence derived from the distant missions on the Brazilian and Venezuelan side of the Savannah. Although Hallelujah undoubtedly owes its origin and the mainstream of its inspiration to the British missions it would be unreasonable to eliminate the probability that more than one source of information influenced and formed it during the course of its establishment.

THE NATURE OF BICHIWUNG'S REVELATION

Bichiwung was taken to England and while staying with the missionary and his relatives he learnt more English and was given more Christian teaching. We might guess, from the tenor of the several versions of the story related by Akawaio, that the clergyman had his doubts about whether Bichiwung was ready to become a full member of the church. The clergyman confided in his relatives and Bichiwung apparently overheard and misinterpreted the conversation concerning his unsuitability for immediate confirmation or baptism into the church. He certainly became dissatisfied with the teaching and suspected that the white people were deceiving him by not giving him the 'strength' which they had received from God and by not enabling him to 'see God' and take God's Words immediately and for himself. 'God gave the parson good strength to give to everyone else. They hid it from Bichiwung,' it is related. Another version says, 'He was told that he could see God. He looked for God but could not find Him,' suggesting that Bichiwung took the clergyman's words to mean that he would be able to meet God and talk to Him, much in the same way that a shaman is said to meet spirits and talk with them during his seances. When he failed to achieve this direct and personal contact Bichiwung suspected that he was being 'fooled'. Nevertheless, he was eventually baptized. One account says that he was afraid to go in the church but that eventually he was baptized with boiling water; in another, there is reference to oil and being baptized in boiling oil.

Of Bichiwung's first revelation and of his visit to heaven the fullest account is from King George (formerly of Kataima, now of Jawalla village), and he said as follows: 'One day Bichiwung asked how he could find God. A path was pointed out to him and he was told that if he went along it he would meet God. When he was left to guard the parson's house he took this trail and he met God.' Another, similar, version of the story, from King George of Chinawieng, is that 'Bichiwung asked some people where he would find God and a trail was pointed out to him leading to a small hill. He went up the hill and prayed and his spirit went to heaven, following three boys. The three boys got through the door of heaven but Bichiwung could only get half way through. He asked God, whom he saw, to let him in but God said that he could not go in because of his sins.' The less colourful, but perhaps more authoritative accounts, simply say that after baptism 'Bichiwung found God' or, 'Bichiwung went up somewhere to God.' The most comprehensible one of all is 'He slept and his spirit went to heaven to find God'.

According to all versions it is plain that Bichiwung definitely believed that there was a path to God and that if the white people were telling him truly he could reach God and heaven by following it. It is equally plain that this path to God was not merely that of right conduct and Christian living followed over a lifetime, as a missionary might try to teach, using figurative language for the purpose. To Bichiwung's way of thinking it was a very real trail which would lead him—his spirit—in a dream or in prayer to heaven, just in the same way as a path led him from one village to the next. In other words, he took his teacher's words more concretely than they had been intended and understood the path to be a reality, having a specific direction, and not a symbolic path of moral conduct sustained by Christian faith. Bichiwung's 'way to God' was the shaman's way and this is further suggested by the fact that in two of the accounts his spirit is escorted or propelled there by spirit guides. In one instance he followed three boys, whose spirits were entering heaven, presumably after death. In a second instance it is said that the Queen's spirit sent Bichiwung to heaven.[6]

[6] This refers to Queen Victoria, who may be said to have sent the missionary concerned to show the Amerindians the path to heaven and the way to God.

As the present-day Leader of Akawaio Hallelujah said, 'Bichi-wung saw God exactly.' There is some interesting information given by the Akawaio concerning this meeting. 'When Bichiwung got to heaven God said, "What do you want?" Bichiwung said he had come to see Him and he wanted to be let in. God let him in and Bichiwung saw a wonderful garden and he wanted to go there, but God said no, he must go back the way he had come and he must not stay.' Some versions state that God would not let Bichiwung into heaven at all because of his sins or because he had not yet died; in one version, which I have already quoted, he could only get half way through the door of heaven!

In spite of this Bichiwung obtained some wonderful things from God and he was taught about Hallelujah. One of the main reasons why Bichiwung was anxious to see God was to find out if all that the white people had told him was true, so when God asked him what he wanted Bichiwung told God what the parson had said and asked whether he had been told truly. According to Jawalla King George's version (and I should perhaps remark that this King George has had considerable experience outside the Akawaio tribal territory and has become increasingly ambitious and also anti-foreigner), 'God said that He had not Himself told the priest these things he was teaching. The English Bible was left a long time ago and Christ came a long time ago; it was now out of date. The Indian Bible was to be the guidance for Edam, he was not to show it to the priest or anyone and not use it until he returned home. He was to keep it in his canister.'[7] The other versions, putting it less strongly, merely maintain that the white people were 'fooling' Bichiwung and God gave Bichiwung a letter or piece of paper[8] which was to be the Indian Bible. One version has it that Bichiwung wrote down in a book what God told him, but the general opinion is that he was given the Bible. 'God gave Bichiwung a small bottle of white medicine, or oil, and this was

[7] The canister is a tin box, trunk, or suitcase obtained through trade. It is highly valued by Akawaio as the container of all their most valuable goods which they often wish to conceal from others.

[8] This is the *kaleda* (also pronounced *kareda, kaleta,* and *kareta;* sometimes the 'k' becomes a 'g' sound). It is probably derived from the Spanish word *carta,* meaning 'letter', since the Amerindians had no knowledge of writing or paper before the Conquest. The Akawaio use the word *kaleda* to mean book, letter, or paper, or anything which is written on or which has the form of writing.

wrapped in paper—the Indian Bible! God also gave him some bananas and cassava[9] to plant and these garden things he took back with him and planted in his garden, so he got plenty of food.' Bichiwung also 'got Hallelujah from God then' and was given the commission of preaching to other Indians.

'When Bichiwung was speaking to God he saw his wife and children,' said Lydia of Chinawieng. 'After he saw his wife and children he wanted to go to them; God said he mustn't go that way to his wife and children, otherwise he would fall down dead. He wanted to go back to them without passing over the sea but God said he must go back the same way that he had come. Then Bichiwung said that he had no money so God told him to borrow from Queen.'

According to all my informants Bichiwung would have liked to stay in heaven, but God would not allow him. Instead, He told the Makusi to return to the parson's house and to continue guarding all the wealth and boxes of money which were inside, as the white man told him to do. However, before Bichiwung left God he was told to help his family and to get money and buy things. God told Bichiwung exactly how to obtain wealth; He said that the goods bought should not be paid for in money but in blow-pipes, baskets, and the various Indian manufactured goods which his friends and relatives should be told to bring to Georgetown to sell on Bichiwung's return there.

Whether Bichiwung left the parson, who was said to have been treating him badly, and lived alone for a time before returning home, as Lydia of Chinawieng stated, or whether he returned with the parson is not certain. He is certainly said to have come back 'having got much wealth', to have been given two canisters full of things (some say four canisters), and a gun and various other goods which he had earned. At this point the story-teller, usually with great relish, goes into considerable detail concerning the wealth which Bichiwung attained and has to be prompted to go on if the story is not to lapse into a list of the goods and a detailed discussion of the merits of each item.

Once in Georgetown Bichiwung's friends were summoned to bring their possessions to exchange for trade goods and to take him and his belongings back to the Rupununi. In the Kanuku

[9] The bitter cassava, *manihot utilissima,* is made into cassava bread which is the staple food of these tribes.

Mountains the returned traveller settled with his family again. Then he began to preach. After an initial misunderstanding with his wife, owing to his insistence on a restful Sabbath and his rather suspicious behaviour with their daughter, he converted his family to Hallelujah and they went about preaching of Hallelujah and of all that Bichiwung had seen in heaven and that God had told him. In dreams and while he was praying Bichiwung's spirit went to heaven and he saw God again. 'The Hallelujah religion became apparent to him.' He unlocked his canister and produced the book from God—some paper which, it is said, got lost soon after his return. He taught the words and songs he had got from God.

Bichiwung's preaching became famous and although some people continued to disbelieve him he obtained a number of disciples (*baidoludong*, lit. 'nephews', 'sons-in-law', 'helpers'). People from other tribes even began to come and hear him and to pay him in return for teaching them Hallelujah words and songs. Meanwhile, the family gardens were large and flourishing and in some of the accounts the fruits which Bichiwung received from heaven and the miraculous gardens which he came to possess are described. During one of his periodic spirit visits to see God he received one seed of every garden product, one banana, one plantain, one huge calabash, and so forth. He planted these in his garden and when they were grown his wife made drink and everyone came and there was enough drink made from the fruit of the one banana tree, served in the immense calabash, to last for four days. Bichiwung told his wife to cut the banana and plantain trees right at the bottom so that they would grow again and bear fruit and every time they grew these two miraculous trees bore their huge fruit.[10]

It is difficult to explain for certain why this emphasis is placed on Bichiwung's gardens. Perhaps his miraculous garden was merely a particularly fertile one planted with good plants which he might have brought back from the coast of British Guiana. Amerindians are always quick to seize on any good strain and to bring back cuttings and roots obtained during their travels. His renown as a preacher would have enabled him to attach to himself a large following of relatives, friends, and helpers and these, automatically, would have made their gardens with his and helped to enlarge his

[10] Banana and plantain trees are always cut off at the base when all the fruit has been taken. This allows the old tree to sprout again and bear a new crop of fruit.

own. There is too, the possibility that the miracles of Our Lord had been related to some of the Makusi, such as the miracle of the loaves and fishes or the turning of the water into wine, and their imagination may have been caught by these to the extent of inspiring a local version concerning Bichiwung and his banana wine.

Whatever the origin of this particular point, all accounts are agreed on the many drinking sprees and feasts which Bichiwung gave, so that his hospitality, bounty, and wealth began to be linked up with his religious zeal for Hallelujah.

Earlier on I mentioned the fact that in these stories of the origin of Makusi Hallelujah there appears to have been an accumulation of myth. Some of the versions are straightforward, historical accounts; others have fanciful details embroidered into them. One story which is related of this initial period of Hallelujah, shows very clearly the type of lore which frequently becomes attached to the more straightforward account. It was related by the son of Danny of the Kamarang River, who had heard it from his father. 'One of Bichiwung's followers, known as Plega or Plegoman, was a Hallelujah prophet who used to pray until he got God's Word. He had plenty of chigoes[11] in his feet so perhaps God was sorry for him. People would not believe him and his words about Hallelujah so he prayed alone. Suddenly Plegoman started to fly away. His spirit went away to heaven and his body was left. It became rotten and turned into leaves, *arosa* leaves, which is why Danny won't eat *arosa*.'[12]

Bichiwung's death is also the subject of some imaginative detail. Though one account says soberly that 'some Makusi killed him with a knife' other versions describe at length the efforts made by sorcerers (*edodo*) to kill him and the use of the medicine from heaven which at first thwarted their efforts. Bichiwung's resurrection, with the aid of the heavenly medicine, on two (sometimes three) occasions, is interesting but his final death through *edodo* is a typically Amerindian one. Scarcely anyone, according to

[11] The chigoe is a small species of flea (*pulex penetrans*) which usually burrows under the skin and toe nails and there lays its eggs and causes a violent itching. It and the eggs are easily removed with a pin.

[12] *Arosa* usually refers to deer calaloo (*phytolacca icosandra*). The leaves are boiled and eaten, when they look and taste like spinach. Calaloo is not planted in the gardens but seeds are carried there by the birds. These take root in the mature gardens and the women collect the leaves during their weekly harvesting and give the berries to pet toucans and parrots.

Akawaio beliefs, dies from a natural cause such as old age; the great majority are always said to have died from *edodo,* the secret killer or sorcerer. The mainspring of sorcery is jealousy and envy of other people's possessions and achievements as well as a desire for revenge for an active wrong. It is no wonder then, according to Amerindian conceptions, Bichiwung's goodness and material wealth in food and his following as a 'big man' caused him to be the object of envy and malice and *edodo* tried to kill him. According to some accounts the sorcerers (*edodo*) ambushed Bichiwung on his way from his garden to his home and chopped him up. This happened several times but each time he was put together again and saved by the medicine which was an oil.[13] According to Austin of Chinawieng the sorcerers once drowned Bichiwung when he went to the waterside by going behind him and pushing him into the river and holding him under. However, he recovered when his wife rubbed the oil on him. 'Then', said Austin, 'they tried to kill him in another way: they chopped him up and threw him in the water in pieces, so his wife couldn't find his body to rub the oil on him. Before he died he should have shared this oil so that people here should have got it.'

However it may have occurred Bichiwung eventually died. After his death his disciples (*baidoludong*) and others continued preaching Hallelujah but much was lost and, as the Akawaio say, no one has been able to have contact with God in quite the same direct way since.

II AKAWAIO HALLELUJAH: THE STORY OF
ABEL OF AMOKOKUPAI

Hallelujah spread not only among the Makusi but also among the neighbouring Carib-speaking tribes, the Patamona, Arekuna, and Akawaio. All these tribes are said by the Akawaio to have Hal-

---

[13] *Kalaböl* (*karaböl, kalapöl,* or *karapöl*) is the word used to describe this medicine. It is a word referring specifically to oil made from the seeds of the crabnut tree (*Carapa guianensis*), but it can also be used as a general term for oily substances. The process of chopping up someone seems to have a fascination of its own, for it is related that there was a Makusi shaman called Sonny who, when chopped up, used to put himself together again! It is probable that, as in Bichiwung's case, this process is conceived to be entirely spiritual, as are so many of the shaman's activities, and is not done visibly and in the flesh.

lelujah still, the same as themselves. In fact, they are all very much subject to mission teaching now, so that it is uncertain how much of the Hallelujah religion continues amongst them and whether further Christian teaching has not turned it into more or less orthodox Christian practice.

The way in which Hallelujah came to the Akawaio tribe is probably typical of its advent in other Carib-speaking tribes, spreading from its Makusi source. The story runs thus: After Hallelujah became established among the Makusi and while Bichiwung and his followers were preaching, visitors from the Kwatin River Group[14] of the Akawaio went and heard about Hallelujah from them. They made at least two visits. Aibilibing of Amokokupai relates that 'The first time people from the Kwatin went to get Hallelujah they couldn't get it. They returned. Then they thought how to pay for Hallelujah so that they could catch it. They offered fish hooks, knives, axes, and various things to pay Bichiwung in order to get Hallelujah. They were not charged, they paid of their own free will. Through that they got Hallelujah.'[15] The names of the Kwatin people who first learnt Hallelujah songs and words from the Makusi are still remembered; they included Agaruchimang (or Akaluchimang), Engimang, Johnging (probably the Akawaio version of the English name 'Johnson'), and a woman called A'mok (or Yamok). These were listed by more than one informant but other names, remembered by individuals only, are, Wakowyaming, Agono, Agonowai (who may be the same as Agono), Kurabid, and Abonai.

[14] These are Akawaio living in the neighbourhood of the Kwatin River, which is the name given to the upper reaches of the Cotinga River, flowing South into the Rio Branco and eventually into the Amazon. These Akawaio live on Brazilian territory, a few miles only from the edge of the Gran Sabana. They are somewhat cut off from the rest of the tribe owing to the mountain range, the watershed of the Essequibo and Amazon river systems, which divides British Guiana from Brazil. Nevertheless, the Kwatin Akawaio have intermarried with other Akawaio and have an especially close relationship with the Ataro River Group and, to a lesser degree, the Kukui River Group beyond.

[15] This was a broad hint to the author. To charge for Hallelujah information is directly contrary to the teaching of Abel which was that everyone should be taught Hallelujah if they came to hear it. The Amokokupai people, knowing that they could not rightly charge, wanted to intimate that they were able to receive gifts and, in fact, expected them. It is the custom to give something for any skill or knowledge learnt from another unless the teacher is a close relative, returning a favour, wants to create an obligation, or is particularly generous.

The story of Hallelujah told by Bichiwung and including his words and songs, was brought back to the Kwatin River Group of the Akawaio and from thence it spread to the rest of the tribe. The story of its establishment centres on a man called 'Abel', who lived at Amokokupai in the Kukui River Group area. His Akawaio names were two, Wetnapa (Etnapa) and Uraiak; but although these are occasionally recalled in Hallelujah songs, nearly always he is called by the English name of Abel which he eventually adopted. It is pronounced variously as 'Apel', 'Abelu', or 'Apelu'. Abel is the great prophet and founder of Akawaio Hallelujah. He has the same position among the Akawaio that Bichiwung holds among the Makusi; the only real difference between the two is that Bichiwung was the very first to get Hallelujah from God and was therefore the original source of inspiration.

The way in which Abel became converted to Hallelujah was best told by Kwiabong of Amokokupai who, when he was a very young man, knew Abel and had heard him preach; but the account which I give is from a number of informants, all of whom agreed on the chief details of the origins of Hallelujah but whose information, taken as a whole, makes a more complete version than any single story.

It is related that some of the Kwatin people who had learnt Hallelujah from the Makusi left their native river area, in Brazil, and settled on a savannah called 'Pötökwai' and built a church there. Pötökwai savannah is in fact situated between Amokokupai landing (called Pilipai) on the Kukui River and Amokokupai village itself which is in the midst of the forest, about two and a half hours' walk inland from the river bank. Why these Kwatin people settled there no one seems to know now but Kwiabong said that at Pötökwai they drank too much *cassiri*[16] and quarrelled and fought each other, so perhaps quarrelling in the Kwatin also caused the initial split and kinship ties with the Kukui people led some of them to select Pötökwai as their new home.[17]

---

[16] *Cassiri* is a fermented drink made of bitter cassava pulp and purple potatoes boiled together for several hours. It is the best known of present-day Amerindian drinks.

[17] Kwatin and Ataro people still go and stay with relatives in the Kukui area. A religious sect from the U.S.A. called Pilgrim Holiness has just set up a mission school at Pilipai. The Ataro and Kwatin families who send some of their children to school there have built a large shelter on Pötökwai savannah, at the back of Pilipai, in which they can stay when on visits. It

Amokokupai, which is the religious centre of the Hallelujah Akawaio to-day, was apparently in existence before Abel, for his father and grandfather had lived there. In those early days it was called Woita, which was the name of the hill on which the houses were perched. The story is told that Abel's grandfather[18] attended a spree and got very drunk. He went to the foot of the hill to bathe in the small creek there. Being in a drunken stupor he fell into the water and was drowned. This incident gave the place a new name, Amoko-kupai, meaning the bend in the stream which makes a pool or inlet (*kupai*)[19] of the old man (*amoko*). 'Old Man's Inlet' or Amokokupai, became Abel's elder brother's place and the entire family lived there. It was, therefore, only a family settlement before it became the centre of Hallelujah and turned into a large village occupied by many families.

Abel was a shaman and, as my informants said, used to roam the mountains and consult the spirits. His evil deeds are stressed, for before Hallelujah affected him he is said to have been wicked, a sorcerer (*edodo*), and had killed many people. He went as a visitor to the neighbouring church of the Kwatin people at Pötökwai and there he first heard about Hallelujah. At the beginning he laughed at the new religion as related by the travellers returned from Makusi country, but he kept thinking about it. Then he tried praying to God and he tried to see God. He found that he was unable to see God among the mountains[20] or on his spirit flights during his seances, but only when he prayed did he see Him, so he gave up shamanism. Also he gave up his wicked ways and became a good man. He found that he could approach nearer to God when he prayed so he prayed and thought all the

---

is typical that they should have chosen the site with which their river groups had a past association and that they have also kept themselves aloof from the houses of the Kukui River residents. Although the trail to the Ataro and on to the Kwatin branches off at Pötökwai it would have been more convenient for fishing and water supplies if they had built with the Kukui families in the mission village itself.

18 He may not have been a real grandfather, or even Abel's grandfather's brother who would be a classificatory grandfather. The term *tamogoli* sometimes means a male ancestor of long ago.

19 *Köpai* (variously pronounced *kupai, kubai, köbai, gubai, gupai*, etc.) is a bend in a river or stream which makes a pool. The suffix seems to be a compound of *kupö* or *gupö* meaning a pool, and *pai* or *bai*, a suffix meaning place.

20 The spirits which the shaman meets and interrogates are often thought to gather together on the mountain tops, or to live there.

time, and when he went hunting or to his garden he prayed within himself.

Abel built a church at Amokokupai at God's command, the first Hallelujah church there, and he prayed for long periods in it. The Pötökwai church was meanwhile under the leadership of a Kamarang Akawaio called 'Christ' who had married a Kukui woman and was residing in her home settlement in accordance with the custom of matrilocality. There was probably some rivalry between the Pötökwai and Amokokupai churches for some people say that Christ was an evil man who became good like Abel and others say that he was always bad and could not change. After Christ's death the Pötökwai church and settlement broke up for many people died of sorcery (*edodo*), it is said, and the survivors returned to the Kwatin. The Amokokupai church with Abel as the Leader was left predominant and Abel went around preaching and teaching the other Akawaio, encouraging them to found Hallelujah churches. He taught people from all the river groups of the Akawaio and in this way Hallelujah spread throughout the tribe and even beyond, to the neighbouring tribes such as the Arekuna. As with the story of Bichiwung there are certain points which require comment and which can be amplified from the numerous different sources of information.

HALLELUJAH AND THE KWATIN PEOPLE

The information concerning Hallelujah activities in the Kwatin River Group and among the Pötökwai people from the Kwatin was obtained mainly from Amokokupai (Kukui River Group) and U'Wi (Ataro River Group) village settlements. The Mazaruni people sometimes state that Abel went to Makusi country and brought back Hallelujah from Bichiwung, or that he heard about Hallelujah somehow, had divine revelations in a dream and so founded the new Akawaio religion. However, the detailed information concerning the Pötökwai church, the recollection of the names of some of those Kwatin Akawaio who visited the Makusi, together with the assertion, from my most authoritative informants, that 'Abel never met Bichiwung', make it certain that the account which I have presented is the correct one.

Although the initial inspiration and the mainstream of information on Hallelujah came from the Makusi through the Kwatin, it is also certain that this was not the only route. At Chinawieng village (Mazaruni River Group) on the Ayanganna plateau[21] a number of Makusi Hallelujah songs are still sung by King George, who learnt them from his mother who had in turn obtained them from her parents. They are said to have been brought to the village by Makusi, before Abel brought Hallelujah to Chinawieng, and to have been learnt by an Akawaio there called Cragik. The source of Akawaio Hallelujah is therefore Makusi but the knowledge of the new cult seems to have travelled northwards by more than one route.

Whether my informants knew about the Kwatin and Chinawieng people or not they all agreed on one point, that Abel was the man who was the real founder of Hallelujah and that present-day Akawaio Hallelujah is derived directly from his teaching. It is quite likely that in a generation's time the knowledge of the Pötökwai people will have been lost; already the Chinawieng people are hazy about their former importation of Hallelujah from the Makusi. Abel, then, will stand alone as the original founder. He is the central figure and the reason for this will be plain when we come to examine the process of the spread of Hallelujah and Abel's influence, from Amokokupai to the rest of the Akawaio.

ABEL'S REVELATIONS

The most important point concerning the revelations of Abel is that, like those of Bichiwung, they are said to have occurred while the spirit (*akwalu*) was wandering apart from the body. Sometimes the spirit flight took place while Abel was asleep, sometimes while he was praying fervently. The initial revelations, when Abel first experienced Hallelujah and visited heaven, seem all to have been during sleep. 'A man had a dream—his spirit went up to heaven,' asserted Danny of the Kamarang River Group referring to Abel. The present-day Prophet Leader of Hallelujah explained it thus: 'Abel got Hallelujah from Bichiwung. He didn't get it directly from him but he used to dream and his spirit went

[21] Chinawieng is at the beginning of a trail leading from Akawaio territory to Patamona territory in the southern Pakaraima Mountains. This is also one of the routes to the Makusi tribe beyond the Patamona. Probably the Chinawieng people also heard about Hallelujah from the Makusi via the Patamona.

to heaven; then he used to wake up and tell people they must believe because it was good, so he used to get Hallelujah exactly.'
According to one old woman, whose lifetime coincides with the
origins and establishment of Akawaio Hallelujah, 'Abel slept six
days, then he got Hallelujah from God. When he awoke he said
to his people that he was bringing *kapong ewang'* (lit. 'Akawaio
heart spirit').[22] 'God spoke many things to Abel when he was
asleep and when Abel woke up he said what God had told him.
. . . When Abel died, or nearly so, for he slept for almost a week,
his wife and children were crying. They blocked up the path to
heaven, which is like a big sea, so that he couldn't get past it. He
said to them on waking up that *kapong* (i.e. Akawaio), mustn't
cry when people die, otherwise the deceased can't get to heaven.
The mourner must just pray; after the body is put in the grave people can cry, but not before.'

Thus the first prophet of Akawaio Hallelujah owed his knowledge to spirit experiences during dreams and spirit flights during
prayer, just as the first prophet of the Makusi and the originator
of Hallelujah did. Let us now consider the nature of some of
Abel's spirit flights as they are related by present-day Akawaio.
According to King George of Jawalla, 'Abel tried to get God. He
prayed and thought and sought for God but could not find Him.
Three times he went in spirit (*akwalu*) to heaven but he met only
Indians. The first time he met a brother-in-law killed by sorcery
(*edodo*). Eventually, he got to the gates of heaven but the door
was closed. He knocked but could not get in. Then it opened a
little and God said, "What do you want?" Abel said, "I want
You." God said, "No, you come as Indian, you have to wait until
you have died; you have sinned."'

The versions given by Aibilibing of Amokokupai, the present-
day Hallelujah Prophet Leader, is as follows: 'Abel wanted to find
out where Hallelujah came from. He kept dreaming in order to
find it. He wanted to look for it in heaven but couldn't pass because
of the great wind. When he was dreaming he saw animals, howler

---

[22] *Ewang,* or *ewöng,* heart spirit. Each part of the body, particularly where
the pulsation of an artery can be felt, has an *ewang,* a heart spirit. The heart
spirit which is in the heart itself (*ewang töbu* = literally 'heart spirit seed',
or 'stone'), is the sum of all the various heart spirits of the body and is
therefore equivalent to, and in fact is said to be the same as, the *akwalu*
which is the spirit of the entire body.

monkey, jaguar, and others, in the path. When he was dreaming
a second time he found a big sea; he passed this and he found
many nature spirits (*imawali*)[23] with good musical instruments
(*liga*).[24] These nature spirits had their own Hallelujah, but he
didn't bother about that. Then he dreamt again and he saw a river,
Igök,[25] somewhere in England perhaps, but he didn't know where.
Then he saw a big village by Igök. Then he found Noah. Noah
had a big boat and Abel saw many animals in this boat. He dreamt
again, then his spirit (*akwalu*) walked on the trail. Then he saw
one trail which went to the East[26] and one which went to the
West. He followed the eastern trail. Then he climbed a hill and
found many people dancing Hallelujah there and he joined them.
While they were dancing he saw a big gourd come on its own,
without being carried. Everyone drank from it. Before he got some
of the gourd, which came in front of him, it went away. He hadn't
been able to drink because someone was speaking to him. The
gourd moved away to other people on its own volition. Abel
dreamt again that he saw a door open in front of him. He tried to
go in but the door closed in front of him, leaving a small hole. He
tried to push his head in but couldn't pass through. Then he
prayed—while he was still sleeping all this time—and he got his
head through only. He couldn't pass any further on. Then
someone spoke to him but he couldn't see who. Then he was
told by God who was speaking to him that he must pray for the
women. Men can pray by themselves because they know how
to pray properly, but girls don't know anything about praying.
When Abel got to heaven's door and had got his head through it,
he saw all sorts of things. He didn't want to return to earth after
seeing all the nice things there. He cried about all the Headmen

[23] *Imawali* is strictly the name of an order of forest spirits and is known
as the 'Bush Spirit' in translation. All forest, water, mountain and other nature spirits are often referred to in a general way as *imawali*.
[24] *Liga* is strictly speaking a mouth organ but the word is often used in
the sense of 'music from heaven' or 'a musical instrument used in heaven'.
[25] This name is unidentified. The name of a river is the most likely name
that an Akawaio would remember since rivers are the basis of their own
territorial divisions and the highways in their communication system.
[26] East = *wei yenu yebu wina*, lit. 'sun's eye (or sunlight) comes side';
west = *wei yenu utö wina*, lit. 'sun's eye goes side'. It is significant that
he chose to follow the path to the east, to the sunrise, and the way to *akwa*,
which is light and life in the sun's place. (See Butt 1954.)

(*ebuludong*) living on earth, the Chibanioli,[27] Coolie, all the people. He was sorry for them because he had found heaven before them. When he woke up he told his wife to light the fire; everyone was asleep.'[28]

Concerning Abel's dream experiences Austin, Leader (*ebulu*) of Chinawieng, said: '*Akono*[29] from the sky had many things, food and drink. So when you see God you see many things on the way. *Akono* are the people dancing Hallelujah; they have a book and musical instruments. You pass these to go to heaven and you pass other things. Then Abel saw a little drink in a bottle, it was a very little. There were angels (*engelödong*) praying and one angel started giving this drink to everyone and the cup started to move on its own, so Abel said.'

When we come to examine closely the nature of many of these dreams, what Abel saw on his way to heaven and what happened in heaven, we are presented with a glorious mixture of traditional beliefs and items of imperfectly understood Christian teaching. Just as Bichiwung desired to find out if the white people had told him truly, so Abel was possessed of the initial curiosity to find out where Hallelujah really came from. His spirit flights to achieve this are of a shamanistic nature. He encountered on the path many different animals; these are animal spirits which the shaman frequently brings down and questions at his seances. Then he encountered many nature spirits, particularly those of the order of forest spirits called *imawali*. These are the most important of the shaman's spirit contacts, his entire professional training being devoted to one object, that of being able to call on *imawali* to help him in his cures. Characteristically, Abel found *imawali* dancing, drinking, and feasting among the hills and mountains and, just as a shaman does, he joined them in their celebrations. However, whereas the traditional *imawali* spirits would be dancing the old spree dances of *tugoik* and *palishara* these were dancing Hallelujah! Another innovation in his shaman's spirit flight is his meeting

[27] *Chibanioli* is an indianized version of Español, i.e. Spanish. Coolie is the name given by all Amerindians to describe East Indians.

[28] This is a typical remark. At the beginning of a shaman's seance the fires are deliberately extinguished so that there is darkness in the village. At the end of the seance the shaman, whose spirit has returned after its wanderings, customarily tells the families to light the fires inside the house. This is the woman's task.

[29] *Akono*, or *agono*, is the indianized version of 'archangel'.

with Noah and his ark full of animals. Also introduced, according to Austin's version of the dreams, are angels (*engelö*) who were praying and the *akono* who also do not belong to traditional beliefs. The *akono,* situated between God in heaven and the people on earth, had books and musical instruments (namely, mouth organs, or *liga*), and were dancing Hallelujah. They appear to be Archangels who have become indianized in name and occupation.

Even the account of Abel's attempted entry into heaven is reminiscent of a typical shamanistic task. Very often in Akawaio beliefs a sick man's spirit (*akwalu*) is taken by an evil forest spirit (*imawali akwalu*), and locked up in *imawali's* round house among the mountains. To cure his patient and prevent his death, following on permanent loss of spirit, the shaman must travel the path to the house, passing through various spirit regions. On arrival he has to get strength to break through the door of the house and to obtain the captured spirit and restore it to the sick owner. Then, after the seance, the victorious shaman announces to the people that he has in fact brought back the sick person's spirit and that he or she will now get strong and well. According to an account already quoted, when Abel awoke after his spirit flight to seek Hallelujah, 'he said to his people that he was bringing *kapong ewang*,'[30] that is, he had got the heart spirit (*ewang*) of the Akawaio (*kapong*) from God and that he was going to give it to them. Therefore, just as a shaman in his seance customarily gets back a sick person's wandering spirit and in this way restores his or her strength, so Abel, during his dream, got from God in heaven the good spirit which he brought back to increase Akawaio strength. The conceptions of thought in both instances are too close to be unconnected and, as all informants asserted, Abel was a shaman (*piai'-chang*) before he was converted and became an Hallelujah Prophet (*Hallelujah pogenak*).

The Hallelujah doctrines and injunctions, based on what God told Abel during his revelations, form the subject of another paper. Here I merely wish to point out that during his spirit visits to heaven Abel obtained God's Words and also music from heaven. Concerning God's Words: one account states that God told Abel words which he wrote down on a piece of paper. This he put in his canister on waking up, having been told by God not to show

[30] See note 22.

the white people for they would steal it, just as they had stolen the English language! Later, Abel opened his canister and showed it to his followers. Other informants stated that they had never heard that Abel got a book or paper from God. 'Abel had nothing like that; just that he said that when people prayed good they might one day get God's Words and a book from heaven.' Since there is some contradiction here it may have occurred that the story of the Hallelujah Bible of Bichiwung got transferred to the accounts of Abel's wonderful achievements in heaven. There is also the fact that although the Makusi traveller could easily have possessed several pieces of paper and religious tracts it would have been more difficult for Abel to produce even one since he never attended a mission; for dwelling in the Upper Mazaruni District he could have had comparatively little opportunity of acquiring anything of the kind at that period. Nevertheless, other prophets and religious leaders, following in the footsteps of Abel, claimed to have received a heavenly literature even if Abel did not. Kwatin Akawaio say that they have received several letters, pieces of paper with writing on them, from God in recent years. One of these arrived from heaven shortly before my visit in 1957 but they did not wish to show it to me. Such incidents clearly illustrate the great value in Amerindian eyes of paper with words written on it, a value which was no doubt begun and fostered by the habit of the early missionaries, led by W. H. Brett, of sending out illustrated tracts to arouse curiosity in distant tribes and so entice them to the coast missions.

Another important aspect of Abel's revelations relates to the prophecy concerning the coming of white people to Akawaio territory in the Upper Mazaruni District. Here again the similarity to the story of Bichiwung and also the anti-foreign flavour which always seems to be a part of these religious movements cannot be ignored. One version of Abel's revelation, as I have already recounted, states that God told Abel to hide the Indian Bible so that the white people should not steal it, as they had already stolen the English language. This same account continues: 'He had another dream. His spirit was told that if Indians followed Hallelujah always they would have white people as their servants (*baidoludong*). If they did not, they would become the servants of white people. He told people this and also said that priests would come and they must not believe what was said but keep to Hallelujah. And so it has come to pass. Indians have heeded Adventists[31] and are servants of the white man.'

At Amokokupai an enquiry about Abel's teaching similarly resulted in the assertion that he had foretold the coming of white people, teaching them another religion from a book. Abel had enjoined them always to believe Hallelujah and then they would have the white people as servants and have all the things they wanted, guns, cloth, powder and shot, knives, much food, etc. According to yet another version (from Austin of Chinawieng), 'When Abel was sleeping after praying he saw how white people would be coming this side: he knew this through God's spirit. Then he woke up and said that other people, many white people and negroes and others, would come and take over the land. He said that when white people come they would open a store and sell things.'

Abel's death, according to Akawaio accounts of the present day, is not subject to the elaborate details which are recorded for that of Bichiwung, but it is said that he similarly died of sorcery (*edodo*) and was buried at Amokokupai. Sorcerers are said to have attacked him three times; on the first two occasions he came back to life but on the third he was unable to revive. In outline, there is a striking similarity between Abel's death and Bichiwung's but it probably amounts to no more than the fact that every 'big' and important man is liable to sorcery attacks. At first he resists them but eventually the sorcerers are successful, so he dies. The present-day Leaders of villages assert that *edodo* is trying to kill them too, but, since sorcerers are believed to devote most of their attention to important people, to say that they are after oneself is an indirect way of asserting one's own importance. The attention which sorcerers paid to Bichiwung and Abel is a good indication of the status of these two prophets in the eyes of their followers and descendants.

While I was at Amokokupai I asked to see Abel's grave. This request was greeted with some amusement, for the Akawaio have no sentimental feelings for the graves of people who are not close relatives and who, moreover, died a long time ago. The approximate position was indicated; it was overgrown with bush and

---

31 The Seventh Day Adventist sect has two missions up the Kamarang River which is the home river group of Danny, my informant, who has been very much opposed to the missions.

undergrowth so that, in spite of his status as founder of Akawaio
Hallelujah and the supreme prophet of the tribe, no more notice
is taken of his grave than that of any other. He is finished and
gone[32] and there is nothing to mark the earthly remains. Instead,
the Akawaio are concerned with his spirit (*akwalu*) of which
they are constantly singing and which, they believe, is with God
in heaven.

DATING HALLELUJAH

It is impossible to give any date for the origins of Makusi Hallelujah and the main events in its dissemination. On the other hand,
the evidence which is available does enable us to date the origins
of Akawaio Hallelujah approximately.

The kinship charts collected and the memories of present-day
Leaders assist in this task. John Charlie of Kataima, Edmund of
Imbaimadai, Joseph Grant of U'Wi, Amoko of Chinawieng, and
other old people who have died since my first period of research,
stated that they never knew Abel properly since they were but
lads when he died. Kwiabong, the old Prophet Leader at Amokokupai, had known Abel very well and had in fact acquired his
knowledge of Hallelujah directly from him, but being so old and
tired had forgotten much about him. An even more useful piece
of evidence was provided by Mr Forbes[33] of Kurupung, Lower
Mazaruni District, who personally told me that he had been with
the Akawaio in the Upper Mazaruni District on and off since
1908. He remembered that Abel and William (who was to be
Abel's successor as Prophet Leader), used to preach a lot at
Amokokupai and people would flock to hear them. Amokokupai
was then a big place. Forbes, though not sure of the exact date,
thought that Abel died about 1911. This made the village Leaders,
at the time of my research in 1951, between forty-eight and fifty-

[32] Akawaio for 'dead' is *matapu;* the word for 'finished' is *makapu.* The
two are very closely connected and sometimes the similarity of form and
meaning is played upon, much as we talk of something, such as a bottle of
alcohol, as being 'dead'.

[33] Only two Guianese were in prolonged and regular contact with the
Akawaio before the establishment of a Government Station in 1946. One of
these was the coloured diamond seeker, F. W. Kenswil, who wrote a short
pamphlet on the Akawaio entitled *Children of the Silence.* The other was
Mr Forbes who followed a similar occupation and also had a workshop in
which he mended guns for those Akawaio who possessed them.

six years old probably, and the very old men and women, such as Amoko and Kwiabong, anything from about sixty-five onwards, which seemed to me about right as far as appearance and descendants could tell.

Abel himself, according to all accounts, lived to a ripe old age. His youngest daughter, who was but a small child at the time of his death, is still alive and though very active is an oldish woman. Her son, Abel's grandson, is a young man of about twenty-eight. Abel probably lived to about the age of seventy-five (though the way in which Akawaio stress his advanced age suggests about eighty-five or ninety), and was probably born about 1836.

As there is no information concerning the time of life at which Bichiwung died it is practically impossible to do more than guess whether he was older or younger than Abel, or about the same age. If he was older and born in the eighteen-twenties he may have obtained a slight knowledge of Christianity from the Rev. Thomas Youd himself, who was at Pirara in 1838. Attempts were certainly made among the Makusi to follow Youd's teaching with their own native interpretation of Christianity, for we have on record a significant statement made by the botanist C. A. Lloyd in 1895. 'Mr Youd died at sea on his way to England, from poisoning,[34] and the Indians assert that the man (a Macoushi) who poisoned him was subsequently struck dead by lightning while in the church one Sunday imitating a parson preaching.' Presumably therefore, it was in this atmosphere of deliberate imitation and the seeking for religious experience after Youd's departure that Bichiwung's own ideas were fostered. Later, Bichiwung himself attended one of the coast missions which were founded during the period between 1840 and 1870. His visit to England was certainly after Queen Victoria's accession in 1837 because 'Queen' figures in the story of his spirit experiences.

Makusi Hallelujah therefore, was most probably born some time during the period of forty years between 1845 and 1885. Youd left Pirara in 1841 and no other mission was established in the Rupununi until 1909, but im Thurn reported an excessive

[34] It was later ascertained that he died from yellow fever contracted in Georgetown just before he embarked. The Indians may have thought that he died from poisoning. They use the word 'poison' when they have blown on someone and charmed them with special words. Youd's Amerindian enemy probably so charmed the food which was then said to have been 'poisoned' and caused him to die some months later. (See Butt 1956.)

religious zeal among the Carib-speaking tribes in the eighteen-eighties. Abel was perhaps teaching Hallelujah among the Akawaio from 1885 onwards, just about the time that im Thurn climbed Roraima, so that, as I said at the beginning, his account of the 'Hallelujahs' among the Indians there may be a record of the very beginning of the Hallelujah cult among the Carib-speaking tribes north of the Makusi. Although Hallelujah dancing began before Abel's death in about 1911, the old traditional dances of *tugoik* and *palishara* and the *imawali* dance cycle did not entirely cease until about 1920–26. It is therefore likely that although there were Hallelujah churches in all river groups during Abel's lifetime, Hallelujah had not completely taken over the traditional spree activities until some time after his death. Among the more conservative and elderly of the tribe a time-lag is to be expected in such circumstances.

Based on the evidence I have presented and on the probability that it took only a few years for the knowledge of Hallelujah to spread from the Makusi to the Akawaio, my guess is that the eighteen-seventies and eighteen-eighties saw the birth and establishment of Hallelujah in the Carib-speaking tribes of the western borderlands of British Guiana. Although it is difficult to be accurate where time-reckoning and Amerindians are concerned, there is one significant correlation which must be stressed: missionary zeal from 1840 onwards gave the core of the Christian teaching which was eventually reproduced in Hallelujah. The failure of the missions among the Makusi and the delay in establishing new ones inside the tribal territories of the Carib-speaking areas gave the opportunity for this newly-acquired set of beliefs to develop in isolation from the rest of the colony. Only the occasional visits of tribesfolk to the missions nearer the coast may have added to the doctrinal basis of the incipient church. When, eventually, the Rupununi and Pakaraima missions started in this century the situation was that, of all the religious movements which had been reported and the churches built, Hallelujah alone remained and this had become a complete and assimilated religion, just about extending itself to the furthest limits of the Carib-speaking group of tribes of this region. The details of its spread, owing to the teaching of the two founding prophets, Bichiwung and Abel, is worth recording, if only to show the way in which such cults may be

propagated in a simply organized tribe without any religious hierarchy to impose them.

III   THE SPREAD OF HALLELUJAH AMONG THE AKAWAIO

All the present-day Hallelujah Leaders in all the Akawaio River
groups, state that they obtained their knowledge of the religion
from Abel, either directly or indirectly. By consulting each Leader
(*ebulu*) in turn and his helpers (*baidoludong*) I obtained a coherent account of Abel's teaching and the way in which Hallelujah
began to spread. The centre of the cult at the beginning, as now,
was at Amokokupai and Abel was the religious Leader there.

AMOKOKUPAI: THE CENTRE OF HALLELUJAH TEACHING
AND RESIDENCE OF THE PROPHETS

'At first God told Abel to tell only his family, his daughters, about
Hallelujah; but they had many sins (*magoi*) in them and would
not listen. He eventually told only his son, Moses, and his elder
brother's daughter,[35] but after a time the new Hallelujah message
was preached widely in Akawaioland and in *all* river groups.'

According to Lydia, the old woman at Chinawieng who had
known him, 'Abel said what God had told him. He was told that
he must teach the children so that if he should get killed by his
relations his children should not lose his customs.'[36] There were
some bad people among his relations, it is recalled, and this suggests that Abel was meeting with some opposition in his attempt
to set himself up as a prophet of the new, revealed, religion.

Bichiwung's preaching and Abel's took similar courses. At first
they both taught their female relatives only, their daughters in
particular. Then because of scepticism (sins in the women), they
taught the men. At first I was unable to understand why both
prophets tried to teach the women before the men, and I assumed
it might have arisen from the missionaries' practice of telling their
Amerindian visitors, who most frequently would be parties of men
come to work on the coast, to teach the women and children on

[35] He would call her *dengi*, daughter, since a man's brother's children are
like his own children.
[36] Custom is used here in the sense of 'Hallelujah way of life' or 'knowledge'.

their return home. However, the Amerindian interpretation of the story of Adam and Eve, illustrative of the weakness of women, seems to be the cause.

After a while Abel's immediate family, like Bichiwung's, became converted, and after them the wider circle of relatives, living in the same settlement or in nearby settlements, were taught and converted. Soon after his revelations began and when his first converts had been made Abel built the first Hallelujah church at Amokokupai. His sanction came from God who told Abel, during his sleep of six days' duration, that people should always live there. 'Abel told people that this place is nearer to heaven than anywhere else. It is the shortest road to heaven. So it comes about that although this place is really far too old to live in, people still do inhabit it,' so the story of Amokokupai village is told to-day.

Abel was renowned for his preaching and all assert that he spent much of his time engaged in this and in praying in the church. Of his manner of teaching Lydia recalled that Abel used to ask his listeners directly if they believed what he was telling them. 'If anyone believed good exactly, they used to say *"await"* ("yes" or "all right") when Abel asked them if they believed his words. If they said *"await"* without actually believing, it would be a sin' (*magoi*). It is also said that 'when Abel first prayed about Hallelujah people didn't know anything about it so they just followed him. This, people did'.

While Abel was sitting on his stool in the church and praying, his spirit used to leave him and go up to God and he got Hallelujah songs from God which he then used to sing in the church, just as Bichiwung sat in church and his spirit sang and got words and music from heaven. While he was still active Abel used to go about praying and teaching and visiting distant settlements and other river groups. 'Abel went around teaching everywhere, saying that Hallelujah was good,' said John Charlie of Kataima. When he got old however, he used to sling his hammock in the church at Amokokupai and pray and preach and sing from it.[37]

One name which requires notice in connexion with Abel's teaching is Moses, Abel's son, who was converted by his father and was zealous in support of his father's propagation of Hallelujah. He is chiefly remembered to-day for having introduced dancing into

[37] This is a practice which very old people still follow.

Hallelujah church ritual, an innovation which he may not have achieved without a struggle with his father. According to one account, Moses maintained that he had a revelation and words from God and it appears that his revelation conflicted somewhat with that of his father! Abel apparently maintained his position, asserting that his own revelation was the right one, but he did allow his son to introduce dancing in the church and to combine it with Hallelujah songs and prayers. Abel himself never danced for he was too old by then, but he watched from his hammock and continued to lead the prayers and to sing the chants. Moses never became a Prophet Leader of the church because he died before his father, but it was his inspiration which gave Akawaio Hallelujah a special character of its own because, according to all informants, none of the other tribes danced Hallelujah in church although they had their own songs.[38]

There have been five Prophet Leaders (*Pogenak*) at the head of the Akawaio Hallelujah church since its foundation and each was, in turn, Leader of the Amokokupai church as well:

1. *Abel:* The founder of Akawaio Hallelujah; was known to Mr Forbes of Kurupung from 1908 on until his death as a very old man, *c*. 1911.

2. *John William:* Both were taught by Abel and were his as-
3. *William:*   sistants before succeeding him in turn. Both were met by the Jesuit Father Cary-Elwes on visits to Amokokupai in 1917 and 1921. That they worked in such close association is partly explained by the fact that they were brothers, John William being the elder. Amokokupai people to-day say that they came from the Kwatin River group originally and took wives in the Amokokupai area. They were related to Queen Mulē by marriage, through taking his brother's daughters as wives.

4. *Kwiabong:* (Also known as 'Captain' or 'Edmund Spencer'). He died as a very old man in 1953. He was my chief in-

---

[38] The most noticeable characteristic of Hallelujah among the Akawaio is this dancing and no foreigner can avoid noticing it while it is being performed. This is not so with the prayers, songs, and preaching which could easily be overlooked by someone unacquainted with the language. This may be the reason why Makusi Hallelujah was never reported as such by travellers and missionaries in the Rupununi. There was no dancing to attract attention to it and to differentiate it from activities which might otherwise appear to be wholly Christian.

formant on Hallelujah for my first research period 1951–52.
Most of his knowledge was derived from direct teaching from
Abel, John William and William.

5. *Aibilibing:* The present Prophet Leader of Hallelujah. A
blind man of advanced age. He was too young to remember much
of Abel but learnt from succeeding prophets. He is endeavouring
to obtain revelations direct from God on his own account. One
of my chief informants for a second period of research in 1957.

All five of the past Leaders lived at Amokokupai and although
they travelled a great deal and preached the faith actively, their
main work centred on Amokokupai. In their old age they were all
confined to the village and immediate neighbourhood, as is the
present Leader, Aibilibing, on account of his blindness. Kinship
relationship has played no part in determining the succession to
the leadership of the Hallelujah church. Devotion to Hallelujah
and knowledge of it, ability, experience, fairly advanced age, acceptance by the people, and willingness to use Amokokupai as a
centre of activity appear to be the main qualifications necessary
for a leading Hallelujah Prophet (*Pogenak*).

According to Kwiabong three separate church buildings have
been erected at Amokokupai, apart from repairs carried out on
each from time to time. The present one, built a few years ago, is
the third and deviates from the normal style by having board sides
instead of the more pleasing tree bark. These were made with the
help of equipment on loan from the Government Station at Kamarang Mouth.

The impression I received in speaking with Akawaio about
Hallelujah in its earliest days at Amokokupai, is one of tremendous
religious enthusiasm and activity, of people pouring into the settlement to hear Abel preach and to pray and sing in the church.
Those who lived at a distance and in other river groups came and
camped there for days at a time in order to learn the Hallelujah
beliefs, songs and ritual. A second impression is of people returning to their homes and founding churches in their villages, teaching
and preaching in all the settlements however remote from
Amokokupai. As one informant said, speaking of Amokokupai
years ago, 'Saturday and Sunday were observed as Sabbaths. People would come from all directions into Amokokupai on the
Friday and would dance Hallelujah all night Saturday and Sunday.

In the day-time they would sleep and eat. Thus Agaman, Edmund's father, used to visit Amokokupai from his place on the Kukui, some hours away by trail, every week-end.'

It is difficult to ascertain exactly how much exaggeration there is in these accounts of old-time practice, but certain facts are clear. There was a multiplicity of churches founded in all parts of Akawaio territory and even beyond it in Patamona country. In the Kukui valley particularly, the names of various settlements with churches and their leaders are recalled by Akawaio to-day. All such churches owed their inspiration to Abel and his followers at Amokokupai. Abel himself must have been an exceptional personality. As Kenswil wrote, 'Abel seems to have been regarded with deep reverence by the people of his tribe, and even to-day, there are many who speak with reverence of him and his teachings. He lived to be very old, they say, then he died whilst worshipping one day.' Amoko, a crusty old man of the Chinawieng village area, described a communal meal at which, as a young man, he had eaten with Abel. He mentioned the fact with pride and little memories such as these, which are not usually recalled or considered of any account among Akawaio, frequently arise when Abel is the subject of the conversation. Mr Forbes of Kurupung, who was with the Akawaio at this early period of Hallelujah, stated that Abel was just an ordinary Indian to him. Nevertheless, Abel must have appealed to his fellow-tribesmen in an exceptional way for he roused them to enthusiasm over the new religion for a number of years and his influence still lingers on. To be able to keep such a loosely organized and independent-minded people as the Akawaio enthusiastic over the same thing for a long period of time is no mean achievement. In the normal course of events a local Leader can rarely influence those who live at a distance and who are not closely related to him, and although enthusiasm can be aroused quickly, it melts away equally quickly during the course of everyday activities and apathy sets in. Akawaio go their own way and maintain an individual independence and aloofness which is staggering to a European, who has been bred under a governmental and church system in which an official hierarchy and body of temporal and ecclesiastical law aim to enforce or maintain certain approved modes of conduct. Abel's shamanistic training must have helped him, as it seems to have helped many of the early Hallelujah adherents and leaders, although they all cast aside their conventional shaman's practice once they started preaching. However, whereas the literature shows that many of the leaders of the religious movements previous to Hallelujah either met a violent or ignominious end, or simply lost their followers, Abel, apparently, was revered and supported right up to the time of his death at a ripe old age and afterwards his memory was similarly revered.

THE VILLAGE FOUNDERS OF HALLELUJAH CHURCHES

The Akawaio preserve in their songs and prayers, as well as in their memories, the names of some of the men who went to Amokokupai and learnt from Abel and who then returned as religious leaders to their individual village settlements. These

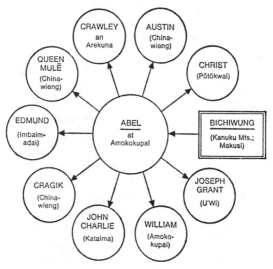

Figure 2. Idealized version of the spread of Hallelujah (as given by John Charlie of Kataima).

leaders taught their relations and founded churches and preached and taught Hallelujah, just as Abel had taught them in the beginning. They continued to visit and re-visit Amokokupai and in spite of being local Leaders (*ebuludong*) in their own right they were, in addition, all Abel's helpers or disciples (*baidoludong*).

As an illustration of how Hallelujah spread from Bichiwung to Abel and then on to the other Akawaio Leaders in the village settlements through Abel's teaching, John Charlie of Kataima drew a diagram with a stick in the sandy floor at my feet. (See Figure 2.) This does not take into account the fact that a few, like Christ, derived much of their knowledge from the Kwatin people who had been to see Bichiwung and also that Abel had first heard about Hallelujah through them. The majority of the Akawaio, as I have already shown, are beginning to simplify the history of the origins and foundation of Hallelujah and to produce a pattern based on the personalities and trends which later appeared to them to be the most important. Abel, as the all-important founder, excludes others with a considerable share in the founding of the religion because his was the personality which perpetuated itself in people's memory. The account of Hallelujah origins, as being commonly related by people to-day, is becoming less of an historical account of actual events and more an idealized pattern commemorating a few outstanding personalities who first preached Hallelujah. This can easily be seen by comparing the more complicated Figure 3 with the simplicity of Figure 2. The former represents some of the interrelationships in an historical growth and development, the latter represents an idealized pattern of social and religious values.

Some information on the deceased Leaders who founded Hallelujah churches in their settlements can be obtained from their successors alive to-day. Each account stresses information on the region in which the informant lives and the way in which he and his family learnt about Hallelujah.

a   *Christ*

Christ came from the village of Warimabia, Kamarang River group. He married a woman from the Kukui River group and resided at her family place for much of the time, in accordance with the requirements of matrilocality. He could not get a wife in his own river group, it is said.

At first he was a bad man, a sorcerer (*edodo*) who killed a number of people. Then, according to some, the Holy Spirit (*God Akawalu*) worked in him and wrought a change. He prayed and became good. According to others he confessed his evil deeds to Abel who 'told him he must not do these bad

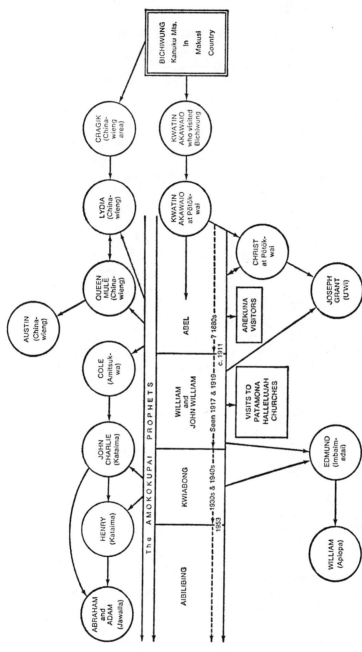

Figure 3. Diagram showing main agents through whom Hallelujah knowledge was acquired by village leaders. (Note: All the Amokokupai Prophets had some influence on the village leaders either directly, or, indirectly through their predecessors.)

things'. Christ was converted to Hallelujah and was from thenceforth a good man and taught God's Word. Some believed in his conversion to a good life but others did not, and these continued to point out the evil he had once done. Even to-day informants are divided over whether Christ really became a good man or not.

Christ founded an Hallelujah church at Sukabi, a small savannah near Warimabia village of the Kamarang River. He preached there during his visits to his parental river group and he used to stay at a place called Kaiape, near Warimabia. He also became Leader (*ebulu*) of the church at Pötökwai near Amokokupai which had been started by the Kwatin people, and no doubt he was in the midst of the quarrelling and drinking feasts which are said to have occurred in the village.

Of Christ's miraculous powers there are stories told. 'A man had pains from a stick inside,[39] and Christ prayed over him for a long time and removed this stick.' Another story of his power, from the Kamarang River people, tells that 'he used to pick a cassava stick which has a silver colour. When he slept he dreamt and saw the cassava stick spirit (*pleli akwalu*) who agreed with him and gave him the cassava stick spirit song.[40] Then, when they made drink they would take some into the church at Sukabi and pray on it and they would take this drink and pour some of it on the cassava plants in the garden. This and the song helped to make the gardens grow good.'

Christ was killed by sorcery (*edodo*) and the church at Pötökwai and the settlement were abandoned. One of his wives, Lydia, lived at Amokokupai after her husband's death; she died during my first period of research (1952). His daughter by another wife still lives at Amokokupai. Since all his helpers and disciples (*baidoludong*) died early on, he seems to have left few

---

[39] In beliefs concerning sorcery the sorcerer (*edodo*) knocks his victim unconscious, thrusts a stick up the anus, and twists the intestines into a knot with it. Akawaio believe that death is inevitable when such cases are diagnosed, but Christ miraculously removed the stick, presumably by prayer and spirit healing.

[40] *Pleli akwalu*, the cassava stick spirit, is frequently contacted by the shamans during their seances. Like all nature spirits it has its own special song. The shaman gets this spirit to sing to make the gardens grow well. The pouring of drink, such as *cassiri* (*kasiri, kasili*), as an offering to nature spirits connected with garden growth is a traditional practice. The admixture of a Christian element with the traditional is particularly striking in this story.

successors who obtained direct inspiration from him. Joseph Grant, late Leader of U'Wi village, Ataro River group, learnt some Hallelujah from him. Exactly how much Abel learnt from Christ, and Christ in turn from Abel, is not certain. Many of my informants, no doubt speaking ideally, implied that Abel converted Christ from his bad ways, as he did many other Akawaio, but since we know for certain that Abel's initial contact with Hallelujah beliefs came from the Pötökwai church, (but whether before Christ was a member or after is uncertain), we should regard their information sceptically.

Kenswil has some interesting, but misleading, information on Christ's career.

'After Abel's death an unscrupulous individual arose, called himself Christ, and took firm leadership of the tribe. This being is said to have pretended to perform miracles, such as turning water into *kassirri* and other drinks, producing sheets of paper with writings on them from no-where and various other doubtful performances. He often went into trances sleeping for days, and when he came out of such trance, he would give the tribe some new instruction, which, he would tell them, he had received from greater spirits than Abel or his predecessor ever knew. This fellow it seems, ruled with a strong and terrible will. He is said to have once committed murder while they were worshipping, and told the tribe he was instructed to do this by the spirits. He was a medicine-man,[41] and is said to have used his profession to commit various murders, his victims being mostly young women who refused to submit to his vicious approaches. He had several wives, and would now and then take some young girl and go away into the mountains.[42] If she pleased him, she returned as his wife, if not she never returned. Naturally such a being incurred the hate of his fellow tribesmen, who eventually murdered him and threw his body to the crows.'

There is little doubt from the way Akawaio still talk of him that Christ was an unsavoury character and there was much quarrelling and fighting at Pötökwai. Nevertheless Kenswil let

[41] That is, a shaman (*piai'chang*).

[42] Probably he was accused of taking a girl's spirit with him on his shaman's spirit flight among the mountains. If a girl died after sickness then he would be accused, perhaps, of keeping her spirit (*akwalu*) away from her body permanently and thus causing death. Akawaio normally never go to stay in uninhabited mountain country alone or even in small numbers unless on a short visit and for a special purpose. Lack of food in such areas, no garden produce, fish, or game, would result in starvation once supplies carried with them gave out.

his imagination run away with him in certain respects. Firstly, Christ died some time before Abel who, as already stated, lived to be a very old man. He never had the leadership of Hallelujah, except locally at the Pötökwai church. His evil deeds are said to be those of a sorcerer (*edodo*) or of an irresponsible shaman. Whether he made more direct attempts at murder it is impossible to say now; probably not, for there is no tradition to the effect that he himself was assassinated. Sorcery is said to have killed him as it did other Pötökwai people and as it always is believed to do with the majority of Akawaio everywhere, then as now. This means that in fact they probably succumbed to disease! It is possible that Christ himself claimed to be an evil man before his conversion, so as to give greater effect to it and to inspire more respect. Abel and many of the other Hallelujah converts claimed to be reformed by the new beliefs, in this way. The possibility of rivalry between the incipient Hallelujah church at Amokokupai and the church at Pötökwai ought not to be discounted, as well as friction which rowdy neighbours derived from another river group might engender. Christ was Leader of the church from which Abel first learnt about Hallelujah and yet, while Abel's efforts met with such outstanding success that his church became pre-eminent in the tribe and the great evangelizing centre, Christ's church gradually disintegrated. Although the survivors continued with Hallelujah in the Kwatin the Amokokupai prophet and his followers were left as the unchallenged leaders of the new cult.

b   *Cole and the Mazaruni People*

Cole, whose Akawaio name was Cezing, learnt Hallelujah from Abel. He became Leader of Hallelujah at Amitsukwa, a village near Amokokupai, from which he went out preaching and teaching. It was through Cole that the Mazaruni Leaders of to-day obtained their knowledge of Hallelujah.

John Charlie, recently deceased Leader of the old village of Waramadokmapu and of Kataima,[43] related how he learnt about

---

[43] The village moved from Waramadokmapu in about 1949, to Kataima. On John Charlie's death in 1952 the village began to break up again and people gradually moved to Jawalla, on the banks of the Kukui River, near its junction with the Mazaruni. Here, John Charlie's successor, Henry, died before the new village and church were fully established.

Hallelujah. His mother and father received some teaching from
Abel and they taught him a little. John Charlie himself did not
remember Abel because he was only a child when he was taken
on a visit to Amokokupai by his parents and when the old man
died. On reaching a suitable age, however, John Charlie, who
had been born at Waramadokmapu, left his home and stayed
near Amokokupai, learning Hallelujah from Cole. He stated that
it took him six years but this ought not to be taken too literally.
Akawaio are always moving about and staying with relatives so
that he might have spent many months in each year away from
Amokokupai and Amitsukwa. After his training he returned to
Waramadokmapu which became the centre of his activities again
and later he became Leader (*ebulu*) there and head of the
church. Henry became his official helper (*baidolu*), having learnt
his Hallelujah from John Charlie. His father, who might have
taught him, died very young.

On John Charlie's death in 1952 Henry became Leader of the
recently established village of Kataima and of the church there
but he died shortly afterwards. To-day, those who are active in
the present church at Jawalla all owe most of their knowledge
to John Charlie and Henry.

The Leader of Waramadokmapu previous to John Charlie
was a man called Goi, who is said to have learnt Hallelujah directly from Abel. In this area of the Mazaruni therefore, the religious Leaders either acquired Hallelujah directly from Abel or
indirectly from him, through Cole.

Those Akawaio who, until the last six years, used to live
further up the Mazaruni River near Imbaimadai, learnt their
Hallelujah in a similar way. Agaman, the father of Edmund the
recently deceased Leader of Imbaimadai, used to go from his
home in the Kukui River area to Amokokupai every Sunday. He
learnt from Abel and later on from Cole and then he made his
own church at Alwai village in the Mazaruni River group. When
Alwai was abandoned he made another church at Kaija'ekwa.
Edmund himself was too young to learn much from his father
and he got his Hallelujah knowledge from William, Abel's successor at Amokokupai, and also from Cole. Edmund (called
Awaima by Kenswil who used his Akawaio name) took over
Hallelujah at Kaija'ekwa and also built a church at Imbaimadai
when Kaija'ekwa was abandoned. William, present-day Leader of

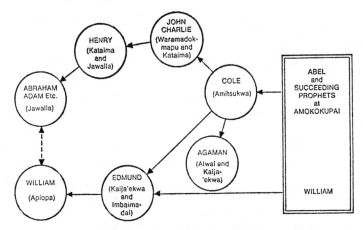

Figure 4. Diagram showing some of the main agents through whom Hallelujah knowledge spread among the people of the Imbaimadai and Kataima area of the Mazaruni River group. Influence from the Amokokupai prophets has been constantly exerted on all religious leaders among the Akawaio. Only the main channels of personal teaching are indicated in this diagram.

Apiopa village, learnt much of his Hallelujah from Edmund, paying for the chants which he obtained; he and the remnants of the population of the Imbaimadai area have a share in Hallelujah activities at Jawalla because they have not yet built a church of their own in their new settlement.

c   *Queen Mulē and the Chinawieng People*

Queen Mulē was a Kukui River group man. He lived in a settlement called Bipo, near Amokokupai, and at Kaimanitai he had a garden place. He used frequently to go to Amokokupai to receive instruction and he became a disciple of Abel.

At this time the village of Chinawieng was founded on the Ayanganna plateau savannah, near the source of the Mazaruni and about two days' walk by trail from Amokokupai. The new village was founded by Kukui people, the previous village settlement there having been abandoned some time previously. A man called Waking, father of Joseph who is the helper of the present Leader of Chinawieng, determined to build an Hallelujah church there. The kinship relationship between Waking and Abel is interesting: he was Abel's elder brother's son and therefore stood

as Abel's son in the Akawaio kinship system. Amokokupai was
his home. However, before his intention could be carried out he
died, and it was a man called James, living at Mortopulu just
below Imbaimadai, who built the church. James had gone to the
Kukui, seen Queen Mulē's church and when he afterwards went
to Chinawieng he founded a similar one. Not content with this
he also founded a second church somewhere further down the
Mazaruni River.

Queen Mulē went to Chinawieng on his marriage to a girl
who was living in the newly-founded village. She was the daughter
of Cragik. In spite of his youth and because of his knowledge and
experience in Hallelujah Queen Mulē became religious Leader at
Chinawieng. Austin, the present Leader, learnt from him. Queen
Mulē became a famous propagator of Hallelujah for he travelled
round the countryside teaching assiduously, and the memory of
him and his preaching is still strong. Eventually he fell ill and a
shaman consulted the spirits for him. He got better and then fell
ill again. He was taken from Chinawieng to a place on the Mazaruni in Chai-Chai gorge where he died. *Taling,* or ritual blowing,
was believed to be the cause of death, coming from U'Wi village,
Ataro River group. Queen Mulē's widow Lydia is still alive at
Chinawieng and is a vigorous preacher herself. Until very recently she was constantly travelling about and teaching. She was
one of my best informants and a reliable one for she had known
Abel personally and, as her fellow villagers say, 'she knows
Hallelujah from the beginning.'

Of Queen Mulē Kenswil wrote:

> 'In the meanwhile a young man was secretly gaining influence with
> the tribe, so when Christ was put out of the way, they made him
> leader. This fellow was named Queen-Mu-le, Queen is the name of
> a very great spirit, and mu-le means child in their language. Queen
> mu-le, pronounced mu-lay, is said to have influenced his people for
> good. He adhered to all the teachings of Abel, abolished all of
> Christ's teachings, and told his tribe that every one was personally
> responsible for his actions to God. He told them that one day God
> would destroy this world, and make a new one, placing all those who
> are obedient to Him there to live for ever. It will be noted how
> close to the teachings of Christianity this man's teachings were, al-
> though, so far as I can gather, he never left his home to go any
> place where he might have heard such doctrine expressed.'

Queen Mulē, in fact, never became religious Leader of the tribe for he was never Leader (*ebulu*) of the Amokokupai church, the religious centre established by Abel. Moreover, as his teaching suggests, he may have come into contact with the Seventh Day Adventist mission which had by this time started teaching among the Taulebang, Arekuna, and the Kamarang Akawaio. His wife Lydia has relatives in the Kamarang area, where the mission headquarters were established, and she has often been to stay with them so that influence from these during her husband's lifetime cannot by any means be discounted. This would certainly help to account for his preoccupation with the ending of the world and the eternal life promised for the virtuous. Queen Mulē's name is derived from Queen Victoria and means simply 'child of Queen'. Among the Chinawieng people 'Queen' is still popular as a name or part of a name; a fair sprinkling of 'Kings' and 'Queens' is also found throughout the tribe.

The present Leader (*ebulu*) of Chinawieng, Austin (or Queen Dez!) learnt his Hallelujah from Queen Mulē whose helper (*baidolu*) he was; he also learnt a little from his father. Austin Senior came from the Kukui and learnt Hallelujah from Abel. He married into the Mazaruni River group in the Imbaimadai-Kaija-'ekwa area and founded a church at Patabaima. His son Austin married within his maternal river group, but into the Chinawieng area further up river.

The story of Hallelujah and its spread to Chinawieng is not complete without mention of Cragik. His Akawaio name was Panalgok according to some and Paletwaik according to others: he may have had both names. He lived at Krumyabong, near Chinawieng. His daughter Lydia married Queen Mulē and was the cause of the latter settling in Chinawieng and eventually taking over the church there. Another of his daughters lives in Chinawieng still, and also a son, a very old and now feeble man called Francis.

It appears that Cragik obtained his knowledge of Hallelujah before a church was founded at Chinawieng. He is said not to have obtained it in the usual way, through inspiration and teaching from Abel or Abel's disciples. According to the Chinawieng people he had revelations straight from God. According to Kwiabong, the old religious head at Amokokupai, he got his Hallelujah directly from the Makusi instead of from Abel. This fact probably

explains why it is that some of the Chinawieng people know a
good number of Makusi Hallelujah songs. Orthodox Akawaio
Hallelujah and church practice came into the area later with
Queen Mulē from the Kukui River group. There is little doubt
that Lydia, as Cragik's daughter and Queen Mulē's wife, blended
the Hallelujah knowledge coming into Chinawieng from two different directions and propagated it in her church activities. For
her, however, Hallelujah as taught by Abel of Amokokupai is
all important as being the true Hallelujah.

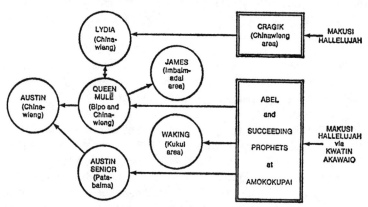

Figure 5. Diagram showing some of the main agents through
whom Hallelujah knowledge spread among the people of Chinawieng village, Mazaruni River group.

d *Other Disciples of Abel*

Apart from Cole, Waking, James, Queen Mulē, Austin Senior,
and Agaman whom I have already mentioned, Abel also taught
his grandson Noah, the father of King George of Chinawieng.
Similarly, he taught Selukamarai (Imbaimadai Edmund's wife's
father from the Kukui River group), and Kaleda who had a
church near Amokokupai. He also taught his successors at
Amokokupai, John William and William and Kwiabong.

These are the major names of the past which Akawaio still
recall in connexion with Hallelujah and its spread amongst them.
Of course many others went to Amokokupai to learn how to sing,
dance and pray Hallelujah and no doubt the mass of the tribe
went at one time or another to see what was happening there.

Even the independent leaders, like Christ and Cragik, who derived their Hallelujah directly from the Makusi or from the Makusi via the Kwatin people, must have been affected by Abel's teaching; to-day, even the Kwatin people acknowledge Abel as the supreme Prophet (*Pogenak*) and originator of their Hallelujah. Only the Kamarang Akawaio, attached to the Seventh Day Adventist missions of Paruima and Waramadong do not care to acknowledge Abel in this way. With these exceptions and according to all other accounts, the present-day religious Leaders (*ebuludong*) in all river groups, obtained their knowledge of Hallelujah from men who had previously obtained it from Abel and his chief disciples at Amokokupai. As Lydia, Queen Mulē's widow asserted, 'All Hallelujah came from Amokokupai; all was obtained from Abel.'

It is noticeable that nearly all the most important religious Leaders, Abel's helpers, were Kukui people. They were either born in the Kukui or married into the river group. Thus, Queen Mulē, Kaleda, Cole, and lesser men such as Austin Senior, Agaman, Waking, Selukamarai, as well as the Amokokupai Leaders, were all born in the Kukui and Christ married into the Kukui group. This pre-eminence of one area may be due to the fact that the Kwatin and Kukui River groups first heard about Hallelujah and so had a start on the others. Abel's personality and zeal are the chief reasons for the continuation of the Kukui as the heart of the Hallelujah area. Abel established his own settlement as the centre of the new religion and it naturally followed that his relatives learnt first from him and then themselves propagated the new faith along the lines of kinship and affinal relations which linked the Kukui people to the other river group peoples in the tribe.

Some of the Leaders remained in the Kukui and went into other river groups for the specific purpose of preaching during short visits to relatives. Others married out and took Hallelujah with them. These, such as Queen Mulē, Austin Senior, and Agaman, became religious Leaders in their adopted river groups and either founded churches there or brought increased activity to those already in being. Marriage and its accompaniment, matrilocality, were important factors in the spread of the new religion from the Kukui to the Mazaruni, Kako, and Kamarang villages.

It seems therefore, that Abel taught his relatives and river

group kin and many of these, by example and through marriage,
attracted and taught their affinal kin in their adopted river group.
In this way, the new religion spread with the maximum speed
and in accordance with the network of kinship and locality ties
by which, to a great extent, Akawaio society is organized.[44]

IV HALLELUJAH AND OTHER CARIB-SPEAKING TRIBES

Just as Akawaio visitors went to listen to Bichiwung among the
Makusi and to learn Hallelujah from him, so members of adjacent tribes came to Amokokupai to hear Abel. Among these
visitors the names of three Arekuna are still recalled: Crawley,
Cradine, and Apeyu.

Information suggests that the traffic was not all one way in
religious exchange. Danny of the Kamarang River Group stated
that Hallelujah came from Caroni head in Arekuna country and
it is likely that some news of Hallelujah came to the Kamarang
people from these regions for the Taulebang and Arekuna and
Kamarang Akawaio were occasionally in contact with each other,
in former times as now.

Patamona and Akawaio Hallelujah were closely interconnected
in the past for it is related that some of the Prophets of Amokokupai used to visit Hallelujah churches in the Patamona villages.
My Akawaio informants seemed to think that, in the first instance, the Arekuna and Patamona tribefolk got most of their
Hallelujah knowledge direct from the Makusi, and this is probable because the two tribes have always had frequent contact
with Makusi. The Patamona, although they are related most
closely to the Akawaio in language, are territorially situated between the Akawaio, to their north, and the Makusi, to their
south. The Arekuna and Taulebang are closer to the Makusi in
language than they are to the Akawaio.[45] There were always
some contacts via the connecting trails between the Roraima
region and the South. This contact was intensified after the dis-

[44] I should emphasize that neither the Akawaio nor neighbouring Carib-
speaking tribes have a clan or lineage system, but the wide network of kinship ties is nevertheless a very important feature of the organization of the
society.

[45] Both the Akawaio and Patamona call themselves by the same name,
Kapong yamök. The Makusi, Arekuna, and Taulebang call themselves
Pemonggong.

covery of Roraima because of the explorers, orchid collectors, botanists, and mountain climbers who passed that way with Makusi and Arekuna carriers, and because fighting had ceased between the tribes by that time. The trail to Roraima would be a natural route in the propagation of Hallelujah. There was always a certain amount of interchange between localities, due to trading visits, intermarriage, natural curiosity, and desire to travel, and to the reputation of certain Leaders attracting visitors. Hallelujah, like other more material commodities such as urali poison, hammocks, pottery, cassava graters and guns, must have spread throughout the Carib-speaking tribes of the Pakaraima area and, having been carried over certain recognized trade paths, it developed under the influence of these contacts.

Territorial proximity and ethnic similarity meant that interchanges of this kind, whether of the traditional or of a newly developed type, were inevitable. As Makusi Hallelujah paled into insignificance after Bichiwung's death and when the onslaught of Anglican, Catholic and Seventh Day Adventist missions began in the first decade of this century, Akawaio Hallelujah at Amokokupai became the chief centre of inspiration for those who continued to believe in and practise this religion.

Scraps of information suggest that the Arekuna, Taulebang, and Patamona at one time experienced a widespread adoption of Hallelujah analogous to that which, at the same time, was occurring among the Akawaio. Kenswil mentions two outstanding religious leaders among the Arekuna: one was called 'Pre-ri Ba-shi' who lived at the headwaters of the Kamarang River on the Gran Sabana in Venezuela. She was regarded as a great prophetess, according to Kenswil, and like Abel foretold that white men would bring a book and try to teach them from it.

> 'She said that some of these white men would tell them that one day was the correct one on which to praise and worship and that other white men would come after them and say that their predecessors were wrong and name another day.[46] She also said that they would be told by these men to abstain from certain meats and fish, also to put away their native drinks.[47] She said that their children

[46] Seventh Day Adventists regard Saturday as the Sabbath, not Sunday. They keep to this very strictly, not working or doing anything active from sunset Friday to sunset Saturday.

[47] The Adventists, following the injunctions of the Old Testament, forbid the eating of unclean meats. For the Amerindian this means not eating pec-

would be encouraged to leave their homes, and go and live with these white men and be taught their beliefs.'[48]

She told her followers not to have anything to do with these white men and 'she also called her doctrine Hallilieujah. . . . At a certain time of the year delegates from the various tribes would gather where she was, to receive instructions from her. The Indians say she also performed miracles' (Kenswil 1946).

Preri Bashi had obviously had contact with the Seventh Day Adventist mission, which had been at work since 1909 on the Gran Sabana and since 1932, lower down the Kamarang River in British Guiana. Probably she also had knowledge of Roman Catholic teaching through the visits of Father Cary-Elwes and the Brazilian priests who took over from him. Anglican missionaries also had been in the Roraima area, although they, too, never did more than make short visits. No resident mission has ever been permanently established in the Roraima district, but several denominations made the same round of the Taulebang and Arekuna villages. The prophecies of Preri Bashi concerning the different types of teaching which were to come were therefore soundly based on experience! The Adventists were the most persistent in their efforts and effected a permanent establishment in the Kamarang area; this may account for the fact that before she died (in about 1939 according to Kenswil), she told the Arekuna at the Seventh Day Adventist missions to throw away their tracts and retire to their homes; her messenger was a man called Noah.

The second leader recorded by Kenswil is Akwa, who belonged to the Eruwani River Group, also on the Gran Sabana in Venezuela and near Roraima. It would appear from his teaching, which prohibited the use of alcoholic drinks and the eating of peccary, that he had been influenced by the Seventh Day Adventists even more positively. Yet, like Preri Bashi, Akwa told his followers not to listen to the white people and their religion. The interesting point which arises from Akwa's teaching is the

---

cary (bush hog), tapir (bush cow) or various small rodents such as *aguti*. Thus, practically all the main meats are forbidden to them and so also are skin fish. Deer and bush birds are allowed. Fermented drinks are prohibited, as well as tobacco and anything which can be regarded as a stimulant or narcotic.

[48] Children are encouraged to live at the missions and attend school and church there while their parents frequently dwell in distant settlements.

fact that the Amerindians were not unwilling to take over the doctrines which they had been taught by the missionaries but, having adopted them, the prophets claimed the doctrines as their own and rejected the authority of the missionaries who had first propounded them.

The two prophets, Preri Bashi and Akwa, were probably not Arekuna but Taulebang. Certainly the people of the Eruwani River Group to-day are known as Taulebang and nominally they are Seventh Day Adventists and have a church near their main village of Uraianda.[49] Their own religious Leader, Prataluding, is supposed to work under instructions from the nearest Seventh Day Adventist mission headquarters, at Paruima on the Kamarang River in British Guiana. On my visit to the Taulebang in 1957 I was told that 'none of the Taulebang to-day know Hallelujah', but I was told that they have a cult called 'Chimiding'.

Chimiding is yet one more piece of evidence of the intense interest that the Carib-speaking tribes took in missionary teaching and of their ability to adapt portions of it to their traditional life. 'All the Taulebang used to sing *palishara* and *tugoik*. After being taught Seventh Day Adventist songs they wanted to have songs to sing and to pray at Christmas time and at sprees,[50] so they developed Chimiding,' a Taulebang Leader related. Chimiding (also pronounced 'Chimiting') is said to be an English word and is probably the Amerindian version of 'Church Meeting'. Augustine, Leader of Uraianda village, stated that his father's brother had got Chimiding from 'Smithy' from Bartica. It appears that a Rev. Mr Smith from Bartica on the Essequibo River, visited the Taulebang on an evangelizing tour of the Roraima area and taught them the Chimiding songs. He told them to sing them when they prayed, adding the injunction that they were to sing them without troubling the girls![51]

I recorded many of these Chimiding songs but on attempting

[49] The church is at a small settlement in the neighbourhood, called Kumalakapai. Uraianda is four days' walk from Paruima and as might be imagined the people are rather lax in their interpretation of the main Seventh Day Adventist doctrines and prohibitions.

[50] 'Spree': I use the general Guianese term for the Amerindian festival which consists of feasting, drinking, dancing, and general jollification combined with ritual practices.

[51] Amerindian sprees are frequently occasions for a certain amount of sexual licence, particularly among the youths and girls.

to take down the words found that they were a jumble of sounds, of the meaning of which the Taulebang have no idea. Here and there a few English words are distinguishable, including such phrases as 'Oh Mose drenking water'; 'one, two, tree'; and 'where's my Lor?' Nor are the tunes recognizable as any particular English hymn tunes but they are reminiscent of both English and Amerindian songs. The original 'Church Meeting Taulebang' must have learnt Mr Smith's songs parrot-fashion and, as time went by and they were passed on to the next generation, the words got thoroughly mixed up and the tunes began to take on the lilt of the native music. To-day they are an intriguing and tuneful mixture from both sources.

Unlike Hallelujah, Chimiding has no church and no particular set of doctrines. It consists merely of a number of songs sung at festive times and with a religious association. Chimiding is not a religion, any more than is any collection of songs expressing religious sentiments.

The Arekuna, to the north of the Taulebang, had Hallelujah and still have it, though probably not to the same extent as the Akawaio. Many of the Arekuna have for years been subject to both Seventh Day Adventist and Roman Catholic mission teaching. The Arekuna dance Hallelujah at one of their settlements and a few Arekuna Hallelujah chants have been learnt by some of the Kamarang Akawaio with whom they have intermarried in recent years. These chants I have recorded as well as some which were sung at my request by a Savannah Arekuna visiting Paruima mission in 1957. The source of Hallelujah inspiration amongst the Arekuna, as among the other tribes, is also by revelation through dreams. It is said that one Arekuna Leader, called 'England', slept for two days and 'had Hallelujah'.

Although the Akawaio sometimes assert that the Wai-Wai, a Carib-speaking tribe on the southern borders of British Guiana, have Hallelujah, this is not the case. Neither the Wai-Wai, nor the Wapisiana[52] (Arawak-speaking), who lie between the Makusi and Wai-Wai, have Hallelujah. The Maionggong (or Makiritare), a Carib-speaking tribe in Venezuela at the head-waters of the Orinoco, is not a Hallelujah tribe, nor are the

[52] For this information I am indebted to Dr J. Yde of the National Museum, Copenhagen, who kindly made these enquiries for me during his research expedition of 1954.

Barama River Caribs or a small community of Akawaio in the north-west district of British Guiana and Pomeroon area.

Hallelujah seems to have been confined to those tribes of the Carib group who call themselves *Kapong yamök* (i.e. the Akawaio and Patamona), and *Pemonggong* (i.e. Makusi, Taulebang, and Arekuna)[53] who live in adjacent areas in the Pakaraima Mountains and the Gran Sabana, on the borderlands of British Guiana, Brazil, and Venezuela. To-day, only the Akawaio practise Hallelujah assiduously, though a few Arekuna also perform it in their more remote settlements. The position of Hallelujah among the Patamona and Makusi requires investigation. Since it has not been remarked on by the Guianese living amongst these tribesfolk it has probably either died out, or is carried on only in the areas remote from missionary and colonial influence and in such a way as not to attract attention.

CONCLUSION

Some significant generalizations may be made concerning the origins and dissemination of Hallelujah. The dissemination of the new religious beliefs contained in Hallelujah was confined to a group of tribes on the borderlands of British Guiana, Venezuela, and Brazil. This is due to two combined factors: these tribes are territorially contiguous and they also have the greatest similarity in all aspects of social life, language, culture, and concepts of thought. We should add that conditions were favourable for the dissemination and development of the new religion, for had there been intensive mission activity in any one of these tribes before the introduction of Hallelujah, it is unlikely that this religion, in its present form, could have taken a hold on the people there. Territorial, cultural, and historical factors all reinforced each other therefore in making possible the birth and spread of the new religion.

From the information available it seems that Hallelujah was first introduced to each tribe, from its Makusi origin, in a similar way: namely, by the reports of visitors travelling between the

[53] The Kamarakoto also call themselves Pemonggong but whether they have Hallelujah is not known. They are the most distant from the Makusi of all the tribes of this group and are therefore furthest from the original centre of the diffusion of Hallelujah.

tribes. Hallelujah also spread and developed in a similar way within each tribe. Although this similarity in development can be attributed in part, to the process of cultural diffusion in that there was a certain amount of interchange, teaching, and copying between the tribes, it can also be attributed to parallel development arising out of the very similar organization and patterns of thought within them.

It is noticeable that the religion spread through the agency of certain people who taught and preached and who, by personality and force of example, impressed their fellow tribesfolk to the extent of persuading them to cast aside, or adapt, their traditional beliefs and practices in favour of the new. Hallelujah was not imposed by force or persecution of any kind and it is typical of the organization of this tribal group that this should be so. There was, and is, no central authority and no person or group of persons who could enforce conformity in the way that religious concepts have been enforced from time to time in history by authoritarian governments or church hierarchy. Concomitantly, there was no organized opposition to the new cult; people could take it or leave it and indeed, as the old form of traditional feast continued into the first quarter of this century some of the older people for the most part did leave it. Personality and force of example, the typical qualities of leadership among the Carib-speaking peoples, were the only compelling agents in Hallelujah.

The course of the spread of Hallelujah within the tribes proceeded via kinship and affinal relationships, indicating the importance of the network of kinship ties as the effective channels for transmission of ideas. The pattern seems to be as follows: A man is converted or has some spiritual experiences. He converts his immediate family and close relatives. This conversion next spreads to the village settlement and neighbourhood, containing somewhat more distant relatives. Strangers arrive from other river groups and other tribes, hear and carry off what they have learnt, so taking it back to their own families and settlements where the process begins again. Intermarriage between people of different settlements and the practice of matrilocality also assist in setting up similar processes in other areas. Personality and force of example, directed along lines of affinity and kinship, arbitrated in the diffusion of Hallelujah in and between river groups of each tribe.

Some significant generalizations arise from the comparison of the experiences of the various Hallelujah prophets as these are recalled to-day.

There is, most obviously, a close similarity in the nature of the revelations and spiritual experiences of Bichiwung, Abel, and of the lesser prophets. All claimed to see, hear, or in some way achieve direct contact with God and other heavenly spirits; from heaven they obtained pieces of paper, words, music, bottles of oil, medicine, or some miraculous liquid. They also obtained messages from heaven, the promise of a heavenly abode after death, and goodness and material prosperity of one kind or another in this world. The prophets were told to preach of their experiences and to persuade others of the truths they had witnessed. Experiences frequently included contact with traditional spirits, such as the nature spirits, as well as Christian ones, such as angels and archangels, and in all the revelations this mixture of traditional beliefs and newly adopted ideas garnered from the teaching of the Christian missions is evident.

The methods of obtaining revelations also show basic similarities. Some of the prophets shut themselves up in their houses and went to sleep, seeking spiritual contact with the upper regions through the flight of their spirit in dreams. Sometimes spirit flight was achieved by means of prayer and song and for this purpose the stress is placed on getting the right words from God or from some important spirit. The majority of the early Hallelujah prophets were shamans by training and the method of seeking spirit contact with God and the type of spirit flight and revelation envisaged are obviously reflections of the traditional shamanistic procedures. Although, so far as we know, all the prophets abandoned the practice of fasting and of drinking tobacco juice and all the traditional shamanistic procedures of this kind, they nevertheless continued with the basic underlying idea of making direct spirit contact, though this was with God and the other occupants of heaven and not with nature spirits and ghost spirits only. The experiences and the spirits met with during such flights and the seeking after certain benefits for their people, such as bringing down their heart spirits from God, are all feats of a shamanistic nature. The use of the right words, the right songs, gaining assistance of spirit helpers and guides, such as Queen and Noah, also underline the fundamental similarity in method between the new and the old forms of spirit contact.

Another feature noticeable in the development of Hallelujah and apparent in the teaching of all the prophets is the common reaction to the encroachment of the white man, his society, culture, and teaching, on Amerindian life. The reaction is ambivalent, perhaps necessarily so. There was, and still is, an obvious admiration of the material products obtained through trade and also of the knowledge displayed by the colonists: a respect and liking for white folk is also not wanting in many instances. Accompanying this is, and was, a feeling of opposition and hostility natural to the subordinate Amerindians in their relationship to a dominant foreign society. These feelings appear to have expressed themselves in the belief that, by imitating Christianity and acquiring spiritual knowledge from the white people Amerindians too would obtain equivalent prosperity, knowledge, and future salvation.

The practical expression of this combination, of this admiration and desire to attain all the advantages possessed by the foreigners and the opposition and distrust in face of actual inferiority, is to be seen in the efforts of the prophets to redress the balance between the two societies. Certain anti-white features occur in the prophets' teaching. Bichiwung for example, claimed that the white folk had been trying to deceive him and later prophets said that they must not listen to the teaching of the missionaries or all would become the servants of white people. The stress in the stories is always on the belief that the prophets themselves got their *own* revelations and for Amerindian benefit alone, or at least, the benefits are to be dispensed by Amerindians to the rest of mankind. Thus Bichiwung got Hallelujah on his own, so it is related, and he got an Indian Bible from God; this is constantly emphasized and not very much attention is paid to the fact that he first acquired a knowledge of the Christian idea of God and the Bible—the out-of-date Bible—from a white missionary.

In building up their own system of beliefs, revealed by God to Amerindian prophets only, these Carib-speaking tribes countered the Christianity of the colonists with the Amerindian semi-Christian religion of Hallelujah, the creation of the new religion being in part an expression of a fundamental opposition between two different societies and cultures.

I should like to express my gratitude to the Colonial Development and Welfare Corporation, the International Federation of University Women, and the London Central Research Fund for their generous financial assistance which made my field work possible. I also wish to thank Professor Evans-Pritchard, Institute of Social Anthropology, Oxford, for advice concerning this article.

This article is a product of field research carried out in 1951–52 and again in 1957. A complete account of the origins of Hallelujah requires a consideration of the various religious movements among the Guiana Indians and also an account of the establishment of the mission churches which gave rise to the movements. These subjects, as well as an appraisal of the importance of Hallelujah in relation to other semi-Christian religious movements amongst other peoples, have had to be omitted here owing to considerations of space.

BIBLIOGRAPHY

AGAPITOV, N. N., and M. N. KHANGALOV.
1883 "Materially dlia izucheniia shamanstya y Sibiri" (Materials for the Study of Shamanism in Siberia). IVSOIRGO (*Journal of the East Siberian Section of the Imperial Russian Geographic Society*), vol. 14, pts. 1–2, pp. 1–61.

ALLAN, C. H.
1951 "Marching Rule: a nativistic cult of the British Solomon Islands," *Corona* 3 (3).

ANAGARIKA ANANDA.
1955 *A supreme enterprise for the establishment of Buddhasasana.* Matara.

ANDERSON, J. N. D.
1954 *Islamic law in Africa.* London.

ANDRÉ, P. J.
1924 *L'Islam noir: contribution à l'étude des confréries religieuses islamiques en Afrique Occidentale, suivie d'une étude sur l'Islam au Dahomey.* Paris.

ASHTON, H.
1955 *The Basuto.* London.

ASSEMBLIES OF GOD MISSION.
1934 *Report of the Assemblies of God Mission to the Mossi, Upper Volta.* Springfield, Mo.

BALANDIER, G.
1955 *Sociologie actuelle de l'Afrique Noire.* Paris.

BANZAROV, DORDŽI.
1891 *Chernaia Vera* (The Black Faith). (G. N. Potanin, ed.) St. Petersburg.

BARTHOLD, V. V.
1928 *Turkestan Down to the Mongol Invasion.* (Gibbs Memorial Series 5.) London.

BATAROV, P. P.
1890 "Buriatskie poveriia o bokholdaiakh i anakhaiakh" (Buryat Beliefs Regarding *boxoldoy* and anaxay). ZVSOIRGO (*Memoirs of the East Siberian Section of the Imperial Russian Geographic Society, Ethnographic Section*) vol. 2, pt. 2, pp. 10–14.

BATESON, G.
1936 *Naven.* Cambridge.

BEATTIE, J. H. M.
1958 "Nyoro marriage and affinity," *Africa* 23 (1).
1960 *Bunyoro: an African kingdom.* New York.

1961 "Group aspects of the Nyoro spirit mediumship cult," *Rhodes-Livingstone Journal* 30.

1963 "Sorcery in Bunyoro," in: Middleton, J., and E. Winter (editors), *Witchcraft and Sorcery in East Africa*. London.

BERNDT, R. M.
1952–53 "A Cargo Movement in the Eastern Central Highlands of New Guinea," *Oceania* 22.

1954 "Reaction to contact in the Eastern Highlands of New Guinea," *Oceania* 24.

BOGDANOV, M. N.
1926 *Ocherki Istorii Buriat-Mongol'skogo Naroda* (Studies in the History of the Buryat-Mongol People). Verkhneudinsk.

BOULDING, K. E.
1962 *Conflict and Defense*. New York.

BOUNIOL, J.
The White Fathers and their Missions. London.

BREWSTER, A. B.
1922 *The Hill Tribes of Fiji*. London.

BROWN, J. T.
1921 "Circumcision rites of the Becwana tribes," *Journal of the Royal Anthropological Institute* 51.

BRYANT, A. T.
1949 *The Zulu People as they were before the white man came*. Pietermaritzburg.

BUTT, A. J.
1954 "The burning fountain from whence it came," *Timehri* 33; *Social and Economic Studies* 2 (1).

1956 "Ritual blowing: *Taling*–a causation and cure of illness among the Akawaio," *Man*.

BUXTON, J.
1958 "The Mandari of the Southern Sudan," in: Middleton, J., and D. Tait (editors), *Tribes Without Rulers*, London.

CAMPBELL, D.
1922 *In the Heart of Bantuland*. Philadelphia.

CARSTAIRS, M.
1957 *The Twice Born*. London.

CASTRÉN, ALEXANDER.
1857 *Versuch einer Burjatischen Sprachlehre*. St. Petersburg.

CHEREMISOV, K. M.
1951 *Buriat-Mongol'sko-Russkii Slovar'* (Buryat-Russian Dictionary). Moscow.

CHESNEAUX, J.
1953 "Le révolution Taiping d'après quelques travaux récentes," *Revue historique* 1953.

CHINNERY, E. W. P., and A. C. HADDON.
1917 "Five new religious cults in British New Guinea," *Hibbert Journal* 15.

CLARIDGE, G. C.
1922 *Wild bush tribes of tropical Africa*. London.

COLSON, E.
1953 "Clans and the joking relationship among the Plateau Tonga of Northern Rhodesia," *Kroeber Anthropological Society Papers* 8–9.

CONSIDINE, J. J.
1954 *Africa, world of new men.* New York.
COOKSEY, J. J., and A. MC LEISH.
1931 *Religion and Civilization in West Africa.* London.
COOPER, J.
1946 "The Araucanians," *Bulletin of the Bureau of American Ethnology* 1946, ii.
COPE, J.
1955 *The Fair House.* London.
COPLESTONE, R. S.
1892 *The Twice Born.* London.
COSER, L. A.
1956 *The Functions of Social Conflict.* Glencoe.
COWAN, J.
1910 *The Maoris of New Zealand.* Wellington.
CRAZZOLARA, J. P.
1933 *Outlines of a Nuer Grammar.* Vienna.
1938 *A Study of the Acooli Language.* London.
CUNNISON, I.
1959 *The Luapula Peoples of Northern Rhodesia.* Manchester.
CURTIN, JEREMIAH.
1909 *A Journey in Southern Siberia.* Boston.
DALE, G.
1896 "An account of the principal customs and habits of the natives inhabiting the Bondei country," *Journal of the Royal Anthropological Institute* 25.
DAVIS, M. B.
1938 *A Lunyoro-Lunyankole-English and English-Lunyoro-Lunyankole Dictionary.* London.
DELAFOSSE, M.
1912 *Haut-Sénégal-Niger.* Paris.
DELEGORGUE, M. A.
1847 *Voyage dans l'Afrique australe.* Paris.
DELOBSON, D.
1934 *Les secrets des sorciers noirs.* Paris.
DIAMOND, S.
1963 "The search for the primitive," in: Galdston, I. (editor), *Man's Image in Medicine and Anthropology.* New York.
DRIBERG, J. H.
1923 *The Lango.* London.
DUBOIS, F.
1896 *Tombouctou la mystérieuse.* Paris.
DUPONT, A.
1949 "La rapide évolution des Africains dans la Haute Volta," *Marches coloniaux* 5 (163).
DURKHEIM, E.
1915 *The Elementary Forms of the Religious Life.* London.
DYRENKOVA, N. P.
1930 "Poluchenie shamanskogo dara po vozzreniiam turetskikh plemen" (The Acquisition of the Shaman's Gift in the View of the Turkic Peoples), *Sbornik Muzei Antropologii i Etnografii,* vol. 9, pp. 267–91.
ELKIN, A. P.
1931a "The rainbow-serpent in north-west Australia," *Oceania* 1 (3).

1931b　"The social organization of Australian tribes," *Oceania* 2 (1).
1932a　"The social organization of the Worimi," *Oceania* 2 (3).
1932b　"Social organization in the Kimberley Division," *Oceania* 2 (3).
1932c　"The secret life of the Australian Aborigines," *Oceania* 3 (2).
1933a　"Totemism in northwestern Australia," *Oceania* 3 (4).
1933b　"Totemism in northwestern Australia," *Oceania* 4 (1).
1933c　"Studies in Australian totemism," *Oceania* 4 (1).

ELWIN, V.
1947　*The Muria and their Ghotul.* Bombay.
1949　*Myths of Middle India.* Madras.
1955　*The Religion of an Indian Tribe.* Bombay.

EVANS-PRITCHARD, E. E.
1929　"Some collective expressions of obscenity in Africa," *Journal of the Royal Anthropological Institute* 59.
1937　*Witchcraft, Oracles and Magic among the Azande.* Oxford.
1948　*The Divine Kingship of the Shilluk of the Nilotic Sudan.* Cambridge.
1949a　"The Nuer *col wic*," *Man* 49.
1949b　"Nuer totemism," *Annali Lateranensi* 13.
1949c　"Burial and mortuary rites of the Nuer," *African Affairs* 48.
1949d　"Nuer curses and ghostly vengeance," *Africa* 19.
1949e　"Two Nuer ritual concepts," *Man* 49.
1951a　*Social Anthropology.* London.
1951b　*Kinship and Marriage among the Nuer.* Oxford.
1951c　"Some features and forms of Nuer sacrifices," *Africa* 21.
1956　*Nuer Religion.* Oxford.

EVANS-PRITCHARD, E. E., and A. C. BEATON.
1940　"Folk songs of the Sudan I," *Sudan Notes and Records* 23.

FARON, L. C.
1961a　"On ancestor propitiation among the Mapuche of Central Chile," *American Anthropologist* 63.
1961b　*Mapuche Social Structure.* Urbana.
1962　"Symbolic values and the integration of society among the Mapuche," *American Anthropologist* 64.

FEHLINGER, H.
1921　*Sexual Life of Primitive People.* London.

FÉLIX JOSÉ DE AUGUSTA, FRAY.
1934　*Lecturas araucanas.* Valdivia.

FERGUSSON, V. H.
1921　"The Nuong Nuer," *Sudan Notes and Records* 4.

FIRTH, R. W.
1951　*Elements of Social Organization.* London.
1955　"The theory of 'Cargo Cults': a note on Tikopia," *Man* 55.

FISON, L., and A. W. HOWITT.
1880　*Kamilaroi and Kurnai.* Melbourne.

FORDE, D.
1949　"Integrative aspects of Yakö first fruits rituals," *Journal of the Royal Anthropological Institute* 79.

FORTES, M.
1936　"Ritual festivals and social cohesion in the hinterland of the Gold Coast," *American Anthropologist* 38.
1945　*The Dynamics of Clanship among the Tallensi.* London.

1954 "Mird," in: Evans-Pritchard, E. E. (editor), *The Institutions of Primitive Society*, Glencoe.

FORTUNE, R. F.
1932 "Manus religion," *Oceania* 2.

FOURIE, L.
1928 "The Bushmen of South West Africa," in: *The Native Tribes of South West Africa*. Capetown.

FRAZER, J. G.
1911 *Taboo and the Perils of the Soul*. London.

FRY, H. K.
1933 "Body and Soul," *Oceania* 3 (3).

FÜRER-HAIMENDORF, C. VON.
1936 "Zur Religion einiger hinterindischer Bergvölker," in: Buxton, L. H. D. (editor), *Custom Is King*. London.
1948 *The Raj Gonds of Adilabad*. London.
1953 "The after-life in Indian tribal belief," *Journal of the Royal Anthropological Institute* 83.
1954 "Religious beliefs and ritual practices of the Minyong Abors of Assam, India," *Anthropos* 49.
1955 *Himalayan Barbary*. London.

FÜRER-HAIMENDORF, C. VON, and J. P. MILLS.
1936 "The sacred founder's kin among the Eastern Angami Nagas," *Anthropos* 31.

GEORGI, J. G.
1776–1880 *Beschreibung aller Nationen des Russischen Reichs*. St. Petersburg.

GLUCKMAN, M.
1935 "Zulu women in hoecultural ritual," *Bantu Studies* 3.
1949a *An Analysis of the Sociological Theories of Bronislaw Malinowski*. Oxford.
1949b "The role of the sexes in Wiko circumcision ceremonies," in: Fortes, M. (editor), *Social Structures*. Oxford.
1954a "Political institutions," in: Evans-Pritchard, E. E. (editor), *The Institutions of Primitive Society*. Glencoe.
1954b *Rituals of Rebellion in South-east Africa*. Manchester.
1959 *Custom and Conflict in Africa*. Glencoe.

GLUCKMAN, M., J. C. MITCHELL, and J. A. BARNES.
1949 "The village headman in Central Africa," *Africa* 19.

GMELIN, J. G.
1751–52 *Reise durch Sibirien von dem Jahre 1733 bis 1743*. Göttingen.

GOODY, J.
1957 "Fields of social control among the LoDagaba," *Journal of the Royal Anthropological Institute* 87.

GORER, G.
1935, 1949 *Africa Dances*. London, New York.

GOUILLY, A.
1952 *L'Islam dans l'Afrique Occidentale française*. Paris.

GREENBERG, J.
1946 *The Influence of Islam on a Sudanese Religion* (Monographs of the American Ethnological Society 10). New York.

GUEVARA SILVA, T.
1898 *Historia de la civilización de Araucanía*. Santiago.

GUIART, J.
1952–53   "The John Frum movement in Tanna," *Oceania* 22.
GULLIVER, P., and P. H. GULLIVER.
1953   *The Central Nilo-Hamites.* London.
HAHN, C. H. L.
1928   "The Ovambo," in: *The Native Tribes of South West Africa.* Capetown.
HAMBLY, W.
1930   *Ethnology of Africa.* Chicago.
HARVA, UNO.
1938   *Die Religiösen Vorstellungen der Altaischen Völker* (F. F. Communications no. 125).
HAYLEY, T. S. S.
1947   *The Anatomy of Langoreligion and Groups.* Cambridge.
HERSKOVITS, M. J.
1934   "Freudian mechanisms in primitive Negro psychology," in: Evans-
Pritchard, E. E. *et al.* (editors), *Essays Presented to C. G. Seligman.*
London.
1938   *Dahomey.* New York.
HOBLEY, C. W.
1910   *Ethnology of A-Kamba and other East African Tribes.* Cambridge.
1938   *Bantu Beliefs and Magic.* London.
HODGSON, A. G. O.
1933   "Notes on the Achewa and Angoni of the Dowa district of the
Nyasaland Protectorate," *Journal of the Royal Anthropological Institute* 63.
HOERNLE, A. W.
1925   "The importance of the sib in the marriage ceremonies of the
South-Eastern Bantus," *South African Journal of Science* 22.
HOFMAYR, W.
1925   *Die Schilluk.* Vienna.
HOGBIN, H. I.
1935   "The native culture of Wogeo," *Oceania* 5.
1947a   "Local government for New Guinea," *Oceania* 17.
1947b   "Native trade around the Huon Gulf," *Journal of the Polynesian
Society* 56.
1947c   "Shame," *Oceania* 17.
1947d   "Sex and marriage in Busama," *Oceania* 17.
1948   "Native Christianity in a New Guinea village," *Oceania* 18.
HOWITT, A. W.
1904   *Native Tribes of South-east Australia.* London.
HUFFMAN, R.
1929   *Nuer-English Dictionary.* Berlin.
1931   *Nuer Customs and Folk-lore.* London.
HUNTINGFORD, G. W. B.
1953a   "The Northern Nilo-Hamites," *Survey of Africa, East Central
Africa.* London.
1953b   "The Southern Nilo-Hamites," *Survey of Africa, East Central
Africa.* London.
1955   "The Galla of Ethiopia," *Survey of Africa, North-Eastern Africa.*
London.
HUXLEY, A.
1954   *The Doors of Perception.* London.

IM THURN, SIR E.
 1885 "Roraima," *Timehri* 2.
JACKSON, H. C.
 1923 "The Nuer of the Upper Nile Province," *Sudan Notes and Records* 6.
JUNOD, H. A.
 1913 *The Life of a South African Tribe.* Neuchatel.
 1927 *The Life of a South African Tribe.* London.
KABERRY, P. M.
 1941 "The Abelam tribe," *Oceania* 11.
KAMMA, F. C.
 1954 *De Messiaanse Koreri-Bewegingen in het Biaks-Noemfoorse cultuurgebied.* 's-Gravenhage.
KARSTEN, R.
 1935 *The Head-hunters of Western Amazonas: the life and culture of the Jibaro Indians of eastern Ecuador and Peru.* Helsinki.
 1954 *Some Critical Remarks on Ethnological Field-Research in South America.* Helsinki.
KEESING, F. C.
 1941 *The South Seas in the Modern World.* London.
KENSWIL, F. W.
 1946 *Children of the Silence.* Georgetown, British Guiana.
KHANGALOV, M. N.
 1888 "Zegete-Aba, oblava na zverei drevnikh Buriat" (Zegete-Aba, the Hunting Surround of the Ancient Buryats), IVSOIRGO, vol. 19, no. 3, pp. 1–27.
 1890 "Novye Materialy o shamanstve u Buriat" (New Materials on Shamanism), ZVSOIRGO *po Ethnografii,* vol. 20, pt. 2.
 1891 "Neskol'ko dannykh dlia kharakteristiki severnykh Buriat" (Some Data to Characterize the Northern Buryats), *Ethnograficheskoe Obozrenie* 3.
 1894 "Iuridicheskie Obychai u Buriat" (Juridical Practices of the Buryats), *Ethnograficheskoe Obozrenie* 4.
 1898 "Svadebnye Obriady . . . u Buriat . . . Balaganskago Okruga" (Marriage Rites . . . of the Balagansk District Buryats), *Ethnograficheskoe Obozrenie* 10.
KHORI-BURIATY.
 1899 (Khori Buryats). St. Petersburg.
KIGGEN, J.
 1948 *Nuer-English Dictionary.* London.
KLEMENTS, D.
 1924 "Buriats," in: Hastings, J. (editor), *Encyclopaedia of Religion and Ethics.*
KLEMENTS, D., and M. N. KHANGALOV.
 1910 "Obshchestvenniya okhoty u severnykh Buriat" (Communal Hunts of the Northern Buryats), *Materialy po Ethnografii Rossii* 1.
KRIGE, E. J.
 1950 "Individual development," in: Schapera, I. (editor), *The Bantu-speaking Tribes of South Africa.* London.
KRIGE, E. J., and J. D. KRIGE.
 1956 *The Realm of a Rain-Queen.* London.

KROL', M.
1894 "Brachnye obriady i obychai u zabaikal'skikh Buriat" (Marriage Rites and Practices of the Trans-Baikal Buryats), IVSOIRGO 25.
1895 "Okhotnich'e pravo i zverinyi promysel u Zabaikal'skikh Buriat" (Hunting Law and the Trade on Wild Game of the Trans-Baikal Buryats), IVSOIRGO 25.

KUPER, H.
1961 *An African Aristocracy.* London.

LA FONTAINE, J.
1959 *The Gisu of Uganda.* London.

LANG, A., and C. TASTEVIN.
1937 *La tribu des Va-Nyaneka.* Corbeil.

LATCHAM, R. E.
1924 *La organización social y las creéncias religiosas de los antiguos araucanos.* Santiago.

LAWRENCE, P.
1954 "Cargo cult and religious beliefs among the Garia," *International Archives of Ethnography* 47 (1).
1955 "The Madang District cargo cult," *South Pacific* 8 (1).

LE CHATELIER, A.
1899 *L'Islam dans l'Afrique Occidentale.* Paris.

LEHNER, S.
1930 "Geister und Seelenglaube der Bikaua," *Mitteilungen aus dem Museum für Völkerkunde.* Hamburg.
1935 "Balum cult of Bukaua," *Oceania* 5.

LÉVI-STRAUSS, C.
1955 "The structural study of myth," *Journal of American Folklore* 68.

LIENHARDT, G.
1954 "The Shilluk of the Upper Nile," in: Forde, D. (editor), *African Worlds,* London.
1961 *Divinity and Experience.* Oxford.

LINTON, R.
1943 "Nativistic movements," *American Anthropologist* 45 (1).

LITTLE, K. L.
1951 *The Mende of Sierra Leone.* London.

LLOYD, C. A.
1895 "Stray notes from Pirara," *Timehri* n.s.2.

LOUDON, J. B.
1959 "Psychogenic disorder and social conflict among the Zulu," in: Opler, M. K. (editor), *Culture and Mental Health,* New York.

LOWIE, R. H.
1936 *Primitive Religion.* New York.

MACLEAN, C. B.
1858 *A Compendium of Kafir Laws and Customs.* Mount Coke.

MAC MILLAN, W. M.
1929 *Bantu, Boer and Briton: the making of the South African problem.* London.

MAIR, L. P.
1948 *Australia in New Guinea.* London.
1953 "African marriage and social change," in: Phillips, A. (editor), *Survey of African Marriage and Family Life.* London.

MALINOWSKI, B.
1938 "Anthropology of changing African cultures," in: *Methods of Study of Culture Contact in Africa* (International African Institute Memorandum 15).
1945 *Dynamics of Culture Change*. New Haven.
MANZONI, A.
1951 *The Betrothed*. London.
MARTY, P.
1917 *Etudes sur l'Islam au Sénégal*. Paris.
MARWICK, B. A.
1940 *The Swazi*. Cambridge.
MARWICK, M. G.
1950 "Another modern anti-witchcraft movement in East Central Africa," *Africa* 20.
MATHEWS, R. H.
n.d. *Ethnological Notes on the Aboriginal Tribes*.
MC CONNEL, U. H.
1931 "Symbolism as a mental process," *Psyche* 46.
MEAD, M.
1934 "The Marsalai cult among the Arapesh," *Oceania* 4.
1935 *Sex and Temperament in Three New Guinea Societies*. New York.
1956 *New Lives for Old*. New York.
MEEK, C. K.
1931a *A Sudanese Kingdom*. London.
1931b *Tribal Studies in Northern Nigeria*. London.
MEYEROWITZ, E.
1951 *The Sacred State of the Akan*. London.
MIDDLETON, J.
1960 *Lugbara Religion: ritual and authority among an East African people*. London.
MIKHAILOVSKIY, V. M.
1892 "Shamanstvo" (Shamanism), *Antropologii i Etnografii* 75.
MILLIN, S. G.
1928 *The Coming of the Lord*. London.
MITCHELL, J. C.
1956 *The Yao Village*. Manchester.
1959 "The Yao of southern Nyasaland," in: Colson, E., and M. Gluckman (editors), *Seven Tribes of British Central Africa*. London.
MOESBACH, E. W. DE.
1930 *Vida y costumbros de los indigenas araucanos en la segunda mitad del siglo XIX*. Santiago.
MONTAUBAN, P.
"Le grand rêve Buka depuis la guerre," *Missions Maristes d'Océanie* 15.
MOONEY, J.
1892–93, 1896 *The Ghost Dance Religion and the Sioux outbreak of 1890*. (14th Annual Report of the Bureau of Ethnology, Smithsonian Institution), Washington.
NADEL, S. F.
1947 *The Nuba*. London.
1951a *A Black Byzantium*. London.
1951b *The Foundations of Social Anthropology*. Glencoe.
1952 "Witchcraft in four African societies: An essay in comparison," *American Anthropologist* 54 (1).

1954 *Nupe Religion.* London.

NASH, P.
1955 "The place of religious revivalism in the formation of the inter-cultural community on Klamath Reservation," in: Eggan, F. (editor), *Social Anthropology of North American Tribes.* Chicago.

NASSAU, R. H.
1904 *Fetichism in West Africa.* New York.

NEBEL, A.
1936 *Dinka Dictionary.* Verona.

NEUHAUSS, R.
1911 *Deutsch Neu Guinea,* Vol. II. Berlin.

NORBECK, E.
1961 *Religion in Primitive Society.* New York.

OHLMARKS, AKE.
1939 *Studien zum Problem des Schamanismus.* Lund.

OKLADNIKOV, Å. P.
1937 *Ocherki iz istorii zapadnykh Buriat-Mongolov* (Studies in the History of the Western Buryats). Leningrad.

O'REILLY, P., and J. M. SÉDÈS.
1949 *Jaunes, Noirs et Blancs.* Paris.

PALLAS, P. S.
1771 *Reise durch verschiedene Provinzen des Russischen Reiches,* 6 vols. St. Petersburg.

PERISTIANY, J. G.
1939 *The Social Institutions of the Kipsigis.* London.

PETRI, B. E.
1923 *Shkola Shamanov u Severnykh Buriat* (The Shamans School of the Northern Buryats). Irkutsk.
1925 *Vnutri-Rodovye Otnosheniia u Severnykh Buriat* (Inner-Clan Relations among the Northern Buryats). Irkutsk.
1928 *Staraya Vera Buriatskogo Naroda* (The Ancient Faith of the Buryats). Irkutsk.

PLOTNICOV, L.
1962 "Fixed membership groups: the locus of culture processes," *American Anthropologist* 64.

PODGORBUNSKIY, S. I.
1891 "Idei Buriat shamanistov o dushe" (The Ideas of the Buryat Shamanists about the Soul). IVSOIRGO 22.

POPPE, N. N.
1925 "Zum Feurkultus bei den Mongolen," *Asia Major* 2.
1934 "Problemy Buriat-Mongol'skogo Literaturovedeniia" (Problems of Buryat Literary Studies), ZIV 3.

POS, H.
1950 "The revolt of Manseren," *American Anthropologist* 52 (4).

POTANIN, G. N.
1881–83 *Ocherki Severo-Zapadnoi Mongolii* (Northwestern Mongolia), 4 vols. St. Petersburg.

PRINS, A. H. J.
1953 *East African Age-Class Systems.* Groningen.

QUELLIAN, A.
1910 *La politique musulmane dans l'Afrique Occidentale française.* Paris.

RADCLIFFE-BROWN, A. R.
1918 "Notes on the social organization of Australian tribes," *Journal of the Royal Anthropological Institute* 48.
1929 "The sociological theory of totemism," *Fourth Pacific Science Congress* 3.
1930 "The social organization of Australian tribes," *Oceania* 1 (2).

RADCLIFFE-BROWN, A. R., and D. FORDE.
1950 *African Systems of Kinship and Marriage.* London.

RATTRAY, R. S.
1954 *Religion and Art in Ashanti.* London.
1955 *Ashanti.* London.

READ, K. E.
1952 "Missionary activities and social change in the Central Highlands of Papua and New Guinea," *South Pacific* 5 (11).

READER, D. H.
1954 "Marriage among the Makhanya," *International Archives of Ethnography* 47.

RICHARDS, A. I.
1935 "A modern movement of witchfinders," *Africa* 8.
1956 *Chisungu.* New York.
1961 *Land, Labor and Diet in Northern Rhodesia.* London.

ROHEIM, G.
1933 "Women and their life in Central Australia," *Journal of the Royal Anthropological Institute* 63.

ROSCOE, J.
1911 *The Baganda.* London.
1915 *The Northern Bantu.* Cambridge.
1923a *The Bakitara.* Cambridge.
1923b *The Banyankole.* Cambridge.
1924 *The Bagesu.* Cambridge.

RYAN, B.
1953 *Caste in Modern Ceylon.* New Brunswick.

SACHS, C.
1937 *World History of the Dance.* New York.

SACHS, W.
1947 *Black Hamlet.* Boston.

SAMUELSON, R. C. A.
1929 *Long, Long Ago.* Durban.

SANDERS, R.
1953 *Meet the Mossi.* Springfield, Mo.

SANDŽEYEV (SANDSCHEJEW), GARMA.
1927–28 "Weltanschauung und Schamanismus der Alaren-Burjaten," *Anthropos* 27.

SARMA, H.
1930 "Some problems connected with Brahmanical asceticism," *Archiv orientalni* 11.

SAYERS, G. F. (editor).
1930 *Handbook of Tanganyika.* London.

SCHLOSSER, K.
1949 *Propheten in Afrika.* Braunschweig.

SCHMIDT, W.
1949, 1951 *Der Ursprung der Gottesidee.* Münster.

SCOTCH, N.
1960 "A preliminary report on the relation of sociocultural factors to hypertension among the Zulu," *Annals of the New York Academy of Sciences* 84.

SECRET HISTORY OF THE MONGOLS.
1948 (Eric Haenisch, translator, *Die geheime Geschichte der Mongolen.*) Leipzig.

SELIGMAN, C. G., and B. Z. SELIGMAN.
1932 *Pagan Tribes of the Nilotic Sudan.* London.

SHASHKOV, S.
1864 "Shamanstvo v Sibiri" (Shamanism in Siberia), ZIRGO 2.

SHAW, A.
1915 "Dinka songs," *Man* 15.

SHEPPERSON, G.
1954 "The politics of the African Church Separatist Movement in British Central Africa, 1892–1916," *Africa* 24 (3).

SHIROKOGOROV, S. M.
1935 *Psychomental Complex of the Tungus.* London.

SHOOTER, J.
1857 *The Kafirs of the Natal and the Zulu Country.* London.

SIMMEL, G.
1908 "Der Streit," in: *Soziologie Untersuchungen über die Formen der Vergesellschaftung.* Leipzig.

SMITH, E. W., and A. M. DALE.
1920 *The Ila-speaking Peoples of Northern Rhodesia.* London.

SMITH, W. R.
1902 *The Prophets of Israel.* London.
1927 *Lectures on the Religion of the Semites.* London.

SNAITH, N. H.
1944 *The Distinctive Ideas of the Old Testament.* London.

SOCQUET, MSGR.
1956 *L'église catholique en Afrique Noire.* Paris.

SPENCER, B.
1914 *Native Tribes of the Northern Territory.* London.

SPENCER, B., and F. J. GILLEN.
1899 *The Native Tribes of Central Australia.* London.
1927 *The Arunta.* London.

STANNER, W. E. H.
1953 *The South Seas in Transition.* London.

STAYT, H. A.
1931 *The Bavenda.* London.

STEWARD, J. H., and A. METRAUX.
1948 "Tribes of the Peruvian and Ecuadorian Montana," in: Steward, J. H. (editor), *Handbook of South American Indians* 3. Washington.

STIGAND, C. H.
1923 *A Nuer-English Vocabulary.* Cambridge.

STIRLING, M. W.
1938 *Historical and Ethnographical Material on the Jivaro Indians.* Washington.

SUNDKLER, B. G. M.
1940, 1948 *Bantu Prophets in South Africa.* London.

TALBOT, P.
1912 *In the Shadow of the Bush.* London.

1923 *Life in Southern Nigeria.* London.
1927 *Some Nigerian Fertility Cults.* London.
TAUXIER, L.
1912 *Le noir du Soudan.* Paris.
1927 *La religion Bambara.* Paris.
TEN HAAFT, D. A.
1948 "De Manseren-beweging op Noord-Nieuw-Guinea, 1939–43," *Tijdschrift Nieuw-Guinea* 8th year and 9th year.
THOMAS, E. M.
1959 *The Harmless People.* New York.
THOMSON, B.
1895 "The Kalou-Vu (ancestor-gods) of the Fijians," *Journal of the Anthropological Institute* 24.
TITIEV, M.
1951 "Araucanian culture in transition," *Occasional Contributions from the Museum of Anthropology, University of Michigan* 15.
TORDAY, E.
1925 *On the Trail of the Bushongo.* London.
TRACEY, H.
1948 *Chopi Musicians.* London.
TRENCH, R. C.
1871 *Synonyms of the New Testament.* London.
TRILLER, R. P.
1932 *Les Pygmées de la forêt équatoriale.* Paris.
TURNER, G. D.
1958 "Alternative phonemicizing in Jivaro," *International Journal of American Linguistics* 24.
TURNER, V. W.
1952 *The Lozi Peoples of North-western Rhodesia.* London.
VAMBOTSYRENOV, E.
1890 "Aba-Khaydak, oblava u khorinskikh Buriat" (Aba-Khaydak, the Hunting Surround of the Khorin Buryats), IVSOIRGO 21.
VAN GENNEP, A.
1909 *Les rites de passage.* Paris.
VLADIMIRTSOV, B. Y.
1948 "Le Régime Social des Mongols, Féodalisme Nomade," in: Carsow, M. (translator), *Obshchestvennyi Stroy Mongolov* (Mongol Social Structure). Paris. (Russian edition, 1934, Leningrad-Moscow.)
WALLACE, A. F. C.
1959 "The institutionalization of cathartic and control strategies in Iroquois religious psychotherapy," in: Opler, M. K. (editor), *Culture and Mental Health,* New York.
WARD, B.
1956 "Some observations on religious cults in Ashanti," *Africa* 26.
WARNER, W. L.
1932 "Malay influence on the cultures of North-eastern Arnhem Land," *Oceania* 2.
WEBER, M.
1947 *The Theory of Social and Economic Organization.* Glencoe.
1958 *The Protestant Ethic and the Spirit of Capitalism.* New York.
WEEKS, J. H.
1913 *Among Congo Cannibals.* Philadelphia.
1914 *Among the Primitive Bakongo.* London.

WESTERMANN, D.
  1912a "The Nuer language," *Mitteilungen des Seminars für Orientalische Sprachen.*
  1912b *The Shilluk People.* Philadelphia.
WILLIAMS, F. E.
  1923 *The Vailala Madness and the Destruction of Native Ceremonies in the Gulf Division* (Papua Anthropological Reports, 4).
  1928 *Orokaiva Magic.* London.
WILSON, M.
  1959 *Divine Kings and the "Breath of Men."* Cambridge.
WIRZ, P.
  1954 *Exorcism and the Art of Healing in Ceylon.* Leiden.
WORSLEY, P.
  1957 *The Trumpet Shall Sound.* London.
YALMAN, N.
  1960 "The flexibility of caste principles in a Kandyan community," in: Leach, E. R. (editor), *Aspects of Caste in South India, Ceylon and Northwest Pakistan.* Cambridge.
  1962a "On the purity of women in the castes of Ceylon and Malabar," *Journal of the Royal Anthropological Institute* 92.
  1962b "On some binary categories in Sinhalese religious thought," *Transactions of the New York Academy of Sciences* ser. 2, 24.
  1964 "The structure of Sinhalese healing rituals," *Journal of Asian Studies* 23.